British Women Writers
and the Writing of History,
1670–1820

■

British Women Writers
and the Writing of History,
1670–1820

■

DEVONEY LOOSER

The Johns Hopkins University Press

Baltimore and London

© 2000 The Johns Hopkins University Press
All rights reserved. Published 2000
Printed in the United States of America on acid-free paper
2 4 6 8 9 7 5 3 1

The Johns Hopkins University Press
2715 North Charles Street, Baltimore, Maryland 21218-4363
www.press.jhu.edu

ISBN 0-8018-6448-8

For my parents,

SHARON *and* LEROY,

and my grandparents,

VIRGINIA *and* ANCHOR

Contents

■

Acknowledgments

■

This book owes its existence to the helpful advice, expert direction, and boundless generosity of many people. I gratefully acknowledge the financial assistance of the National Endowment for the Humanities, the William Andrews Clark Memorial Library, and the University Research Committee of Indiana State University. The training in archival research and the feedback provided in Paula Backscheider's 1994 NEH summer seminar at the Public Record Office, London, were especially formative. The Center for Twentieth Century Studies at the University of Wisconsin–Milwaukee (under the directorship of Kathy Woodward), where I was a research associate in 1996–97, also proved a marvelous community to work in.

Those who read, heard, commented on, or otherwise encouraged my scholarly work at its earliest stages have not been thanked sufficiently. Boyd Koehler, Cathie Nicholl, and Ron Palosaari offered direction during my years at Augsburg College. At SUNY–Stony Brook I benefited from the professional support of Pat Belanoff, Helen Cooper, Drucilla Cornell, E. Ann Kaplan, Ira Livingston, Adrienne Munich, Clifford Siskin, the late Michael Sprinker, Susan Squier, Kathleen Wilson, and Rose Zimbardo. I also thank Linda Frost, Ellen Gardiner, Martha Heller, Mike Hill, Jhan Hochman, Maria Jerinic, Greg Laugero, Pam Moore, Mona Narain, Jillian Meyer Quinn, Patti Sakurai, Chris Semansky, Barbara Smith, Tony Vaver, and Jeff Williams.

At Indiana State University I am grateful for help from colleagues Ron Baker, Matt Brennan, Jim Broaddus, Keith Byerman, the late Madelyn De Gaetano, Myrna Handley, Darlene Hantzis, Harriet Hudson, Jake Jakaitis, Linda Maule, Michael Shelden, and Joe Weixlmann. I acknowledge the students I had the pleasure to teach and learn from, particularly the master's students in my spring 1995 Literary Theory and fall 1995 Eighteenth-Century Novel seminars. At the University of Wisconsin at Whitewater, my thanks go to Becky Hogan and Star Olderman. Those at the Johns Hopkins University Press who have been tireless in their support of this project include Doug Armato, Linda Tripp, and especially the unflappable Maura Burnett. The expert copyediting of Alice Bennett caught many errors. I also thank the Press's external reader, Martine Watson Brownley, whose suggestions for revision were an impressive amalgam of challenge and support.

Some had no institutional reason whatever to give me assistance but nevertheless graciously provided it, including Nancy Armstrong, Joan Austen-Leigh, Craig Dionne, Alistair Duckworth, Diane Elam, Margaret J. M. Ezell, Jane Gallop, Anne Goldgar, Bert Goldgar, Claudia L. Johnson, Deborah Kaplan, Mary Jo Kietzman, Gene Koppel, Kate Levin, Juliet McMaster, David Norbrook, Ruth Perry, Al Rivero, Peter Sabor, Barbara Brandon Schnorrenberg, Judy Slagle, Alison Sulloway, Ruthe Thompson, Laura Mooneyham White, and Kathy Woodward. Paula Backscheider, Miriam Elizabeth Burstein, Antoinette Burton, and Catherine Ingrassia were especially generous with their time, reading parts or all of the manuscript and offering valuable feedback and corrections.

Others who have given years of sage advice and encouragement include Amy Hanson, Lisa Kivirist, Sandra Le Duc, Dutch Toenjes, and Becky Wyganowski. The generosity of my father-in-law and my Turkish in-laws the Cemalis made possible a visit that brought alive the context of chapter 3. To the Looser and Sarslow families (and more recently, to the Justice and Monser families), thank you for your warmth, guidance, and patience. I especially thank my parents and grandparents, to whom this book is dedicated. Last, I acknowledge with gratitude George Justice, who helps me to find the joy in doing this work—and in everything—even at the most trying of moments.

Earlier versions of several chapters have been previously published. Portions of chapter 3 appeared in very different form as "Scolding Lady Mary Wortley Montagu? The Problematics of Sisterhood in Feminist Criticism" (*Feminist Nightmares: Women at Odds: Feminism and the Problem of Sisterhood,* ed. Susan Ostrov Weisser and Jennifer Fleischner [New York: New York University Press, 1994], 44–61; used with permission). Material from chapters 1 and 7 was published in "(Re)Making History and Philosophy:

Austen's *Northanger Abbey*" (*European Romantic Review* 4.1 [1993]: 34–56; used with permission). A version of chapter 7 was published as "Reading Jane Austen and Rewriting 'Herstory'" (*Critical Essays on Jane Austen,* ed. Laura Mooneyham White [Boston: G. K. Hall/Macmillan, 1998], 34–66; used with permission of the Gale Group). I gratefully acknowledge the Gilder Lehrman Collection on deposit at the Pierpont Morgan Library, New York, for permission to quote from the Catharine Macaulay papers.

*British Women Writers
and the Writing of History,
1670–1820*

■

Introduction: British Women Writers and Historical Discourse

I

∎

Received feminist wisdom has conceived of history as a male enclave devoid of women subjects and practitioners, particularly before the twentieth century. As Ann Forfreedom put it in 1972, "From Herodotus' to Will Durant's histories, the main characters, the main viewpoints and interests, have all been male" (1). Second-wave feminist accounts of the 1970s and 1980s viewed history as overwhelmingly "his," coining the term "herstory" and presenting it as a compensatory feminist practice.[1] Herstory designated women's place at the center of an alternative narrative of past events.[2] Rosalind Miles's description restates the popular view: "Women's history by contrast has only just begun to invent itself. Males gained entry to the business of recording, defining and interpreting events in the third millennium BC; for women, this process did not even begin until the nineteenth century" (xii). The herstorical method provided a means for feminist historians to explore issues and materials by and about women that had previously been neglected or ignored. Herstory promoted curricular transformation in schools and was used as a slogan on T-shirts, pencils, and buttons. Exposing historians' tacit and intentional sexism, herstorians set out to correct the record—to show that women held up half the historical sky.

Despite the great scholarly gains made behind the rallying cry, herstory's popular myths—particularly about the lack of women who have recorded history—require revision. Herstory may accurately describe second-wave feminists' efforts to construct female-centered accounts of the past, but the term inadvertently blinds us to women's important contributions to historical discourse before the nineteenth century. History has not been an entirely male preserve, though feminists are justified in faulting its long-standing masculine contours.[3] In fact, criticism of history's sexism is not of recent origin. Early eighteenth-century feminist Mary Astell protested that "the Men being the Historians, they seldom condescend to record the great and good Actions of Women" (206–7).[4] Astell, like those who echoed her sentiments two and a half centuries later, must be credited for admirable zeal in setting out to right scholarly wrongs, but her supposition that historians were only male is inaccurate. Her perception is especially strange because she herself wrote a historical work, *An Impartial Enquiry into the Cause of Rebellion and Civil War* (1704). Astell's judgment is at the same time understandable, given that much historical writing by women of the late seventeenth century was not published until the nineteenth century. Despite their courage and their rightful anger, Astell and her descendants overlooked early modern women writers' contributions to historiography.

Future feminist investigations into women's contributions must define "history" more broadly and must acknowledge that women writers used historical material with widely diverging interests, aims, and results. A sustained look at British women's writings of the "long eighteenth century" (from the Restoration through the Regency) illustrates that women were much more involved in the burgeoning genre of history than we have formerly thought. The ways women writers drew on historical discourse in their texts varied enormously, from direct engagement with political history, to the use of historical forms in letters or travel writings, to manipulations of historical material in fictional works. Throughout this book I use the term "historical discourse," following Michel Foucault, to designate "the rules that come into play in the existence of" history, that give it "value and practical application" at the time it is written and accepted (*Order* xiv). Historical discourse refers not only to histories per se but to "the ensemble of written texts" that make up history and in so doing "define, limit, and describe it" (L. Davis 7). In addition to discursive practices, I retain an interest in individual authors (and texts by and about them), information that enriches our knowledge of how subjects participate in and shape textual modes. As a relatively fluid and immensely popular genre, history provided a rich area of discourse for women writers to mine. Historiography was changing rapidly throughout the period, moving from a memoir-based, politically volatile, or annals-saturated form—largely the province of eyewitnesses, gossips, and antiquarians—to one of greater scholarly, scientific, stylistic, and professional pretension, drawing on documentary remnants in an emerging print culture. Women did not stand by and watch these changes occur. They participated, tangentially and head on, in debates about history writing that effected change.

Closer scrutiny shows that eighteenth-century women writers' use of historical discourse did not usually adumbrate "herstory." Women's writings were not necessarily more feminist or more female-focused than those of their male counterparts. I argue here that though British women writers of the long eighteenth century contributed significantly to the period's historiographical developments, it was rarely in the uncomplicated, foremotherly, and protofeminist ways that many of us hoped to discover. One example that demonstrates the point is Charlotte Cowley's seven-hundred-page *Ladies History of England; from the Descent of Julius Caesar, to the Summer of 1780. Calculated for the Use of the Ladies of Great-Britain and Ireland; and Likewise Adapted to General Use, Entertainment, and Instruction* (1780). As a female historian who writes for women, Cowley might seem a likely candidate for the label "protoherstorian." Histories of England written both *by* and *for* women were unusual before 1780. Cowley's history was therefore groundbreaking in its form, though written by an author about whom little is known and who apparently published nothing else. Her *Ladies History of England* is a compilation that includes "all the remarkable events recorded by other historians [and] is intended to convey to posterity a faithful picture of the characters of our most illustrious women for a long series of ages" (n.pag.). If the subscription list is a fair indication, the *Ladies History* was designed for purchase by girls' boarding schools.[5]

Cowley's *Ladies History* understands itself as a text exploring new generic and historiographical ground. Her epigraph makes clear why she contrasts her history to the writings of her female contemporaries:

> Idly too long the Female Pen has stray'd
> Thro' Fairy Bower, or gay enamell'd Mead
> Content in Trifles to exert its Art,
> Play round the Fancy, but not reach the Heart;
> Mine be the Talk to swell th' Historic Page,
> And paint my Sex's Worth in every Age.

Distancing herself from the trifles of fanciful, idle romances written by women, Cowley attempts to link women's heartfelt writing to historical narratives like her own. She writes English history to entertain and to instruct, to paint her sex's worth across centuries, and to reach both hearts and minds. The peculiar thing about Cowley's expansive *Ladies History,* however, is that her book features approximately the same amount of material on women as histories of the era that do *not* make such gendered claims.

Cowley's work is not as centered on female achievements as she would have us believe, nor does it ultimately give extraordinary attention to women as readers. She tells her female readers that in taking up this book their curiosity is "truly laudable," because "the acquirement of knowledge, especially that of our own Country, may be fairly reckoned among the most useful of our pursuits" (1). Throughout her history, Cowley offers a handful of references to her "proposed plan" of discussing illustrious women, but the project is not followed through with any regularity. The illustrious women in Cowley's history become germane primarily when they are queens. Cowley's coverage is even, with each monarch or historical epoch receiving approximately the same number of words, though the section on Elizabeth I is generous and the eighteenth century gets more than its share of space. In the end, Cowley's attention to "the ladies"—at least in the narrator's address—virtually disappears. She concludes with a return to the arena of the heart: "We shall now retire from an arduous employment, happy in the reflection, that the produce of our labour will contribute to increase the knowledge, improve the judgment, and mend the hearts of mankind" (704). The "fair sex" has melded into "mankind."

A brief examination of Cowley's *Ladies History* provokes questions of consequence to the study of dozens, if not hundreds, of female-authored texts of the period. How did women writers contribute to historiography as it metamorphosed throughout the eighteenth century? Did women's writings demonstrate self-consciousness about the distinctions and mixings among genres, subgenres, and their gendered associations, as Cowley's did about trifling women's romances and histories for the heart? Toward what ends did women employ historical discourse in genres other than political history? Did female writers of historical texts consider their productions derivative, sui generis, or something else? Finally, were women's historical writings noticed by reviewers and readers, and if so, how were they received? The chapters that follow consider these questions for six British women writers active from the late seventeenth century to the early nineteenth: Lucy Hutchinson, Lady Mary Wortley Montagu, Charlotte Lennox, Catharine Sawbridge Macaulay, Hester Lynch Piozzi, and Jane

Austen. Taken as a whole my research furthers our knowledge about the ways historiography developed, beginning the process of expanding the picture to include female writers active during the long eighteenth century. The book sketches the ways women writers accepted, rebelled against, adapted to, and co-opted history's generic parameters.

To understand why feminist scholars invented herstory, we must first comprehend early women writers' roles in the development of history writing, well before its nineteenth-century professionalization and institutionalization in Great Britain. The mid- to late nineteenth century, rather than the eighteenth, has been a popular starting point for investigations of British women and history. In *The Ends of History: Victorians and "the Woman Question"* Christina Crosby investigates the ways "woman" was placed outside history just as it emerged as a discipline.[6] Working largely from literary documents, Crosby maintains that women are the ideological and unhistorical Other of history in the nineteenth century, against which men are defined as worthy of history and history making. As subsequent work has shown, however, in practice women were fundamentally important to history writing of that period. The history of the past two centuries "has *not* been mostly written by men or even been concerned mostly with men," as Bonnie Smith points out (*Gender* 6). Historical biographies (especially of queens) were produced in great numbers by nineteenth-century women (Maitzen, "Feminine" 371): Billie Melman identifies sixty-six women historians who among them wrote 782 works ("Gender" 7). Miriam Elizabeth Burstein's essay on Agnes Strickland demonstrates that women historians of the Victorian era enjoyed noteworthy financial success. But there is truth to Crosby's implicit charge that British women's contributions to nineteenth-century historiography either went unremarked or were disrespected. British women were rarely seen as the most able historians.

We do not yet know how many British women published histories. There is no reference work exploring early modern women's historical texts. No dictionary of British women historians of the eighteenth and nineteenth centuries, or even a full-length survey, has yet been published, even though dictionaries and anthologies of eighteenth- and nineteenth-century British women writers have appeared in substantial numbers in the past decade. Most writers described in these sources are highlighted as novelists, poets, literary critics, and playwrights.[7] Scholars who work on British women historians have concentrated on the years since 1800—a time when women in the West had "a lively, productive, and growing interest in the genre" (Smith, *Gender* 6). Before 1800, however, many women writers made contributions to historiography. Scholars have begun to compile statistics about the era's writings by women (especially fictional texts) and to draw tentative conclusions about their authors' careers.[8] Cheryl Turner's *Living by the Pen,* for example, illustrates that "there was not a simple, continuous growth in women's fiction during the eighteenth century" (38). By comparison, women's writing in genres other than fiction has received markedly little attention.

Second-wave feminist studies of British women historians focused on a few female trailblazers but downplayed the larger context of their work.[9] One of the first feminist scholars to turn her attention to British women's historical writings was Natalie Zemon Davis, who asked whether women historians held subjects in common, shared distinctive voices, or were viewed similarly by contemporaries ("Gender" 154). Positing a tradition of historiographical progress in which women historians were eccentric rarities, Davis discusses Margaret Cavendish, duchess of Newcastle, Hutchinson, Catharine Macaulay, and Madame de Staël. She concludes that there was a movement among women historians from family to national and then to general history writing (165). Davis's version of progress reads back from the nineteenth-century historiographical outcome, invalidating earlier women's history writing as more primitive rather than investigating the conditions and norms of its production. Gerda Lerner's chapter "The Search for Women's History" in *The Creation of Feminist Consciousness* (1993) expands Davis's survey. Lerner notes that "current scholarship holds that women made no significant impact on the writing of History until the late eighteenth century" but that "there is significant and almost constant effort on the part of women to create Women's History from the seventh century A.D. forward" (249). Lerner's suggestive chapter looks only to women writers of "women's history," however, neglecting those who were not explicitly protofeminist. Both important essays directed attention to the need for further scholarship, but their preliminary paradigms for women's historiography require reworking.

Toward this end, additional studies have appeared. Bonnie Smith's *The Gender of History* is the first single-author book on women's historical writings in the West after 1800. Smith's study "examines how, between 1800 and 1940, [women historians] struggled over definitions of historical significance; how they variously imagined historical topics and meaning; and how they produced scholarly selves out of historical practices and the iteration of historical rules" (13). Smith's book is useful and theoretically provocative. As an introduction to women historians, however, it disappoints. Although she writes that she "gathered information on hundreds of women [historians]," she includes little of it (244 n. 14). It remains for future scholars to examine and interpret the work of these hundreds. This task has begun in short studies, including pioneering essays by Burstein, Kucich, Maitzen, Melman, Mitchell, Rendall, Thirsk, and Woolf. Rohan Maitzen has published a book on Victorian women and history writing. D. R. Woolf is writing a book on the gendering of history in England between 1500 and 1800, and Greg Kucich is writing on British Romanticism, gender, and historiography. Burstein is finishing a study of histories of women and historical fiction in Great Britain from 1770 to 1870. Each promises to move the field ahead a quantum leap. To date, we know much more about American women writers of history. A book on early American women historians has been published by literary critic Nina Baym, and a thought-provoking but incomplete biographical dictionary of American women historians has appeared (Scanlon and Cosner).[10] British women's contributions to historical discourse have not yet received similarly sustained scholarly attention.

Despite this dearth of information, feminist theories about women's historiography continue to appear. Isobel Grundy, for instance, argues that women's historical writing before the late eighteenth century deserves study and that we must include epic or fictionalized history, biography, scandalous court memoirs, and family history in our research. Grundy believes that these writings provide "a history of a whole female culture. Together they make up one of those barely explored subgenres which are now emerging in such numbers among works written by women" ("Women's History?" 126). She locates a pre-nineteenth-century "feminine" relationship to history that women enacted. Joan Thirsk, too, believes that "differences can be identified between the historical interests and style of the history men and those of the history women, the men clustering at one end and the women at the other end of the spectrum" ("History Women" 5). I am skeptical of Grundy's and Thirsk's views in that I do not believe there was a characteristic women's relationship to history. Instead, the information I have gathered suggests that early modern British women writers enacted various and often competing relationships to historical discourse, depending on their political commitments and class affiliations, their perceptions of developing genres and markets, and their ability to manipulate authorial circumstances and reputations. It is difficult and dangerous to make sweeping generalizations about women writers' engagements with history, particularly before we have given sufficient attention to the myriad individual authors and texts. My work builds on the scholarship of Natalie Zemon Davis, Grundy, and Thirsk, putting us in a better position to understand women writers' complex interactions with historical discourse while incorporating theoretical insights gained from literary and feminist studies of the past decades.

In addition to our needing a better grasp of the contributions of women historiographers, many questions remain about the gendering of history as a genre. Until recently, few people asked how history was gendered during the long eighteenth century, perhaps because the answer seemed obvious.[11] Studies of gender and genre, among the most popular enterprises within literary studies, are finally turning to history writing, with "the acknowledgment [that] gender contributed to history's emergence as both a major branch of literature and a field of knowledge prior to 1800," as Woolf states (647). We have a long way to go to understand history's multiple genderings, whether in mainstream political histories or in less recognized but nevertheless popular eighteenth-century historical subgenres such as antiquarian pursuits, secret histories, memoirs, autobiographies, annals, and compilations. Some writers understood the genre of history in feminine terms. In the late seventeenth century, one writer called history the "mistress of life" and the "mistress of civil conversation" (Wheare 15, 299). Others argued for history as the signature of maleness. In 1746 Peter Whalley styled history a "manly composition" (22). History's status—gendered and otherwise—fluctuated throughout the long eighteenth century, depending on a complex of factors including what kind of history was produced, who produced it, and who was reading it.

It is now well established that in the eighteenth century history and literature were engaged in a struggle for discursive prestige and power. By the nineteenth century these struggles had come to a head. As Linda Orr puts it, "History wanted out of literature just as literature was finally going to let it in. . . . It is as if history awakes in the nineteenth century surprised and even horrified to see how closely it is coupled with fiction" (1). Part of that horror was related to an increased coupling with female writers. One way to distance women from history was increased professionalizing and scientizing. As historiography gained scientific credentials and as fiction gained readers and respect, gendered associations adhered to each genre in a more subtle way. History was never completely "male" in its production or content, just as novels were not wholly "female," but the effect of nineteenth-century historical scientificity—though it did not literally force women out of historiography—appears to have limited how far audiences were prepared to see women's historical writings as authoritative or successful. The conditions for women's historiography that came before that moment remain unclear and largely unexplored.

British Historiography in the Long Eighteenth Century

"No other age," one scholar claims, "had such a voracious interest in historical literature as the eighteenth century. Everyone read and talked history" (J. W. Thompson 2: 94). Standard accounts of eighteenth-century historiography—focusing on a few "great historians"—have obstructed our vision of the large and varied body of history writing published throughout the period. More detailed histories have been published by Martine Watson Brownley, Philip Hicks, Donald R. Kelley, Karen O'Brien, and Laird Okie, among others; additional histories of history will certainly continue to be written. In the interest of producing more nuanced accounts of individual female authors' contributions to history writing, however, in this section I rehearse generalizations of historiographical practices that may themselves be worthy of revision. I leave it to subsequent scholars to describe those subtleties. What remains clear is that both male and female historians wrote in a climate that required knowledge of the most popular and respected historical texts.

Histories were published frequently and sold with great success throughout the long eighteenth century. In terms of quantity published, histories (especially histories of England) far surpassed novels, though not quite equaling the number of religious works (Feather, "British Publishing" 42–43). Market demand was for leisure reading, but leisure reading did not mean light reading, as John Feather notes: "Indeed, the largest single category of books produced by British publishers in the eighteenth century was in the field of religion. . . . books of voyages and travels were among the most popular of the century, and . . . history, both domestic and foreign, was also in heavy demand" (*History* 96). Historical works enjoyed strong popularity throughout the century, experiencing a revival from 1791 to 1800, when their number doubled from the already significant quantity published in the 1780s. In the eighteenth century an estimated ten thousand books were published on British history alone, compared with three thousand novels (Feather, "British Publishing" 42–43). A scholarly focus on fiction to the exclusion of other genres does not accurately depict the market for books.[12]

Traditional histories of British history writing concentrated on the works of a few remarkable historians: Edward Hyde, the earl of Clarendon; Bishop Gilbert Burnet; David Hume; William Robertson; and Edward Gibbon. Generations of scholars have labeled the seventeenth and early eighteenth centuries "poor in historiography" and have therefore believed that only a handful of historians before Hume were worthy of attention (J. W. Thompson 1: 626). Hume, Robertson, and Gibbon were seen as historical geniuses who rose above the poor historiographical productions that surrounded them to create great works. When eighteenth-century histories were discussed outside a "great historian" framework, it often involved weighing accuracy and describing competing party politics—for instance, comparing the bishop of Peterborough White Kennett's Whiggish *Complete History of England* (1706) with his rival Laurence Echard's Tory *History of England* (1708–18). Competing party approaches illuminated eighteenth-century political and contested historical interpretations, but these approaches did not go far enough in explaining the changing features of historiography.

During the eighteenth century, the content of history was widening (M. Thomson 16). The public's taste for modern history had been growing since the sixteenth century, though the explosion of print in the late seventeenth century and the eighteenth century promoted the rise of modern history. "Modern history" in the long eighteenth century designated accounts of the distant as well as the recent past and was, of course, opposed to ancient history—the former being accessible to readers without a classical education and the latter being the only history legitimately taught at university. Modern history was read, if not studied, and there were laments in 1734 that " 'nothing is now hardly read but Burnett's romance or libel, call'd by him *The History of his own Times*. 'Tis read by men, women, and children' " (qtd. in Wordsworth 148–49). Hardly the province of elite, well-educated males, modern history's early linkage to romance and to women and children—or to men without a classical education—contributed to its second-class, feminized status.

In 1724 George I established the Regius Chairs of Modern History and Modern Languages, but they proved little more than sinecures; history (apart from ancient history) did not become part of the curriculum.[13] The professorship demonstrated to some the "depths to which learning had fallen," but it had little impact because the holder of the chair was under no compulsion to lecture (Wordsworth 149; Kenyon 59). Few who held the professorship throughout the long eighteenth century felt themselves so compelled.[14] Modern history was taught to boys in dissenting academies, but ruling-class boys learned modern history, if anywhere, from "the lawyers at the Inns of Court" (Kenyon 7, 6). Modern history was a subject that educated males pursued as a hobby, a marginal genre one might read recreationally. That modern history was not a well-regarded field influenced its status and growth, as Arnaldo Momigliano notes: "There is of course an intrinsic relationship between the fact that history was an ill-defined subject and the fact that history entered the schoolroom so late as a discipline in its own right" (190).

Modern history's emergence as a popular genre may have influenced its reputation as historiographically substandard, but so did the assessments of late seventeenth- and early eighteenth-century British writers and philosophers. A frequent complaint during the period was that the best historians of Great Britain were not British. "By the middle of the eighteenth century, Englishmen had complained for over two centuries about the quality of their historical writing," Philip Hicks declares (1). Histories of England and other popular histories were being translated from French and Italian authors. The British saw their own historians as inferior to their European counterparts, a view shared on the Continent. French historian Paul de Rapin-Thoyras's ten-volume *History of England* (1723–27) was translated into English by Nicholas Tindal starting in 1726. In its sundry abridgments, Thoyras's work remained the most respected history of England until Hume's. Hume too had a low opinion of British history writing, although the *Annual Register* believed his *History of England* (1754–62) "discharged our country from this opprobrium" that the nation produced inferior historians (qtd. in Kenyon 50). As late as 1766 one writer believed that from his own countrymen "we have yet not very good history of our own country, nor I fear ever shall" (*Directions* 11). Hume, Robertson, Catharine

Macaulay, and Gibbon would convince critics that the British could produce historical genius; they had many less-known and less-respected forebears and contemporaries.

What "improved" British historiography? Greater attention to structure and narrative synthesis at midcentury is frequently credited—the same pattern we find with novels. But midcentury "innovations" reveal little about previous conceptions of effective writing in the genre. Despite its unfair reputation today as lacking in science (an anachronistic judgment), history writing in all its forms in the late seventeenth century demonstrates few concerns for creating universal, detached, and well-synthesized stories. Historians were divided into at least two camps, long described as "scholars and antiquarians" versus "literary historians" (Pocock, *Ancient Constitution* 6). For antiquarians the emphasis was on documentation rather than on literary style, a trend that continued until the decline of medieval studies in the mid-eighteenth century (Fussner 115). Antiquarians collected history for the sake of history, often without moral purpose or attention to narrative form. These amateurs are now pictured as men whose efforts involved gross misinterpretations of the past as well as deadening prose. Women were also "directly involved in the gathering of information that concerned the antiquaries," as D. R. Woolf points out (653). Most visible today among these women is Elizabeth Elstob (1683–1756), antiquarian and grammarian. Elstob defended antiquarians, refusing to apologize for her sex in her scholarly venture: "I will not involve the whole Sex, by pleading Woman's Frailty. I confess I thought it would be to little purpose to write an English Saxon Grammar, if there was nothing of Worth in that Language to invite any one to the study of it" (*Rudiments* xxxiv). David C. Douglas contends that Elstob's contributions to the antiquarian movement may have been exaggerated because of the "romantic piquancy" of the circumstances of her work's production, but he believes the role of women in antiquarian enterprises of the long eighteenth century deserves further attention (87).[15]

History's status as an art form and a literary genre—as "belles lettres" rather than as a scholarly pursuit—provides an alternative branch in late seventeenth- and early eighteenth-century historiography. The names that have come down to us from the period are those of the literary historians— Clarendon, Burnet, Edmund Ludlow, Lord Fairfax, and Sir Philip Warwick. The Civil War and its aftermath prompted many men and women to document what they had witnessed, including personal, political, and theological observations—the combination of which was understood as history. Historicizing was perceived as a directly political and didactic act, and as a result, interpretations of modern English history took on great weight. Charles II appointed a historiographer royal, James Howell, to generate what we might today call the monarchical spin. Depending on which position a historian took, history writing could be a dangerous proposition. The Licensing Acts of 1662–79 and 1685–94 stifled publication of histories that were critical of the monarchy or that promoted a Commonwealth agenda. Despite restrictions, critical histories were—as we know now—nevertheless being written, perhaps with an eye to a posthumous audience, which some achieved during the subsequent century.

The early 1680s provided a window during which histories were published in greater numbers. The Revolution of 1688 further stimulated the writing of history. There was "a brisk market for authentic material" at the turn of the century, and "for the next fifteen or twenty years recent history was the very stuff of political debate" (Kenyon 28). Literary historians regularly mixed reminiscences, chronological accounts, and character sketches. Life writing and historical narrative not only were compatible but were viewed as essentially identical in the late seventeenth and early eighteenth centuries (Mayer 80), almost all "memorialist in form" (Fitzsimons 133). Clarendon's celebrated conflation of historical narrative and autobiography in *History of the Rebellion* (1702–4) is said to have inspired Gilbert Burnet to turn his life into a narrative history.[16] Late seventeenth-century women historians—most of whose writings were not published until the nineteenth century—chose similar vehicles.

There were few professional historians in the current sense. Many of the century's most notable literary figures "dabbled in history," including Daniel Defoe, Jonathan Swift, Henry Fielding, Samuel Johnson, Tobias Smollett, Oliver Goldsmith, and Edmund Burke (Okie 9). Although historiography's literary importance did not disappear, in the mid-eighteenth century emphasis turned to a more scholarly, scientific, and cosmopolitan basis for history writing, which led gradually to nineteenth-century professionalization. Original documents were used to create historical narrative of unwitnessed modern history as early as 1679, with Burnet's *History of the Reformation in England,* but that method did not become a historical imperative for many decades (Sutherland 281; Kenyon 34). Despite the publication of works addressing how best to write history (some of them by women), historiographical dictates were by no means rigid. Historical evidence came into print, including "large and small collections of letters and State papers, not drawn from the national archives, but derived directly or indirectly from the families of the statesmen whose activities they recorded" (Firth 31). Beginning in the 1730s and continuing throughout the century and beyond, "every four or five years some fresh collection came out" (Firth 31).

The change was not simply in available evidence. There was also a sea change in philosophical approach. Midcentury historians' "cosmopolitanism" involved an "attitude of detachment towards national prejudice" and "an intellectual investment in the idea of a common European civilisation," as Karen O'Brien has maintained (4). Many British historians of the middle and later eighteenth century embraced French historiographical innovations, holding antiquarians in low esteem and viewing history as a didactic form and a training ground for virtue and citizenship (J. Black 31). Following Voltaire, historians branched out from political and military topics to include social history and manners. They took seriously the aesthetic dimensions of historiography and engaged in research.

Though he did not consult primary documents, Hume believed history writing was a science (the study of man and his environment). His history sought causes, stretching beyond well-rehearsed accounts of wars and monarchs. By contrast, Robertson has been called the "pioneer of scholarly apparatus" among British historians for his use of source material (Kenyon 63). Hume's aversion to documentation increasingly became the minority view. Many midcentury historians quote at length from extracts and original documents, following the preferences of eighteenth-century readers for "history in the raw" (Kenyon 63). When we think of historians using primary documents, we envision travel to archives, but that was not the usual method. Some historians, like Catharine Macaulay, utilized the newly established British Museum (after 1753) or sought access to privately held papers. Travel was expensive, and gaining access to documents was not easy because of "the miserliness with which the possessors of archives guarded their treasures" (Gooch 12). Those historians who could not get direct access to archival material had acquaintances gather and send it; Gibbon received information in this manner, despite his great contempt for compilers (Kenyon 61). Hester Lynch Piozzi (a self-professed compiler) asked family members and friends to send her books so that she could complete her world history. Historical "research," when done at all, had very different protocols in eighteenth-century Great Britain.

The works of Gibbon, Voltaire, Hume, and Robertson were tremendously popular in Great Britain and throughout Europe. Catharine Macaulay also had a devoted following, particularly abroad. Writers of history could now become celebrated figures based on their writing alone, since history was no longer the exclusive territory of eyewitnesses or political heroes. At the end of the eighteenth century, revolutionary activity and nationalist feelings in Great Britain and on the Continent increased people's desire to understand the past, perhaps as a way to explain the present. History gained readers among the middling and even working classes in the latter part of the century, when literacy rates for men averaged one in two and for women, one in three. History appealed to writers not just for the acclaim but also for the money. Robertson's *History of Scotland* (1759) earned him £600, and his publishers were said to have made £6,000 (Kenyon 57). Even long-forgotten histories were profitable. Robert Henry's thematically organized *History of England* (1771) has been called "dull and conventional," but it earned £3,300 in royalties (Kenyon 58).

In the late eighteenth and early nineteenth centuries, history writing was an occupation not only for ambitious literary workers and statesmen but for dilettantes and hacks. Little education and few special skills were required. The budding historiographer no longer needed public experience. We would expect, then, that some women writers—especially those looking for a lucrative and polite genre—would choose historical forms. It is only recently that we have begun to assess the career of the most visible of British female historians, Catharine Macaulay. Macaulay wrote an eight-volume *History of England* (1763–83) that was influential in its own day and is becoming better known in our own. But merely adding Macaulay to our accounts of eighteenth-century historiography does not go far enough in addressing women's supposed absence from historical discourse. Macaulay may well have been the first eminent British woman historian of England, but she was by no means the only woman of her day who wrote history. A full century before she published her history, women writers wrote accounts of the Civil War, including works by Margaret Cavendish, Lady Ann Fanshawe, Lady Anne Halkett, Lady Brilliana Harley, Lucy Hutchinson, and Alice Thornton. Many more Restoration and eighteenth-century women writers grappled with history in their texts. Cowley, Mary Hays, and Mary Wollstonecraft deserve attention as historiographers. Writers we would be more likely to categorize as literary workers also played a part in the development of historical discourse. The histories, biographies, letters, and miscellaneous prose of Mary Astell, Anna Laetitia Barbauld, Mary Berry, Elizabeth Griffith, Elizabeth Hamilton, Ellis Cornelia Knight, Lady Mary Wortley Montagu, Ann Murry, Hester Lynch Piozzi, Sarah Scott, Ann Thicknesse, Priscilla Wakefield, and Helen Maria Williams—and the fiction and translations of Jane Austen, Aphra Behn, Frances Brooke, Maria Edgeworth, Sarah Fielding, Sophia Lee, Charlotte Lennox, Delarivière Manley, and Charlotte Smith, among many less-known others—struggled with what it meant for women to narrate actual or embellished history.[17] Countless female-authored essays, secret histories, conduct books, biographies, memoirs, travel narratives, historical translations, fictional narratives, and poems responded to, participated in, and contributed to the development of history writing during the long eighteenth century. It is imperative that we begin to count, categorize, and comment on them.

Women as Readers of History

One reason we should investigate more carefully women writers' use of history is that more eighteenth-century girls were being encouraged to *read* history. Certain males were thought to need an education in history too, of course. History was a subject "much more fitted for an active than a studious Life, and therefore much more useful for Gentlemen than scholars," and it was considered the conduct book of a future statesman, according to Edmund Bohun (1694) (qtd. in J. Levine 280). Understood by some as cyclical in its pattern, history was believed to provide lessons of the past (whether negative or positive), taking on a powerful conduct book force. Not to know the mistakes of previous epochs was to put yourself at direct risk of repeating them—especially if you were a powerful male. For the most part, however, well-educated boys studied the classics, and the little English history that was available was considered too lightweight for their more rigorous needs (Kent, "Learning" 60).

At the end of the seventeenth century "voices deploring the poor education of women were everywhere," and "lightweight" subjects were just the thing to improve females' ignorant condition (Hunter 269). Histories were offered as among the most appropriate kinds of reading for girls, although in practice many educational programs stressed female accomplishments over "strenuous" study. The belief that history could serve as a moral guide for women readers was imported to England from France in the late seventeenth century: Archbishop François Fénelon advised "wellborn mothers to expose their daughters to 'the history of France . . . and of other neighboring countries,' for this would 'elevate their minds and stimulate them to noble thoughts' " (qtd. in Davis, "Gender" 155). According to Davis, "A few of the boarding schools for wealthy girls in France and England began to include history in their advanced classes, basing its study at least on vernacular texts, if not the Latin ones used in the grammar schools and Jesuit colleges for boys" ("Gender" 155). Fénelon wrote, "Use no monstrous Fictions to divert her with; but either ingenious Fables, or real Histories" (*Accomplish'd Governess* 25).[18] He also saw women as agents of history, which required that girls be schooled in historical matters to learn about the potential consequences of their actions: "What revolutions in state have been all caused merely or chiefly by the irregularities of women! and thus it appears, that there is a necessity for a right education of daughters" (*Instructions* 4). If the conduct literature is any indication, British females were not often regarded as potential political actors, despite Fénelon's warnings. Instead, his notion that history is a form superior to novels and romances earned it a high ranking among British females' educational subjects throughout the century (Woolf 656 n. 46).

In the first half of the eighteenth century, conduct books began to recommend history as a necessary field of study for girls. Women writers too promoted such reading. In her 1710 *Essays upon Several Subjects in Prose and Verse,* Lady Mary Chudleigh encouraged readers to redeem the "vast Disproportion there is as to intellectual Endowments between the Men and Us" (251). After mentioning logic, physics, metaphysics, geography, moral philosophy, ethics, and the Bible as proper objects of study, Chudleigh recommends history:

When we are tir'd with more intricate Studies, we may apply our selves to History, which that we may read with Advantage, we ought to have some insight in Chronology, and to render what we read the more Intelligible, as well as in order to its making a deeper Impression on our Memories, 'twill be best to understand something of Geography, and to have both the Ancient and Modern Maps before us of those Places to which our Books refer. History is a large Field, we shall there see wonderful turns of Fortune, surprizing Occurrences, and an amazing variety of Accidents, foolish mortals labouring for Trifles, contending eagerly for things they would be much happier without; some curst in having their own Wishes, rais'd to the utmost height of Power and Grandeur, only to be thrown thence with the greater Obloquy and Contempt; others pleasing themselves with their Obscurity, and laughing at the Noise and Bustle that surrounds them. (258)

Chudleigh imagines history as useful to females for its moral examples, since it provides an alternative to experiencing the "large field" of the world itself. Chudleigh's rationale would later become the standard one for including history in women's education. As Kent explains, "The entertainment [of reading history] lay in the excitement, the danger, the glamour of court, battlefield, and bedroom—all the staples of traditional 'high' history. The improvement lay in the fact that it all happened, that it was true, not invented" ("Learning" 61). History's improving qualities were beneficial to women readers as substitutes for experience, standing in for those parts of the world that "ladies" should not see. Reading history provided a way for women to gain the benefits of understanding aspects of life they were not supposed to have access to without encountering problems of decorum in experiencing them.

Mary Astell was less enthusiastic about the study of history than was her contemporary Chudleigh. Astell advanced the view that history was most profitable to those who had an opportunity to effect change in the political life of a country (i.e., statesmen), not to women:

But to what Study shall we apply our selves? . . . [Men] allow us Poetry, Plays, and Romances, to Divert us and themselves; and when they would express a particular Esteem for a Woman's Sense, they recommend History. . . . History can only serve us for Amusement and a Subject of Discourse. For tho' it may be of Use to Men who govern Affairs, to know how their Fore-fathers Acted, yet what is this to us, who have nothing to do with such Business? Some good Examples indeed are to be found in History, tho' generally the bad are ten for one; but how will this help our Conduct, or excite in us a generous Emulation? since the Men being the Historians, they seldom condescend to record the great and good Actions of Women; and when they take notice of them, 'tis with this wise Remark, that such Women acted above their Sex. By which one must suppose they wou'd have their Readers understand, that they were not Women who did those Great Actions, but that they were Men in Petticoats! (206–7)

Astell takes history to task for its male-centeredness and its lack of female role models. Despite Astell's concerns about history's sexism and its inappropriateness for women readers, history was gaining a reputation as improving women's conduct.

By the mid-eighteenth century, popular historical texts were being included in the new periodicals for women. Jasper Goodwill's *Ladies Magazine* (1749) featured as a regular column in its two-year print run "The History of England by Question and Answer." The questions begin very simply, addressing female readers as if they were completely uninstructed and uninformed: "Q. What Country is [it] that you term Great-Britain? A. The Island which comprehends the Kingdoms of England and Scotland" (2).[19] Goodwill's questions address geography, naming practices, ancient inhabitants, kings and their families, kinds of government, and powers of the monarch. Readers are informed that "the Crown is hereditary, and the Women are allowed to succeed to it" (2). Subsequent issues dealt with laws, the clergy, the nobility and gentry, and the British in general. All the information provided is in the third person and directed to beginners. The assumption is that females must start from their historical ABCs.

Not all texts spoke of or to women with so little faith in their historical knowledge or capabilities. Lady Sarah Pennington's *An Unfortunate Mother's Advice to Her Absent Daughters* (1761) outlines a typical recommended course of study for polite education that included religion, English (speaking, writing, and grammar), French, Italian, arithmetic, music and drawing (for the talented), natural philosophy, and history:

Acquire a good Knowledge of History; that of your own Country first, then of the Other European Nations; read them, not with a View to amuse, but to improve your Mind; and to that End make Reflections on what you have read, which may be useful to yourself, and render your Conversation agreeable to others; learn so much of Geography, as to form a just Idea of those places you read of; this will make History more entertaining to you. (24)

Pennington's advice, too, is echoed long after the century's end. History came to be valued as morally acceptable entertainment, but it also had the advantage of making its female readers more entertaining and thus more sought-after company—presumably for the opposite sex. Pennington does not recommend novels and romances because "though many of them contain some few good Morals, they are not worth picking out of the Rubbish intermixed" (39). In addition to "truth," histories were believed to have features that novels did not. Histories could make a woman more satisfied with an inactive life, and they could also help her attract a higher-quality husband.

Yet too much history reading could be detrimental to women. Some feared that women would become too learned and therefore unattractive. Eighteenth-century conduct books "advised women that happiness could be secured only by subverting the desire to be educated, or, at the very least, by hiding one's education" (Rafferty 57). Despite this directive, many also express the fear that women will not learn enough, making them insipid companions who devour novels, tea-table gossip, and card-table games. Ann Murry's *Mentoria, or The Young Ladies Instructor, in Familiar Conversations* (1776) devotes a dialogue to history and the "necessity of your making it your peculiar study," describing the kinds of history that are acceptable: sacred history, natural history, biography, the history of your own country, and ancient history (1791, 135–36). The Edgeworths (Maria and her father Richard) were more wary about assigning histories to younger girls. They acknowledge that history is considered a "necessary accomplishment" for females but maintain that "we ought, however, to distinguish between that knowledge of history and of chronology which is really useful and that which is acquired merely for parade" (1: 135). Their *Practical Education* (1798) shows concern for children who read history that must strike them as "absolute nonsense"; without any background in policy, commerce, civilization, and literature, history could not hope to catch their interest (1: 345).

Mary Pilkington's *Mirror for the Female Sex: Historical Beauties for Young Ladies* (1798) also worries about girls' reading history, though the book is a strong supporter of its study: "Of the advantages to be derived from an acquaintance with history, every person of a liberal education must be sensible" (xi). Pilkington fears that young ladies, especially while at school, have "no time for acquiring the least idea of general history, as they enjoy no leisure for reading, or digesting what little they may read" (ix). Studying history remained less valued work than acquiring accomplishments such as drawing, needlework, dancing, and music. When young women were finding time for leisure reading, especially late in the century, it was assumed that they were reading novels and romances, believed to damage them with too narrow a view of the world. In such cases they were given histories so that they "may learn that love is not the only, nor always the predominant, principle in the hearts of man," according to Reverend Broadhurst's 1810 treatise (qtd. in Armstrong, *Desire* 104).

The injunction throughout the conduct literature of the eighteenth century is that women were to become not narrow specialists but noble generalists of history. If ideal women readers were noble generalists, it seems possible that women writers saw openings for themselves as historiographers. Reading history was viewed as a desirable substitute for women's experience outside the domestic or social sphere, but writing history (as the previous section explained) began to change its relation to experience too. Historians needed less "real world" political experience to succeed in the genre. The distinction between specialist and generalist, then, was less about participation in "public life" than about acquiring historical knowledge and rhetorical skill. Despite the potential for opening up the definition of historical expertise (and widening possibilities for who could achieve it), the eighteenth century appears to have produced relatively few female "narrow specialists" of history writing, especially given the tremendous number of histories published. Perhaps, however, we have perceived a dearth of women's contributions to historical discourse because we ourselves have been looking too narrowly.

Questions of Genre and Gender in the Eighteenth Century

Recent scholarship on generic classifications demonstrates why the task of studying historical discourse in the long eighteenth century is so complicated. History as a genre (like fiction) did not appear neatly defined and fully formed. Concomitantly, mapping the messy permutations of a single genre may be a fool's errand. To study a genre exclusive of the other kinds of writing it was competing with (and defining itself against) skews our perception of the early modern market of letters. Genres did not neatly "develop," nor did they simply "progress." As Suzanne Gearhart writes, "The boundary between history and fiction . . . has a history, but that history is not continuous and uniform" (11).[20] Many have argued that fiction and history were contested and fluid categories throughout the long eighteenth century. Leo Braudy's *Narrative Form in History and Fiction* (1970) paved the way for comparing similar narrative structures in historical and literary accounts in eighteenth-century prose. He points out that "*The History of Tom Jones, A Foundling* has more than a merely verbal similarity to . . . *The History of the Decline and Fall of the Roman Empire*" (3–4).[21]

Studies like Braudy's demonstrate that to investigate history without considering fiction (or vice versa) prevents our achieving a more complete understanding of either genre. Scholarship of the 1980s and early 1990s demonstrates that history and fiction share narrative features as well as labels and functions. Some argue that the novel's eighteenth-century "rise" provided the major textual vehicle for promoting a sense of history as a chronicle of human development and subjectivity, but others more accurately describe history's and fiction's functional interconnections. Michael McKeon points out that in the seventeenth and early eighteenth centuries the terms "romance," "history," and "novel" evidently were used interchangeably (25).[22] Lionel Gossman claims that "as late as the eighteenth century, and probably beyond, history was still a literary genre" (3). Michel de Certeau suggests that fiction and history are "quasi-identical" in the early modern period (xi). Ian Haywood's *Making of History* charts the interconnections and ambiguities of fiction and history up until the period of Sir Walter Scott and the formation of the historical novel (11–12).[23] J. Paul Hunter asserts that "historiography was undergoing significant changes just as the novel began to emerge as a historical form, and the popularity of histories may have helped lead, at least indirectly, to the popularity of novels" (339).[24] All these studies reform our understanding of early modern genres, propelling our investigations of historiographical and fictional practices into more dialogic terms.

Despite their strengths, many studies examining historical and fictional prose in the long eighteenth century overstate the similarities between the genres. History and fiction were distinct enough kinds of writing that, from what we can gather, few readers would have gone to Robertson's *History of Scotland* in search of a comic romance or to Fielding's *The History of Tom Jones* for British history lessons. As Robert Mayer puts it, "the closeness of historical and novelistic discourse at the beginning of the eighteenth century in England should not be taken to indicate that readers were confused about the difference between the two" (94). History and fiction, despite many similarities, were not interchangeable genres, though occasionally mistaken for each other. Each genre was struggling with other types for authority, status, and readers. Novels in particular, according to Everett

Zimmerman, were "providing a critique of historical studies as a way of making a place" for themselves (*Boundaries* 4). Recent studies establish history's fraught relationship to fiction and vice versa, from which we learn that fiction writers likened their productions to histories in order to achieve status through association with a more respectable genre.

Our greater comprehension of fiction *and* historiography also requires considering gender as a category of analysis—something most studies lack. "The distinctions between fiction and history which are made in the 17th and 18th century . . . are often made in gendered terms," Jane Spencer contends ("Not Being" 319). Thus any study of eighteenth-century genres would do well to give attention to gendered differences as they took shape. Fiction may have been more often classed as feminine (in terms of both its supposed creators and its intended readers) and history more often as masculine, but that generalization tells us too little. It does not investigate the sex of the contributors to these genres, why they may have chosen to write as they did, or how their writings were received when their sex was known. Nor does it tell us about the varying gendered assignments given to subgenres or to mixings of historical and fictional writing. For example, romances (with their "feminine" associations, fanciful stories, chivalrous heroes, and historically remote locations) were sometimes seen as more history-like than novels, despite novels' more probable and contemporary settings.[25] We have a great deal of work to do to understand how male and female writers—individually and collectively—faced changing gendered, generic, and evolving professional dictates in their encounters with historical discourse during the long eighteenth century.

My book contributes to this ongoing work. Drawing on the theories of Nancy Armstrong, Margaret J. M. Ezell, and Joan Wallach Scott, among others, it takes gender as a central category of analysis in its examinations of historical discourse, focusing on women writers. The various chapters stake local claims in what promises to be thriving scholarly territory. In each chapter I examine how one woman writer of the long eighteenth century perceived, used, and manipulated the genre of history in her texts. I then look at how her texts were evaluated by critics and other members of the reading public. In my revisionary account, British women writers frequently fall short of our feminist hopes for them. I argue that many trailblazing women writers did not identify with or construct a *women's* historiographical tradition to be joined, copied, or perpetuated. Rather than paving the way for "herstory," some early modern British women writers employed generic strategies that may even have contributed to women's dismissal from what Thomas Babbington Macaulay would later call "history proper." A more urgent task than looking for feminist historiographical foremothers, I believe, is gaining a sense of the complex, local, particular, and sometimes contradictory ways that British women writers concerned themselves with mainstream historiographical practices.

Although she wrote at a time when there were few published women writers or established markets for their work, Lucy Apsley Hutchinson, the focus of chapter 2, would become a chief beneficiary of those markets some 125 years after her death. As a historian, autobiographer, poet, translator, religious writer, and political player during the Civil War, Hutchinson presents a fruitful case through which to investigate women's changing relation to historical discourse, reasserting her legitimate place in our histories of history. By examining reviewers' and readers' assessments of Hutchinson's *Memoirs of the Life of Colonel Hutchinson,* I demonstrate that what was historiographical work at the time Hutchinson completed it was not understood on those terms when it was published in the early nineteenth century. A reception history of Hutchinson's texts affords a measurement of the changes in history and fiction from the Restoration to the Romantic era. Though Hutchinson does not label her own writings romance, by the time her works were published they were valued for their romantic and novelistic qualities. Her immense nineteenth-century popularity (as well as her relative twentieth-century obscurity) has everything to do with the generic changes of the eighteenth century.

Chapter 3 discusses Lady Mary Wortley Montagu's unrecognized contributions to historiography. Comparing Montagu's historical writings with Burnet's, I point out that her "Account of the Court of George I" and her recently published fiction show similar concerns for the status of historical personalities and fictional characters as subjects. Montagu employs the features of romance to communicate her historical and political truths. Next I turn to a discussion of the "Turkish Embassy Letters," showing how Montagu creates a space for herself at the apex of historical narrative. In doing so she removes Turkish women from historical time and alters the ways they were depicted and understood. Influenced by past representations of Eastern and Western women, Montagu affected future ones. Montagu's writings, some of which were taken up by historians as reliable records, are influential not just as documents in histories of women, literature, and Orientalism but in histories of history as well.

In chapter 4 I examine Charlotte Lennox's encounters with history writing, concentrating on her prose. That Charlotte Lennox was well versed in historiographical methods is demonstrated by a brief discussion of her proposed history, *The Age of Queen Elizabeth*. The bulk of the chapter looks at *The Female Quixote* (1752), a central text for investigating midcentury historiography, fiction, and gender, showing how Lennox alternately embraces, ridicules, rejects, and reshapes history in ways that do not fall evenly into gendered sides. Lennox usurped some of history's discursive features to create a more highly valued fictional form in *The Female Quixote*. Examining the Bath section of the novel, I disagree with critics who view Arabella's interactions with the dilettante historian Mr. Selvin as proof of Lennox's wish to construct herstory rather than history. I show instead that Mr. Tinsel's "Adventures of Illustrious Persons" are presented as the novel's generic menace. *The Female Quixote* is more dismissive of tinsel—fanciful discourse without integrity—than of Selvin's shallow knowledge of ancient history or of Arabella's immersion in modern French romances. I describe Lennox's philosophy of history in relation to Bolingbroke and Voltaire, with whom she had philosophical and authorial connections.

Chapter 5 considers the grande dame of British history writing, Catharine Sawbridge Macaulay. Macaulay is best known for her *History of England,* but I concentrate on an unusual and rarely discussed piece of historical writing from her "middle period," *The History of England from the Revolution to the Present Time: In a Series of Letters to a Friend* (1778). Macaulay was not the first writer of epistolary history, but her choice of the subgenre signals an attempted shift from a scholarly form to a more popular one. I speculate on the reasons for her shift and on the consequences to her reputation as a female historian and public figure. Resistance to the *History in Letters* may have had less to do with the epistolary historical form than with her idiosyncratic execution of it and her inability to understand the implications of her own identity in that genre. I consider the public's changing perceptions of Macaulay and her writings in 1777–78 as they were affected by her romantic life and choices. Macaulay (later Graham) was savaged in print for her marriage to a younger man of lower social class. Her seeming inability to envision audience expectations and generic implications adds an additional layer of meaning to help us make sense of her *History in Letters* and of her own unfortunate textual role in laying the groundwork for her unfairly damaged reputation.

Hester Lynch Piozzi's historical magnum opus, *Retrospection* (1801), is the focus of chapter 6. *Retrospection,* panned by reviewers, did not achieve the critical or financial success that Piozzi envisioned. Rather than agreeing with the received critical wisdom that this failure arose from poor writing or insufficient research, I argue that *Retrospection* failed because its reviewers and readers did not know what to make of it as a kind of writing and because the author could not effectively execute the ambitious book she promised to deliver. Piozzi's contributions to historiography, in the form of historical anecdotes or "meditations upon history," were not recognized as properly historical by a public that increasingly looked to women writers to address other women or children, to turn history into appropriate moral lessons, and to defer to historical authorities. Examining reviewers' commentary as well as Piozzi's rebuttal in the *Gentleman's Magazine,* it becomes clear that issues of quality were not the only things at stake. As one reviewer put it, Piozzi's book did not succeed because world history is " 'unadapted to a female pen . . . as requiring at once infinite and exact reading.' " Looking at *Retrospection*'s composition, contents, and reception, I show that the kind of history Piozzi designed contributed to her critical downfall; she misread how women's relation to historical discourse was changing at the turn of the century.

Chapter 7 concentrates on Jane Austen's *Northanger Abbey* (1798/1818) and *The History of England* (1791). Whereas Piozzi failed to achieve popular acclaim, Austen eventually succeeded. Though many would be tempted to see Austen's success as the mark of her transcendental genius, I look at the ways her generic choices influenced her ability to build a readership. My investigation provides information that explains why, for nearly 150 years, arguments about Austen's connection to matters historical were viewed as untenable. Using Catherine Morland's statements on history and women as a starting point, I propose that rather than making a plea for "herstory," *Northanger Abbey* ridicules histories and defends novels, usurping elements from historiography while making romance probable. Austen combined genres that were said to be masculine or feminine into a new kind of text that retained elements of both. Her attempts to inflate the value of the novel may have inadvertently contributed to the whittling away of women's

associations with the genre of history, however. Rather than avoiding historical discourse, Austen engaged it directly and refashioned it for her own
purposes.

My book furthers our knowledge of the individual careers of eighteenth-century women authors, of whom some have long been substantial sidelights in literary history (Austen, Piozzi, and Montagu) and others
were until recently ignored (Hutchinson, Lennox, and Macaulay). I do not
offer an overarching, teleological narrative for understanding their writings
within histories of historiography or within histories of women's literature.
Instead, I find that the writers under consideration differed greatly as a result of their political, religious, class, historical, and historiographical affiliations. Despite their profound differences, however, these writers share
an interest in and a commitment to writing history. The chapters of this
book collectively demonstrate that women writers were not divorced from
matters of historiographical import but were intimately involved in debates
over and conversations about the genre of history, as revealed within their
own writings and in the reception their texts met.

British women writers of the long eighteenth century struggled with
what counted as historical in their own writings and in those of their contemporaries, producing (whether purposefully or accidentally) inventive generic combinations. Like their male counterparts, they manipulated generic conventions in their attempts to reach a wider audience, to make more
money, or to instruct readers with greater authority. What women had to
face that men did not, of course, was the "problem" of their sex, assigned
by a culture that usually did not imagine for them an equivalent place in
history or in history writing. Eighteenth-century readers and critics of both
sexes asked not only if women could write historically but if they should.
The following chapters demonstrate, to borrow Charlotte Cowley's words,
that women's writings unquestionably swelled the historic page, albeit with
varying degrees of acceptance and success.

2

The True and Romantic History of Lucy Hutchinson's *Memoirs of the Life of Colonel Hutchinson*

■

The ladies will feel that [Hutchinson's *Memoirs*] carries with it all the interest of a novel, strengthened with the authenticity of real history.—Julius Hutchinson (1822)

Lucy Hutchinson (1620–81) is familiar to scholars of the English Civil War and of seventeenth-century women's writings, but she was formerly known to a more extensive audience. Hutchinson's *Memoirs of the Life of Colonel Hutchinson* (ca. 1671, published 1806), a Puritan account of the Civil War with an ostensible focus on her husband, John, was celebrated throughout the nineteenth century. Despite her political sympathies, Hutchinson gained a posthumous reputation as a national treasure, and her memoir was among the most popular texts from the era (Hutchinson, *Memoirs* [1906] ix). In 1914 Alice Meynell wrote that "all Englishmen know the name of Lucy Hutchinson" (195). Furthermore, according to Doris Mary Stenton, "None of the picturesque royalist heroines was so widely known and praised in the nineteenth century as Lucy Hutchinson" (164). Three editions were exhausted before 1810, two in quarto and one in octavo. A fourth edition of the *Memoirs* was prepared by editor and descendant Julius Hutchinson in 1822. During the next hundred years the *Memoirs* was republished at least seven times (including an abridged edition).[1] In an era when British women writers of previous centuries were reviled or forgotten, Lucy Hutchinson was remembered, recreated, and made a celebrity, but she was often not perceived as a historian.

That the seventeenth and eighteenth centuries in Great Britain produced a great deal of poetic and fictional writing by women is now abundantly clear, but a century ago at least one scholar thought that history was early modern women's forte. Historian Alice Stopford Green's *Woman's Place in the World of Letters* lists history as the only pre-nineteenth-century genre female writers excelled in, and she mentions just two contributors to it: Lucy Hutchinson and Catharine Macaulay (15–16).[2] A century after Green published *Woman's Place,* history is one of the last genres critics turn to when looking for women writers of the early modern period, and Hutchinson is only beginning to be taken seriously in histories of history writing (Mayer 76). Recognition of her position as a pioneer historian has been slow to take hold, despite Green's arguments. Interest in Hutchinson was rekindled in the 1980s in work by feminists Antonia Fraser, Margaret George, Germaine Greer, and Dale Spender. Attention to Hutchinson continues to grow as a result of newly discovered writings, more complete editions, and more frequent anthologizing. In 1995 the *Memoirs* reappeared in a paperback edition—an honor not yet paid to the Civil War account by Margaret Cavendish, duchess of Newcastle, with whom Hutchinson has been frequently and unfavorably compared (Upham; Nicolson; MacCarthy; MacGillivray, "Upham Thesis"; Italiano; Mendelson).[3] David Norbrook's recent positive and tentative attributions of many poems to her provide additional insight into Hutchinson as a writer ("Devine Originall"; "Lucy").[4]

Revived attention, however, is no guarantee of Hutchinson's receiving her due as a *historian* of importance. She has more often been returned to us as a memoirist and literary figure rather than as a historiographer. Literary scholars focus on the belletristic aspects of her prose, and historians have been suspicious of her historiographical credentials and accuracy. Hutchinson is not alone among seventeenth-century writers in being neglected by historians, as Robert Mayer notes. He describes how Hutchinson, along with Edward Hyde, earl of Clarendon, and Richard Baxter, melds life writing and historiography—a combination that was commonplace and accepted as historical discourse around 1700 but that today's "scholars have trouble classifying and therefore mostly ignore" (76). When seventeenth-century historical writings are attended to, they are often presented as literary masterpieces or as biased contemporary curiosities, as in Taylor's *The Origins of the English Civil War* (1960). That short textbook contains essays by historians as well as excerpts from writings by Hutchinson, Clarendon, Baxter, and Thomas Hobbes. More frequently, Hutchinson has been noticed and treated by literary critics. In 1993 the *Norton Anthology of English Literature* added a short selection from one of Hutchinson's texts, marking her as a canonical figure in literary studies.

Relatively few nineteenth- or twentieth-century scholars have praised Hutchinson's writings for historiographical innovation. To give one early example of her distance from the category of history, we might look to George Handley's *Notes on the Memoirs of Colonel Hutchinson* (1905), a volume in the Normal Tutorial Series, claiming to offer teachers and teacher candidates an indispensable study guide. A predecessor to *Cliff's Notes,* The Normal Tutorial Series included such feminine subject areas as "Domestic Science" and "Needles and Cutting-Out" as well as "History" and "Notes on the English Classics." Rather than categorizing Hutchinson's text as history, the series presented it as an English classic, advertised alongside volumes summarizing the works of De Quincey, Dickens, Pepys, Scott, Tennyson, and Thackeray. Most of the company Hutchinson kept in that series has been claimed for literary studies. How was Hutchinson chosen as the lone female author of an English classic? Why was her *Memoirs* grouped with works of fiction, poems, and diaries? Finally, what is at stake in reclaiming Hutchinson's text as early modern historiography?

Lucy Hutchinson made significant—and not sufficiently recognized—contributions to history writing in the late seventeenth century. Melding genres (romance and history, which included life writing) and registers (family, local, and national), she dealt with historiographical problems in remarkable and self-conscious ways. Her popularity in the nineteenth century seems astonishing given the way she and her works were belittled or ignored during much of the twentieth. Many theories might be proposed to explain Hutchinson's emergence, disappearance, and reemergence in the popular and scholarly world of letters, including arguments about the mercurial status of women writers. One largely unexplored reason for the fluctuations in her popularity, however, is the uncertainty of her text's generic assignment.[5] Hutchinson's prose writings became linked to fiction as they would not have been in her own lifetime, when "readers were habituated to accepting highly personal, even clearly biased, accounts as works of history" (Mayer 76).

Nineteenth-century understandings of historiography allowed—perhaps even compelled—Lucy Hutchinson's generic marginalization as a historian. Through a study of Hutchinson and her reception, we can draw conclusions about changes in gendered historical discourse from 1670 to 1820—and well beyond. As early modern generic categories once again undergo critical scrutiny, her *Memoirs* has resurfaced as a text that illustrates women's rejection of mainstream national histories. To understand Hutchinson through this formula is to miss a great deal. Indeed, the aspects of her writings that have been taken up by recent critics threaten to repeat the mistakes of the past two centuries—assuming that the *Memoirs* is worthy of study mainly for its descriptions of Lucy herself or for its colorful characterizations. It is important that Hutchinson's *Memoirs* be understood as a historiographical contribution—one that used selected mainstream historical forms and rejected others—as we seek to explain how her text came to be perceived as something other than history.

Lucy Hutchinson and Authorship

Though she is best known for writing *Memoirs of the Life of Colonel Hutchinson* (hereafter the *Memoirs*), Lucy Hutchinson's body of work is far more substantial. In the 1660s she wrote an autobiographical fragment titled "The Life of Mrs. Hutchinson Written by Herself," a character study of her husband addressed "To My Children," and a record called the "Note Book" or the "diary." [6] Earlier in her life, she translated Lucretius's *De rerum natura*. [7] It was once believed (mistakenly, it appears) that she also translated the *Aeneid*. [8] Verses and religious writings by Hutchinson are also extant and continue to resurface. [9] A few letters have been published as appendixes to earlier editions of the *Memoirs*. Unlike Margaret Cavendish, whose work was published during her lifetime, Hutchinson either chose not to pursue publication or could not do so. [10] Many of her texts were collected and printed more than a century after they were written, a fairly typical outcome among her contemporaries. [11] The Reverend Julius Hutchinson (great-grandson of Colonel John Hutchinson's half brother Charles) published the *Memoirs* in 1806. Its publication met with enough encouragement that Julius Hutchinson later edited two of her treatises on religion, *On the Principles of Christian Religion* and *On Theology* (1817). He apparently believed the latter was original, although it has been revealed as a translated work (Narveson).

Despite Hutchinson's significant written output, some critics have dismissed her as a private or family author, arguing that she did not seek an audience or that she did not view herself as a "serious" writer. It has also been asserted that because she remained patronless and unpublished she therefore did not want her texts to be read.[12] Recent scholarship debunks these views, illustrating that our narrow conception of publication as the sole means of finding an audience for one's writing does not hold for seventeenth-century England. Margaret J. M. Ezell and Harold Love have documented the existence of manuscript circulation and "scribal publication"—the levels on which Hutchinson may have sought readers.[13] Evidence exists that Lucy Hutchinson's texts were read in manuscript while she lived. She is known to have presented her translation of Lucretius to Arthur Annesley, the first earl of Anglesey, a friend who may even have constituted a kind of "patron" (Norbrook, "Lucy"; Greer et al. 215). Anglesey was the first peer who devoted time and money to the formation of a great library—"a scholarly man and a great book collector," as Hugh De Quehen puts it (Lucretius 10). Hutchinson may have had the preservation of her own authorial efforts in mind when she dedicated her translation to him. Or he may have requested her manuscript. Regardless, Hutchinson's gesture demonstrates that despite her protestations to the contrary, she was not averse to building a readership.

After Hutchinson's death, her manuscripts continued to enjoy an audience and a reputation. Historian Catharine Macaulay and others were said to have lobbied Hutchinson's Royalist descendants unsuccessfully for the publication of the *Memoirs* in the late eighteenth century. According to Julius Hutchinson, "*The Memoirs of the Life of Col. Hutchinson* had been seen by many persons, as well as the editor, in the possession of the late Thomas Hutchinson, Esq. of Owthorpe, in Nottinghamshire, and of Hatfield Woodhall, in Hertfordshire; and he had been frequently solicited to permit them to be published, particularly by the late Mrs. Catharine Macaulay, but had uniformly refused" (Hutchinson, *Memoirs* [1822] vii). The family's reluctance to publish ensured that Hutchinson's writings did not attract a mass audience until the nineteenth century. That decision, in turn, made it more difficult for Hutchinson to be read (as Macaulay presumably would have read her) on historical terms.

Though it has less claim to the label "history" than does the *Memoirs,* Hutchinson's autobiographical fragment serves as a useful preview to understanding her historiographical predilections. In it she demonstrates how she imagines her own life in relation to the nation, the world, and the universe. The fragment resembles spiritual autobiographies of the day, but it ranges beyond them in its secular historical concerns. During the seventeenth century more Puritan women were reading and writing, in part because of the emphasis placed on an individual's relationship with God. A growth in literacy rates gave more women the opportunity of redefining themselves on paper, whether for their contemporaries or their descendants (Coleman). Devotional writings were more common, but the events that were happening around them led some Puritan women to compose history. Histories, lives, and autobiographies could illustrate God's hand in world affairs. Hutchinson set out to write her own life in this context.

Hutchinson's text differs from Cavendish's autobiography, *The True Relation of My Birth, Breeding, and Life* (1656) which focuses on family history and offers no national context like that found at the beginning of Hutchinson's fragment. Cavendish's short autobiography dwells on the character and habits of her parents, her brothers, and her husband as well as on her own personality, including her contemplativeness, laziness, anger, and ambitions for fame. Hutchinson's more anecdotal method brings readers from the global to the particular: the history that has led to England, the England that has led to Hutchinson's grandparents, the couplings that led to Hutchinson herself, and the formative details of Hutchinson's upbringing. The fragment joins macro- and microhistorical detail, as universal history sits comfortably alongside national and family material.

Hutchinson begins the story of her own life with a reference to "The Almighty Author" and his "books of providence."[14] She plays down her own authorship, claiming that she writes as a way to avoid overlooking God's part in the smallest concerns of her life, including the hairs on her head (*MJH* 3). Hutchinson moves from God in her own life to God's hand in the formation of the English nation, beginning with the Roman invasion. As she writes, "The celebrated glory of this isle's inhabitants, ever since they received a mention in history, confers some honour upon every one of her children" (4). In the first third of the fragment, Hutchinson describes the fortunes of the Romans, the Britons, the Picts, the Saxons, and the Normans. She remarks that she herself is the product of two seminal lines of English inhabitants—the Normans on her mother's side and the Saxons on her father's. She fashions herself as a true descendant of modern England, perfectly situated to convey its history.

Hutchinson writes that not only was she of fortuitous English lineage but she was born at an opportune moment: "Nor is the place only, but the time of my coming into the world, a considerable mercy to me" (7). Her self-characterization—as a pious, unwilling English martyr, brought into the world with the "right" blood at the "right" time, by the grace of God— was not unusual. Seventeenth-century life writing often included thanks to God for being born then and in England (George 16). What is unusual is the way historical discourse so generously frames her life story—indeed, makes it possible. Hutchinson requires a weighty rumination on her country's history before discussing herself. After commenting on her fortunate, providential birth, she shifts to family concerns. Then, leaving herself aside, in the rest of the fragment she focuses more predictably on her ancestors.

Hutchinson provides information about why she undertakes an autobiographical project. She claims that her autobiography is written primarily for God, to express her thankfulness to him, and to memorialize her parents. Others of her writings, including the *Memoirs,* are said to be set down for her daughter and other children, for diversion, or even in lieu of doing her needlework.[15] Hutchinson echoed her era's authorial conventions for women. In the case of her translation of Lucretius, she says that writing itself causes her anxiety. As she claims in her dedication to Arthur Annesley:

Your Lordship hath skill to render that which in it selfe is poysonous, many ways usefull and medicinall, and are not liable to danger by an ill booke, which I beseech yr Lordship to conceale, as a shame I did never intend to boast, but now resigne to your Lordship's command, whose wisdome to make the defects & errors of my vainly curious youth pardonable, I relie on much more then my owne skill in searching out an apologie for them, and your Lordships benigne favour to me I have so many wayes experienced, that it would be great ingratitude to doubt your Lordships protection against all the censures a book might expose me to.[16]

The censures a devout woman's translation of a controversial pagan work might be subject to are no doubt more real than imagined. However, Hutchinson repeatedly invokes in her writings what Mary Beth Rose calls the "strategy of modesty," frequent in early modern women's writings. Because of the highly formulaic nature of such statements (as well as their repetition within and across texts), it is difficult to accept them at face value. In her autobiography, for instance, Hutchinson writes, "Since I shall detract from those I would celebrate by my imperfect commemorations, I will sum up some few things for my own use" (*MJH* 8). Both assertions—that

Hutchinson held her writing ability in low esteem and that the autobiography was not designed for anyone else's eyes—deserve our skepticism.

The first section of the autobiography resembles political history, whereas the more substantial portion draws on the plot elements of a tragic romance, always brought back to the providential grace of God. In the mid-seventeenth century, sophisticated romances "incorporated actual historical events and political situations, [though] the popular chivalric romance portrayed a world increasingly distant from that of its readers," as Paul Salzman has pointed out (270). Hutchinson's text uses the features of sophisticated romance, but her autobiography does not expound on specific historical events and political situations. That task would be left to the *Memoirs.* Instead, she employs historical generalities in her autobiography. In both texts, romance elements are made accessible to rather than distant from readers. In the seventeenth century, to write a life (one's own or someone else's) was to write "a work of history, not a form of fiction" (Mayer 80). Hutchinson wrote her own life and her *Memoirs* in a form that was framed as political history but that also employed the more idealized conventions of romance.

Hutchinson's *Memoirs* as History

Historiography in the late seventeenth century frequently took the form of memoir. History writing was hardly at an apex in its development during and just after the Civil War, as Martine Watson Brownley argues. She notes that as "historians entered the political arena . . . history became reduced not only to personal polemical views, but also to individual experiences," where issues beyond one's own sphere were rarely tackled (*Clarendon* 7). Those who attempted larger and more "objective" accounts were stymied by their inability to get beyond "dull and prosaic compilation" (8). Hutchinson's approach in the *Memoirs* is neither reductive nor stymied by chronological imperatives. She narrates issues beyond her own sphere with authority and recognizes their larger historical impact. The downfall of the Commonwealth surely posed a "daunting case of conscience" for Hutchinson, as Keeble believes it did for all Puritans who saw the "collapse of the Good Old Cause" (228). Hutchinson belongs in a camp with the likes of John Milton and Richard Baxter, who attempted through historical writing "to perceive and accept God's purpose in and after the Restoration" (Keeble 229).

Hutchinson did not title her work *Memoirs*. The label was chosen by editor Julius Hutchinson. According to the *Oxford English Dictionary*, the meanings of "memoir" in the late seventeenth century included a memorandum, a record of events, and a memorial. The sense of memoir as biography did not come into play until the early nineteenth century. When used in the seventeenth century to designate a record of events, "memoir" was employed in contradistinction to "history." A memoir was considered an incomplete or partial history. In seventeenth-century terms, then, "memoir" is an inappropriate title for Hutchinson's text. She designed it as a complete and impartial "history." Hutchinson, like Clarendon (whose first wife, Anne Ayliffe, was her cousin), describes with candor her personal involvement in the events she narrates, but she maintains her freedom from bias.

Hutchinson's descriptions of local happenings appear to be entirely her own, but her text does not relate only firsthand knowledge.[17] She also incorporates material from other historians, especially Thomas May's *The History of the Parliament of England* (1647). May, secretary to the Long Parliament and a friend of Clarendon's, published in his commissioned *History* what one critic calls "an official apologia for its doings" (Kenyon 26).[18] Hutchinson's use of May's work is acknowledged within her text. She does not simply lift extracts, however. She evaluates the sources she uses and notes specifically how she finds these sources to be lacking. Hutchinson writes of May:

In conducting the state of England in those days wherein he [Colonel Hutchinson], whose actions I am tracing, began to enter into his part in this great tragedy, I have been too long for what I intended, a bare summary, and too short to give a clear understanding of the righteousness of the Parliament's cause; which I shall desire you inform yourselves better of by their own printed papers, and Mr. May's history, which I find to be impartially true so far as he hath carried it on, saving some little mistakes in his own judgment, and misinformations which some vain people gave of themselves, and more indulgence to the King's guilt than can justly be allowed. (*MJH* 75)

The section above is typical of the *Memoirs* as a whole in its authoritative tone, its direct address to its readers, and its penchant for long sentences. Well into her historical task, Hutchinson makes no apologies for her own authorial capability as she did early on in the work. She shows anxiety only for sufficient space and time—how she will reconcile the need to summarize national events with the wish to focus on the actions of her husband, most of which are based in Nottingham and are regional in scope. Hutchinson is conscious of sophisticated historiographical tensions about weighing sources and offering sufficient context to make her local coverage understandable—concerns that are described straightforwardly in the text.

The history the *Memoirs* tells involves the Hutchinsons' changing positions in the Civil War. The course of events can be briefly sketched as follows: A staunch Puritan, Colonel John Hutchinson served as governor of the town and castle of Nottingham, was a member of Parliament, signed the death warrant of Charles I, and served as a member of the Council of State of the Commonwealth. Eventually he came to oppose Oliver Cromwell, after Cromwell had become lord protector. Colonel Hutchinson's renegade position brought trouble to him and his family even before the Restoration. His fate after the return of Charles II was also a difficult one, though he escaped death through his deference to royal authority. He was implicated in the Northern or Derwentdale Plot (a plot to restore the old Parliament), an allegation that Lucy Hutchinson vigorously denies. Colonel Hutchinson was never charged with a crime, but he was imprisoned first in the Tower of London and then at Sandown Castle in Kent, where he died. The *Memoirs* was written some time after Colonel Hutchinson's death in 1664 and completed by 1671. As its readers know, however, the description above is by no means a full summary of the text.

Historians and literary critics alike have found the *Memoirs* engaging from its opening: "He was the eldest surviving son of Sir Thomas Hutchinson, and the Lady Margaret, his first wife. . . . to descend from them was to set up in the world upon a good stock of honour, which obliged their posterity to improve it" (*MJH* 31). Hutchinson provides many hagiographic descriptions of her husband, right up to the *Memoirs*' curious ending, which twice imagines Lucy Hutchinson as a ghost: "He is gone hence and I remain, an airy phantasm walking about his sepulchre and waiting for the harbinger of day to summon me out of these midnight shades to my desired rest" (337). Colonel Hutchinson's life was the vehicle through which Lucy Hutchinson put together her history, but it was not the only focus of her narrative. The *Memoirs* "focuses to an overwhelming degree on public events" (Mayer 79). Unlike the hyperpersonal concentration of most of the late seventeenth-century histories Brownley mentions, the narration in Hutchinson's text collects hundreds of pages of political machinations, local battles, and character descriptions of friends and enemies. Hutchinson wrote history on a larger scale than many of her contemporaries.

Attempts to fuse story (depiction of events) and discourse (analytic commentary) without a strict adherence to chronology were unusual in seventeenth-century histories (Brownley, *Clarendon* 9, 12). Hutchinson's fusing of story and discourse is evident in the transitions she uses in the *Memoirs*. Her segues include: "To take up my discourse of Mr. Hutchinson where I left it" (*MJH* 75); "Instead of digressing, . . . to return therefore to his actions at that time" (87); and an abundance of uses of "in the meantime" (212). The transitions are sometimes jarring and the *Memoirs* is notorious for its lack of punctuation, but it is a narratively skilled text. She includes digressions that delve further back in history, such as considerations of the reign of Elizabeth I.[19] Despite its lack of smoothness, Hutchinson's history juxtaposes local and national events with authoritative commentary, the better to tell her version of what happened and why.

Hutchinson did not directly lay out her theories of history writing, but her contemporary and critical foil Margaret Cavendish did. Cavendish's ruminations on historical writing provide another avenue through which Hutchinson's historiographical concerns might be discerned. Cavendish makes the predictable claim that she is "ignorant of the rules of writing histories," but she demonstrates that she has given the matter a great deal of consideration (xxix). She outlines three types of history writing: general, national, and particular. She defines general history as the "history of the known parts and people of the world," most useful for travelers, navigators, and merchants (xl). National history is the history of a "particular nation, a kingdom or a commonwealth" (xl). She concludes that this kind of history is "political" and "pernicious" because it "teaches subtle policies, begets factions, not only between particular families and persons, but also between whole nations, and great princes, rubbing old sores, and renewing old quarrels, that would otherwise have been forgotten" (xl). Last, particular history is "heroical" in that it recounts the life and actions of a particular person (xl). General history should be written by travelers and navigators, national history by statesmen, and particular history "by the prime actors, or the spectators of those affairs and actions of which they write" (xl).

Cavendish links each kind of history—general, national, and particular—to a kind of government: democracy, aristocracy, and monarchy. The

Royalist Cavendish (who had been one of Queen Henrietta Maria's maids of honor) claims to write "a particular history," which is "the most secure, because it goes not out of its own circle, but turns on its own axis, and for the most part keeps within the circumference of truth" (xl). Cavendish believes it is not inconsistent with her femaleness to write of wars, as long as they are wars among her own countrymen, whose customs and inclinations she knows well (xl–xli). Experience is what creates her ability to write true history. Those (important individuals) who experienced the war could rightly claim status as historians. In Cavendish's schema, women's experiences should be valued rather than denigrated for their particularity, as well as for their superiority to statesmen's warped accounts. Women are likely to make the best historians, and particular history is the form they should elect to write.

Hutchinson and Cavendish did not agree on politics or hold similar ideas of themselves as authors, but they may have shared a commitment to "particular history" as a valuable historical record. Hutchinson would surely not have linked particular history to monarchy, and her *Memoirs* mixes national with particular history. Like Cavendish, though, Hutchinson presents herself as a historical authority because of her firsthand knowledge. "Particular history" may have offered the approach that each woman was best suited to produce as a result of education, proximity to events, and gendered self-understanding. Hutchinson's additional difficulty in making "particular history" suit her purposes involved creating a narrative that could be received as a reflection of her God-given talent for writing well and that could be understood as authoritative in the context of Puritan defeat. To create such a history involved working with intense conflicts and contradictions on political, personal, and generic levels.

Among feminist critics, the most commented-on "conflict" in Hutchinson's *Memoirs* has been the text's construction of two definitive Lucys through the use of "I" for the narrator and "she" for the historical actor described.[20] The narrator and the actor are presumably understood by readers to be the same person, but "she" is employed more frequently than "I" when recording an action that involves both Lucy and John Hutchinson.[21] "I" is used primarily as the author-narrator who makes choices to include or expand on certain events. Some critics have taken Hutchinson's two selves—what I will call the character Lucy (the actor in the text) and the narrator Hutchinson (who comments within the work)—and have argued for one or the other as more representative of the actual woman. To label one of the selves as more true is to miss the point of their combination. In light of the work's other mixings, the use of both first- and third-person pronouns takes on additional meaning. Hutchinson's authorial and narrative complexities need not be solved, but they deserve to be studied, particularly for what they can tell us about the conglomeration of generic features in the *Memoirs*.[22] The text offers a hybrid of history (heroic particular history and national history) and romance, redefined to suit Hutchinson's purposes. She often uses the language of romance but rejects the label.

In terms of its characterization of Lucy, the *Memoirs* also presents a hybrid of narrative history and romance. The character of Lucy in the *Memoirs* tends toward that of the proper wife, and the ways she renders herself deferential provide an illustration of the things Puritan women were valued for. Most sections of the *Memoirs* conform to the gendered ideologies identified in scholarship on early modern women—exemplified in the title of Suzanne Hull's book *Chaste, Silent and Obedient*. Several sections of the *Memoirs* shatter these gendered dictates, which has made Hutchinson more interesting to feminist critics searching for foremothers. The narrator Hutchinson is by necessity unable to keep within a dictate for silence, but the actor Lucy faces similar challenges. Lucy the devoted wife occasionally transforms herself in the narrative into a woman who does not follow the rules for proper feminine behavior.

Every study of the *Memoirs* discusses its so-called mirror section, where Hutchinson displays her commitment to obedient womanhood. Critics have emphasized the section's romantic qualities. However, it is also possible to read the mirror passage as "a Christianized version of Neoplatonic imagery, in which earthly life is seen as a mere reflection of the heavenly, and all human history and social relations form a series of mirrors in which reflection after reflection stretches toward the absolute," as David Norbrook has proposed ("Lucy" 471). Rather than simply mirroring her husband, Hutchinson shows that she mirrors God's will. Lucy Hutchinson writes of herself as eternally silenced ("vanished") at her husband's death, but it is his dying—and her own life as a series of reflections of him—that provides her with the impetus to undertake the *Memoirs* and, subsequently, to achieve textual visibility. She creates a textual mirror that reflects her own image, even though her husband was the inspiration to do so.

Their marriage, which takes place as Lucy is recovering from smallpox, is narrated in the third person and reveals a change in Lucy's antifeminine oddities (*MJH* 52). John is first congratulated for the faithful qualities that would lead him to choose such an unwomanly, studious (and perhaps permanently scarred) spouse.[23] Lucy is said to have had "a melancholy negligence both of herself and others, as if she neither affected to please others, nor took notice of anything before her" (49). Her stony silence toward men and her devotion to quiet study and writing are subsumed into a more appropriate feminine silence when she becomes a wife. After her marriage, many passages (usually told through John's dialogue) describe Lucy as honorable, virtuous, and above ordinary women. Hutchinson claims she kept her proper matrimonial silence from the time of their nuptials to John's death: "[John] soon made [Lucy] more equal to him than he found her, for she was a very faithful mirror, reflecting truly, though but dimly, his own glories upon him . . . but she, that was nothing before his inspection gave her a fair figure, when he was removed was only filled with a dark mist, and never could again take in any delightful object, nor return any shining representation. The greatest excellency she had was the power of apprehending and the virtue of loving his. So, as his shadow, she waited on him everywhere, till he was taken into that region of light which admits of none, and then she vanished into nothing" (51–52). Discounting herself—most pointedly in her life after John's death—Lucy offers the reader a model of the appropriately silent wife.

Norbrook's interpretation of the mirror section as Christianized Neoplatonism can also be used in an argument about Hutchinson's historiography. She uses multiple genres to mirror each other: romance as a reflection of politics as a reflection of providence, stretching toward the absolute. Hutchinson's inclusion of romantic history and political history in the same text, apprehending their interconnected virtues, demonstrates her aims as a wise, compliant, God-centered female historian. She is an apt vessel through which historical truth can be delivered or mirrored because she knows and accepts her position within the patriarchal order, one she redesigns to include writing history.

Hutchinson's use of romance to mirror, reflect, or comment on political history is not limited to describing her own life. In several instances the narrator passes judgment on other women, particularly on whether they are faithful mirrors. The felicity of Queen Elizabeth's reign "was the effect of her submission to her masculine and wise counsellors" (70). Queen Henrietta Maria's influence was pernicious (although this is due in part to her being French and Catholic), since she applied "her great wit and parts, and the power her haughty spirit kept over her husband, who was enslaved in his affection only to her, though she had no more passion for him than what served to promote her designs" (70). A country physician is described as a good man except for "being married to a wicked unquiet woman, she and the love of the world had perverted him to forsake all religious meetings" (328–29). A description of the Hutchinsons' daughter-in-law enumerates the qualities Lucy Hutchinson assigned to a perfect wife: "She was besides naturalized into his house and interests, as if she had had no other regard in the world; she was pious and cheerful, liberal and thrifty, complaisant and kind to all the family and the freest from honour of any woman; loving home, without melancholy or sullenness, observant of her father and mother, not with regret but with delight, and the most submissive, affectionate wife that ever was" (292–93).[24] This daughter-in-law died in childbirth, sealing her martyrdom. All of Lucy Hutchinson's examples of female behavior imply that speaking women manipulate and pervert their husbands and that silent women are the most worthy wives. But female "speech" is not culpable when it entails acceptable kinds of writing, including history, that mirror husband, God, and truth.

Female speech is faulted by Hutchinson when it goes against patriarchal dictates. On several occasions the character Lucy oversteps earlier-drawn gendered boundaries in order to assert herself, ignoring narrator Hutchinson's injunctions about womanly silence. Near the end of the *Memoirs,* after the Restoration, John Hutchinson is in danger of being executed for his part in the regicide and the Civil War. Lucy, flouting her own injunctions to silence, plays a definitive role in furthering family history, if not national history—all against John's purported wishes. She decides that her husband has acted foolishly in his stubborn refusal to ask Charles II for a pardon. Lucy and John disagree over the kinds of placating he should do to reduce or escape punishment. Lucy becomes more and more active on his behalf, serving as a go-between with messages for her husband, who has concealed himself in his house. She writes several letters to complain of the treatment he receives. Letters and messages multiply, some torn up by laughing soldiers, others threatened for publication (270–71).

Hutchinson's account emphasizes her active role as an agent and as an author of history. According to Lucy, John seemed set on turning himself in and being punished. She decides that she wants her husband to be pardoned. For a time, it is Lucy who controls his and their fate. Margaret George sees this section as illustrating a reversal of the roles of husband and wife. George writes of John Hutchinson that "in his uncertainty he was quieted by the strength of her arguments" (31). It is perhaps more helpful to see this episode as evidence of the malleability of the category of wife or public figure than as a temporary usurpation of the category of husband, which respects the boundaries of the categories — something the text itself belies. In her active role Lucy leaves behind her silent self. It becomes clear that John will be punished, and she resolves to step in directly: "Mrs. Hutchinson, whom to keep quiet her husband . . . at this beginning was awakened, and saw that he was ambitious of being a public sacrifice, and therefore, herein only in her whole life, resolved to disobey him . . . she said she would not live to see him a prisoner. With her unquietness, she drove him out of her own lodgings into the custody of a friend . . . and then made it her business to solicit all her friends for his safety" (*MJH* 280). Lucy will not allow John to surrender himself. She "devised a way to try the House, and writ a letter in his name to the Speaker to urge what might be in his favour" (281). She writes a sycophantic letter to the Royalists and forges John's signature to it, suggesting that she wrote many of the letters he dictated and had a hand similar to his (281).[25]

John discovers Lucy's forgery, and she "never displeased him more in her life" (286).[26] He charges her to let him "stand and fall to his own innocency" (311). She claims that she has learned her lesson about usurping power and words, and "remembering how much she had displeased him in saving him before, submitted now to suffer with him, according to his own will" (311). When John is imprisoned, Lucy embraces appropriate wifely silence, and now it is John who "diverts her," commands her, and bids her trust God with him (303-4). Agents of the Crown, looking for evidence against John Hutchinson, later question Lucy, and she is shown a number of letters and papers that she allegedly wrote. She denies knowledge of most of them. The forged letter to Parliament in John's name also resurfaces, but she equivocates, saying that she "could not absolutely say that was her writing, though it had some resemblance" (309). Her public words from this point forward (in the form of letters) are all initiated at John's request. One exception to her appropriate silence must be the writing of the *Memoirs* itself. John Hutchinson dies in the squalid conditions of prison. Although the suspicion of foul play and poisoning is introduced, no mention is made of his commissioning his wife to present the events of his (or their) life (318, 335–36). In the end Hutchinson's text opposes female entry into the world of politics when it is against her husband's will, but it argues on behalf of female entry into history writing when it is for the good of God's aims.

These sections of the *Memoirs* make up a small part of the whole, yet since the book's first publication Lucy and John's courtship has most often piqued readers' interest. When the *Memoirs* was published, its political narration and interpretation may have seemed the text's least engaging aspects. But for Hutchinson the *Memoirs* was designed as personal and providential political history, and the elements of romance were subsumed to her historiographical aims. She is concerned that her *Memoirs* not be mistaken for other kinds of writing, including romance. She insists several times that she does not write romance. Mayer contends that "Hutchinson rejects romance as her model in favor of 'true history'" (88). But if Hutchinson rejects romance, it is primarily its label and not its features that she leaves behind. The *Memoirs* does not steer away from romance elements (including stories of heroism, love, and honor, stylistic elegance, and elaborate descriptions), whether in Lucy and John's courtship or in battle.

In her description of the battle for Nottingham, Hutchinson notes that she could write a romance but that God's involvement prevents it:

If it were a romance, we should say, after the success, that the heroes did it out of excess of gallantry, that they might better signalize their valour upon a foe who was not vanquished to their hands by the inclemency of the season; but while we are relating wonders of Providence we must record this as such a one as is not to be conceived from a relation, in the admirable mercy that it brought forth; but to those who saw it and shared in it, it was a great instruction that even the best and highest courages are but the beams of the Almighty, and when he withholds his influence, the brave turn cowards, fear unnerves the most mighty, makes the most generous base, and great men do those things they blush to think on. (147)

The will of God, not the protection of women, is the stated goal. God encourages gallantry. Hutchinson implies that the events she narrates do not a romance make, but she ultimately eschews a heavenly focus for an earthly domestic one, conceding that the men also wanted to preserve their families and houses (147). God, not man, instigates romance-like heroism.

An additional claim that she is not writing a romance occurs earlier, when she recounts incidents in her courtship with John Hutchinson:

I shall pass by all the little amorous relations, which if I would take the pains to relate, would make a true history of a more handsome management of love than the best romances describe; for these are to be forgotten as the vanities of youth, not worthy of mention among the greater transactions of his life. There is only this to be recorded, that never was there a passion more ardent and less idolatrous; he loved her better than his life, with inexpressible tenderness and kindness, had a most high obliging esteem of her, yet still considered honour, religion, and duty above her, nor ever suffered the intrusion of such a dotage as should blind him from marking her imperfections; which he looked upon with such an indulgent eye as did not abate his love and esteem of her, while it augmented his care to blot out all those spots which might make her appear less worthy of that respect he paid for her. (51)

In this passage Hutchinson implies that her writing cannot be considered "romance" because categorizing it that way would compromise her religious faith and her virtuous reputation. If, as she would have it, she creates a true *history* rather than a romance, her writing, like her husband's love, is ardent and not idolatrous. By claiming that her writing adds to the esteem in which John holds her, Hutchinson makes herself spotless as both wife and historian. The impulse to record history is pure; romance is the morally unthinkable genre. Romance elements, however, are not only acceptable but necessary to honest history writing.

In renaming her passion and their courtship as historical, she can record it within the dictates of purity. Hutchinson's repeated protestations that she is not writing romance differ from those of early novelists, such as Aphra Behn or Daniel Defoe. The *Memoirs* can seem to participate in conflicts over fiction and history only as a result of our latter-day wishes. Hutchinson does not plead for the truth of fictionalized events or for the moral benefits of probable fiction. She aims to create undecorated stories of love, war, and political intrigue, "true romance" that comes (in her view) from God rather than from fancy. Hutchinson may have been familiar with Roger Boyle (who argued in 1655 that history was a mixed romance) or with Sir George MacKenzie (whose 1660 *Aretina* claimed that history described what was done but that romances illustrated what should be done) (qtd. in Barnett). She does not echo their sentiments. In the *Memoirs,* as in her Puritan politics, Hutchinson carved out a place for herself as a dissenting voice. Her history alternately describes what was done and what should be done (or should have been done), using providence and romance to bolster her historiographical enterprise.

Hutchinson insists that romance—like history, politics, and religion—avoid overdressing in preference for the plain truth. By occasionally including romance elements and by classifying them as outside their alleged propensity to falsehood or idolatry, she implicitly presents in her text a new combination of discursive features—a historiographical approach that mirrors many facets of life and events. Hutchinson describes the war as a series of conflicts among those who loved God, country, city, family, power, or themselves in the wrong order or in the wrong amounts. Julius Hutchinson would call this combination a "memoir," but in her own day the *Memoirs* was more generically innovative than has been previously credited (Keeble 238).[27] Although scholars have begun to recognize and discuss Hutchinson's contributions to historiography (among them Keeble, MacGillivray, and Mayer), some continue to see her history as female-focused, compensatory "herstory." Roger Hudson sees all Civil War women's writings as circumscribed by their limited female concerns. He writes, "It is time to turn from the 'sad spectacle of war,' its causes and effects, to the more immediate concerns of these six ladies: dowries, husbands' and fathers' incomes, childbirth, illness, and family ties" (xvii–xviii).[28]

Hudson's own selections from Civil War women's writings disprove his contentions. Women writers of the Civil War repeatedly demonstrate that their "immediate concerns"—especially in Hutchinson's case—are the causes and effects of war and the place of the war in history. Hudson may "like to think also that womenfolk such as the ladies in this book reminded their men of the claims of humanity and common sense when passions were running high" (xx), but "womenfolk" were doing—and writing—things that ignored prescriptions for ladylike, morally superior behavior. Hutchinson and her contemporaries, male and female, were centrally involved in the activities and arguments of wartime. Her *Memoirs* incorporates a great deal of "masculine" subject matter in the form of minute descriptions of battles, military and political. What makes her text unusual is that she simultaneously embraces "feminine" material and ventures so far beyond it. Skewed assumptions about Hutchinson's feminine, humanizing relation to Civil War history (and the simultaneous virtual erasure of her military descriptions and political commitments) were inventions of the nineteenth century.

The Reception of Hutchinson's *Memoirs*

Rather than design her historical mixture as pleasant fancy, Hutchinson promoted the *Memoirs* as historical truth, despite its occasional use of romantic tropes and stories. By the nineteenth century and its first publication, the *Memoirs* found itself in a vastly different generic landscape. The ways Hutchinson's texts were assimilated by nineteenth-century readers and critics provide a stark contrast to her own productions. Her reception history offers information to help us make sense of the "Hutchinson" we have inherited and are now reassessing. Lucy Hutchinson was transformed by her first mass readership into a kind of writer that would have been unthinkable to her. By the early nineteenth century, the generic conditions of the late seventeenth century under—and against—which she wrote her text were long forgotten. What were artificially remembered in their place were anachronistic visions of Hutchinson herself. These visions illustrate the ways a seventeenth-century woman historian was erased or, at best, elided into a quasi-novelist. As D. A. Hobman speculated in 1949, Hutchinson "in a later age might well have become a famous novelist" (118).[29] Sifting through fictional portraits of Hutchinson helps us understand how she was removed from the category of historian by her critics and readers. The categorical uncertainties—her own and her readers'—show how women's historiography was largely dismissed during the nineteenth century.

Before its publication in 1806, the *Memoirs* had gained a readership. Catharine Macaulay was likely interested in Hutchinson's *Memoirs* as a Republican historical document. By the time it was published, the *Memoirs* was more often marketed for its *novelistic* qualities and for its author's idealized domesticity than for its political or historical material. The book was trumpeted as superior to novels because it was true, but it was otherwise always in the shadow of fiction. As the Reverend Julius Hutchinson put it in his preface (which the epigraph to this chapter partially quotes):

The ladies will feel that [Hutchinson's *Memoirs*] carries with it all the interest of a novel, strengthened with the authenticity of real history; they will no doubt feel an additional satisfaction in learning, that though the author added to the erudition of the scholar, the research of the philosopher, the politician, and even the divine, the zeal and magnanimity of the patriot; yet she descended from all these elevations to perform, in the most exemplary manner, the functions of a wife, a mother, and mistress of a family. (Hutchinson, *Memoirs* [1822] xxvi)

Julius Hutchinson's descriptions created the conditions for decades—perhaps centuries—of representations. Lucy Hutchinson is moved out of the arena of politics, philosophy, religion, and scholarship and put on the pedestal of historian-cum-novelist and proper woman.

In his introduction to the *Memoirs,* he apologizes for Hutchinson's writing and manner while simultaneously praising the masculine understanding of her prose and the delicate feminine touch of her pencil (Hutchinson, *Memoirs* [1822] xxv).[30] In 1817, publishing Hutchinson's treatises on religion, he had grown confident enough in her authorial reputation and merit to claim:

The talents of Mrs. Hutchinson as a writer are so well known, and have been so justly appreciated, that it will be unnecessary to say more in this place, than that it is presumed the present work will be found to shed fresh lustre on her character, from the uniform moderation, rationality, and mildness of the principles it discovers; from the liberal, elegant, and dignified deportment of mind it displays, and the pure and gentle spirit of Christianity which pervades every sentiment, and actuated every motive of the Author. As such, it was considered a duty to her memory to rescue from oblivion another most eminent proof of her singular talents and virtues, that they may bloom anew for the future edification of her sex. (Hutchinson, *Principles* iii–iv)

Hutchinson's prose style is described as nervous (meaning muscular or strong), elegant, and unaffected. The tradition of seeing Hutchinson as an ideal English Christian woman who wrote ideal English Christian (if politically misguided) works was well on its way to being established.

According to Julius Hutchinson and myriad nineteenth-century critics, Lucy Hutchinson's writings should be appreciated for their colorful characterizations, proper femininity, and didactic effects—the very qualities for which the novel was earning value. Julius Hutchinson compared her to Samuel Richardson, among others, in his editor's introduction. In *Buds of Genius, or Some Account of the Early Lives of Celebrated Characters: Who Were Remarkable in Their Childhood* (1818), Hutchinson is considered alongside Sir Isaac Newton, Alexander Pope, Samuel Johnson, William Cowper, and Hester Chapone, making her a "child" of eighteenth-century letters. In his personal copy of the *Memoirs,* Samuel Taylor Coleridge likens Lucy Hutchinson to a painter, applauding her characterizations: "As a portrait painter, Mrs. H unites the grace and finish of Vandyke with the life and substantive Reality of Rembrandt."[31] Lady Louisa Stuart (Montagu's granddaughter) wrote in an 1807 letter to her sister that she preferred Hutchinson to "Humes and Robertsons," and that it is more interesting to see "what people say of their own times than what is said of them," especially when it is written in the "best style" — "much better than the present" (*Gleanings* 3: 183). Although neither published the commentary, their views were widely held: Hutchinson's characterizations, like Clarendon's, were her master-piece; her style was amusing. The *Eclectic Review* compared the "goddess" Hutchinson to Sterne and the *Memoirs* to an "ancient romance," appreciating its "miniatures" or character sketches (16–17). Even when the *Memoirs* was congratulated for its historical efforts, rarely was it classified as what Christopher Kent has called "school-room history" or as what I have else-where termed "history-as-fact" (Kent, "Learning"; Looser, "[Re]Making"). Reading Lucy Hutchinson in the day of Sir Walter Scott's historical novels further changed readers' expectations of her writings. The political history she narrated was seen as the background, and the family happenings were classed as the main plot.

I must trace a more detailed path to illustrate how Hutchinson was, in effect, set at one remove from the label of historian, both by readers sym-pathetic to her Republican cause and by those who would have preferred to erase the Civil War from national history. A short but significant part of this path involves Hutchinson's reviewers, who set in motion her alliance with fictional material. The reviews of the *Memoirs* were largely positive, unlike those of Hester Lynch Piozzi's historical magnum opus *Retrospection,* pub-lished five years earlier in 1801. The *Edinburgh Review*'s Lord Francis Jeffrey lavished one encomium after another on the character of Lucy Hutchin-son and declared that he had "not often met with any thing more inter-esting and curious than this volume" (1). He welcomes Hutchinson's (ad-mittedly scanty) disquisitions on "the manners and conditions of women in the period" chiefly through "what she is led to narrate or disclose as to her own education, conduct, or opinions" (4). Jeffrey gives much space to listing the personal attributes of Mrs. Hutchinson, most of which involve her support of her husband and her peerless carrying out of wifely duties. Jeffrey's commentary focuses on Hutchinson's characters rather than on the events she describes.

The sections that Jeffrey and most other reviewers chose for quotation or paraphrase are among those that have captured the attention of today's feminist scholars—a fact that in itself should give us pause. Jeffrey even makes apologies for his relentless focus on Lucy Hutchinson: "In making these miscellaneous extracts, for the amusement of our readers, we are afraid that we have too far lost sight of the worthy Colonel, for whose honour the whole record was designed" (20). His review then delves into some of the colonel's affairs, but not for long. Within a few paragraphs the focus returns to Lucy, the character and idealized figure — not, however, to Hutchinson the historian. What Hutchinson has contributed to the world of letters, if Jeffrey is to be believed, is her own moral example. Jeffrey writes, "England should be proud, we think, of having given birth to Mrs. Hutchinson and her husband; and chiefly because their characters are truly and peculiarly English; . . . we may safely venture to assert, that a nation which produces many such wives and mothers as Mrs. Lucy Hutchinson, must be both great and happy" (24). In his assessment the English character — the safety of the nation — is linked to the achievements of wives and mothers, albeit not in their capacity as writers and historians. It is the likes of Colonel John Hutchinson who are lost to history in the *Memoirs'* nineteenth-century reception.[32]

Lord Jeffrey's final suggestions for editor Julius Hutchinson are the most telling in light of the *Memoirs'* generic assignment. Jeffrey advises that in the next edition he should "omit about 200 pages of the siege of Nottingham, and other parish business" (25). In other words, Jeffrey would like to see more concentration on the characters (particularly, from all appearances, the female ones) and less on local political events. What would be left of the *Memoirs* after Jeffrey's suggested cuts would include a mélange of macrohistorical details (largely drawn, as noted, from May and other contemporary historical sources) and anecdotes about Lucy and John Hutchinson. Jeffrey does not cast the *Memoirs* out of the genre of political history, but his review paves the way for seeing the text and its author as most compelling for personality or character.

Other reviewers made similar critical moves. *Flower's Political Review and Monthly Register* deemed the *Memoirs* "a fund of information, and entertainment" (364). The reviewer notes, "It is not easy to determine which is most to be admired, the character [of John Hutchinson] held up to view, or the writer by whom it is described" (105). The reviewer sees Hutchinson's text as valuable in *not* being a novel, while still recommending it to women readers: "We are happy to find that so interesting a work has within the short space of a few months reached a second edition; and we sincerely hope

it will excite the attention in particular of the female sex: . . . the respectability of the sex consists—not in . . . acquiring vitiated sentiments from the
innumerable volumes of modern trash published under the name of Novels,
but in duly furnishing their minds with useful knowledge" (105). Throughout this review, the audience of the *Memoirs*—imagined as female—is told
to value the work as entertainment and domestic instruction. The work is
worthwhile not as history but as a conduct book, not as a record of events
as they happened but as a manual delineating ideal female behavior. This
is amusing, given the potential parallels early nineteenth-century readers
might have drawn between the English and French revolutions while reading the *Memoirs*. Hutchinson is especially notable not as a revolutionary,
but as an example of a learned woman who has not forgotten her domestic
place. The reviewer appreciates her less for her historiography or her political involvements than for her avoidance of the wrong kind of sentimentality
and her strong commitment to female propriety.

The *Censura Literaria* discusses the *Memoirs* for its own history—that
is, for the history of its road to publication. This publication history resembles in no small way the plot of eighteenth-century gothic novels. The
reviewer writes, "The memory of Mrs. Hutchinson has slept for a century
and an half, in an obscure MS the sport of carelessness or stupidity, thrown
about in corners of deserted mansions, exposed, perhaps, to the rats; to
the weather; to the dirty lighters of fires. . . . Now it is that Mrs. Hutchinson starts into life again, as if from the tomb; and lives in the eye of the
world, with a luster of fame, which never fell upon her, during her actual
existence here!" (55–56).[33] Hutchinson, steeped in the world of Ann Radcliffe, is imagined not only as heroine but as present-day supernatural force.
This device of imagining Hutchinson as a ghost may be traced back to her
own fascinating and phantasmic ending to the *Memoirs,* described in the
previous section. The strange fact, however, is that the ghost section was
suppressed in the version published by Julius Hutchinson—the only one,
presumably, to which this reviewer would have had access. The *Critical Review* speaks of Hutchinson's vivid representations of events, her abilities to
describe scenery, her taste, and her literary merit in similar tones. As the
reviewer writes, "It is not without good grounds that the repositories of
the House of Hutchinson have been ransacked to fill the pages of this volume . . . which have thus unexpectedly escaped from the dust of ancient
records to revel in the magnificence of modern typography" (66–67). The

review concludes by praising the contributions of the text as political history, but then it predicts that "its greatest merit will be allowed to rest on its excellency as a literary composition" (89). As these reviewers' gothic scenarios for Hutchinson's text imply, the *Memoirs*' removal from the genre of history was also effected by turning Hutchinson herself into a fictional character.

In her *Epistles on Women* (1810), Lucy Aikin memorialized Hutchinson in verse, referring to her as "the high historian of the dead" and a "patriot," a "martyr," and a "heroine" (89). An idealized Hutchinson was featured at greater length in the aforementioned *Buds of Genius*. The book's anonymous female author created a series of dialogues among "Mamma" and her two children, Louisa and Henry. The chapter on Lucy Hutchinson is one of three describing the childhood of girls in a work that most often deals with boys. Hutchinson's childhood is reproduced from her own descriptions, using wording drawn from the autobiographical fragment and the *Memoirs*. Some of the descriptions take liberties with Hutchinson's writings. When Henry asks, "And pray, mamma, was [Lucy Hutchinson] a *good* little girl?" Mamma replies, "Yes, my love; her mind was seriously impressed when very young. Her parents were careful to give her suitable religious instruction. . . . When her mother's maids were engaged in idle discourses, she used to exhort them, and endeavour to turn the conversation to something profitable" (15). Mamma's is not the full account from the autobiographical fragment. Just after this statement on idle discourses Hutchinson writes that she was "*not* at that time convinced of the vanity of conversation which was not scandalously wicked" and that she became "the confidante in all the loves that were managed among my mother's young women" (*MJH* 15). By her own admission, Hutchinson's mind was not always of a serious cast.

Buds of Genius commits little more than a sin of omission in its characterization of Hutchinson. Later texts were not so subtle. Elizabeth Sandford's *Lives of English Female Worthies* (1833), dedicated to Queen Victoria, downplays Lucy Hutchinson's political views in its ample entry on her. There are copious apologies for Hutchinson's politics but a relative glossing over of her actions and involvements. Sandford reforms Hutchinson into an exclusively dutiful helpmeet. The *Memoirs* is held up for its asides, apologies, and apotheosis of Lucy Hutchinson. It is as though the Civil War were virtually forgotten as the backdrop for the *Memoirs,* which is duly summarized in purple prose. Sandford's Hutchinson is far more deferential than the *Memoirs* shows her to be:

Mrs. Hutchinson never obtruded [her] advice, or made any show of [her] power: [her] counsel was asked because it was needed, and followed because it was found to be of value. The influence of such like women has not been confined to domestic life, but has often embraced and adorned an ampler sphere. To say nothing of the silent effect of their example, the success that has sometimes attended them as authors may be considered a gratifying tribute to their usefulness. Society will acknowledge the debt it owes to those of them who, as moral and religious writers, have attracted public attention, and so materially affected the tone and habits of their sex. (xiv)

Hutchinson is described not only as obedient and silent but as impelled by her husband to devote herself to his political cause, as if wifely duty explained away her Republican views. As Sandford puts it, Hutchinson "enters, indeed, into details upon subjects which would scarcely in themselves be of any interest to her; and entirely forgets herself, and her own concerns, in narrating matters which refer exclusively to her husband" (182). Hutchinson is found to have only one fault—her political allegiance—but even this is overcome within Sandford's dehistoricizing schema. Sandford concludes, echoing Julius Hutchinson, that if Lucy Hutchinson "lived in the present day, she would not have been a republican, but would have perceived that a constitutional monarchy is the best guarantee for individual liberty" (258). In effect, Hutchinson lived a kind of afterlife "in the present day" in works by Sandford and others, often reincarnated without her Republican politics. The "new" Hutchinson exemplifies an "almost blameless" "example well worthy the imitation of her sex," who displays "courage, self-devotion, and cheerful resignation of her own will" through her faith (259).

Two decades later H. G. Adams's *Cyclopedia of Female Biography* (1857) announced that Hutchinson's *Memoirs* "has taken its place as an English classic" (396). An American work, *Women of Worth: A Book for Girls* (1861), included Hutchinson as a "pattern of domestic virtue" and summarized her "romantic courtship" with John Hutchinson (132).[34] Their celebrity allowed John and Lucy Hutchinson to make appearances as fictional characters in at least four Victorian literary efforts: Eliot Warburton's *Reginald Hastings: Or, A Tale of the Troubles in 164–* (1850); John Henry Brown's play *Love's Labyrinth* (1876); J. Antisell Allen's "drama in verse" *The True and Romantic Love*

Story of Colonel and Mrs. Hutchinson (1885); and Lina Chaworth Musters's *Cavalier Stronghold: A Romance of the Vale of Belvoir* (1890).[35] These texts continue the tradition of fictionalizing Lucy Hutchinson into the late Victorian era, downplaying, if not erasing, the historical contributions of the *Memoirs*.

Warburton's *Reginald Hastings* is a fictional autobiography of the eponymous cavalier. As Warburton claims, Hastings's fictional "confessions" have been written to illustrate the social life of the period and to render "more familiar its leading characters; not only such heroic characters as inspire emulation, but also such as may deter from future evil, by showing of what base matter that evil was composed" (iv). The evil revolves around the Parliamentarians, though the Hutchinsons are curiously excepted from that imputation. The novel is in the main a romance, full of the usual shipwrecks, imprisonments, nunneries, and other such obstacles to true love, and Lucy Hutchinson's role is minor.

Reginald Hastings is in love with Zillah, a woman he has known since childhood. Zillah has both Royalist and Puritan relatives, the Hutchinsons among the latter. Zillah embraces Puritan doctrines in the "folly" of her youth.[36] Colonel Hutchinson is introduced several times as Zillah's cousin before we are told, by Zillah's Royalist sister Phoebe, of the colonel's "tiresome wife" (35). Mrs. Hutchinson herself appears much later on as Hastings's nurse, while he is imprisoned at Nottingham: "I had been dangerously ill for a fortnight; that Mrs. Hutchinson, the Governor's wife, had been very anxious about me, and had even visited me more than once."[37] Colonel Hutchinson too is identified as a "mild, good man" who shows kindness to the trounced Cavaliers (82). While he is concealed from view, Hastings first sees Mrs. Hutchinson with his long-lost love Zillah. Hastings overhears their conversation: Mrs. Hutchinson alludes to Zillah's unmistakable preference for the prisoner. Mrs. Hutchinson leaves Zillah alone, allowing a rendezvous between the star-crossed lovers.

Ultimately Mrs. Hutchinson and Reginald Hastings meet when Hastings is released. Hastings describes her thus:

Mrs. Hutchinson's appearance was by no means puritanical, no more than that of her care-worn but soldier-like looking husband. He wore his hair long, in the fashion of our cavaliers, and his fair wife likewise indulged in rich auburn curls, that set off her serene and delicate beauty to advantage.

This amiable and accomplished lady instantly adapted herself to her husband's manner toward me, and with grave sweetness hoped that as their guest I would be able to forget that I had been their visitor in any other light. I returned to her my sincere and hearty thanks for all the courtesies that I had received, but especially for the great kindness which I felt had been extended toward me in my illness. Mrs. Hutchinson glanced involuntarily toward Zillah, and declared that she had done but little—only a small part of the duty that she owed to her Christian profession, and that she was, after all, but an unprofitable servant. (86)

Lucy Hutchinson is described as fair and beautiful, not as someone careless of her appearance. In a footnote, Warburton lets us know that he takes his description "from the life," that is, from a portrait of Lucy Hutchinson in the possession of Sir Robert Bromley at Stoke Park (86).[38] Hutchinson not only is endowed with great beauty in Warburton's account, she is made "un-puritanical"; the colonel's hair and hers are likened to the Cavaliers'—long and rich. Hutchinson, it is also implied, is a knowing insider when it comes to love. She "glanced involuntarily" at Zillah before responding to Hastings about what she "owed" him and her God. Lucy Hutchinson is depicted as a worthy Puritan in a Cavalier romance—an unlikely transposition.[39]

The most remarkable moment concerning Hutchinson in Warburton's novel comes in an aside. Warburton makes mention of Sir John Gell and his men and notes that Mrs. Hutchinson "by no means seemed to approve of them" (86). Gell, the subject of a substantial digression in Hutchinson's *Memoirs,* was a sheriff of Derbyshire and Parliamentarian general. Hutchinson describes him as "violent," barbaric, and as a man who had no judgment of equity, no piety or holiness, and who was a "foul adulterer" (*MJH* 92). Gell comes in for some of the harshest criticism in the *Memoirs*—and rightly so, according to Keeble. Keeble notes that, though the *Dictionary of National Biography* intimates that Hutchinson exaggerates in her description of Gell, her charges against him are "substantially sound" (*MJH* 357). Not so to Warburton's sensibilities. Warburton inserts a rare footnote in the novel after Gell and Mrs. Hutchinson are mentioned, arguing that Mrs. Hutchinson's accounts of Gell are not to be taken at face value because "the good lady was not writing history, and therefore, perhaps, did not feel obliged to tell the whole truth" (86). In Warburton's *Reginald Hastings,* it is not just the woman "Mrs. Hutchinson" who is fictionalized, de-Puritanized, and romanticized. Lucy Hutchinson's *Memoirs* is also taken out of the category of history writing and placed, one can only conclude, on a par with Warburton's own text—in a sea of nineteenth-century historical novels.

John Henry Brown's *Love's Labyrinth: A Play* resembles *Reginald Hastings* only slightly in its plot and politics. Brown's drama features the heroine Agnes, daughter of a Royalist soldier, who is in love with Francis Thornhagh of the Parliamentary army, a man described in Hutchinson's *Memoirs*. In the end King Charles vows to overcome hate and prejudice to allow Thornhagh and Agnes to marry, encouraging their "artless troth" and disproving Lucy Hutchinson's earlier claim that the king is "trothless." The Hutchinsons appear in act 5, where Lucy is portrayed as against the lovers because she is willing to sacrifice all forms of love for the Puritan cause. She would brand Thornhagh and Agnes "traitors." Brown's characterization retains and foregrounds Lucy Hutchinson's politics more than most portraits drawn of her in the nineteenth century, though all her politics are expressed as family, wifely allegiances.

J. Antisell Allen's *The True and Romantic Love Story of Colonel and Mrs. Hutchinson: A Drama in Verse* makes character changes similar to those in Warburton's novel but on a much larger scale, perhaps in reaction to the rise of the feminist new woman, which one suspects horrified the likes of chivalrous Allen. Allen's eighty-eight-page drama in verse focuses solely on the courtship of John and Lucy Hutchinson, expanding the story in the *Memoirs* with fictional material. Calling them "hero" and "heroine," Allen introduces the Hutchinsons as "too remarkable personages even in this, the heroic age of English history, to be suffered to pass into oblivion" (6). Quoting Lucy Hutchinson's statement that she will "pass by all the little amorous relations, which . . . would make a true history of a more handsome management of love than the best romances describe," Allen asks, " 'Will not many regret that she passes so transiently over these scenes of tenderness and sentiment?' " (6–7). Allen claims he has been "let into the secret" and can therefore "bridge over this very gap in their history" (7). He says he chose verse as the most appropriate medium "through which to reach the loved one's ear and heart" (7).

The story Allen tells is tediously melodramatic from start to finish. He builds up the section from the *Memoirs* in which John Hutchinson is afraid that the absent woman he has fallen in love with (without actually having seen her—merely from being told of her intellectual accomplishments and temperament) may return married. Miss Lucy Apsley remains single, however, and John must contrive a way to meet this "most femininely feminine" of women. One must read three-quarters of the way through Allen's text before John convinces Lucy that he is worthy of her and they kiss "passionately" (64), leading John to exclaim, "And now we're one; now and for ever one, / Folded and locked in one life-long embrace" (64). John and Lucy are compared to Romeo and Juliet. The verse drama ends with an epilogue by a Puritan who knew and outlived them both, likening their love to a strong oak blasted by lightning (Allen 87–88). Lucy and John are presented as saints, though she occasionally fears she cannot measure up to his idealized vision of her. Allen implies that she more than measures up. Her *Memoirs* have displayed her love but have made her the heroine, regardless of her wish to shine only on her husband. A martyr to marriage, Lucy Hutchinson inadvertently saves herself for posterity by sacrificing herself for her husband.

The most remarkable part of Allen's text again occurs in a footnoted disclaimer. He worries that his interpretations of Lucy stretch the account the *Memoirs* gives:

I have not, I find on a reperusal of the *Memoirs,* been portraying her as, historically, she was, but rather as, from her general character, I had conceived of her ideally. And this warns us how unlike the historic reality may be the ideally-conceived picture of any man with whose writings and doings and character we are not intimately acquainted. Let any man read the latest life of (say) the Earl of Strafford, and when he has done so, let him read the Earl's own letters and despatches, and ask himself if the ideal statesman and the man of history be the same man.

Now, however, I have to do with the life and love-making of this noble high-strung Puritan woman, an ornament of her age and sex, and with those of her brave and high-souled husband. (20–21)

Allen's note is confusing in its stance on historical accuracy; he asserts that many texts purporting to be histories fall short of the truth. He points up such shortcomings in historical texts, but he purposefully enacts them in his verse. A "general character" is linked to ideal representations rather than to historical ones. The ideal is given a higher status, perhaps because he believes poetry need not follow the dictates for history. The view of Lucy Apsley as entirely, appropriately feminine despite her intellectual leanings provides the fabricated aspect of Allen's text. He shows no compunction about having created an ideal version of a historical personage; he believes his "general character" of Lucy is the more valuable. In no other text are the Hutchinsons more fully evacuated from historical and political discourse and transplanted into romance than in Allen's production. Apparently some

readers found the change convincing and charming. Allen's text cites glowing reviews from half a dozen periodicals in England and Canada.

If Allen idealizes Lucy Hutchinson as a character while dismissing her
as a historian, Lina Chaworth Musters does the opposite. Musters's *Cavalier
Stronghold* is far more steeped in the history of Nottinghamshire in the Civil
War, not in the least because this fictional novel (predominantly featuring
historical characters) sets out to make a "local hero" of one of her ancestors, John, Lord Chaworth, the "defender of Wyverton" (387). The center
of the novel is a love story—a fabricated one between Juliana De la Fontaine
(ca. 1630–1722) and Prince Rupert (1619–82), nephew of Charles I. Their
love story turns tragic as a result of the events of the Civil War. *A Cavalier
Stronghold* may qualify, in Joan Thirsk's definition, as a nineteenth-century
woman's contribution to local history, but its differences from Hutchinson's *Memoirs* are more striking than its similarities (Thirsk, "Women Local
and Family Historians" 499).

The role of the Hutchinsons in Musters's story provides a cross between
the demonizing of them in Brown's play and their Cavalierizing in Warburton's novel. In *A Cavalier Stronghold*, Lucy Hutchinson is mentioned frequently as a writer and less often as a character in the novel. John Hutchinson is given a more polite, even-tempered personality, whereas Lucy first
appears to us as a lover of court gossip and as someone ambitious for her
husband's political career (13). Musters often draws directly on Hutchinson's *Memoirs* in crafting her own fictional tale. One such sketch taken from
the *Memoirs* involves Hutchinson's lying to one of Prince Rupert's men
so that her husband is not arrested. In anger, she tells a captain that her
husband is in the house, leading to the mistaken arrest of the man who is
actually present, her brother-in-law George Hutchinson.

In using this incident from the *Memoirs* in her novel, Musters short-
ens Hutchinson's narrative, adds some parenthetical remarks, and leaves
out two crucial facts: John Hutchinson was in danger, and Lucy Hutchinson was several days away from delivering a child. Including these elements
might have changed the sympathies of Musters's readers.[40] But Musters
focuses on Hutchinson's telling a lie: "In all probability the Captain could
hardly bring himself to believe that a well brought up young lady, of strict
religious principles, and an old friend of his own, would tell him so gra-
tuitous and uncalled for a falsehood" (92). Royalist characters in Musters's
novel never dream of prevaricating to promote their cause or protect their

ground. In Musters's text, Hutchinson and her allies are made worse, rather than better, than the *Memoirs* would have them perceived.

Strangely, though, Musters cites liberally from Hutchinson's *Memoirs*, usually including tags such as "so Mrs. Hutchinson tells us" (249) or "says the wife of that despotic Governor" (293). The thirty-page appendix to the novel clarifies Musters's aims, as she summarizes her historical research on the people featured in her novel, discussing precisely how she has deviated from the historical record in the plot. She is also very interested in family trees. For instance, she notes that Sir Richard Byron's son (Biron in Hutchinson's text) and his wife Elizabeth Chaworth were the direct ancestors of the Romantic poet George Gordon, Lord Byron and also of Lina Chaworth Musters herself (378). Richard Biron was the nephew of John Hutchinson's mother, Margaret Biron, making the Hutchinsons distant cousins of poet Byron as well as of novelist Musters, though that particular connection is not highlighted in *A Cavalier Stronghold*.[41] Musters writes, "The lives of Colonel and Mrs. Hutchinson are so minutely described in the latter's celebrated memoirs that nothing more need be said about them here" (383), other than relating their connections and descendants. The Hutchinson connection that is trumpeted most loudly is a Royalist one: that of John Hutchinson's father, Sir Thomas Hutchinson, and his second wife, Lady Katherine Stanhope—sister of Lord Chesterfield. Lady Katherine seems to have been responsible for John and George Hutchinson's being cut off from their father's property. All this information could be chalked up to the genealogical and local historical interests of a writer who has perhaps gotten carried away with proving her latter-day place in Civil War history.

Another connection might be made. In framing herself as the direct descendant of these characters—as a woman with a literary pedigree who is a cousin to Lucy Hutchinson—"the historian of the Civil Wars in Nottinghamshire" (383)—Musters charts for herself a birthright as a historical novelist. In *A Cavalier Stronghold*, she provides correctives to Lucy Hutchinson's *Memoirs*' "one-sided" (381) account—one with "unreasoning admiration" (382) for her "worthy, honest, narrow, tyrannical, domineering Puritan" husband (382)—turning Hutchinson's words back on themselves for use in the Royalist cause. Is it possible that Lina Chaworth Musters is an amalgam of what Lucy Hutchinson herself could have been had she lived two hundred years later, expressed an interest in history, and looked for an authorial outlet? Musters herself might have so wished. Many nineteenth-century critics, in the ways they reformed Lucy Hutchinson to suit their own purposes, seem to have obliged.

Hutchinson's dismissal from histories of history has to do not just with her sex. Even male amateur literary historiographers were discredited by the 1860s, as Ian Small notes, pointing to the influx of German historical standards to explain the change (47–50). Restoration historiographical methods and concerns were not shared by the "scientific" historians of the nineteenth century. But the situation of a seventeenth-century *woman* historian was indeed differently conceived by later readers and critics. The ultimately decisive "rise of the novel," its association with female readers, and its many female practitioners made it difficult for texts like Hutchinson's, which utilized romance elements (however tangentially), to be seen as anything but quasi-fictional. That many have subsequently read her writings as marginally or secondarily historical, as overdressed or as charmingly ornate, tells us more about what ultimately happened to women, history, and fiction than it tells us about Hutchinson's contributions to historiography.

Many of us, like our nineteenth-century forebears, remain more interested in the elements of Hutchinson's texts that conform (or fail to conform) to our expectations and tastes. Repeating a nineteenth-century view of Hutchinson's authorship as most interesting for its gender markers or for its romantic qualities may reinforce previous marginalizations rather than open them to further investigation. Future work on Lucy Hutchinson should not make its central quest to replace her in the discourse of history as a "herstorian."[42] We should not attempt to add Hutchinson to literary studies as a protonovelist.[43] Instead, we ought to continue to investigate what was or was not believed to qualify as "history" in women's writings, including but not limited to political historiography, from the Restoration to the present. By so doing we will come to a better understanding of the ways writers like Hutchinson adapted to and affiliated themselves with emerging historiographical practices, as well as the ways audiences accepted, amended, or refused them these associations.

Lady Mary Wortley Montagu: Historian of Her Own Time

■

3

Lucy Hutchinson's "afterlife" in the popular imagination was, on the whole, an apotheosis, though it dampened her historiographical credentials. Subsequent eighteenth-century women writers of history were not generally put on a pedestal by their nineteenth-century audiences. Those who managed to stay in the cultural spotlight, like Lady Mary Wortley Montagu (1689–1762), often were subject to posthumous insinuations and recriminations. Like Hutchinson, Montagu published no work under her own name during her lifetime. Her famous *Letters of the Right Honourable Lady M——y W——y M——e: Written during Her Travels in Europe, Asia and Africa* (1763) was published a year after her death.[1] These "Turkish Embassy Letters" (as they are by convention called) were written from 1716 to 1718 while her husband, Edward Wortley Montagu, was ambassador to Turkey. The letters contributed to the establishment of what has been called the "Montagu cult that grew up in the years immediately after her death" (Pointon 148). By the mid-nineteenth century a mass reading audience knew of Lady Mary, her letters having undergone thirty-one printings between 1763 and 1853 (Ezell, *Writing* 106).

Despite Lady Mary's popularity, not all the information circulating about her life was flattering.[2] Her granddaughter, Lady Louisa Stuart, anonymously published her "Biographical Anecdotes of Lady M. W. Montagu" (1837) to clear her grandmother's name.[3] Stuart knew her task was a difficult one. She believed her problems as a biographer arose in part because "the incidents of [Lady Mary's] life were in no respect linked to those historical or political facts which fix in men's memories even trifles if connected with them" (*EP&S* 6).[4] According to Stuart, it was difficult to create a true picture of Lady Mary because her life had nothing to do with history and politics. Her statement that Lady Mary's life lacked connection to history and politics was wishful thinking. Between 1700 and 1760, "every major writer and many minor writers contributed to contemporary political debates" (Speck 14). Stuart was certainly wrong about Lady Mary and politics. In a sense, however, she was right about Lady Mary and "history," as history was understood in the mid-nineteenth century. Montagu's "Turkish Embassy Letters" were not then understood as historiographically important, though they had been seen as such in the late eighteenth century.

It is my argument that Montagu's prose writings were and are historically, politically, and historiographically informed and influential. Lady Mary had more nineteenth-century fame than most of her female compatriots, "never [having] been completely 'lost' although . . . thoroughly patronized" by literary history (Ezell, *Writing* 64). Despite never being lost to history, Montagu is rarely discussed as a writer of it. Her short historiographical work the "Account of the Court of George I" was published decades after its composition (and her death), which likely contributed to its misclassification as a trifling diary entry. Many of her writings had their genesis in the early decades of the eighteenth century, when the most respected histories of Great Britain were imports, except for historical and scandalous memoirs that attracted a large readership if little critical acclaim. Montagu's fiction, which remained unpublished until the 1990s, also reveals her investment in historical discourse through its use of real people as characters. The fiction provides important points of comparison with the "Account," rounding out Montagu's view of political and romantic history as they are and as they should be. The final text I consider, Montagu's "Turkish Embassy Letters," perhaps constitutes the eighteenth-century document most important in establishing women's history in its cross-cultural dimensions. In it Montagu cements her place as a woman making history as well as a woman narrating it.

The best opportunities for understanding Montagu as a historian have been denied to us by the writer herself. In the 1750s Lady Mary, in the middle of a self-imposed twenty-year exile in Italy and France, wrote—and then progressively destroyed—a work she referred to in her letters as "the History of My Own Time."[5] Her history, she confessed to her daughter Lady Bute in 1752, was her "chiefe Amusement," based on her "exact knowledge both of the Persons and Facts that have made the greatest figure in

England in this Age" (*CL* 3: 18–19). Firsthand knowledge allowed her to "take pleasure in putting together what I know, with an Impartiality that is altogether unusual. Distance of Time and place has totally blotted from my Mind all Traces either of Resentment or prejudice" (3: 19). Lady Mary considered herself an able, if private, historian, concluding, "I speak with the same Indifference of the Court of G[reat] B[ritain] as I should do that of Augustus Caesar. . . . I can assure you I regularly burn every Quire as soon as it is finish'd, and mean nothing more than to divert my solitary hours" (3: 19).[6] Several fragments of Montagu's writing that fit this description have survived (including her "Account of the Court of George I"), but we can only speculate about the kinds of details she chronicled in the longer work. It is possible that her history had much in common with her fictional romance writings. She may have written her own historically focused scandalous memoirs, following Delarivière Manley, whose method she liked (1: 16). Montagu's history may have—like her famous letters—reconstructed her travels and observations. Had her history survived, she might have been known to us as the early eighteenth-century female answer to Clarendon or to Gilbert Burnet, the historical (though not political) counterpart of Lucy Hutchinson.[7]

The differences between Hutchinson and Montagu are more obvious than their similarities. Lady Mary, though she too was loath to style herself an "author" (3: 19), traveled in literary and social circles far more active than any we can document for Hutchinson. Both women were poets and scholars of language who circulated their manuscripts among friends; both clearly considered themselves knowledgeable about political and historical matters. During her lifetime Montagu surreptitiously sought out publication, writing nine numbers of a pro-Walpole periodical, *The Nonsense of Common-Sense* (1737–38). Had she been publicly charged with writing these essays, one supposes that her protestations to the contrary would have been louder than anyone's.[8] Lady Mary appeared as a character and a muse in the published writings of friends and enemies alike (Alexander Pope serving alternately in each role).[9] Publication of her own writings occurred posthumously and continued with additional texts throughout the nineteenth century and up to the present.

Montagu's writings do not reveal a programmatic political agenda (feminist or otherwise), nor do they convey consistent generic affiliations. Like the masquerade she was so fond of in several cultures, Montagu tried on a variety of writerly guises in regard to genre.[10] Despite the wide cast of her writerly net, many of her texts deserve to be studied in our histories of history, especially because her textual role as what Cynthia Lowenthal has called a "reader of history" proved convincing to subsequent readers and scholars of her writings (132). Lady Mary's letters in particular were taken up as reliable historical documents for many years after her death. The "Turkish Embassy Letters," unlike Montagu's other writings, contributed directly to the establishment of "women's history," as she created a space for herself at the apex of historical narrative. Through her descriptions, Montagu changed the ways Turkish women were depicted and understood in Great Britain, although disagreement persists over whether her changes were happily progressive, unintentionally elitist, or maliciously racist. For my purposes it is less useful to label Montagu as definitively "feminist" or "Orientalist" (I see her as both) than to recognize how she used other women in her textual negotiation of authorship, gender, and historiography. Montagu implicitly argues for the validity of women's history and for women as historians, but in the process she removes Turkish women from historical time. The "Turkish Embassy Letters" imply that Turkish women are unhistorical or ahistorical, simultaneously reinforcing her own position as an appropriate female historian. Before examining the "Turkish Embassy Letters," however, I first turn to Montagu's other prose writings in order to describe her wider commitments to historical form. Her "Account" and her recently published fiction show concern for the status of historical personages and fictional characters as subjects, using the features of romance to communicate truths.

The Historical Accounts of the Montagus

When Montagu's "Account of the Court of George I at His Accession" was first published (in the 1837 edition of her *Letters and Works*), it was given a privileged position as the lead-off text. The "Account" followed three introductions—Lord Wharncliffe's "Preface"; James Dallaway's error-riddled "Memoir of Lady Mary Wortley Montagu" (reprinted from the 1803 edition of Montagu's letters); and Lady Louisa Stuart's "Biographical Anecdotes."[11] The "Account," a ten-page description of romantic and political court intrigues, may have been put in a prime location because it was a new addition rather than an important one. Immediately following Montagu's "Account" the editors placed a parallel work written by her husband, Edward Wortley Montagu, titled "Of the State of the Party, at the Accession of George I." His account is half the length of hers and, according to Stuart, not nearly as polished: "His sketch, ten times more shapeless than hers, is a mere rough copy, so blotted and interlined as to be scarcely readable. . . . He, in short, dwells upon grave and solid politics. Lady Mary, slightly noticing these, keeps to the chapter of court-intrigue; which, in a government like ours, may possibly influence them but little, though at a certain distance of time it furnishes better entertainment to careless, idle readers. She therefore is led to give details, and portray individuals; and we must admit that her touches are (as usual) rather caustic. Her husband enters into no particulars of the kind" (Montagu, *Letters* [1837] 97–98). Given Stuart's initial disparagement of Edward Wortley's writing as "shapeless," it is surprising that in the end she shows a preference for his account over Lady Mary's. Stuart describes Lady Mary's version as historically and morally suspect, comparing the historical accuracy of the two accounts, particularly on the issue of the worth (or rather unworthiness) of Sir Robert Walpole. Stuart faults Lady Mary's history for its appeal to careless, idle readers who might even misguidedly appreciate its ill-chosen caustic tone. Seeking to protect readers from the improprieties of Lady Mary's historical "Account," Stuart simultaneously tries to protect Lady Mary's reputation from critics' "inaccurate" versions of her alleged improprieties. One reviewer disallowed both possibilities in one swoop. John Wilson Croker's review of Montagu's *Letters* (1837) claims that Lady Mary is "a suitable historian" of George I's extramarital affairs (181).

In her anecdotes Stuart appears to have anticipated responses like Croker's. She may have tried to forestall these criticisms by shifting her subject. For several pages in her "Biographical Anecdotes," Stuart quotes from, summarizes, and comments on Edward Wortley Montagu's account rather than Lady Mary's. Stuart concludes her discussion of these "somewhat similar" texts with final musings on Wortley's "Of the State of the Party": "This account of what was passing cannot well be called impartial, since the writer obviously leans—does more than lean—to one side; but he sets down his real opinions, formed on the spot, and recorded only for himself: and surely it may be desirable, though but as a matter of curiosity, to learn how the facts and characters at which we are now looking back through the telescope of time, through the long series of years that has made them historical, appeared to the eyes of their contemporaries" (Montagu, *Letters* [1837] 100).

Does Stuart mean to couple Lady Mary's "facts and characters" with her husband's in this conclusion? Is Lady Mary, along with her husband, to be congratulated for setting down her "real opinions," "on the spot," and "recorded only for" herself? Is Lady Mary considered able to help readers look back through the telescope of time? Given her defensiveness, it seems unlikely that Stuart would say yes. Although it is Lady Mary who reports that she writes her account for herself, Stuart attributes the sentiment of recording history for oneself only to Wortley. Lady Mary's "Account" goes editorially unremarked in Stuart's conclusion, subsumed in Wortley's "grave and solid politics."[12] That Stuart chose to end her anecdotes with homage to Edward Wortley Montagu suggests that she herself preferred not to use Lady Mary's writings to look back through time. Stuart apparently did not see Lady Mary's "Account" as historiography.

The final pages of Stuart's "Biographical Anecdotes of Lady M. W. Montagu" deal almost exclusively with Edward Wortley Montagu and his political position. Her discussion serves as an excuse to give readers her own thoughts on Walpole, Wortley, Halifax, Harley, Whigs, and Tories, leaving little doubt that her allegiance is with the Tories.[13] Edward Wortley gets the last word. It is difficult to determine whether Stuart's choice tells us more about her, about Wortley, or about Lady Mary. Robert Halsband and Isobel Grundy seem to be among those who conclude that the final section of the anecdotes is not relevant to Lady Mary. Their recently reprinted selections from the "Biographical Anecdotes" are abridged to omit Stuart's discussion of Edward Wortley's "Of the State of the Party." There is no doubt that Halsband believed Lady Mary Wortley Montagu's "Account" was worthy of attention, since he calls it her "most important piece of miscellaneous prose" (*EP&S* 4) and notes that it "has recently been accorded historical importance" (Halsband, *Life* 272).

Halsband and Grundy's omission may have something to do with the fluctuating status accorded to Montagu's "Account" as historical writing. To some nineteenth-century historians, the history she produced seemed perfectly accurate. Her focus on sexual intrigues did not bother them as it did the socially correct octogenarian Lady Louisa Stuart. The "Account" was used as "a reliable historical source by at least two eminent German historians" of that era, according to Halsband (*EP&S* 82).[14] It is difficult to imagine such treatment for the "Account" today, though Ragnhild Hatton complained in 1978 that Montagu's assessment of George I "has largely been accepted by British historians without independent evidence" despite being "full of traps for the unwary and more important for the development of myths . . . than for historical insight" (172).[15]

Stuart's discussion of Edward Wortley's "Of the State of the Party" is significant for what it says and for what it does not say, revealing one of the first assessments of Lady Mary Wortley Montagu's "Account" as (not) history. Stuart also appears to be the first to link Lady Mary's "Account of the Court of George I" to her destroyed "History of My Own Time." After quoting from that letter, Stuart maintains that the "account . . . is evidently a fragment of that history, which, by accident or oversight, escaped the flames; as it has neither beginning nor end" (Montagu, *Letters* [1837] 97). Subsequent critics have either accepted Stuart's assessment or proposed an earlier date of composition, perhaps as early as 1715.[16] Whether written in 1715 or 1750, the "Account" displays her historiographical assumptions more clearly than any of Montagu's other texts and offers one possibility for imagining the content and form of her "History of My Own Time."

The description—or, if it may be so called, title—of Montagu's "History of My Own Time" echoes Burnet's *History of His Own Times,* the first volume of which was published in 1724, eight years after his death. In his *History,* Burnet, according to Horace Walpole, "only did, what Tacitus, the Cardinal de Retz, and other most approved historians taught him to do, that is, speak the truth" (*Memoirs* 1: 160). Swift was not so enthusiastic: "[Burnet's] Secret History is generally made up of coffeehouse scandals . . . his vanity runs intolerably through the whole book. . . . He is the most partial of all writers that ever pretended so much to impartiality" (5: 183–84). Lady Mary, whose *Letters* were praised and excoriated in similar terms, knew Burnet well as an old friend and mentor. She sent her translation of Epictetus's handbook of stoic advice, *Enchiridion,* to Burnet in 1710 (Halsband, *Life* 31, 14; *CL* 1: 43–46). Burnet's *History* may not have been a direct influence on Montagu, but when compared with her "Account" it shows similar historiographical contours.

The "Account," unlike Burnet's *History,* initially resembles an autobiography. Montagu begins her history in absentia: "I was then in Yorkshire; Mr. W[ortley] (who had at that time that sort of Passion for me, that would have made me invisible to all but himselfe, had it been in his power) had sent me thither" (*EP&S* 83). After mentioning Wortley's possessive passion, Lady Mary writes a full paragraph before arriving at the "new Court with all their Train." Her court scene is framed from an observer's point of view. Montagu writes that the court arrived "before I left the country." Lord Townshend, Robert Walpole, and his sister Dolly are introduced. The narrative centers on Dolly, whose "Folly had lost her Reputation in London," after which her brother arranged to "get rid" of her by marrying her off to an unsuspecting Townshend (*EP&S* 84). Montagu again makes an abrupt transition to the king, ostensibly the central character in this fragmented history: "When King George ascended the Throne, he was surrounded by all his German ministers and playfellows male and female" (*EP&S* 84). The rest of the account describes the all-too-serious play of the playfellows, focusing on the machinations of men and women alike. The account resembles the anecdotal and gossip-filled secret histories of the day. Secret histories were usually written "from the perspective of an insider, not as one who has participated in the events but as one who has heard what happened from well-placed informants" (Mayer 100). That Montagu used narrative elements of secret histories should not lead us to see her work as "unhistorical," for, as Robert Mayer notes, secret histories are "where historical and fictional discourse can be viewed in closest conjunction" (94). Montagu reports on happenings she may have witnessed as well as events that were likely reported to her by others, but she regularly punctuates her narrative with assessments of political implications and consequences.

The most notorious sections of Montagu's "Account" involve George I. It is obvious why historians quote these sections, even when their accuracy is dismissed, because they are at once colorful, straightforward, and damning:

The King's character may be compriz'd in a very few words. In private Life, he would have been call'd an Honest Blockhead; and Fortune that made him a King added nothing to his happyness, only prejudic'd his Honesty and shorten'd his days. No man was ever more free from Ambition; he lov'd Money, but lov'd to keep his own without being rapacious of other men's. . . . He was more properly Dull than Lazy, and would have been so well contented to have remain'd in his little Town of Hanover that if the Ambition of those about him had not been greater than his own, we should never have seen him in England; and the natural honesty of his temper joyn'd with the narrow notions of a low Education made him look upon his acceptance of the crown as an Act of usurpation, which was allways uneasy to him. But he was carry'd by the stream of the people about him in that, as in every other Action of his Life. He could speak no English and was past the Age of learning it. . . . He was passively good natur'd, and wish'd all Mankind enjoy'd Quiet, if they would let him do so. (*EP&S* 86)

To describe the king as an honest blockhead who was passively good-natured and free from ambition is to present him as the opposite of regal.

Montagu's descriptions resemble those of Burnet, who also took a free-speaking tone and moved through his description of Charles II in a similar progression, from personal character to romantic liaisons to affairs of state:

The King was then thirty years of age, and past, one would think, the levities of youth and extravagances of pleasure. He had a good understanding, was well acquainted with the state of affairs both at home and abroad, and had an easy affability and softness of temper that charmed all who came near him. . . . His apprehension was quick, and his imagination and memory good, which enabled him to tell stories with a good grace; but these being sometimes too long and sometime too often repeated, made him become an everlasting talker. . . . His private opinion of people was very odd. . . . No one, he fancied, served him out of love, and therefore he endeavoured to be quits with the world by loving others as little as he thought they loved him. (32–33)

Montagu's and Burnet's descriptions are not carbon copies, any more than George I can be said to be a replica of Charles II. But Montagu may have looked to Burnet when coupling her incisive critique with generous assessment. Both writers' descriptions focus on temper (honesty vs. affability), likability (dull vs. charming), and conversational foibles (passive vs. garrulous) as well as on how the monarch found happiness (quietude vs. excessive pleasure) and how he understood himself in court circles (drawn along by others vs. cynically detached).

The structure of Burnet's description of Charles II continues to be echoed as Montagu's account proceeds. Burnet segues to Charles II's mistresses, as they proved his "ruin." Montagu takes up George I's mistresses, including Mademoiselle Schulenburg, who was "duller than himself and consequently did not find out that he was so" (*EP&S* 86–87). Montagu is even more particular in her discussion of Madame Kilmansegg. Kilmansegg had a "vivacity" in conversation; she loved reading and polite learning, was of an easy humor, and was well bred and inclined to gallantry (*EP&S* 88). The last woman linked to the king, the countess of Platen, gets the most lengthy treatment, and Montagu makes an apology for it: "Perhaps it will be thought a digression in this place to tell the story of his [George I's] amour with her, but as I write only for my selfe I shall allways think I am at Liberty to make what digression I think fit, proper or improper, beside that in my own Opinion nothing can set the King's character in a clearer Light" (*EP&S* 89).

Digressions feature in Burnet's *History* as well, though there they are tagged with transitional phrases such as "I now turn to," "I now come to," or "I look next to" rather than with claims to be writing only for himself. Readers should doubt the sincerity of Montagu's statement about writing only for herself because such claims are so formulaic in early modern women's writings. As early as 1838 Montagu's claim seemed dubious. Editor J. A. St. John, remarking on her statement, concludes, "Now it demands no particular sagacity to detect the absurdity of sophistry like this" (Montagu, *Letters* [1838] xxiv). For one thing, referring to other readers' reactions ("perhaps it will be thought") would be unnecessary in a document meant only for her own eyes. Montagu's other alleged reason for the Platen digression, that it would "set the King's character in a clearer Light," is also an unusual thing to remind oneself of.

The Platen digression narrates a story of romance and of jockeying for court influence, which Montagu follows into a discussion of several men of power in the court, including the duke of Marlborough, Lord Fairfax, diplomat Paul Methuen, and finally the Prince of Wales. Montagu's ordering here, too, follows Burnet's book 2 on Charles II, moving from descriptions of mistresses to men of the court. In Montagu's much shorter (and much less governmentally focused) "Account," however, the two strands are woven together more tightly. Rather than staging history on the battlefield or in Parliament, Montagu shows that the "real" battles for political change occur as men of power are manipulating or ingratiating themselves with the king's women. Her "Account" implies that Parliament is a secondary arena when jockeying for power. The primary space is instead the king's closet— a reasonable enough supposition.

Montagu's historiographical choices both resemble Burnet's and significantly differ from them. Whereas Burnet uses ancient personages as foils for his royals (e.g., Tiberius for Charles II), Montagu prefers the heroes of seventeenth-century French romance. As Montagu writes, "If you will believe Mr. Methuen's account of himselfe, neither Artamenes or Oroondates ever had more Valour, Honnour, Constancy, and discretion" (*EP&S* 92). Montagu's interest in French romances was lifelong, but her use of such comparisons in historical writing is notable. Seventeenth-century French romances were historical fakes, loosely adapted from ancient chronicles that were themselves replete with artistic license. Montagu's choice of Arta-menes (of Madeleine de Scudéry's *Grand Cyrus*) and Oroondates (of La Calprenède's *Cassandra*) as foils comments on the ways court personalities tried to create fictions about themselves—fictions they hoped would take hold as historical fact. Montagu may also have been attracted to French romances as a historiographical tool because they blurred the gendered boundaries of public and private spheres of influence, a strategy required by her view of historical causality (Donawerth 311). Most of Montagu's anec-dotes offer likenesses not of the heroes and heroines of romance, however, but of the villains. None of her court personalities are inspired by love. They are motivated most often by greed and ambition and only occasionally by lust and jealousy. Montagu's "Account" begins with Edward Wortley Mon-tagu's jealous love and ends with "schemes being laid by various persons of gratifying their Ambition or makeing their fortune by particular attach-ment to each of the Royal Family" (*EP&S* 94). The "Account" starts as a secret history but ends as somber historical commentary.

In her "Anecdotes" Stuart tried to separate Edward's masculine history ("grave and solid") from Lady Mary's feminine history ("intriguing and careless"), but a comparison of the "Account" with Burnet's *History of His Own Times* shows that solid politics and romantic intrigue were not so op-posed in early eighteenth-century historical texts as Stuart would have us believe. Montagu's generic choices conform to trends for popular histories in her day, especially if we assume that she wrote the "Account" about 1715. Montagu couples the interest she had displayed in the romance tradition (and would continue to display) with the aims and features of political his-tory. History for Montagu is revealed as a failed masquerade of romance, in which few of the players have noble motivations or heroic qualities. They are instead petty and base. Histories and romances share sensibilities in her "Account": both suggest that events of lasting importance have their gene-sis in the bedroom, later spilling onto the battlefield (whether figurative or literal) of the public sphere. Montagu couples Burnet's immensely popular historiographical innovations with a penchant for romance fiction in order to communicate the realities of historical agency and political life. She did so not just to tell a good story but to reveal the nefarious characters, moti-vations, and schemes of the country's ruling elite.

Court Tales: Montagu and Fiction

In Montagu's fiction the moral inclinations of villains are every bit as low as those of their real-life examples in the "Account." Her good characters, by contrast, soar higher than their human counterparts. For those who have read only Montagu's letters, it may seem strange that she wrote fiction at all. Montagu was dismissive of most contemporary fiction. Though she unapologetically devoured romances and novels, she "disliked most fiction because it lacked realistic moral instruction and demeaned the upper classes (sometimes by dignifying the lower ones)," according to Halsband ("Lady Mary" 156). Montagu's surviving fictional writings were not products of youthful folly, either. Some fiction survives in the juvenilia, most notably the epistolary *Indamora to Lindamira,* written when she was fifteen years old. Most of Montagu's fiction was written when she was much older, while "in her European 'exile' beginning in 1739" (*RW* xiii). Montagu wrote in her commonplace book that "romances should be wrote for the use of old women" (qtd. in *RW* xxiv). She appears to have put that belief into practice as both a reader and a writer, even though by the 1740s her favored French romances had fallen in popularity, replaced by the more realistic English bourgeois novel. Lady Mary's "lifetime of seventy-three years spanned a period of radical change," as Halsband reminds us ("Lady Mary" 145). Literary and historiographical forms, too, experienced radical change.

Lady Mary knew of developments in British fiction during her years in Europe.[17] She arranged for recently published books (many of them novels) to be shipped to her as they appeared. In her own fictional writings, Montagu was aware that she was writing an outmoded kind of story. "During her lonely exile she consoled herself with such nostalgic exercises," according to Halsband ("Lady Mary" 147). She did not merely resuscitate an older genre, however. Montagu's romance writings were not wholly derivative, since they "resist categorization" (*RW* xxvi). None of the texts are clearly datable. They do not have titles (except as editor Isobel Grundy has assigned them), and many exist in fragmented form. The texts range from an epistolary novel and a series of tales written in English to an autobiographical memoir in Italian, to romance fragments written in French. Grundy has made valuable, detailed commentary available on Montagu's "Italian Memoir," a work that offers much material for speculation on issues of gender, historiography, and narrative form ("Lady Mary Wortley Montagu's 'Italian Memoir'").[18] I will forgo a discussion of it in favor of those romance writings that have been less thoroughly scrutinized: "The Sultan's Tale" and "Court Tales 2: Louisa." Both tales demonstrate how Montagu shaped her fiction by romanticizing historical fact.

Montagu's "Sultan's Tale" "may have been a unit in a large composite whole like the series (perhaps complete, perhaps not) of the 'Court Tales'" (RW xiii). It begins and ends in the middle of a sentence, and it is possible that "someone detached the gathering which contains it from a larger unit," though the tale itself appears to be complete (xiii). At the beginning of the tale, a sultan and a sultana converse about the superstition that flowers retain their freshness if worn by a virgin but wilt if worn by a sexually experienced woman. The sultan offers to tell a story he has just read that explains the natural or supernatural origin of the tale, in which he purports to believe. The sultana is far more skeptical. The sultan wants to tell the tale because "once in my Life I may have the pleasure of making you own I knew something you did not. Besides, I have now nothing else to do and am tired of hearing the Vizir's Nonsense, and tho' I don't remember that any of my ancestors condescended to relate a Story themselves, I don't see why I should not set the example of it to my Successors" (17).

Revealing Montagu's fictional aims, the tale offers "pleasure" and "instruction," but in the form of fanciful ("supernatural") knowledge. It is also offered as a perfect break from inactivity and from political activity ("the Vizir's Nonsense"). Finally, the sultan believes it is acceptable for even the most highly placed people to tell such "ridiculous" stories, though doubting the historical precedent for doing so. If there is no precedent, he declares, there ought to be one; he himself will set it. It is difficult not to imagine the sultan as Montagu's mouthpiece. Montagu, alone and bored, takes a break from other activities (perhaps from her "History of My Own Times"?) to indulge in lighter material. Though there are few precedents for someone of her class writing fantastical stories (Margaret Cavendish, the duchess of Newcastle was one), Montagu herself will blaze the trail. One need not agree with the interpretation that the sultan as narrator mirrors Montagu to explore this text, however.

The tale continues by describing the goddess Diana coming down among mortals to help Princess Emma purify her court. Diana offers the help of the goddess Flora's magical powers. Assuming the form of one of Emma's ladies, Diana tells Emma of the secret property of flowers to assess a woman's purity. The rest of the short, humorous tale explains how the princess "weeded out" all but the virginal in her entourage using this test. In retaliation, the excluded women (with supernatural help) rig a contraption to keep their flowers artificially fresh. Despite the initial success of their ruse, they are finally revealed as cheaters. The tale's conclusion presents Flora in person, acknowledging that Jupiter has decreed that she should be "adored in every Garden of the Island" but that he has taken away the detective power of flowers.

Montagu's tale is set on an "Island" that Grundy believes must be Great Britain (*RW* 20), though the place is never named. The setting is implicitly Western and the time contemporary, but the story is an Eastern sultan's tale with Greco-Roman elements. Contemporary English and French dances—minuets and rigadoons—are incorporated in the tale (26). The anglicized names (Emma, Bettina, etc.) suggest British characters, as do the references to historical people. Grundy speculates that the tale may use Augusta, princess of Wales, as its Emma and Elizabeth Chudleigh as Iphegenia, an "Inchantress" who assists the fallen women in feigning chastity (25). The real-life Chudleigh, whose virtue was in doubt, had served as a maid for Princess Augusta, as did Lady Mary's daughter, Lady Bute.[19]

Seeing this tale merely or entirely as the descendant of the secret histories of the 1710s and 1720s—a present-day morality tale disguised as fanciful distant fiction—would be a mistake. Grundy notes many inconsistencies in the text that prevent her from drawing definitive conclusions about the status of the "Sultan's Tale" as secret history. Montagu's story mingles Eastern and Western traditions to tell a fantastical story, but in the "Sultan's Tale," as opposed to the "Account," the story takes precedence over the characters, who are stock ones at best. A secret history worthy of the label would have presented characters easily recognized and ridiculed, linking them to "fabulous anecdotes and traditional gossip" (Firth 27). In the "Sultan's Tale" Montagu flirted with secret history, but like the tale's narrator she chose a less scandalous fictional path for considering (and moralizing about) contemporary behavior.

Montagu's French tale "Louisa" shares textual features with the "Sultan's Tale," but "Louisa" is a somber tragedy with direct historical references and memorable, round characters. Set in the court of Louis XIV in the 1690s, "Louisa" concerns a war orphan, "the Beautifull Louisa," who is brought up in a seminary of female orphans by the purportedly kind but actually scheming Madame de Maintenon. The charming, married duke d'Enguien falls in love with Louisa, and he approaches Madame de Maintenon for assistance in making Louisa his mistress. Louisa falls in love with the rakish duke, but she does not sacrifice her virtue, foiling the many contrivances of her guardian and her would-be lover. The duke, unlike *Clarissa*'s Lovelace, professes that he is unable to take Louisa by force.

To remove herself from temptation and ruin, Louisa agrees to marry a much older man, the count de Belforrest—a possessive recluse, suspected of murdering his first wife. In their unhappy marriage, the count watches Louisa closely, but he does not discover the cause of her sadness. When the count leaves town temporarily, the duke reveals that he has followed Louisa to her new home and watched her for weeks, unwilling to live without her. True to her course, she refuses him, despite her broken heart. Her melancholy becomes consumption. Upon his return the count waits too long to send for doctors, effectively ensuring her death. When Louisa dies, her faithful maid Henrietta finds the duke's miniature and returns it to him. The duke "remain'd above a year in a Melancholy that nothing could Dissipate," though the tale ends with him finding his sorrow "supportable" (*RW* 80).

The plot of Louisa's tale has echoes of Richardson's *Pamela* and *Clarissa;* Lady Mary likened the latter to her own life story, though she found it "miserable stuff" (*CL* 3: 8–9). Montagu did not aim to make the plot of *Clarissa* a more probable story, however. Her tale retains the protagonist's saintly status as moral exemplar, though it substitutes a foolish marriage for a rape. Montagu's use of recognizable historical figures as the basis for some of her characters also proves a significant departure from Richardson, who instead chose quasi-allegorical names like Lovelace. Montagu used historical figures as characters for her fantastical, romantic ends. Madame de Maintenon would have been well known to readers as the mistress (or possibly wife) of Louis XIV (*RW* 42), and Montagu makes her own de Maintenon's questionable moral fiber central to Louisa's tale.[20] Montagu's duke d'Enguien (or d'Enghien), on the other hand, refers to an actual person whose life appears not to have provided the model for his romantically drawn character. The Condé heir on whom the fictional duke is based was "short in stature, ugly, and even deformed" rather than the attractive, if morally defective, duke of Montagu's "Louisa" (xvi). "Louisa" uses historically based personalities in stock romance situations in order to deliver Montagu's message—the best of women can be stuck in the worst of situations but remain honorable.

Montagu's "Louisa" may appear to be a response to familiar French and British fictions, but it also deserves credit for its generic innovation. The story is a precursor to Sophia Lee's *The Recess* (1783–85), the gothic romance often called the first British historical novel (Lee; Alliston; Lewis). As Lee would later do, Montagu uses personalities drawn from history to create fantastical stories of love and moral instruction. Like Lee's well-born "orphans" (Matilda and Ellinor, the fictional twin daughters of Mary, Queen of Scots), Louisa grows up in a reclusive setting. But unlike them, Louisa is not of lofty birth. The pseudohistorical basis of both stories is their only grounding in reality or probability. Montagu, departing from the trend among contemporary British novelists, does not claim she is working with actual events, historical documents, or likely scenarios. Departing too from French romances, which used ancient settings as a historical backdrop, Montagu selected modern history as her foundation. Setting her stories among the previous generation of aristocrats (or in the case of the "Sultan's Tale," in an indeterminate year), Montagu linked history and fiction in ways that would not become popular until several decades after her death. Her use of history in her fiction allows her to rewrite it with abandon. She makes it as interesting and instructive as she likes, without recourse to any "truth" other than her own sense of what is right and good. Montagu's moral sensibilities, in her fiction as in her historical "Account," involved representing vice and virtue and showing what happened (or what should happen) behind the scenes of momentous political and romantic events.

Before anyone knew of Montagu as a writer of fiction, her descendant Lady Louisa Stuart was eager for readers to believe that Lady Mary's penchant for reading romances contributed to a useful education. According to Stuart, reading romances could have a positive effect on a woman's learning: "After resolutely mastering Clelia, nobody could pretend to quail at the aspect of Mezeray, or even at that of Holinshed's Chronicle printed in black letter. Clarendon, Burnet, and Rapin had not yet issued into daylight" (Montagu, *Letters* [1837] 52). Stuart would have us believe that romances serve as an instructional warm-up for modern histories, with the latter given a position of priority in her educational hierarchy. Stuart's views of romance and history do not appear to have been Lady Mary's views, however. In her famous letter to Lady Bute about female education, Montagu recommends history, geography, and philosophy as the reading material that gave her a passion for learning (*CL* 3: 23). In other letters Montagu admits that her own "Taste still continues for the Gay part of reading; wiser people may think it triffling, but it serves to sweeten Life to me, and is, at worst, better than the Generallity of Conversation" (2: 473). For Stuart, romance reading laid the groundwork for the proper study of history. For Montagu, history was the groundwork and romance the reward for mature readers. Montagu maintains that in the "second childhood" of her old age, the pleasures of fiction are precisely the thing: "I am reading an Idle Tale, not expecting Wit or Truth in it, and am very glad it is not Metaphisics to puzzle my Judgment, or History to mislead my Opinion" (3: 134). In her "idle tales," Montagu's wit, truth, and penchant for history were combined in ways that updated French romances. She merged passing fictional trends with more original ones. Rather than abandoning modern history because it misleads (as her letter claims), her fiction used historical fact to link the features she most approved of in scandalous histories, French romances, and bourgeois novels.

The "Turkish Embassy Letters," Women, and Historical Time

If surviving output is any indication, Montagu put more writerly stock in letters than in fiction, although these forms were then highly intertwined. As Ruth Perry has noted, women writers tried their hands at epistolary writing because "it was a format that required no formal education"; letter writing had long been encouraged in women as "an accomplishment rather than an art" (*Women* 17). The temptation to consider Montagu's letters in fictional terms is strong. Joseph Epstein, for one, believes that "within [Montagu's] letters one discovers . . . a mother lode of novelistic material" (17). If today's readers find building blocks for a novel, fewer have apprehended historiographical material. Again, to quote Epstein, "Lady Mary's letters contain little of great events, not a vast amount about famous persons, and a paucity of personal confessions" (17). Though the letters contain less of this sort of material than some readers may wish, hers are not apolitical and ahistorical missives, in the mold once assigned to Jane Austen's writings. Montagu's "Turkish Embassy Letters" are immersed in historical discourse, most directly when she offers brief history lessons and treatises on architecture, literature (Turkish and English), manners, and government. Montagu's letters have become most interesting to recent critics, however, for their statements on Turkish women.

In the past decade's resurgence of interest in Montagu's "Turkish Embassy Letters," critical arguments have been put forward in the name of establishing her "Orientalism" or "feminism." Montagu's statements about the freedom of Turkish women led some to regard her as progressive, escaping the ethnocentricity and sexism of her contemporaries. Others have seen her as elitist and ethnocentric, thoroughly implicated in dominant Western oppression. How far Montagu's letters might be deemed to contain sympathetic renderings of eighteenth-century Turkish customs, particularly regarding Turkish women, is now much debated. Her own claims of fairness were traditionally accepted at face value. Halsband says of the letters, "By virtue of their clear-sighted observation, their expansive tolerance, and their candid sympathy for an alien culture, they are Lady Mary's valid credential for a place in the European 'Enlightenment' " (*CL* I: xiv). More recently Michelle Plaisant concludes, "Peut-on imaginer plus belle leçon de tolérance?" (72). Cross-cultural sympathy is one of the reasons Montagu has been named as a protofeminist and an advocate for women. She has been called "a brave spirit who challenged the male domination of the literary world by writing moving letters and ladylike epistles" (P. Rogers 29). For some she "was a staunch advocate of feminism" (Spender, *Women* 68–69).[21] She was "full of appreciation of the exotic cultures she encountered" (McVeagh 8).[22]

Even among those who place Montagu firmly in the feminist or protofeminist camp, however, there is disagreement over the sincerity of her comments on Turkish women. Katharine Rogers disbelieves Montagu's statements on Turkish women, finding it inconceivable that she would think their veils provide them with more liberty. Rogers concludes, "Of course [Montagu] must have realized that this was a frivolous proof of liberty and that Turkish women were even more restricted and less valued than English ones. But this was how she made the point that English women were only supposed to be free" (*Feminism* 94).[23] The "Turkish Embassy Letters," in Rogers's view, are not truer but more *deceptive* accounts of Montagu's feminist views on women. Whether seen as representative of Montagu's feminism or as subversive attempts to disguise her beliefs, these views of the

"Turkish Embassy Letters" have loosely followed the pleas of Mary Astell in her 1724 preface to the "Letters." There Montagu is praised for her female sensibilities; Astell asks other women to join her in praise because Montagu is a woman writer.[24]

Though some have read Montagu's letters with an unquestioning sympathy akin to Astell's, others have been far more skeptical, showing that although the letters may seem at first glance to offer a sisterly attitude toward Turkish women, this sisterhood is only with upper-class women and exists through alternately aestheticizing and Westernizing their attributes.[25] Consequently Montagu has been implicated in Orientalist practices.[26] She has been described as an elitist for her notion that traveling in veils eliminated class distinctions, even though her own letters everywhere reveal such distinctions. G. S. Rousseau and Roy Porter conclude that Lady Mary was among the "most ethnocentric observers" and "saw precisely what she had been expecting to see" (16).[27] Others have taken a middle view, seeing her letters as sometimes taking a "male spectatorial position," though there is a "slippage" in her own more subjective (and presumably sympathetic) position vis-à-vis Turkish women (B. Orr 160).

Despite debates on the political implications of the "Turkish Embassy Letters," few scholars have commented on their historiographical contributions. One early twentieth-century editor, Arthur Ropes, believed they were "not perhaps the most interesting part of her correspondence; for they give rather *too much useful information* and too little of the personality of the writer" (Montagu, *Lady Mary* 69). His views place him in the critical minority. Many readers of the past two centuries have found the "Turkish Embassy Letters" among the most fascinating parts of Montagu's correspondence, discerning an emphasis on personality over useful information. I argue that Montagu's eighteenth-century readers found an adequate supply of both and that it is important to recover the text's entertaining as well as educational effects.

In her letters Montagu observes many parallels between English practices and Turkish ones—including both of them in the "manners of mankind." In some instances she accords superiority to Turkish customs. She continually corrects the excesses of previous travel writers and insists that Turks are not so vulgar as the English have been led to think. In her letters there are at least seventeen references to "lying travellers or their incorrect reports" (Schwartz 68). Montagu recognizes that her anecdotes sound like tales from the "Arabian Nights" but maintains that Turkish customs are indeed reflected in these stories. Like her contemporaries, she shows particular interest in the status of Turkish women. In eighteenth-century England Turkish women were pitied, their plight compared with that of other nations' females. In her *Poems on Several Occasions* from 1696, Elizabeth Singer Rowe contends that English women have reason and sense and are undervalued by English men, using Turkish women as her foil. She writes of "a plain and an open design to render us meer *Slaves,* perfect TURKISH WIVES, without *Properties,* or *Sense,* or *Souls,*" rather than "*Free-born English Women*" (qtd. in Jones, *Women* 144–45). Rowe, accepting these assessments of Turkish women, bristles at English women's being treated in kind. Montagu's representations of Turkish women provide a less dismissive view. She works within and outside dominant English stereotypes of Turkish culture, questioning some assumptions but reinforcing others.

The "Turkish Embassy Letters" outline the differences and the similarities between Turkish and English women's manners. Montagu claims she is the first Western woman to have ventured inside a Turkish bagnio (or *hammam*) and to have spent a good deal of time with Turkish women. Diverging from the views of her contemporaries, Montagu does not find Turkish women to be sinners without souls. Montagu "tried to put right Western misapprehensions about women's rights in Turkey," as M. D. Allen puts it (3). Montagu also sympathetically explains the sexual practices and values of the country. Virginity is not valued in Turkey, Montagu writes, but that is because it is seen as unproductive. Although implying that such a custom is not as rational as that of the English, Montagu finds value in Turkish views of products and production. She notes in her letters that all the ambassadresses follow Turkish customs while they live there and have many children.[28] Many of Montagu's letters also catalog the superior beauty of Turkish women.

The myth of Turkish women's lives with which Montagu most vehemently takes issue is that they are slaves. Montagu sees freedom where others have seen confinement. She writes:

I cannot forbear admiring either the exemplary discretion or extreme Stupidity of all the writers that have given accounts of [Turkish women]. Tis very easy to see that they have more Liberty than we have, no Woman of what rank so ever being permitted to go in the streets without 2 muslins, one that covers her face all but her Eyes and another that hides the whole dress of her head and hangs halfe way down her back. . . . You may guess how effectually this disguises them, that there is no distinguishing the great Lady from her Slave, and 'tis impossible for the most jealous Husband to know his Wife when he meets her, and no Man dare either touch or follow a Woman in the Street. (*CL* 1: 328)

Montagu maintains that "this perpetual Masquerade gives them entire Liberty of following their Inclinations without danger of Discovery" (1: 328). Many Turkish women, Montagu believes, have affairs without letting their "gallants" know who they are. Montagu ends this section with her now famous statement: "Upon the Whole, I look upon the Turkish Women as the only free people in the Empire" (1: 329).[29] Where others before her saw strangeness to be noted and dismissed, Montagu saw exotic freedom.

One letter in particular—describing Lady Mary's visit to the women's public baths—has emerged as among the most debated of her collection.[30] That letter is also among the most crucial to a discussion of Montagu, Turkish women, and historical discourse. In a letter dated 1 April 1717, mysteriously addressed to Lady ——, Montagu described her arrival at a "new World," the centerpiece of which was her visit to the "Bagnio" one morning in Adrianople.[31] She writes, "I went to the Bagnio about 10 a clock. It was allready full of Women. It is built of Stone in the shape of a Dome with no Windows but in the Roofe, which gives Light enough. There was 5 of these domes joyn'd together, the outmost being less than the rest and serving only as a hall where the portress stood at the door" (1: 312–13). She finds one room so hot that "twas impossible to stay there with one's Cloths on" (1: 313). The focus shifts not to the other women in the baths (we have so far met only the portress) but to Lady Mary herself with her clothes on: "I was in my travelling Habit, which is a rideing dress, and certainly appear'd very extraordinary to them, yet there was not one of 'em that shew'd the least surprize or impertinent Curiosity, but receiv'd me with all the obliging civillity possible. I know of no European Court where the Ladys would have behav'd them selves in so polite a manner to a stranger" (1: 313). Montagu well prepares her correspondent Lady —— for what is to follow: the Turkish women bathers themselves. The reader is made ready to view the scene with Lady Mary in the center of it. She, as narrator, is centrally placed as a concrete image.

Montagu's description of the women begins after this stunning architectural and personal introduction. It is worth quoting at length:

I believe in the whole there were 200 Women and yet none of those disdainfull smiles or satyric whispers that never fail in our assemblys when any body appears that is not dress'd exactly in fashion. They repeated over and over to me, Uzelle, pek uzelle, which is nothing but, charming, very charming. The first sofas were cover'd with Cushions and rich Carpets, on which sat the Ladys, and on the 2nd their slaves behind 'em, but without any distinction of rank by their dress, all being in the state of nature, that is, in plain English, stark naked. . . . They Walk'd and mov'd with the same majestic Grace which Milton describes of our General Mother. There were many amongst them as exactly proportion'd as ever any Goddess was drawn by the pencil of Guido or Titian, and most of their skins shineingly white . . . perfectly representing the figures of the Graces. . . . To tell you the truth, I had wickedness enough to wish secretly that Mr. Gervase could have been there invisible. I fancy it would have very much improv'd his art to see so many fine Women naked in different postures, some in conversation, some working, others drinking Coffee or sherbet, and many negligently lying on their Cushions while their slaves . . . were employ'd in braiding their hair. . . . In short, tis the Women's coffee house, where all the news of the Town is told, Scandal invented, etc. . . . The Lady that seem'd the most considerable amongst them entreated me to sit by her and would have undress'd me for the bath. (1: 313–14)

Moving from the subject of Lady Mary to the beautiful bodies and how to represent them on a canvas and to the function of the public baths, the letter returns again to Lady Mary, who discerns from the crowd of bathers as if by magic the most important woman there. Lady Mary's stays are discussed, mistaken as a kind of chastity belt by the Turkish women, who think she cannot join them in the baths because she has been forced by her husband to wear the confining contraption. The letter concludes, "Adieu, Madam. I am sure I have now entertaind you with an Account of such a sight as you never saw in your Life and what no book of travells could inform you of. 'Tis no less than Death for a Man to be found in one of these places" (1: 314–15).

Montagu covers an impressive range of subjects. In letter after letter she proves that she has an eye for detail, that she has been reading histories of the Ottoman Empire, and that she is acquiring the Turkish language. She takes particular pleasure in describing, as in this letter, architecture, interior decoration, and manners. Unlike her fiction, sparse in its description of setting and preferring the realm of allusion and narrative action, the "Turkish Embassy Letters" include little activity. There is instead a prosaic frieze on top of the allusions. The subject that emerges most readily is Lady

Mary herself. The letter quoted above shows the ways her presence shapes the narrative. Rather than a disembodied narrative eye, Montagu creates an altogether embodied one. Her descriptions of herself are often given more prominence than are the descriptions of Turkish women. As Marcia Pointon has argued, "Appropriating the right to look, articulating and interpreting the seen, was one way in which woman could exert power. It was, after all, Montagu's interpretation of what she saw that made her reputation. But, arguably, the conditions that made that attainment possible were prepared by her reproduction of herself in society" (143). Pointon's discussion focuses on portrait painting and on Lady Mary's control of her visually reproduced image once she returned to England, but a similar argument could be made of her self-created image in the "Turkish Embassy Letters." In her letters, Lady Mary grants herself the power of a historian of women.

It would be inaccurate to claim that Montagu provides a solipsistic portrait or that the images of Turkish women are meant to be marginal. On the contrary, Turkish women are Montagu's subject, and later letters include encapsulated life stories of individual women. In the letters describing the women's baths, Turkish women are the only ones who are given lines of dialogue: "Charming, very charming" in Turkish. Again, however, these words refer to Lady Mary. The long description invites readers to imagine themselves in the public baths with Lady Mary standing alongside as a guide— or to imagine themselves in her place. Lady Mary is the only figure in the letters who moves through space and time. She has appointments to meet, while the Turkish women stay in the baths for languid hours. Lady Mary moves from room to room, but the Turkish women enjoy an indolent stasis. Some are said to be working, talking, or drinking, but many are "negligently lying." Lady Mary is active in these letters, but her subjects are largely immobile.

Many angles could be—and have been—taken to make sense of Lady Mary's activity and her subjects' immobility, including histories of Oriental painting and aestheticism, female homoeroticism and voyeurism, and cultural relativism or hybridity.[32] The salient parts of these discussions, for my purposes, involve the temporal aspects of the description, romance conventions, and historical agency. By calling up the names of painters like Titian, Guido, and her own portrait painter, Richard Jervas, in her descriptions of Turkish women in the bagnio, Montagu invokes history. History might seem more of an absence than a presence in discussions of painting, particularly of the type Montagu describes—studies of nude women in Eastern settings. However, one of the features of later paintings of this kind is the "absence of history," as Linda Nochlin observes (35).[33] An indication that Montagu's "Turkish Embassy Letters" provided a great deal of material to the history of painting is offered by Pointon, whose discussion of Montagu and Montagu-inspired portraits notes that the letters were "a major source for orientalist artists of the nineteenth century" (147). Lady Mary was the subject of many portraits, so much so that today "almost every unidentified portrait of a woman in Turkish dress that comes up at auction tends to be labeled 'Lady Mary Wortley Montagu'" (Pointon 148). She has obviously been significant to the history of art. But what did Montagu's artistically framed letters offer to history? To put it another way, how did her painterly descriptions become part of historical discourse that circulated about Turkish women?

The bagnio letter uses art (specifically painting) to place its subjects in time. Cynthia Lowenthal maintains that "Lady Mary views these women through layers of art, and, as a result, perceives them not as unequal, inferior 'others' but as quintessential examples of womanhood: the Graces and Eve. . . . the native inhabitants observed are situated in a timeless present rather than a particular historical moment. Such timelessness certainly exists in the description above, yet it is also the same timelessness that a viewer of a painting might experience" (103–4). Though I am not willing to go as far as Lowenthal does in exonerating Montagu from "othering," I agree that Turkish women in her description are painted as if in a landscape—like characters on a Keatsian vase. I would modify Lowenthal's argument to add that "native inhabitants" are imagined not in a "timeless present" but instead in a timeless *past*. Montagu creates in the bagnio letter the Westernized, Christianized past of a Miltonic Eve—not a contemporary image—despite its representational immediacy in a dated letter.[34] Lady Mary has a distinct date and time associated with her image. The women she describes are static, unchanging, idealized figures.[35] They could just as easily appear in the "Sultan's Tale" as in a letter describing present-day conditions.

The romance tradition that Montagu used in her fiction was fully present in the rest of the "Turkish Embassy Letters," as Lowenthal and others have convincingly argued. I will not rehearse those arguments here, except to note that when Montagu does delve into individual Turkish women's life stories, they "mimic contemporary fiction" (Lowenthal 105). Just as with Montagu's previously discussed "Account" and romance fiction, the "Turkish Embassy Letters" are concerned with the place of women's everyday lives in history, something Montagu rarely separates from romance conventions. The "Turkish Embassy Letters," however, have a different stance toward history in that they are self-consciously aware of themselves as texts that are *making history,* in a way that her other writings are not. It has been said that Montagu "de-romanticizes romance by identifying the factual element in what was believed to be wholly fiction, by showing that what some thought merely imagined could be directly observed" (Knipp 59). Montagu's "de-romanticized romance" is not antiromance. It is historically inspired romance. As Montagu reminds her correspondent, the letter's information is not available from any other source and could not come from a male writer. Montagu's letter (and her anonymous reader's reception of it) constitutes women's history. Her subjects, the Turkish female bathers, are consigned to collective oblivion in being written about. Montagu becomes an English female worthy over Turkish women's undifferentiated bodies.

Montagu highlighted and cemented her role as a historically embedded woman, but she was not able (or willing) to carry out the same mission for Turkish women, who instead are depoliticized through romance conventions and dehistoricized through aesthetics. Even those women who are individualized in the letters are presented as completed stories rather than as women currently having experiences. Because they are timeless graces, Turkish women are a fitting subject for a first Western observation. Their veiling practices may make them the freest women in the empire in Montagu's formulation, but, though freer, they neither make history nor are implicated in it. As Jill Campbell contends, in Turkey Lady Mary interpreted "the culture and landscape around her as outside history" (74). I would add that, even more significantly, she saw the people around her as outside history. Although Turkish women's freedom is described as greater mobility, Lady Mary—and sometimes her compatriot, the French ambassadress— moves through time. She makes (and documents) women's history.

Lady Mary can hardly be said to have invented the "common belief that in travelling east she had traveled back in time as well" (Yeazell 114). She perhaps did more than anyone in her generation or the next to perpetuate this ideology—despite the later efforts of Lady Elizabeth Craven to supplant her as the expert on Turkish women. Montagu's "Turkish Embassy Letters" were used as historical fact. William Alexander's *History of Women, from the Earliest Antiquity to the Present Time* (1779) follows Montagu in claiming that though European women have varied in manners and characters, Eastern women are unchanging:

While the manners and the character of European women have been held out in such a variety of lights; while they have been liable to so many mutations, from the changes of fashion, of government, and religion, the women of the East have exhibited always the same appearance: their manners, customs, and fashions, like their rocks, have stood unaltered the test of many revolving ages; and though the kingdoms of which they are a part, have often changed masters, and yielded to the victorious arms of a conqueror; yet the laws by which they are governed and enslaved, have never been revised or amended. (1: 13)

In Alexander's history of Turkish women, nearly every detail (save an occasional nod to Montesquieu) comes from Montagu, and, according to Alexander, "our hearts . . . glow with the description" (1: 287). She is quoted and paraphrased by Alexander on such matters as courtship, the Turkish female character, and bathing rituals. On Turkish dress, Alexander writes that he will not detail Montagu's own costume: "The Turkish dress of Lady Montague, which we shall not describe, as we presume the generality of our fair readers have read her Letters, shews, that the ladies of Constantinople are far from being destitute of taste" (2: 126). Despite this disclaimer, Alexander summarizes at length the Turkish women's clothing as described by Montagu. He frequently and unqualifiedly refers to Montagu as an expert on Turkish women's history.

Alexander's *History of Women* does not focus exclusively on women worthies or on Western women of royal, military, or literary accomplishments. Instead, Alexander produces social history. He provides information on women of different ages and nations, mentioning everyday issues such as marriage, courtship, divorce, polygamy, shopping, dress, witchcraft, and card playing. As a physician, he was more interested in somatic issues than were other contributors to the genre, and perhaps his knowledge of medicine first interested him in Montagu's "Turkish Embassy Letters." Her account of smallpox inoculation in the letters may have encouraged Alexander to take all of her interpretations as reliable historical fact.[36] That some of her writings were seen as not only credible but authoritative implies that her status as an observer and a recorder of history was higher than her impugned personal reputation. Although she was criticized by some for being morally suspect, she was also understood as a reliable historian of women. For a time, Montagu's "Turkish Embassy Letters" set her up as an eighteenth-century anthropologist or historian of cross-cultural female manners.

In the later eighteenth century and the nineteenth, additional travel writers and historians expanded and amended her account. Historiography took its scientific turn, and Montagu's letters were consigned to history as literary trifles. As we saw at the beginning of the chapter, Lady Louisa Stuart did her share to advance such a categorization of Montagu. Grace and Philip Wharton's *Queens of Society* (1861) furthered Stuart's work without her apologetic finesse. The Whartons wrote that Montagu's "Account of the Court of George I" "shows . . . had she written novels à la Thackeray instead of simple letters, Lady Mary would be hailed . . . as the bold satirist of the follies, if not the reformer of the vices of society" (104). Understanding Montagu as a satirical novelist, the Whartons disallow her historiographical powers. Of the "Turkish Embassy Letters" the Whartons conclude, "Lady Mary's letters during this period are very amusing, and her description of things, as she found them, are really the best ever written about the East, not even excepting Eliot Warburton's." (108). Putting Montagu in the same class as Warburton, the Victorian historical novelist who fictionalized Lucy Hutchinson, the Whartons characterize her as an entertaining and curious object. Their backhanded compliments about her "Turkish Embassy Letters" resemble Montagu's treatment of Turkish women in her letters. In both cases, compliment and condescension are inseparable.

Subsequent popular representations of Montagu continue to disregard her historiographical contributions. Lady Mary and her "Turkish Embassy Letters" were made the subject of fiction. Doris Leslie's *Toast to Lady Mary* (1954), a novelization of Montagu's letters, quotes frequently from the letters but adds many fictional flourishes. Leslie's novel calls Lady Mary's time in Turkey "Mary's Embassy, her triumph, her greatest of adventures to bear her away upon a magic carpet in which the colours are as fadeless still, and fresh as on the day when she set forth upon her pilgrimage through Europe" (191). Seeing Lady Mary's time in Turkey as a magic carpet ride is a cartoon image that also has its parallel in the "Turkish Embassy Letters." To an even greater degree than the Whartons, Leslie's novel describes Lady Mary as Montagu described Turkish women two centuries earlier. *A Toast to Lady Mary* metamorphoses its subject and her story into a changeless, fadeless, Orientalized past, just as the "Turkish Embassy Letters" depict static, fadeless Turkish women. Those who find more Orientalism than feminism in the letters would likely see Lady Mary as getting her comeuppance in Leslie's novel, with its Harlequinized prose and historical sleight of hand. Montagu, however, deserves a more accurate reading. Influenced by past representations of Eastern and Western women, she affected future ones. She consigned Turkish women to ahistorical, classical, or poetic pedestals and altered the ways they were depicted and understood. Her unusual and troubling use of historical discourse nonetheless established the subject of women and cultural difference as worthy of study. Montagu's "Account," her fiction, and her "Turkish Embassy Letters" demonstrate that early eighteenth-century women writers—even those we think we know well as authors in other genres—advanced British historiography.

Charlotte Lennox and the Study and Use of History

4

■

Charlotte Lennox's writings are not histories in any conventional sense. Except for her translations, nothing published under her name would be mistaken for history by today's readers. Yet Lennox is a writer who, Judith Dorn writes, "could be [enrolled] . . . on the short list of women historiographers active in England prior to 1800" (7). The relationship of Lennox's texts to history writing has not been fully explored. It is easy to establish that she was exposed to historiographical debates; she translated popular French histories and discussed historical texts in her essays. But her interest in history goes beyond rendering the ideas of others into her native tongue or sparse didactic commentary. Lennox was, as Jane Spencer has pointed out, "well acquainted with the work of contemporary historians" ("Not Being" 335). Throughout her literary career—spanning forty years and embracing multiple genres—Charlotte Ramsay Lennox (1727?-1804) adopted and adapted historical discourse, often considering its impact on women. Montagu's history writing was in the tradition of Clarendon's and Burnet's—built on participant observation. Lennox influenced and was influenced by midcentury scholarly approaches to historiography, following the likes of David Hume and William Robertson.

Lennox's historiographical ambitions are most clearly demonstrated by her abortive effort in 1759 to publish by subscription "The Age of Queen Elizabeth." Lennox sought advice on her proposed project from Robertson, already a renowned Scottish historian. Her request for assistance is documented in a letter he addressed to her (Isles, "Lennox Collection" [1971] 51). Lennox's side of the correspondence does not survive. Why would Lennox turn to historiography? It is possible that her plan to write "graver history" was based on financial considerations.[1] Histories had already proved an immensely popular and lucrative genre. At this period in her life, Lennox "desperately needed to write what would sell" (Levin 275). She apparently was ill in 1759–60 and may have been in search of an assured professional success. She briefly set her sights on history writing, knowing that Robertson's *History of Scotland* (1759) had "sold exceptionally well" (Isles, "Lennox Collection" [1971] 51).

No parts of the history of Elizabethan England that Lennox proposed have survived. Nevertheless one should not conclude that she dabbled in historical discourse and then abandoned it. On the contrary, Lennox sparred with history writing throughout her career, putting it to use, emulating it, and manipulating its conventions in virtually all the texts she produced. Her mixing of the elements of several kinds of writing—especially history and fiction—reveals the ways one woman writer creatively negotiated emerging genres in the 1750s and 1760s, when many of the eighteenth century's great historical works came into print in Great Britain. Recognizing how thoroughly Lennox's authorship is saturated with history and historical forms provides a new window into developing—and debated—critical views of her life and works.[2]

In recent studies on Lennox, issues of gender and genre have proved fertile ground, prompting valuable readings of how her novels stood in relation to those of her predecessors and her contemporaries. For many critics of Lennox, the genres under consideration have been limited to subcategories of fiction: burlesques, captivity narratives, realistic novels, romances, and satires among them.[3] When history has been considered in her oeuvre, it has usually been viewed as background material or as generic opponent. Philippe Séjourné's study of Lennox led the way in considering history as "background," especially in her novels with settings in colonial America. Séjourné assembled an impressive collection of historical documents from the childhood years that the former Miss Ramsay is believed to have spent in Albany, New York.[4] These documents allowed critics to read the first and last of Lennox's novels as "historically accurate *romans à clef*" (Warfel 216).[5] History has also been interpreted as Lennox's generic foe—usually coded "male"—signaling her prescient turn to women's history or "herstory." Her fictional form is then said to be subversively antithetical to mainstream national histories (e.g., Craft; Schofield 133; Barreca 45). Readings of Lennox's texts that draw on either of these critical models are provocative, but they caricature the differences between historical and fictional discourse at the moment when she wrote rather than demonstrating substantial convergences.

To realize that there might be more to issues of history in Lennox's texts than simple background or subversive divide, one need only think of the often-quoted remarks on history and fiction in Henry Fielding's *Tom Jones* (1749), especially those at the beginning of book 9. Fielding touts fiction as a "true and genuine . . . historic Kind of Writing" that steers clear of historical records (314). Fielding's definitions tempt critics to claim that midcentury writers indiscriminately lumped together historical and fictional genres. Such positions overstate the case. As Bertrand Goldgar argues, "Fielding takes for granted the total disjunction of history and fiction, as did his contemporaries" because "Fielding did not live in a time when the blurring of history and fiction was part of one's everyday cultural furniture" (287, 292).[6] I agree with Goldgar that history and fiction were conventionally understood as discrete forms at midcentury—that few eighteenth-century readers would have gone to Robertson's *History of Scotland* in search of a comic romance or to Fielding's *The History of Tom Jones* for British history lessons. But the mixing of history and fiction is everywhere to be found in that period's texts. We should attend to the possibility that history and fiction were more fluid in practice than by formal definition—again, potentially because they were generic competitors. Lennox's uses of history must therefore be seen as more than protofeminist anomaly or literary realism.

In examining the features of Lennox's encounters with history writing, I concentrate on her prose, focusing briefly on selected novels, critical works, and translations illustrating the multitude of positions that she took in relation to history. Then I look at *The Female Quixote* (1752), a novel central to discussions of midcentury historiography, fiction, and gender. Duncan Isles suggests that *The Female Quixote* examines "the entire relationship between real life, history, fiction, and the reading public" ("Johnson and Charlotte" 37). Jane Spencer asserts that Lennox "plays out a gendered struggle over the meaning of romance and history, the distinction between fact and fiction" ("Not Being" 331).[7] Critics have interpreted *The Female Quixote* as a document of textual and classificatory struggle, whether humanist or feminist—as Lennox's attempt to grant textual sovereignty to (female) characters and to (female) readers and authors. My investigation builds on the work of these critics, adding an additional dimension. I argue that Lennox—in strategies that parallel those of her successor and admirer Jane Austen—alternately accepts, ridicules, rejects, and reshapes history in ways that do not fall evenly into gendered "sides."

In *The Female Quixote,* Lennox was working through (perhaps less than successfully) how women featured in current historiographical debates. Rather than jettisoning the ideas of all the historical "patriarchs" of her day, she embraced some of them, revising them to suit her fictional purposes. Comparing *The Female Quixote* with works by Voltaire and Bolingbroke, I demonstrate that at midcentury well-known historiographical principles were complex and even contradictory. Lennox usurped some of history's discursive features to create a more highly valued fictional form.[8] Rather than writing "herstory"—a female-centered compensatory alternative to standard historical accounts—she created an amalgam: a novelized history that was neither entirely masculinized nor entirely feminized. *The Female Quixote*'s blending might be understood today as generic (or gendered) confusion, as too invested in the advice of too many mentors, or as pandering to the market as she perceived it. It might be seen as progressive, as conservative, or as some combination of these.[9] Given what we know about Lennox, it is likely that she wanted to reach as many readers as possible. Her combination of generic mixing, gender-bending rhetorical elements, and status quo closure was far more successful in *The Female Quixote* than in other attempts to satisfy her audience. I offer generic, philosophical, and market-based reasons why Lennox's writings demonstrate conflicting alliances to history and fiction, especially in *The Female Quixote.*

Lennox's career as an author should be briefly sketched. A poet of some importance early in her life, Lennox published her *Poems on Several Occasions* in 1747. The most famous of her poetic efforts was "The Art of Coquetry," appearing in 1750 in the *Gentleman's Magazine.* Using the rhetoric of wars and battles in recommending artful feminine behaviors, "Coquetry" encouraged women to employ their wiles to subdue men to women's "empire." The poem promises that women will "controul the world by love" if they are careful not to fall in love themselves. Lennox displayed an early interest in the ways women wielded power, even though she restricted that power to a predictable sphere of influence (romance) and voiced frequently rehearsed ideologies of femininity. She turned from poetry to novels, translations, and literary criticism, changing directions again in the late 1760s and 1770s to write for the stage. She was no stranger to the theater, having been a "deplorable actress" (in Horace Walpole's estimation) in 1748 (*Correspondence* 9: 74).[10] Lennox died a pauper in 1804, and a dearth of documentary evidence about her life and career continues to frustrate scholars. Scrambling for facts, critics have created many speculative portraits of the author, among them a protofeminist, a coquette, a starving artist, a liar, a perpetrator of assault, a proper lady, a man's woman, and a doting mother.[11]

Although there are conflicting versions of her life, her contributions to literary history are more easily established. Lennox wrote five (possibly six) novels over the course of forty years, including *The Life of Harriot Stuart* (1751), *The Female Quixote* (1752), *Henrietta* (1758), *Sophia* (1762), and *Euphemia* (1790).[12] In 1760–61 she edited a periodical, the *Lady's Museum*, and provided a good deal of its content.[13] She also published an ambitious work of translation and literary criticism, *Shakespear Illustrated* (1753). Finally, Lennox translated a number of works, including historical, biographical, and fictional material.[14] Like most of her writing contemporaries, she ranged freely among genres, choosing by turns to be poet, novelist, playwright, periodical writer, critic, translator, and historiographer.

The most prolific period of Lennox's career was 1750–61, during which her most critically applauded works were published. The end of that decade saw her plan to write a history of sixteenth-century England, the culmination of a highly active and likely exhausting stretch of work. What motivated Lennox to consider history writing, and what compelled her to give it up? No known documents provide answers. Robertson's letter reveals some of her concerns about undertaking "The Age of Elizabeth." We can infer from his letter that she asked his advice about what books and manuscripts to consult. She apparently invited him to guide her in collecting materials. He responds that his own writing on Elizabeth's reign dealt only with "transactions which related to Scotland," though he was "scrupulously exact in referring to [his] authorities," thus making it easy for Lennox to find out which sources his information came from. Robertson also points Lennox to Hume's history, because it "has taken a larger view of Elizabeth's reign & character, & has displayed . . . all that elegance of composition, & depth of reflection, for which his writings are remarkable" (Isles, "Lennox Collection" [1971] 51–52). From Hume, Lennox might gather "what books it is proper to consult with regard to English transactions" (52). Finally, he recommends Lord Royston's collection of Renaissance documents, materials that would eventually become the British Museum's Hardwicke Papers (52 n. 100).

Robertson's advice to Lennox conceives of her as a capable historian, implying mutual respect. Lennox's description of her proposed history, however, must have been sketchy. Robertson speculates on the kind of history she will compose:

> By the title which you give your work, I imagine that you do not propose to confine yourself wholly to historical transactions, but will treat at some length, the taste, the authors, the manners &c of that age. This last is a curious subject. . . . many facts with regard to this article may be picked up in the numerous Collections of Papers published concerning Elizabeth's reign. These things I make no doubt have already occurred to yourself in a better manner than I can point them out. I mention them only to shew my willingness to obey your commands. (52)

Lennox, Robertson assumes, will illustrate the temper of the times in her book rather than publishing trumped-up annals. Histories composed of "general and rapid narratives of history, which involve a thousand fortunes in the business of a day" were sharply criticized by Samuel Johnson, and it is difficult to imagine that Lennox intended to write in this vein (100).[15] A title like "The Age of Elizabeth" allies Lennox with the "curious subject" of taste and manners rather than with a parade of historical transactions.[16] Her proposed title echoes Voltaire's *The Age of Lewis XIV*—a work Lennox finished translating during the same year that she published *The Female Quixote*. Lennox's previous writings would make one assume, as Robertson does, that her inclination would be toward literary-rhetorical historiography rather than general, rapid collections of facts. She had not earned a reputation as a scholar or an antiquarian. If she was considered learned at all, it would have been as a scholar of language and literature, broadly conceived.

The two roles—historian and scholar of language and literature—were closely identified in Lennox's day, as is evinced by the professorships in modern history and modern languages established at Oxford and Cambridge earlier in the century. At the time Lennox wrote, the official distance between a scholar of language and literature and a scholar of modern history was slight. Describing the schooling of nineteenth-century historians in the making like Thomas Babbington Macaulay and Leopold von Ranke, Bonnie Smith contends that "history was an aside, a by-product or diversion in the study of languages" (*Gender* 75). In Lennox's day, the language-history connection was far less institutionalized, but the seeds of such educational philosophies had been planted. Lennox, as an amateur scholar of languages, may thus have been considered a *more* likely candidate for modern historiographical work. She was familiar with French and Italian and moved easily among kinds of writing. Although she translated the same number of works as she wrote novels, Lennox's efforts as a translator have received short shrift from today's critics.[17] Her translations deserve further attention.

At the time Lennox wrote *The Female Quixote,* for example, she was involved—seemingly *more* happily—in translating historical works. In a letter dated 3 February 1752, perhaps written to Samuel Johnson, she entreats the recipient to exert his "interest with the Booksellers to procure me some employment in the translating way, as this would be a great deal easier than composition" (Lennox, Letter). Her translations (which included memoir, history, and fictional works) were in a sense in competition with her original fiction in the market of letters. The ideological commitments and philosophical views expressed in the works she translated and those expressed in her own texts were not in alignment. Regardless, we need not label one activity or the other as more representative of her ideals. She may have been hedging her financial bets by simultaneously investing both in original fiction and in translations of different genres.

The Lennox translation that has been discussed most frequently, *Shakespear Illustrated* (1753), is difficult to classify as historiography, but Lennox considered her translations of the "original" documents on which Shakespeare based his plays to be historically valuable. *Shakespear Illustrated* is the only work of translation by Lennox that is accompanied by her own extensive critical remarks.[18] She criticizes the Bard for adding improbable or unnecessary events to his plays. His powers of invention did not measure up to the texts on which he based his dramatic work. Lennox praises Shakespeare when he conforms to historical chronicles and chastises him for violating "history" or changing earlier texts in any way.[19] *Shakespear Illustrated* should be of interest to those who study the history of the novel, according to Jonathan Brody Kramnick: Lennox "registered the impact of the novel on the ordering of literary culture . . . by arguing that the novel is the canonical genre," seeing it as deserving a place in literary history that ranks above Shakespeare's plays (431). Lennox gives to novels "the imaginative authority of history itself" (444). Kramnick's position resonates with

The Female Quixote, which he briefly explores. Interpretations of Lennox's aims to make the novel canonical must be complicated, however, by the fact that at midcentury she was involved in elevating other genres. In 1753 she may not have even thought of herself primarily as a novelist.

Lennox and Quixotism

Although there are many areas of possible inquiry for historically informed studies of Lennox, the recent critical explosion has focused almost exclusively on *The Female Quixote.* Scholarship has begun to appear on a wider range of Lennox's writings, but even those critics who deal with other texts return to it as an authorial touchstone. There are good reasons for returning. By today's standards the novel remains an entertaining read, despite the complaints of some critics that it is long-winded and sloppily concluded.[20] More important, *The Female Quixote* is pivotal to Lennox studies because the author herself has long been grafted onto Arabella, her quixotic protagonist. The coupling of Lennox and Arabella began soon after the novel was published and continues today, in those arguments suggesting that Arabella intentionally or unconsciously represents her author's intentions or desires. When Sir Joshua Reynolds painted a portrait of Lennox (now apparently lost) he cataloged it in his records as "Lenox, Mrs. Arabella." His record may have been "a compliment, or a mistake" (Séjourné 14). Less ambiguous is George Colman's prologue to Lennox's play *The Sister* (1769), based on her successful 1758 novel *Henrietta.* Colman writes (and Mrs. Mattocks spoke):

> Boast not your gallant deeds, romantic men!
> To-night a Female Quixote draws the pen.
> Arm'd by the Comic Muse, these lists she enters,
> And sallies forth—in quest of strange adventures!
> War, open war, 'gainst recreant knights declares,
> Side-saddles Pegasus, and courts Apollo,
> While I (you see!) her female Sancho follow.

Lennox may have welcomed the comparison to her well-known character, since *The Female Quixote* kept her name in circulation through periods when her written output had fallen off. Many of Lennox's works are signed "By the Author of *The Female Quixote,*" a device she used to sustain or recapture her market appeal. Lennox "carefully monitored the reception of her writing and worked hard to promote it," as demonstrated in a letter to Lord Orrery in which she asks for his help because she is "not without some little ambition" (S. Green 249).

Though readers maintained the identification of Lennox and the female quixote, the mysteries of Lennox's life compounded the imaginative connection.[21] The late nineteenth-century critic W. H. Craig followed this trend to its logical conclusion when he contended that Lennox herself was quixotic. Craig asserted that the professional assistance Lennox received from Samuel Johnson addled her brain. In a famous Boswellian anecdote from 1784, Johnson is reported to have said, "I dined yesterday at Mrs. Garrick's with Mrs. Carter, Miss Hannah More, and Miss Fanny Burney. Three such women are not to be found: I know not where I could find a fourth, except Mrs. Lennox, who is superiour to them all" (Boswell 1284). Sentiments like Johnson's, according to Craig, made Lennox susceptible to Arabella-like qualities: "Such adulation from the Monarch of Letters turned the poor lady's head, who began to give herself airs, with the result that, as we learn from Mrs. Thrale, 'while her books are generally approved, nobody likes her'" (133). Lennox, with her head "turned," became less likable, but her character Arabella's turned head charmed as much as it annoyed. Recent literary criticism has linked Lennox to Arabella in ways that are far more sympathetic, though perhaps no less suspect. The story of Lennox *and* history (as well as of Lennox *in* literary history) requires an account of *The Female Quixote*.

The Female Quixote is "perhaps the first mid-century novel by a woman to start biting its way into the canon" (Woodward 857). Well received in its own time, it enjoyed a second edition within months of its publication, was reprinted at least eight times by 1810, and was eventually translated into German, Spanish, and French (Small 249–50). Lennox's name did not appear on the title page until 1783, but her authorship was generally acknowledged and was referred to in some reviews (Small 13). Though it did not spawn anything like the *Pamela* craze of the 1740s, *The Female Quixote* was a highly influential novel.[22] Itself an imitative book (Cervantes' *Don Quixote* being its obvious progenitor), *The Female Quixote* spawned many imitations of its own. It can count among its literary offspring at least two novels currently in print: Tabitha Tenney's *Female Quixotism* (1801) and Jane Austen's *Northanger Abbey* (1798/1818).[23]

Lennox, who sought advice on her novel from both Johnson and

Samuel Richardson, was concerned with issues of probability and proper instruction as they might be parlayed into fiction.[24] Her novel dealt with an integral issue in eighteenth-century female education—the importance of reading the right books—as well as with courtship and filial piety. *The Female Quixote* (subtitled *The Adventures of Arabella*) focuses on a young heiress whose sheltered life is guided entirely by knowledge gained from frivolous seventeenth-century French romances, what Jane Spencer has called "feminocentric fictions" (*Rise* 189). Though Arabella was not the first female in literature misled by reading the wrong books, she remains one of the most colorful and memorable. Rather than a stock character in amusing situations, Arabella emerges as a quirky, intelligent, and spirited woman, albeit with a naive, hubristic flaw.

The plot of *The Female Quixote* is by now familiar to many. Arabella's father, an exiled marquis, has raised her single-handedly since her mother died in childbirth. The marquis, who allowed Arabella to read romances indiscriminately throughout her childhood, dies early in the novel, but he directs Arabella to marry her cousin Glanville. Should she not, she will forfeit her inheritance. Because Arabella adheres to a skewed worldview (dictated almost entirely by the romances of Madeleine de Scudéry and Gautier de Costes La Calprenède), she refuses Glanville, saying, "What Lady in Romance ever married the Man that was chose for her?" (27). Arabella supposes that "Romances [are] real Pictures of Life, [and] from them she drew all her Notions and Expectations" (7).[25]

In the adventures that follow, mishaps occur because Arabella "had a most happy Facility in accommodating every Incident to her own Wishes and Conceptions" (*FQ* 25). The novel's primary focal points are courtship and reading. Arabella mistakes a series of men for noblemen when they are actually servants. She mistakes her prospective father-in-law for a suitor, and she allows no man to make declarations of love to her. She allows few declarations of any kind from men. Arabella tries to force her ideas about romance on others, sometimes through her predictably dim-witted maidservant Lucy, her female Sancho. Arabella demands that Lucy be her chronicler, that she prepare to write Arabella's life story. Lucy, the reader knows, will never be up to this task. Regardless, Arabella faces or creates adventures with the sensibility of a heroine whose actions will be of great import to posterity. In her most desperate hour, after many mishaps and misunderstandings (some of her own design and some engineered by others' trickery), Arabella is "cured" by a clergyman-doctor. She marries Glanville, the honest man intended for her.

The implied wedded bliss of the novel's ending is not as interesting as the adventures leading up to it, as many have noted. Arabella's "madness," like Don Quixote's, is far more compelling than the normality of those around her. When she is cured, she is no longer Arabella the outlandish figure but Arabella the commendable wife. Arabella's implicit transformation poses difficulties for recent critics, who struggle with the novel's ending. Many prefer to view the flamboyant Arabella as the "real" one, rather than accepting the denouement's promise of her as obedient, virtuous, and dull. Such readings are often not sensitive enough to writerly concerns, including those of audience, market, and genre.

In the past twenty years, excellent articles and chapters have been devoted to Arabella's eccentric behaviors and unlikely charms.[26] Most critics have shown that in trying to escape "harmful" French romances, *The Female Quixote* does not entirely leave behind the romance tradition in its own plotting. Nor does it disavow a connection to history; French romances have "some basis in history," as Sally Hoople notes (120). Critics have concluded that Arabella threatens to escape the novel's surface intentions for her, serving as a cautionary tale (Warren 378), a subversive message to women readers (Barreca 60), a sign of Lennox's coercion by the male literary elite (Malina 289), an echo of writerly disguise and cross-dressing (Marshall 127), or a readerly tension between skeptical and credulous approaches to texts (Motooka, "Coming" 270). Arabella's multifaceted characterization has been thoroughly discussed and debated, particularly in regard to her and the novel's relation to binaries such as fantasy and reality, fiction and fact, madness and sanity, romance and novel, femininity and masculinity, and feminist versus antiwoman. One binary prong—history—occasionally has been coupled with the novel or masculinity, or both, and has been seen as the Other, the enemy discourse Lennox must contend with.

The historical sensibilities Lennox displays in *The Female Quixote* are multilayered and complex, but history is not the Other against which Lennox writes. There are many scenes that could be used to illustrate the point, but I concentrate on one illustrative moment for gender and history before proceeding to issues of context and reception. That moment occurs in the Bath section of the novel, when Arabella's curious approach to the world catches strangers unaware. In Bath Arabella's adventures occasionally involve Mr. Selvin, a man whom she predictably mistakes for a suitor hopelessly in love with her. Selvin, unlike any of Arabella's other alleged admirers, loves ancient historians and his own pretended knowledge of them. Selvin is forced to address Arabella's "knowledge" of the ancients and her undeniable fascination with them. Nothing brings Selvin more happiness than to impart his trivia to interested (or uninterested) listeners, a quality he shares with Arabella. Selvin, however, is of a "graver Cast" and "affected to be thought deep-read in History" (*FQ* 264). Arabella is rarely grave, for all her seriousness, and she actually is "deep-read" in romances. Selvin gathers his knowledge from things "he heard introduced into conversation." He collects ancient history minutiae on scraps of paper, which he keeps in reserve to "retail them again in other Company" (273). Selvin treats history as one might a good joke, whereas Arabella treats laughably inaccurate romances like grave history.

In a chapter titled "Containing Some Anecdotes, the Truth of Which May Possibly Be Doubted, as They Are Not to Be Found in Any of the Historians," Arabella meets in Selvin her intellectual (though not her romantic) match. She had matched wits with men before Selvin. Her legitimate suitor, Glanville, tries to read romances in order to win Arabella, but he cannot stomach them.[27] Though he feigns familiarity with romances, his ignorance is quickly exposed by Arabella's pointed questions. Arabella's illegitimate suitor, Bellmour, knows romance conventions well, and he consistently (and not skillfully) attempts to use them to manipulate Arabella's behavior.[28] Selvin differs from these men in that he does not aim to please or to trick Arabella, except to convince her and the rest of the company of his historical expertise.

Unlike the now thoroughly comprehending Bellmour and Glanville, Selvin remains ignorant of Arabella's misunderstandings. Both Arabella and Selvin are blinded by their own naïveté. Selvin reads Arabella as he "reads" history—strictly on the surface and without nuance. Selvin also reads Arabella as Arabella reads romances. The two have an intellectual kinship. Selvin is amazed at Arabella's seemingly superior knowledge of the ancients. Unknown to him, however, her information has been culled from the historical fantasies and heroic gleanings of French romances— and worse yet, in bad translations. Selvin himself "never failed to take all

Opportunities of displaying his Knowledge of Antiquity, which was indeed but very superficial." He told the same few anecdotes over and over to anyone who would grant him an audience. As a result, he "passed among many Persons for one, who, by Application and Study, had acquired an universal Knowledge of antient History" (*FQ* 264). When he spoke of any event, he would bombastically and irrelevantly describe the year by Olympiad number: "It happened, he would say, in the 141st Olympiad" (265). As a historian, Selvin is a charade.

Although extremely comical, Arabella and Selvin's exchanges are also among *The Female Quixote*'s most revealing on historiographical issues. In a key scene, before a small audience, Arabella begins a speech comparing the medicinal waters at Bath to the "fine Springs at the Foot of the Mountain Thermopylae in Greece" (265). Her fictional information, taken from Madeleine de Scudéry's *Artamenes, or The Grand Cyrus: That Excellent Romance* (1690–91), may be more factually reliable than has been formerly thought, according to Margaret Dalziel (418). In the world of the novel, however, we know that both Arabella and Selvin exaggerate their command of historical information. Selvin, "with all his reading," had never heard of the springs at Thermopylae that Arabella mentions. Unable to join the conversation, he feels that the silence of the company is directed toward him. Arabella holds forth as if she were a learned, gifted orator on historical subjects. She out-Selvins Selvin.

Accustomed to displaying his own expertise, Selvin experiences "Shame . . . at seeing himself posed by a Girl, in a Matter which so immediately belonged to him" (265). Arabella and Selvin then enter into the following contest:

he resolutely maintained, that she must be mistaken in their Situation; for, to his certain Knowledge, there were no medicinal Waters at the Foot of that Mountain.

Arabella, who could not endure to be contradicted in what she took to be so incontestable a Fact, reddened with Vexation at his unexpected Denial.

It should seem, said she, by your Discourse, that you are unacquainted with many material Passages, that passed among very illustrious Persons there; and if you know any thing of *Pisistratus* the *Athenian*, you would know, that an Adventure he had at those Baths, laid the Foundation of all those great Designs, which he afterwards effected, to the total Subversion of the *Athenian* Government.

Mr. Selvin, surprised that this Piece of History had likewise escaped his Observation, resolved, however, not to give up his Point.

I think, Madam, replied he, with great Self-sufficiency, that I am pretty well acquainted with every thing which relates to the Affairs of the *Athenian* Commonwealth. (265–66)

Arabella holds her ground. The two continue to debate Athenian affairs, Selvin on the level of policy and security and Arabella on the level of love and courtship. Arabella offers a string of examples that overwhelm Selvin, who finally concedes his opponent's "wisdom": " 'I protest, Madam,' said Mr. Selvin, casting down his Eyes in great Confusion at her superior Knowledge in History, 'these Particulars have all escaped my Notice; and this is the first time I even understood that Pisistratus was violently in Love; and that it was not Ambition, which made him aspire to Sovereignty' " (266).

Selvin runs down the list of authors he has consulted on the matter—Plutarch, Herodotus, and Thucydides—and says that he does not remember any such details as Arabella mentions. Arabella informs him, "Very likely, sir, . . . but you will see the whole story . . . related at large in Scudéry" (266). When Selvin admits that he has never read that historian, Arabella informs him "then your Reading has been very confined" (266). Glanville steps in, pleased to see his rival Selvin's "ignorance" and affectation exposed. Glanville proclaims that he is surprised Selvin has not read Scudéry because the other writers he mentions "quote him so often" (267). Arabella does not correct Glanville's erroneous assertion (and she rarely misses an opportunity to correct someone), so presumably she believes Glanville is knowledgeable on the matter. It is unclear whether Glanville comprehends the difference between ancient and modern writers, but from what we know about his lack of desire to read, he is likely improvising to help Arabella show up Selvin.

When Arabella reveals that Scudéry is French, Selvin tries to redeem himself. He loftily explains that he reads only the ancients, not the moderns, because he has no taste for that way of writing (267). Glanville asks Selvin how Scudéry could possibly be a "modern" when the ancients themselves quote him. Glanville's fabrication is again allowed to stand, as Selvin is reduced to confusion and silence. A beau who has been privy to this debate, Mr. Tinsel, continues with "a thousand sarcasms" at Selvin's expense (267). Tinsel's comments defuse the argument between Selvin and Glanville, as well as the argument between Arabella and Selvin. As everyone becomes disgusted with Tinsel's sarcastic remarks, Arabella shifts the conversation to a consideration of the appropriate uses of raillery. The chapter ends: "Mr. Sel-vin, tho' he bore [Arabella] a Grudge for knowing more History than he did, yet assur'd her, that she had given the best Rules imaginable for railly-ing well. But the Beau [Tinsel], whom she had silenc'd by her Reproof, was extremely angry" (269). Tinsel, earlier described as the youngest member of the party and a "Pretty-Fellow, a dear Creature, and the most divert-ing Man in the World," is most thoroughly the casualty of the historical-turned-moral debates (264). Tinsel alone remains angry at Arabella. In a failed attempt to revenge himself on her, he flirts with her cousin Charlotte Glanville. Tinsel emerges as the clear loser of the conversational contests.

Most critics find the competition to be one of Arabella versus Selvin, a limited conception of the scene. Arabella emerges triumphant over Selvin and Tinsel, but it is the gossipy Tinsel who is the enemy, not the quasi-historical Selvin. Arabella bristles at the vices of Tinsel more than at the supposed ignorance of Selvin. Critics have noted that proper names are important in Lennox's novels. Lennox "goes out of her way to include allu-sions to the Stuart family in her work" (Motooka, "Coming" 254). Her characters' names have also been convincingly interpreted as reversals of those used in Richardson's *Clarissa* (Bartolomeo 164). The connotations of "Glanville" and "Bellmour" and "Lady Bella" are easily discerned. Mr. Tin-sel and Mr. Selvin are less obviously allusive. Tinsel is the easier to unpack, denoting ornamental gold and silver threads in cloth or an alloy. In its late eighteenth-century usage, according to the *Oxford English Dictionary,* the word became linked directly to a man of pleasure or fashion as opposed to a man of integrity. Selvin's name calls up more benign possibilities, like "self-interested," though any form of "self" or even "sylvan" ("silvan" in eighteenth-century usage—either a rustic or a mythical spirit haunting the woods) would be possible interpretations. Arabella herself is once referred to as "quite a Rustic" by her uncle Glanville (*FQ* 63). If we see Selvin as self-interested or as linked to rustic qualities, he and Arabella again share similar faults.

Because Arabella and Selvin disagree over what counts as history, Ara-bella's triumph in this section has mistakenly been labeled as constituting a feminine or feminist recasting of history. Such an approach labels *The Female Quixote* as a kind of her-story in besting Selvin's his-story and telling a woman's fictional tale in its stead. Interpretations of Lennox as a writer of herstory ignore the fact that all the characters involved in the Bath scene's arguments are set up as mistaken, hubristic, and ridiculous. Arabella opposes herself not to history but to "tinsel"—to fanciful discourse without integrity. If anything, Lennox allies Arabella with the historical Selvin, who was "naturally timid in the Company of Ladies" (288) and who treated women with shyness and deference. Selvin reveals Tinsel as the one who "had the least Respect for your Ladyship, and is more worthy of your resentment" (289). Lennox "transfers to the male the restraint and modesty commonly expected of respectable women," as Joseph Bartolomeo writes, but this describes Selvin, not Tinsel (166). Selvin does "nothing unbecoming a Man of Honour," whereas Tinsel spins lies and puts words in others' mouths, playing Arabella off against her cousin Charlotte (291). What some critics have called his-story (Selvin's) and her-story (Arabella's) have much more in common with each other than they do with Tinsel's malicious gossip. Selvin exits the narrative not by dying, as Arabella mistakenly believes, but with an uncharacteristic laugh at her expense, despite his usual gravity (314). Tinsel leaves the novel with an empty promise not to tell the world of Arabella's distemper (303). Tinsel, not Selvin, is Arabella's nemesis.

When we view Arabella and Selvin's debates about history as a satiric treatment of the Augustan battle of the ancients versus the moderns, the genderings of history involved become no clearer. At least one critic finds the gender divisions clear-cut. Helen Thomson sees the "feminine" moderns as defeating the "masculine" ancients in *The Female Quixote*: "The universally admired historian, Mr. Selvin, in reality very poorly read in the Ancients he cites as authority, is unmasked as a sham in conversation with the better (romance) read Arabella. Here the Ancients are quite clearly associated with the masculine, the Moderns with the non-canonical romances of the feminine discourse—which is victorious" (120). What Thomson's view about Lennox's victorious modern women does not account for is that Selvin, though a dilettante, is not that much more "poorly read" than Arabella. Viewing ancient history as masculine and modern history as feminine in *The Female Quixote*'s schema misses the point that the conversational debate scoffs at the weakest disputators on both sides.[29] Further complicating the debate is that Arabella believes she cites ancient wisdom; she thinks she is on the side of the ancients. Wendy Motooka contends that "*The Female Quixote* does not gender rationality as masculine and quixotism as feminine in any straightforward way. Instead, it conflates reason and quixotism, making their gendered associations suspect" (*Age* 141). I believe Lennox does the same thing with history and romance, ancients and moderns. She does not gender one as masculine and the other as feminine. Instead, she makes aspects of both suspect.

Arabella and Selvin have flawed perceptions of history. Selvin's historical vision omits the kinds of information that Arabella provides—motivations deriving from the personal lives of the "heroes." One might argue that he omits this information because it does not belong in a proper history. But lust, love, and personal losses were not absent from the histories that Lennox and her contemporaries were reading. Voltaire's controversial *Siècle de Louis XIV* (1751) gave detailed coverage to the private history of great men and women as it intersected with public or political history, coupled with social history or manners. Lennox had recently translated Voltaire's work into English as *The Age of Lewis XIV* (1752). Voltaire may have understood women as "avid readers of tales that signify nothing" (Gearhart 86), but Lennox's characterizations suggest that women who are avid readers of tales may be no more foolish than men, despite men's supposedly weightier reading. In *The Female Quixote*, a novel that emulates and implicitly comments on histories such as *The Age of Lewis XIV*, Lennox laughs at her characters' expense in the process of making a more serious point about history writing. The importance Arabella assigns to amatory relations in the historical process echoes the content of *The Age of Lewis XIV*, while Selvin's historical missteps demonstrate that even well-respected historical tales may signify nothing to a flawed reader.

Arabella believes history includes only details of romance, and Selvin believes it includes none; both go too far. Arabella mistakenly thinks that the romantic histories of women and men determine political history, but the opposite (that romantic histories have no relation to political history) is equally false. Her error derives in part from an inflated sense of her own role in making history. She "anticipates her own history as construct," as did Richardson's Clarissa (K. Green 48). Arabella "believes romance is history—told from a perspective that makes women central figures" (Ross 464). She is neither entirely right nor wrong on these points. Lennox need not be seen as writing against history or against the position of the "masculine" ancients in order to make her point that amatory relations (and women, when largely confined to that sphere of influence) can and do determine the course of history. Lennox does not dismiss all historical writing.

She does not discount the possibility of creating "true" history. Instead, she ridicules certain kinds of history—and certain kinds of historians.

Selvin, as a proponent of the ancients, is ludicrous in that he is not well enough versed in history to distinguish ancient from modern authors. He is so out of touch with the recent past that he does not even recognize the name Scudéry—a name that would have been known to modern historians as well as to readers of romance. Madeleine de Scudéry was "the most popular novelist of seventeenth-century Europe" (Donawerth 305). Her brother Georges—under whose name she published—was a French political figure as well as a man of letters in his own right. Some critics have theorized that Lennox herself did not realize that Madeleine Scudéry rather than Georges wrote romances, because Scudéry is referred to several times in *The Female Quixote* as "he." It is extremely unlikely that such a fact would have escaped Lennox's attention. A contemporaneous entry in the *Biographia Gallica* (1752) nonchalantly discusses both Georges and Madeleine Scudéry, focusing on her as the celebrated romance writer and "Sappho of the age" (121). Lennox would also have known of the Scudérys' accomplishments because, as Eric Rothstein notes, Voltaire's *Siècle de Louis XIV* mentions that Madeleine and not Georges de Scudéry is the author of romances ("Woman" 273 n. 25). Did Lennox's scene require a male Scudéry? Ancient female historians may have seemed a less effective comic premise than male ancient French ones. A male Scudéry forces Selvin to believe he is ignorant of an important ancient authority. It allows the badinage between Arabella and Selvin to continue.

For her part, Arabella has obvious flaws in her knowledge of history and historical debates. She fails to realize that she represents the position of the moderns, believing she is crusading on behalf of the ancients. How then should their ancient versus modern conflict be accurately characterized in gendered terms in the novel? The genderings are difficult to untangle, but as the discussion above shows, the ancients cannot be said to represent a masculine position and the moderns a feminine one in *The Female Quixote*. Arabella beats one proponent of the ancients at his own game by citing authorities of dubious veracity with blustering confidence. She believes she presents incontrovertible ancient fact. Selvin sheepishly backs off to let the moderns take the game because he does not recognize a fabricated ancient authority and because he is uneducated in modern political history and literature. Lennox suggests that participants in ancient-modern debates who do not have access to information from both sides of the divide will eventually look foolish.

A subsequent chapter furthers this conclusion. Again, Selvin and Arabella have a disagreement (this time much more genially) over whether Arabella's costume makes her resemble the Princess Julia, daughter of Augustus Caesar. Arabella believes this is a flattering comparison; Selvin tries to convince her it does not do her justice because Julia was licentious. Arabella maintains that Julia's only fault was in allowing herself to be beloved. Julia was in Arabella's version "absolutely chaste" (*FQ* 273). Selvin counters that Julia, "Tho' the Daughter of an Emperor . . . was, pardon the Expression, the most abandon'd Prostitute in Rome; many of her Intrigues are recorded in History; but to mention only one, Was not her infamous Commerce with Ovid, the Cause of his Banishment?" (273). What has changed in this exchange is that Selvin and Arabella share a view of history. Though they differ over an important (perhaps *the* important) interpretation of virgin versus whore, both see the historical process as deriving from women's agency. Neither character's mind is changed regarding Julia's reputation, but they agree that her sexual reputation is the most relevant historical detail.

Reducing women to their sexual reputations is no historiographical innovation on Lennox's part, of course. The Julia scene is derivative of similar scenes in quixote-inspired literature. One of Lennox's likely literary models for *The Female Quixote* was a novel by Perdou de Subligny, translated into English in 1678 as *The Mock-Clelia: Being a Comical History of French Gallantries, and Novels, in Imitation of Dom Quixote*—a send-up of Madeleine de Scudéry's popular romance, *Clelia*.[30] It has been noted that Lennox drew from Subligny the device of having her quixotic heroine throw herself into the river, in imitation of Clelia crossing the Tiber to make her escape (*FQ* 363; *MC* 268; Marshall). Another heretofore unexplored similarity to Subligny's text involves a scene that resembles Arabella's and Selvin's competing interpretations of Julia. In *Mock-Clelia* the heroine, Julliette d'Arvianne, experienced contemporary Clelia-like happenings in her life. Her story is one of many told in interwoven tales as the book proceeds. Julliette behaves normally until someone in the company mentions anything having to do with Rome, at which point she becomes quixotic.

Julliette participates in a historical debate to defend the reputation of a fallen female figure whom she believes is a chaste heroine. Her debate is with a male (the judge), and the figure in question is Lucretia. The judge (like Selvin with Arabella) is not aware of Julliette's distemper, though the rest of the party is. When the judge makes a passing reference to Lucretia's having been raped and therefore dishonored, Julliette, "who heard ill spoken of Lucretia, took up the cudgels and told him, that he ought not to injure the reputation of that Roman Lady, and that in good earnest he was mistaken" (*MC* 178). After this outburst, "the poor young Lady was by degrees falling again in to her Fits" (178). The judge presses the point that Lucretia killed herself, shamed that she had granted what was desired from her—her virginity (179). The rest of the company enjoyed the sport too much to do anything but laugh at the judge:

> Mademoiselle [Julliette] sharply maintained that it was false, which for some time he took much like a Gentleman. . . . He told her however first, That in Titus Livius, and in all the other Historians, who had spoken of that Roman Lady, what he said appear'd upon record; but she made him answer, That Titus Livius, and all the rest lyed; and as he was about to open his mouth to say something, Go, go, said she, all in a rage; that's an infamous calumny, and no body but an old corrupted Senator like your self . . . would have in that manner dishonoured the memory of Chastity itself. (179)

One can see in Subligny the seeds not only for *The Female Quixote*'s scene between Arabella and Selvin but also for their previous debate over the hot springs at Thermopylae. An additional debate over the character of Cleopatra occurs earlier in the novel between Arabella and a "generous stranger," a gentleman (105–6). In *Mock-Clelia,* the historical mistakes and misunderstandings are carried even further in that the judge does not understand that Julliette mistakes him for a Roman senator, and he leaves in a huff. Unlike Julliette and the judge, Selvin and Arabella eventually and moderately warm to each other, finding a degree of mutual respect and understanding, however misinformed.

One difference between *Mock-Clelia* and *The Female Quixote* is in the purpose of these gendered tussles over history and romance. Subligny's text is not interested in delivering anything but a laugh, but Lennox conveys a moral lesson. As Catherine Gallagher proposes, "Satire here is directed at Selvin, the ignorant man pretending a knowledge of history, who cannot refute Arabella's argument because he does not understand the nature of the books from which her information comes" (190). I would add that the satire is also directed against Arabella, who does not understand the sources from which Selvin's knowledge comes either. The point of their exchanges is not just satire but proper instruction, which may be derived from *either* history or fiction. Julia, Lucretia, and Cleopatra are presented by the female characters as worthy historical women who must be presumed chaste. The protagonists' misunderstandings of and respect for historical women (despite their infamous sexual pasts) may be seen on one level as accidental wisdom. Arabella and Julliette see heroines where others have found "prostitutes" and tragedies. What their misreadings illustrate is that young women who are not taught about the sexual innuendo surrounding female historical figures are "protected" in some senses but are not kept from making fools of themselves.

Fiction may cover over historical "fact," but certain kinds of fiction are also capable of revealing history's blindnesses. Fiction shows what might have been or should have been. The usefulness of knowing when fiction is preferable to history is further displayed in a subsequent chapter of *The Female Quixote* titled "Some Reflexions Very Fit, and Others Very Unfit for an Assembly Room." We are again exposed to the bad behavior of Tinsel. At the beginning of the chapter, Selvin acknowledges Arabella's superior historical wisdom (273). Tinsel is not so easily won over, and he prepares to tell Arabella and others some "Adventures of Illustrious Persons" (274). Glanville is immediately skeptical, but Arabella believes that she is about to hear "Histories . . . which may at once improve and delight me; something which may excite my Admiration, engage my Esteem, or influence my Practice" (274). Arabella's list of anticipated benefits are arguably the reasons *The Female Quixote* offers for why one should read probable novels.[31] Where histories can improve, delight, engage, excite, and positively influence readers, they are perfectly acceptable. Where they cannot, novels (such as Lennox's) may rightly take their place.[32]

In the assembly room scene, Arabella needs to learn that she cannot find positive benefits under the title "Adventures of Illustrious Persons." She must recognize that how one labels one's stories may reveal their content and that, while adventures in French romances may be chaste, in eighteenth-century English assembly room prattle they are not considered so. Arabella must learn to judge history's worth to her by its context as well as by its content. Tinsel's history of one of the women at the party, who had been "for many Years the Mistress of a young military Nobleman" hardly meets Arabella's historical or romantic expectations (275). Arabella learns that women's contemporary adventures are unseemly, and she comes to see such licentiousness as distinctly French. Tinsel tells Arabella of another woman of low birth who gives herself airs: "Her Habit, her Speech, her Motions, are all French; nothing in England is able to please her; the People so dull, so aukwardly polite, the Manners so gross" (274). Modesty and honesty are allied with Englishness. The conversation continues until Arabella begins to converse privately with Glanville:

I assure you, replied Arabella, I know not what to make of the Histories he has been relating. I think they do not deserve that Name, and are rather detached Pieces of Satire on particular Persons, than a serious Relation of Facts. I confess my Expectations from this Gentleman have not been answer'd.

I think, however, Madam, said Mr. Glanville, we may allow that there is a negative Merit in the Relations Mr. Tinsel has made; for, if he has not shewn us any Thing to approve, he has at least shewn us what to condemn.

The Ugliness of Vice, reply'd Arabella, ought only to be represented to the Vicious; to whom Satire, like a magnifying Glass, may aggravate every Defect. . . . 'Tis sufficient therefore to shew a good Mind what it ought to pursue, though a bad one must be told what to avoid. (276–77)

Applying Arabella's formula for the ugliness of vice to *The Female Quixote,* we must conclude that Lennox shows poor minds (especially weak female minds) when and how reading can be a vice. The novel offers wayward readers information about what books to read and what to avoid. Impressionable women should put away their French romances for solid, straightforward English texts. An elevation of English over French books cannot have been Lennox's sole position on proper reading, though it may well have been her take on novels. Lennox would surely have been glad at many points in her career if readers chose French books—especially those histories and memoirs she translated into English.

Lennox helps her readers recognize what good English histories and good English fiction should look like, but we might accuse her of not following her own dictates. The "Adventures of Illustrious Persons" section may make historical references. Tinsel's description of the mistress of a military nobleman appears to be drawn from life, as Margaret Dalziel points out. The anecdote "fits the history of Lord George and Lord Aubrey Beauclerk" (408). It is possible that Lennox has written just the kind of ugly, vice-filled history that she has Arabella despise Tinsel for relating. If so, Lennox is assuming the worst of her readers—and perhaps of herself. By including a secret history in her lecture on secret histories, Lennox suggests what mature readers already know: that we often find pleasurable the kind of stories we know we should not enjoy. Even on Arabella's strict moral terms regarding the ugliness of vice, however, a desire for illicit historical detail may not be all bad. According to Arabella, we learn best by reading about the ugliness of vices we tend toward. A "serious relation of Facts" may serve only those readers who are already above reproach.

In the context of Arabella's call for a "serious relation of facts," the stories of Tinsel and the lessons they provoke may be said to condemn some, but not all, historiographical approaches, as well as of some, but not all, gossip. Ronald Paulson has declared that in *The Female Quixote* " 'History' is a perspective that shrinks the business of Bath." Paulson's conclusion is most applicable if Tinsel (and not Selvin) is seen as the representative of Bath business (*Satire* 277). "False" gossip that satirizes or damages reputations is useless history; "true" gossip that teaches a lesson may be permissible or even useful historical material. A history without personalities or manners may be unable to excite admiration, engage esteem, or influence practice. Lennox's ideal qualities for history resemble Johnson's statements in *Rambler* 60, in which we learn that readers are most strongly moved by "narratives of the lives of particular persons" (110). A piece on particular persons may involve gossip, especially when it teaches, as Johnson put it, "what we may hope, and what we can perform. Vice, for vice is necessary to be shewn, should always disgust" (15).[33] Historical gossip can and should consider women—Julias, Lucretias, even mistresses of military noblemen—as long as the aim is to instruct how to (or how not to) conduct one's life.

Rather than working only to increase or decrease the value of history, *The Female Quixote* demonstrates how some fiction can outdo some histories. Lennox used the Bath section in an attempt to inflate the value attached to her fiction, not to dismiss all history. Certain kinds of history and fiction are indeed disparaged. The novel dismisses narratives that describe a timeless past, an ancient world that still exists across the span of centuries. Arabella comes to see her own history as a movement along the files of time and her position as the culmination of this movement. The danger is, as her maid Lucy puts it, that Arabella may end up with "a history of nothing" (305).[34] As a protagonist, Arabella is never in danger of being "nothing." She is only in danger of being a central character in the wrong kind of text, in which the only notable female adventures that make up a history are sexual ones. Lennox shows that Arabella may remain a historical figure (or a literary historical one, at the least) as long as she is free from sexual peccadillos. To have a proper "history," Lennox must bring Arabella to an acceptable marital end, offering instruction on the adventures a woman is allowed. At the novel's conclusion, although Arabella eschews her historical centrality for unobjectionable womanhood, Lennox as the author of the novel does not.

Critics who find the ending of *The Female Quixote* disappointingly conventional should rethink their expectations. Lennox uses romance elements in a probable novel to demonstrate the limited ways women figure as subjects in historiographical discourse. To assume from Lennox's adherence to convention that she was antifeminist or that she did not really mean for Arabella to marry is to misunderstand the function of conventions. Lennox bends some generic "rules" and conforms to others. She does not offer Arabella's end as tragic. On the contrary, Arabella's fictional story attempts to convince readers that proper women can make a historical mark. *The Female Quixote* functions similarly for Lennox; it shows her ability to join fictional and historical discourse in a polite, pleasing narrative. She was not the first to do so, but her contributions were groundbreaking. In her novel Lennox allied features of romance fiction and modern history, creating conditions in which female characters and female authors could be at the narrative center yet retain proper femininity. In the process, she argues for the revision—however slight—of the categories of proper femininity, proper fiction, and proper history themselves.

Lennox's Philosophy of History

Despite her authoritative narrative stance, Lennox was not confident of her novel's chances for success. Her experiences in composing and printing *The Female Quixote* reveal many doubts and fears. She complained about Richardson's "unkindly" treatment of her, probably the result of his actions as printer rather than as editor.[35] Richardson may not have printed *The Female Quixote* in time to meet her publisher Millar's proposed deadline. Lennox may have feared that "the book would not be published before the second week in May, when the London theatrical season was at an end" (Isles, "Lennox Collection" [1970] 342). The London elite would at that time leave for the country, drastically reducing potential sales. The book was published in March 1752. Johnson writes triumphantly to Lennox: "Mr. Millar has you in great esteem, and blames Mr. R[ichardson]. He says he hopes your book will eclipse Lord B[olingbroke']s Letters" (343).

Seeing *The Female Quixote* as a competitor of Henry St. John, Lord Viscount Bolingbroke's posthumous *Letters on the Study and Use of History* may seem a stretch, but there is no reason to doubt Millar's expertise about the book market. By today's standards, Lennox's *Female Quixote* has eclipsed the Tory statesman's treatise in terms of its reprintings, textual availability, and readership. In 1752, however, "in spite of—or perhaps because of—the hostile reception given to the *Letters* from many quarters, [*The*] *F[emale] Q[uixote]* can hardly be said to have eclipsed them in terms of either notoriety or ultimate profitability," as Isles notes ("Lennox Collection" [1970] 343). *Letters on the Study and Use of History* (published on 20 March, exactly one week after *The Female Quixote*) was initially the more popular book. The two works share more than contemporaneous publication. Lennox's novel and Bolingbroke's essay may seem unlikely textual allies, but they share some beliefs about history. Both describe and employ contradictory historiographical philosophies that reveal more about the conditions for history writing at midcentury than about the failures or foibles of either author.

Bolingbroke's works are, according to one mid-twentieth-century critic, "dead junk" (qtd. in Nadel 550). *Letters on the Study and Use of History* has more recently been called incoherent, unoriginal, and inconsistent, though Bolingbroke has also been granted the label "the major English historical thinker of the first half of the eighteenth century" (Woolf 659 n. 58; see also Zimmerman 34; Weinsheimer). Bolingbroke's *Letters* "rather than expressing a position . . . register a contest, or rather a number of contests" (Weinsheimer 74). These contests are largely philosophical and historiographical, leading Joel Weinsheimer to conclude that Bolingbroke "occupies a liminal position, straddling the crevasse between two distinct historical epochs" (74). I believe Bolingbroke and Lennox share that liminal position. Like Bolingbroke, Lennox does not provide consistent historiographical views in her novel. Bolingbroke's often-cited line from the *Letters*, "history is philosophy teaching by examples," is exemplified by *The Female Quixote* (Bolingbroke 1: 15). But Bolingbroke's "examples" and how they are best narrated and absorbed by men (both their readers and their subjects, in Bolingbroke's rhetoric) are as difficult to discern as are Lennox's on the subject of history and women.

Bolingbroke, too, ruminates on the appropriate functions of history versus fiction. His *Letters* even mentions the romance tradition and Don Quixote in its discussion of proper histories:

> When the imagination grows lawless and wild, rambles out of the precincts of nature, and tells of heroes and giants, fairies and enchanters, of events and of phae-nomena repugnant to universal experience, . . . and to all the known laws of nature, reason does not connive a moment; but far from receiving such narrations as historical, she rejects them as unworthy. . . . Such narrations therefore cannot make the slightest momentary impressions, on a mind fraught with knowledge, and void of superstition. . . . the delusion hardly prevails over common sense. . . . nothing less than enthusiasm and phrenzy can give credit to such histories, or apply such examples. Don Quixote believed; but even Sancho doubted. (1: 119–20) [36]

If Bolingbroke's system is applied to Lennox's novel, characters like Arabella cannot be understood as credible and are therefore not probable. Romance and history would be separated by common sense. Bolingbroke continues, however, and reveals a conflict:

> In Amadis of Gaul [a romance], we have a thread of absurdities that are invented without any regard to probability, and that lay no claim to belief: antient traditions are an heap of fables, under which some particular truths, inscrutable, and therefore useless to mankind, may lie concealed; which have a just pretence to nothing more, and yet impose themselves upon us, and become under the venerable name of antient history the foundations of modern fables; the materials with which so many systems of fancy have been erected.
>
> But now, as men are apt to carry their judgments into extremes, there are some that will be ready to insist that all history is fabulous, and that the very best is nothing better than a probable tale, artfully contrived, and plausibly told, wherein truth and falshood are indistinguishably blended together. (1: 120–21)

For Bolingbroke history is neither entirely true nor entirely false. Rather than dwelling on hermeneutic dilemmas such as this one, Bolingbroke himself makes determinations as to what historical material is most beneficial to readers. The right kind of historian, he implies, will choose the right historical details.

For Bolingbroke history must be true, but to be of use it must also be probable: "History must have a certain degree of probability and authenticity, or the examples we find in it will not carry a force sufficient to make due impressions on our mind, nor to illustrate nor to strengthen the precepts of philosophy and the rules of good policy" (1: 139). Problems arise when writers of history fail to adhere to either dictum—for probability or authenticity. History has been "purposely and systematically falsified in all ages," but that does not make it fable (1: 122)—it just makes it bad history. When history is both probable and true, it is good history. In addition, "when histories have this necessary authenticity and probability, there is much discernment to be employed in the choice and the use we make of them. Some are to be read, some are to be studied; and some may be neglected entirely" (1: 139). Bolingbroke's is an attitude we may find "deplorable," as J. G. A. Pocock puts it, but it is a position with a certain amount of sense as well: "[Bolingbroke] had called attention to a real problem: if it was no longer thought that the form of the modern state was directly determined by what had happened in the eleventh century, why should that period be studied at all, except by dry-as-dusts cut off from their own age and incomprehensibly interested in the past for its own sake?" (*Ancient Constitution* 246). Certain kinds of "irrelevant" history could be and should be neglected. Bolingbroke called for a new conception of determining the relevance of historical study, just as Lennox called for a new conception of beneficial fictional "study."

Choosing good history is the most meaningful consideration for Bolingbroke, just as choosing good fiction is paramount in Lennox's *The Female Quixote*. For Bolingbroke, the trick is to choose history that reflects your own experience and worldview: "We ought to apply, and the shortness of human life considered, to confine ourselves almost entirely in our study of history, to such histories as have an immediate relation to our professions, or to our rank and situation in the society to which we belong" (1: 173). Lennox, too, suggests that Arabella must look at the histories of those who are like her in order to get the best results. The doctor chastises her: "Has it ever been known, that a Lady of your Rank was attack'd with such Intentions, in a Place so publick, without any Preparations made by the Violator for Defence or Escape? . . . Does there in the Records of the World appear a single Instance of such hopeless Villainy?" (*FQ* 372). Though we might be tempted to answer yes, clearly we are supposed to affirm with the doctor that women of Arabella's "rank and situation" are not treated to such examples in history and therefore cannot hold these preconceptions.

What use is a history that merely reinforces our own experiences? For

Bolingbroke, history prepares us for more experience, so we should read those histories that most conform to the experiences we have had or expect to have. Bolingbroke's history has an "exclusive concern with the present," as does Lennox's (Weinsheimer 100). Her novel shows that the "histories" we read shape our present expectations, and that if we believe we will be subject to examples like those we read in bad histories, we may find our heads turned in a "phrenzy" similar to that produced by romances. Neither Bolingbroke nor Lennox sorts out the status of fiction in relation to history. Rather than viewing that as an inconsistency or a shortcoming in either author, we might better understand it as in some sense conditional and reflective of currently contested historiographical issues—precisely what Weinsheimer gestures toward in his work on Bolingbroke.

To make a case linking Lennox's and Bolingbroke's historiographical sensibilities, we need not show that Lennox knew Bolingbroke's *Letters* in advance of its publication (though, as George Nadel has claimed, the book may have circulated in manuscript as early as 1738). It is interesting to speculate, though, that Bolingbroke's *Letters* could have influenced one historian who, in turn, influenced Lennox: Voltaire. Nadel believes it is possible that "Voltaire's thought—especially his criticism of the Old Testament and his historical pyrrhonism—was borrowed or at least inspired by Bolingbroke" rather than the other way around, as had formerly been assumed (555).[37] J. B. Black, too, calls Bolingbroke "Voltaire's intellectual father" (31). Regardless of the direction of influence between the two men, they shared an affiliation with French skepticism and Pyrrhonism (Kramnick, *Bolingbroke* 15–16). Both Bolingbroke and Voltaire were more interested in modern than ancient history (or at the least were not willing to squelch the former for the latter). Lennox shares this penchant in her fiction, most of her translations, and her proposed English history. All three writers are willing to emphasize personality over event and manners over "complete" accounts when they believe the situation calls for it. As Voltaire wrote (and Lennox translated): "Every thing that is done does not merit the being recorded. We shall confine ourselves therefore in this history, only to what deserves the attention of all ages, to what may describe the genius and manners of men, to what may serve for instruction, and to enforce the love of virtue, the arts, and our country" (Voltaire 1: 8). History, according to Voltaire, need not include all events. To be judicious and interesting, it must be selective, albeit not quixotically so. Voltaire once used Don Quixote as a comparison to a historical figure, the antihero Charles XII (qtd. in Gearhart 78). Lennox reversed the analogy, comparing her fictional characters to historical figures as well as fictional ones.

Lennox and Bolingbroke may have had something else in common—their ambition for fame. Weinsheimer proposes that Bolingbroke wrote the *Letters* because he "desperately wanted to be not a philosopher of history or even a student of it but instead the subject of history, a historic figure" (73). Lennox, whose far more humble class background prepared her to know better than to see herself as a potential "historic figure," created a fictional situation that demonstrated what could happen to an aristocratic woman who mistook herself for a figure in history. In the process she created a new, legitimate kind of fictional women's history, and she came to stand behind that fictional historical figure. Through her fictional creation, Lennox in her ephemeral celebrity became a subject of history, if only of literary history. Of all the ages that Charlotte Lennox could have selected for her own proposed history, then, it should not surprise us that she would have chosen Elizabeth's reign. Queen Elizabeth offered proof positive that virtuous, powerful women (or at least one such woman) formed a crucial part of the national historical record. Women writers were gaining acceptance as able novelists in the mid-eighteenth century because their works centered on the romantic lives of women. Lennox may have hoped that histories by women chronicling the political power of women (or understanding the role of "feminine" romantic intrigue in the political process) would also receive public approval. Like the novel, history was a malleable genre at midcentury. Historical discourse provided fertile ground for women authors who, like Lennox, were attempting to write themselves into the generic rules.

History did not immediately prove the most suitable genre for women writers, and Lennox did not come down to us as a historian. Had she completed a work of mainstream national history, she might have become the first British Clio, preempting Catharine Macaulay and perhaps altering future women writers' professional paths and receptions. Although Lennox was not a pioneer in political history writing, she used the interplay of women and history in an attempt to inflate the value attached to fictional forms. She recognized one of the signal conflicts facing authors of her generation—the diffuse roles possible for women as authors and textual figures in emerging genres, particularly in combinations of fiction and history. Her recognition may demonstrate the textual machinations of a protofeminist struggling to be heard in a patriarchal marketplace. More likely, however, Lennox's manipulations of gendered, fictional, and historiographical ideologies reveal an instinct for authorial self-preservation during a period of financial uncertainty and relative generic openness.

"Deep Immers'd in the Historic Mine": Catharine Macaulay's *History in Letters*

∎

In 1778, the year Frances Burney published her epistolary first novel *Evelina,* Catharine Sawbridge Macaulay (1731–91) also produced a work in letters. Macaulay had published five volumes of what would eventually make up her eight-volume *History of England from the Accession of James I* (1763–83). She temporarily put aside her multivolume project to work on a different kind of history, titled *The History of England from the Revolution to the Present Time: In a Series of Letters to a Friend* (1778). For Macaulay the *History in Letters* (as I will refer to it) was a sea change in historical form, scholarly apparatus, and time period. Her new project consisted of six letters addressed to Dr. Wilson, a friend who was the "aging nonresident rector" of St. Stephen's, Walbrook, and senior prebendary of Westminster (Donnelly 184). Thomas Wilson's association with Macaulay was well known. His boosterism was common knowledge in Bath and London, where their friendship aroused gossip and speculation. In addressing her historical letters to Wilson, Macaulay may have been demonstrating her gratitude, defying the rumors of their allegedly improper relationship. Regardless of her intentions, her *History in Letters* did little to win the public to her side.

In the widower Wilson, Macaulay—widowed for almost a decade—found for a time a quasi-patron, a supportive friend, and an ardent admirer. At Wilson's invitation, she and her young daughter Catherine Sophia moved into his home, Alfred House, where his library was at her disposal. Wilson and Macaulay's unconventional living arrangement did not go unnoticed. Adding to the speculation about their relationship and his intentions toward her, Wilson (thirty years her senior) made over the deed of Alfred House to Macaulay. He adopted her daughter, with whom he had a portrait painted. He intended to make Macaulay his heir. Her affiliation with Wilson and the book she addressed to him set off a chain of events that irrevocably altered the ways her name came down to us — or failed to — through the succeeding years.

In November 1778 the forty-seven-year-old Macaulay shocked Wilson and her contemporaries when she married William Graham, the twenty-one-year-old brother of her quack doctor, James Graham. Macaulay's unforeseen nuptials brought to an end her contact with a displeased Wilson, who had been unaware of their courtship. By marrying a much younger man from a lower social class, Macaulay (like Hester Lynch Piozzi after her) was cut off from friends who could not countenance the marriage.[1] She astonished them by choosing for a husband what one recent critic has called a "toy-boy" (P. Thomas 11). To call it a time of great personal upheaval for the historian is an understatement. The events of 1777–78 radically altered her life.[2] Months before her second marriage, Macaulay's *History in Letters* was published. By the end of the year few in England would be able to read any of her works without snickering about her scandalous alliances.

Macaulay — known as the "British Clio" and the "celebrated female historian" — was the first British woman to write a full-scale national history. Knowledge of her had formerly come to scholars of the eighteenth century through the condemnatory anecdotes of Samuel Johnson, Hannah More, and Horace Walpole (Schnorrenberg, "Catharine" 226–32). Macaulay's works, despite her notoriety or because of it, did not attract large numbers of nineteenth- and twentieth-century readers. Many of her writings remain difficult to find.[3] As a result, it may be ill advised to begin a chapter on Macaulay with the controversial stories of the late 1770s, thus reinscribing the tradition that these sensational accounts alone define her.[4] To repeat the rumors from this period of Macaulay's life risks giving credit to those who would capitalize on her social missteps in order to dismiss her and her writings. Despite the danger, there are sound critical reasons for covering once again such defamatory ground. For one, in the *History in Letters,* written just before her socially imprudent marriage, Macaulay implicitly encourages readers to ponder her private life. She does so in the work's very title and through her use of first-person narration — something she rarely employed in her other histories. Readers of the *History in Letters* may have believed they were invited into an exchange between Macaulay and Wilson, the "political and platonic lovers."[5] On consulting the work, such readers were surely disappointed. The *History in Letters* raises expectations of intimacy and narrative immediacy that it does not meet.

To further our understanding of the apparently uncalculated risks Macaulay took as a historian in her epistolary venture, we must try to understand the events of her life in 1777–78, especially as they allow us to take seriously the generic contributions and shortcomings of the *History in Letters*. That work—an overlooked text that has alternatively been seen as business as usual or as a break with Macaulay's historiographical methods—has been called both a "ninth volume" of her *History of England* and her "new history."[6] It attempts to serve as a continuation of Macaulay's historiography and as a new standard. In 1778 Macaulay was taking both generic and personal risks. These risks are interrelated and provide us with another picture of her—a brash innovator who could not anticipate (or refused to trouble herself with) the ways her departures from historiographical and social conventions would be punished, ridiculed, and dismissed. Macaulay's apparent failure to understand audience expectations and generic implications adds an additional layer of meaning to help us make sense of the *History in Letters* and, ultimately, of her own unfortunate textual role in laying the ground for her unfairly damaged reputation.

Many feminist critics remain reluctant to discuss biographical details that reflect poorly on historical women. Perhaps it is because we fear that any criticism of their professional or personal lives will support forces arguing for women's burial in the historical record. After a chapter on Macaulay's "Bath period" (1774–78), Bridget Hill's biography of the historian adds an odd postscript, expressing regret for the chapter she has just written and for the one she is about to embark on:

There are times when biographers wish they could ignore part of their subjects' lives. Some of them of course do. But many today tend rather to lay bare every aspect, however unsavoury or belittling, of the lives of their subjects, to reveal all the dirty washing, leaving no bone of a skeleton in the cupboard. Nobody suggests because a man is an insufferable, arrogant, mean bastard, he cannot also be a great poet. Where Catharine Macaulay is concerned there is a strong temptation to gloss over events of the Bath period. . . . In an attempt to have Catharine Macaulay, her history, republicanism, and radicalism taken seriously, why does she have to frustrate her biographer's designs by behaving in such a manner? (*Republican Virago* 103–4)

Hill writes that she does not suppress the unsavory stories of Macaulay's life, though she doubts their relevance and fears their repercussions in future evaluations of Macaulay's writings (*Republican Virago* 104). Hill's reservations (which one reviewer believed resulted in a "descriptive and defensive" biography) affect her interpretations, however (P. Thomas 11). Some Macaulay scholars, like Hill, downplay the events of the Bath period, perhaps in hopes that the way will be clearer for her finally to enjoy the just remembrance by posterity that Mary Wollstonecraft predicted for her (105).[7] "Fate," as John Kenyon has noted, "has dealt unfairly with [Macaulay]" (55).[8]

In attempting to right the record, though, we must have the record in full. For better or worse, these so-called embarrassing actions of Macaulay's from the late 1770s are woven into the fabric of her writings and her reception. Some critics might wish to have it otherwise, preferring to find what Margaret Ezell has called the "shrinking-violet female author" or the unequivocal, strident protofeminist (*Writing* 52). Barbara Newman puts it differently: "Historical women who refuse to fit our criteria for role models may find themselves an easy prey for our pity [and] . . . closely related to pity is the temptation to blame" (703–4). Macaulay frustrates our expectations for female authors, illustrated by the contradictory interpretations found in recent scholarship. One critic deems Macaulay's few remarks on the position of women "spectacularly underargued" (Staves, "Liberty" 165). Others see her bringing women to center stage in a thoroughly feminist manner (Mazzuco-Than 89; Kucich, "This Horrid Theatre"; Kucich, "Romanticism").[9] Regardless of how we understand Macaulay's position on the woman question, the events of the Bath period show that at worst she seriously misperceived the ways authorship and genre differed for women and at best she disregarded them. A biographical excursus is necessary to examine how the choices Macaulay made in life may have influenced the expectations readers had for her *History in Letters*, demonstrating her lack of foresight in designing a popular historical text. Having a publicly known romantic life made it difficult for her to be perceived as an acceptable historian. Particularly in the subgenre she chose—more like a conduct book than her previous publications—Macaulay's own conduct could not be ignored.

The Celebrated Female Historian

For most of her life, Macaulay's public behavior conformed to social expectations, and she enjoyed the privilege she was born to. As the daughter of a Kent family descended from prominent London Whig bankers,
Catharine Sawbridge married the Scottish physician George Macaulay in
1760. Macaulay, affiliated with the London radical Whigs, introduced his
wife to many members of his circle. The only event to raise eyebrows in her
background involved her grandfather Jacob Sawbridge's supposed role in
the South Sea Bubble. Despite Macaulay's high social position and her apparently unexceptionable behavior, once she turned author her habits were
regularly scrutinized. She was, according to one account, "perhaps the first
British woman to spend her adult life in public political controversy. . . .
Enemies reported that she was a disfigured hag (she was in fact rather handsome), given to excessive ostentation and use of cosmetics (conventional
for both upper-class women and men), and a neglectful mother (no evidence)" (Boos and Boos 49, 51).[10] Before the personal attacks became so
virulent, *The History of England* received praise as a Whig corrective to
Hume's history.

Five years after her death, a supporter tried to recreate the aura of Macaulay's earlier reputation. In a "Letter from a Gentleman in Town to His
Friend in the Country, concerning Celebrated Fair Historians" (1796), the
gentleman writes, "You tell me that your mother, aunts, sisters, and the
circle of good women who form the assembly in your neighborhood, ever
since they perused Mrs. Macaulay's history, are upon the tenter-hooks of
impatience to know what kind of a woman she is. . . . You cannot talk with
her ten minutes, without perceiving that she is a woman of sense; but you
may be ten years in her company, without suspecting her to be an author. . . .
I never could discover by her manner or dress that she had been either reading or writing" ("Letter" 91–92). The gentleman attempted to recreate a
properly feminine Macaulay—a version of her that was most sustainable
while her first husband was living. The stereotype of her wifely acquiescence
may have had a real-life basis. Although Dr. George Macaulay has long been
credited with encouraging his wife's historical pursuits, begun early in their
six-year marriage, there is some evidence that he had a tempering influence
on her writing. Marianne Geiger's study of Macaulay's *History* in manu-

script (housed in the New-York Historical Society) concludes that though "Macaulay had remarkably few second thoughts about her composition," her husband suggested places where her vitriolic expressions could be toned down (189).

After being widowed in 1766, Macaulay could no longer claim that she was a wife first and an author second. She did not retreat into seclusion, nor did she soon remarry. She maintained a public role, and she appears to have had no lack of male company or supporters, continuing friendships with the wealthy Old Whig barrister Thomas Hollis (who provided her with many seventeenth-century documents), with those friends surrounding her brother, the member of Parliament John Sawbridge, and with the Wilkites from whom Sawbridge was largely estranged.[11] When she moved from London to Bath in 1774 and took a house in St. James Parade, it seems to have been in search of better health. A testimonial letter attributed to her was attached to the second edition of *A Short Inquiry into the Present State of Medical Practice, in Consumptions, Asthmas, Nervous Disorders, &c.*, written by her physician, James Graham. In this letter, parts of which "smack suspiciously of Graham's overheated style," Macaulay's symptoms are described (Geiger 286).

Macaulay's letter mentions her "delicate constitution" and "weak system of nerves"; she complains of "continual pains in the stomach, indigestion, tremblings of the nerves, shivering fits, repeated pains in the ears and throat" (Graham 18–19). The letter also ties Macaulay's health to her authorship: "In this very weak state of health, I undertook writing the History of the Stewarts; and I do not know whether it is not impertinent to add, that seven years severe application reduced an originally tender frame to a state of insupportable weakness and debility" (19). The account reinforces prevailing ideologies about women being too fragile to complete scholarly work. Graham (if not Macaulay) stood to gain by representations of her weakness and her return to health. Macaulay may even have disclosed physical weakness in order to counterbalance her peremptory prose. Her health was frequently poor. In a 1774 letter to Lord Buchan, Macaulay writes, "My health is thank god much better than it has been for some years" and says that her eyesight is so much improved that she should soon "be able to return to the labors of composition" (GLC 1794.12). A 1785 letter from Catherine Sophia to her mother admonishes her to be careful: "I cannot but apprehend the most imminent danger to so delicate a constitution as yours" (GLC 1795.13). Macaulay's claims of poor health appear to have a basis in fact, but the printed testimonial was beneficial to the professional reputations of both Graham and Macaulay.

Graham treated patients with electricity, and his medical career was at this time a profitable one.[12] Maintaining that his remedies could be administered only under his own supervision (and for a fee), he put his patients on a "magnificent throne" or in a bath and passed electrical currents through them. Another aspect of his treatment, according to the *Dictionary of National Biography*, involved "aetherial and balsamic medicines," milk baths, and dry friction.[13] Presumably some of these methods cured Macaulay, providing the basis of her testimonial. Following Macaulay's letter are those of five other women and two men, relieved of symptoms ranging from headaches to deafness. Their illnesses are far more graphically described than hers, perhaps because she is the most genteel of the group. Macaulay, as Graham's most famous client, was valuable to him. He professed to have treated patients including Catherine the Great of Russia, Georgiana, duchess of Devonshire, members of the British royal family, and other Continental princes and nobility, but none of these claims can be substantiated.[14]

The ways Graham found to thank Macaulay for supporting him and his methods backfired. Along with Wilson (whose house Macaulay had moved into), James Graham hosted a birthday party for Macaulay in April 1777, described in a series of odes. These odes, read aloud at the party, were published soon afterward. The party was derided in the periodical press. Several critics have discussed the lavish gathering, but many have shied away from a full description, perhaps out of respect for the celebrant.[15] The birthday celebration described should have made a modest woman, particularly a republican one, blush. "The praise is so excessive it puts her beyond mortal women," according to Cecile Mazzucco-Than (98). The party was "ushered in by ringing of bells" and was attended by "a numerous, polite, and brilliant assembly" (*Six Odes* vii, iv). At this "elegant entertainment," Macaulay was "elegantly dressed" and sat in a "conspicuous, elevated situation" (vii–viii). She sat as if on a throne, replicating the position of her medical treatments with Graham as well as imitating a monarch.

The birthday odes themselves were read by six men, with "great propriety and expression," and their delivery was compared to the style of David Garrick and Demosthenes (viii). Wilson presented Macaulay with a "large and curious gold medal, struck in the reign of Queen Anne (and presented to her Majesty to one of the Plenipotentiaries at the peace of Utrecht)" (viii). James Graham, presenting a copy of his own book, compared Macaulay to Catherine the Great (x). The party moved between "elegantly furnished" apartments and enjoyed dancing, cards, and conversation until nine in the evening. Then there were sideboards with syllabubs, jellies, creams, ices, wines, cakes, and dried and fresh fruits (especially, we are told, grapes and pineapples). Macaulay divided her attention among the company, sustaining her proper character that united dignity, ease and true politeness until the party broke up about midnight (viv). One need not get beyond the prefatory material to realize that Macaulay was, for one night at least, treated like a queen. A letter to the editor in *Westminster Magazine,* written a year after the birthday party and just after Macaulay's marriage, refers to the "reign of Queen Catharine, the abdicated Queen of Alfred House" (Alfred 681).

Macaulay's hosts rightly anticipated that the odes would "much engage the attention of the public" (*Six Odes* vii). But the hypocrisy of staunch republican Macaulay's allowing herself to be feted as royalty was what most immediately struck readers. In the *Westminster Magazine,* "Alfred" put it succinctly, "the Doctor begged, borrowed, and bought birth-day Odes on the happy occasion; and Catherine [*sic*], the Republican, was enthroned Queen of Alfred House" (681). Bridget Hill's collection of contemporary responses to the party shows that friends and enemies alike found Macaulay's participation in Wilson's party "extravagant and ridiculous," "contemptible vanity," a "farcical parade of foolery," and a "puppet show" (qtd. in Hill, *Republican Virago* 97). The profits from the pamphlet containing the odes were apparently to go to a distressed clergyman and his large family, but the contents of the *Six Odes* hardly called up visions of charitable acts. Some readers may have felt that Macaulay's elevation was their demotion, especially the Bluestockings. Anna Laetitia Barbauld, Hester Chapone, Elizabeth Montagu, and Elizabeth Carter are singled out in one ode as "yielding claimants" who "modestly retir'd" from consideration in a contest in order to let Macaulay be crowned by Britannia (*Six Odes* 43–44). In these odes she is given "the wreath of permanent honour" by Apollo, who was said to have sent James Graham to cure her (20). Macaulay is dubbed by Athena a "matchless fair" on whom "Virtue, Sense, and Honour, fix'd their throne" (22).

Macaulay not only is well regarded among the ancient gods, she is also favorably compared to Titian, Cato, and Livy (24). In the extravagant opinion of the birthday ode poet, she improves on them:

> New were her thoughts, her nervous language new,
> While in the mirror of th' *historic page,*
> Of Britons' woes she trac'd the springs.   (22)[16]

In addition to being an inspired historian, Macaulay is declared a feminine wonder:

> Tho' deep immers'd in the historic mine,
> She bids each fact with truth's bright lustre shine;
> With Science fraught, yet see! she condescends,
> To charm with smiles. . . .
> At friendship's call, she quits the studious chace;
> Unbends her mind; resumes each softer grace.   (19)

An obsequious tone also colors the rest of the odes. Macaulay is characterized as studious but not lofty, as deep but not unbending. She resides at higher heights than most mortals but condescends with her regal smiles and feminine graces.

Gauging by the response of the periodical reviewers, readers could not but laugh at the extravagant praise in the *Six Odes.* As the *Monthly Review* put it, "There is a certain line beyond which if ridicule attempts to go, it becomes itself ridiculous" (145). The snickering review compares Wilson and Macaulay to a painting of "Folly worshipping at the shrine of Vanity" (146). The reviewer quotes the material on the food served at the party, right down to the phrase "PARTICULARLY GRAPES AND PINE APPLES" (147). The reviewer reassures that though "our Readers may possibly think [the detail about fruits] uninteresting . . . they must remember the proverbial hunger of a Reviewer, and the temptation of the scene" (147). Mocking throughout, the reviewer likens Macaulay's "deep immersion in the historic mine" to drowning and concludes that the notion of the ancient gods meeting to discuss Wilson and Macaulay is "*one thing new under the sun* at least" (147–48). The harshest criticism is reserved not for Macaulay but for the "scribblers, boys, and dotards" who wrote the odes (149). She is chastised for allowing them, rather than "men of liberal minds," to provide her with "Incense" (149).

Macaulay's birthday party was likely the idea of Wilson, the "dotard" impugned by the reviewer. Undeterred, Wilson continued his public acts of reverence in subsequent months, creating additional occasions for those who would make fun of him and his houseguest. In September 1777 Wilson had a monument to Macaulay of "Amazonian proportions" erected at St. Stephen's (Fox 138). The statue depicted her as Clio, the muse of history, or as Claire Gilbride Fox has suggested, as a "formidable Minerva, goddess of war and wisdom" (138). Wilson angered many by putting the statue in his church. The controversy was discussed in the *Gazetteer and New Daily Advertiser,* the *Gentleman's Magazine,* and the *Westminster Magazine* (Fox 137–39; Hill, *Republican Virago* 99–102; Pierpoint). The poem that was chiseled on the statue (since erased) has been attributed to Lord Lyttleton. That poem wished that one woman in every age would prove that genius is not confined to sex; still, the poet hoped for no more than one Mrs. Macaulay (Fox 138). Church officials pressed for the statue's removal, but the following year Wilson voluntarily had it pulled down, presumably outraged by Macaulay's marriage to Graham.

If Macaulay was embarrassed by Wilson's excesses, there is no evidence of it. Her *History in Letters,* on the contrary, implies her continuing approval of him and publicly displays her appreciation. In an example of life imitating art, several months after the *History in Letters* was published she is said to have written Wilson a private letter defending her marriage to Graham. Rather than an epistle on political and historical matters, as was the *History in Letters,* her private letter was alleged to be confessional and apologetic. Geiger has claimed that "Macaulay apparently wrote an ill-advised, almost crazed letter to Wilson, saying that she would have married him, but for his impotence" (289). Most critics have remained more skeptical of the rumor that Macaulay cited Wilson's alleged impotence in her letter. John Wilkes noted that Wilson threatened to publish Macaulay's letter — an unlikely threat if the letter made him look ridiculous (Hill, *Republican Virago* 111–14). The letter apparently does not survive. Its contents appear to have shocked Wilkes, although he did not give specific details (Beckwith, "Catharine" [1953] 52). In any case, Macaulay wrote a letter of a personal nature to Wilson. Wilson reportedly held others of her letters too, all of which he wanted to publish in an attempt to discredit her.

Macaulay's letters were not published, but mock letters predictably appeared. *A Bridal Ode* gives the Macaulay-Graham marriage a plot like *The Taming of the Shrew.* "Kate" gives up history for love after questioning herself over and over about whether she is doing the right thing. There are the expected digs at Wilson, the "not young" rival: "No *Epitaph* in Alabaster, / No *Panegyric* can plaister / Th' impolitic Disgrace" (14, 11). *A Remarkable Moving Letter!* another satire in verse, full of double entendres, pretends to be the actual letter Macaulay wrote to the "Delightful Doctor" to explain her constitutional grievances, to adduce the physical causes of her late union, and to bring about a coalition of parties. Macaulay calls on her "epistolary pow'rs" to "restore Historic energy" such as she used in her *History of England* (6). Wilson, referred to as her "parent," is faulted for his lack of "pow'rs that Heav'n allots to younger men" (6). Love wins over history, and Graham's youth wins over Wilson's age, though Macaulay and Graham will watch over their "patron" and his will until his death, afterward sticking him in the niche at St. Stephen's formerly earmarked for Macaulay (10).

The most revealing of the satiric letters, *The Female Patriot: An Epistle from C-t-e M-c-y to the Rev. Dr. W-l-n on Her Late Marriage,* is worth extended discussion. Bridget Hill writes that *The Female Patriot* was "almost certainly" written by Richard Paul Joddrell (Hill, *Republican Virago* 117). Joddrell, a playwright, included Wilson and Macaulay as characters in his successful farce *A Widow—No Widow* (1779). Susan Staves calls *The Female Patriot* "the most literarily accomplished of the satires," pointing out that although some library catalogs absurdly attribute this poem to Macaulay herself, it later appeared in Joddrell's *Poetical Works* (1814).[17] In *The Female Patriot* the fictionalized Macaulay once again refers to Wilson as her "honour'd parent," a phrase that Joddrell alleges is taken directly from Macaulay's actual letter:

This expression of Catharine is borrowed from the epistle written immediately after her marriage to her venerable benefactor. . . . it is allowed to be a manuscript of the most invaluable curiosity, for no Female ever penned so indelicate a composition. She there assures her aged Doctor, that, had he not been totally incapacitated for hymeneal rites, she would certainly have preferred him to any other candidate as a husband: but, in consequence of his disability, she was obliged, for the gratification of those natural and irresistible passions which stimulate the sex, to apply to another better qualified to satisfy her warmest wishes; that, however sensible he was of those exalted talents of mind which she possessed in an eminent degree, he was an entire stranger to the glowing nature of her constitution; that she must pass the delicious hours of amorous dalliance with her beloved spouse, but she was willing to dedicate the philosophical moments of her repose to her "Honour'd Parent." (Joddrell 6)

This note informs the reader that Macaulay Graham's matrimonial visit to Alfred House is not welcome, that Wilson's large legacy has been withdrawn, and that a Chancery suit has commenced: "The Lady claims the right of Alfred House, as her own by deed; but the Doctor retains possession, as he has a set-off of debts discharged, for paper, pins, pomatum, and parchment, to a very considerable amount indeed" (6). Joddrell portrays Macaulay as a greedy woman who has equally grotesque appetites for sex, beauty, and authorship. In actuality, she did not act greedily concerning Wilson's money. She abandoned Alfred House to Wilson without claim, and Wilson, in a will made several months after the marriage, left £500 to Catherine Sophia Macaulay, although nothing to her mother (Beckwith, "Catharine" [1953] 48; Hill, *Republican Virago* 119–20).[18]

Mere facts need not get in the way of satirists, however, especially on a subject of such prurient interest as Macaulay's marriage to Graham. Joddrell's verse epistle descends into further bawdiness. Alfred House is called a place where "friendship's . . . unsullied by desire" and where "Nor e'er that boist'rous tyrant dar'd to thrust / Which maids call Love, but which Immortals, Lust." Even Macaulay's history is presented as fiery and emblazoned, capable of bringing readers to raptures, rage, and "transport o'er th' Historick page!" (7). Macaulay, the "fair patriot" struggles between ambition and love:

> And in my female, though immortal page,
> The Stuart line shall bleed through ev'ry age.
> But now, my W-l-n, while this trembling lay
> My blushing Muse unfolds to open day,
> Hush'd for a moment be each nobler plot,
> Let Hamden, Sidney, Sawbridge, be forgot!
> Let patriotick thunders cease to roll,
> And tune to metre my Historick Soul.
> Come, gentle Cupid, now invok'd by me;
> Come, lovely Hymen, point my Modest Plea!
> Yet soft poetic murmurs waft your gale,
>
> . . . .
>
> For now, my honour'd Sire, must truth proclaim
> Thy widow'd Patriot is a wedded Dame.
> Last night, last night did Hymeneal vows
> Unite thy Catharine to her second spouse.   (8–9)

Joddrell notes that Macaulay reluctantly yields to love, "but it is now whispered in the ear of the Publick, that in defiance of the law she still adheres to her former appellation, and subscribes herself Catharine M-c-y" (9).[19] The poem implies that if she retains the name Macaulay, she proves she is lustful and ambitious—a woman of ravenous appetites. The title of Macaulay's earlier published pamphlet, "A Modest Plea," is used ironically in *The Female Patriot*.[20]

Though some accounts featured a diminutive husband for Macaulay, because Graham was called "not yet of age," Joddrell's *Female Patriot* imagined him as a fully formed man.[21] In a long, hyperbolic section, Graham is characterized as having mammoth, warlike sexual appetites, with his "spartan fervour," "Hotspur zeal for fair," "broad Atlantean shoulders," "manly clusters," "locks," "well-toned muscles," and "portly legs." Graham is so strong that "His single arm well brandish'd dares withstand / Six Irish chairmen from Ierne's stand." Another note explains the joke: "Catharine, in order not to deviate from historical truth too far, contents herself with comparing her wondrous Hero to six Irish chairmen only" instead of equating him with Virgil's Aeneas, who had the strength of twelve men (10–11). Macaulay exaggerates her lover's worth, Joddrell suggests, just as she exaggerates historical truths. Her appetites make it impossible for her to write history with less warmth or to marry an older man. Graham affects Macaulay's history writing abilities in other ways as well. Not only is she unable to write impartial history, but she is inspired to write only romances:

> Stern Patriotism ceas'd my soul to move,
> And all the Heroine languish'd into love.
>
> . . . .
>
> In my heroick pen the ink grew pale,
> While Fancy whisper'd some romantick tale:
> And in my evening lamp's historick urn
> With fainter lustre did my taper burn.   (12)

Macaulay compares her having been won by Graham to the "Venus's mousetrap." Liberty cannot free her; she is bound by amorous fetters to Graham (15). Joddrell further ribs Wilson, focusing on Macaulay's statue in St. Stephen's; Wilson may not want to be buried next to Macaulay any longer, "unless he obligingly consents that she should lie in the middle between him, and her present Spouse" (18).

An interlude follows in which Macaulay's first husband returns in ghostly form to bless her marriage and hints that she may even have a child (26). The ghost calls her his "quondam Queen," after which another note explains that Macaulay became a queen at Wilson's home: "Our Republican Heroine, as Fame reports, was solemnly enthroned at Bath Queen of Alfred-Palace; where the numerous band of Poets, Patriots, Puppies, Pimps, presented their respective homages to this extraordinary idol in the most humble posture" (25). With the encouragement of Dr. Macaulay's ghost, Mrs. Macaulay and Graham run to the vicar, who performs the marriage. A note reminds us, "To be imparadised in the arms of an immortal Historian, what a sentimental ne plus ultra! no language can express it, nor can the most refined Voluptuary conceive the joy of this literary epicureism" (28). Female historians are accused of indulging in sensual pleasures and gluttony. Macaulay's republican aims dwindle into inextricable historical and sexual lusts. As Macaulay "crashed her way into the writing of history, normally defined as a specifically masculine activity," so for Joddrell she crashes her way into fulfilling her appetites (Pocock, "Catharine" 243).[22]

The line "no language can express it" proves true for Joddrell's fictional Catharine, as she delivers a long speech on why she fails to write more about her connubial bliss:

> But here the aspiring Muse must check her flight;
> For how can language speak my marriage night?
> Tho' oft my pen in bold heroic vein
> Has painted Warriors on th' embattled plain,
> Their heart-felt wounds, their agonizing pains,
> Their falt'ring accents, and their dying strains;
> Yet here connubial combats to describe
> Defies all History's rhetorick pride;
> If all thy eloquence my Muse could steal,
> In vain Love's curtain'd joys could she reveal:
> . . . .
> Thus o'er the sequel of my tale I draw
> The veil of Silence with mysterious awe.   (29–30)

Sex and war are again coupled, but Macaulay is unable to describe the ecstasies of sex, despite her expertise as a narrator of other kinds of "battles." Her inability results from lack of skill, not modesty. Alleged to be more like a romance writer than a pornographer, Joddrell's Macaulay leaves the fleshly aspects to the reader's imagination (and to innuendo and double entendre).

In a final note, *The Female Patriot* asks that the "fair Reader" recall that in this amorous epistle "there is not a single expression to revolt the most scrupulous delicacy" (30). Macaulay may not be modest, but Joddrell is. He sarcastically suggests that his readers may even envy Macaulay's transcendent happiness and wish to be in her place, though they will not want to be forced to exchange faces with her. In his satiric treatment, Joddrell invokes an increasing dichotomy between the skills required for romance and for history writing. Macaulay could not be viewed as both romantically involved and historically competent. Those who defamed her tried to convince readers that her marriage effectively ended her career as a historian. They were too presumptuous; Macaulay continued to write history as Macaulay Graham. Attacks on her ability to create sound history (coupled with profound changes in the political climate during the French Revolution) contributed to her plummeting reputation over the next two decades. Supportive letters to the editor—such as the *Westminster Magazine*'s "Vindication of Mrs. Macaulay's Marriage"—were not able to stem the tide of negative publicity.[23]

History in a Series of Letters to a Friend

Between Macaulay's outlandish birthday party in 1777 and her notorious marriage at the end of the following year, she published the *History in Letters*. Though she had been publishing pamphlets, the *History in Letters* was her first book to appear since the fifth volume of her *History of England from the Accession of James I, to That of the Brunswick Line* (1771).[24] The eight-volume *History of England,* with its groundbreaking use of seventeenth-century source material, has attracted renewed scholarly interest.[25] The *History in Letters,* which covered 1689 to 1742 (using plenty of thematic digression) and was supposed to continue in a second volume to "the present time," has received little attention, perhaps because it is considered Macaulay's least successful book. Barbara Brandon Schnorrenberg suspects that the project was discontinued because "no one, except presumably Wilson, was impressed by it. [Macaulay's] thesis was unchanged: the revolution of 1688–89 and succeeding governments had done nothing to ensure liberty and honest government; but her research was apparently limited to reading some of the periodical press. There is none of the thorough documentation here that characterizes *The History of England, from the Accession of James I.*" [26] Schnorrenberg believes that the *History in Letters* was received with little enthusiasm because "Macaulay's unflattering accounts of men of more recent times turned many against her, among them Horace Walpole, who heartily condemned her portrait of his father, Sir Robert" ("Catharine" 229). Lucy Donnelly puts it less personally: "An experiment of throwing the first volume of her history into the popular form of letters fell flat, for the public showed no disposition to read a twice-told tale" (189). Neither of these interpretations seems entirely convincing. *The History in Letters* fell short of its promise because Macaulay was working in a new genre and miscalculated the efficacy and ramifications of her chosen framing device.

The public disposition toward the *History in Letters* may have had less to do with Macaulay's form than with her sex and her idiosyncratic execution of epistolary history. Her idea to compose epistolary history was a clever generic choice but not an original one. In 1764 Oliver Goldsmith had published his very successful *An History of England, in a Series of Letters from a Nobleman to His Son*. Considered alongside her use of the epistolary historiographical form must be her readers' expectations (sullied by recent gossip about Macaulay and Wilson) and the very act of circulating letters in a charged political climate. Why would Macaulay deviate from her historiographical and chronological course, particularly when her previous efforts had met with success? One critic has proposed that she made the change in response to the lag in sales of her earlier volumes and to criticism of their "pedantic literary style" (Fox 136).[27] It has also been proposed that Macaulay struck out on a new path because while living in Bath she did not have access to the resources of the British Museum, or because of her poor health, or because she meant the work as a gesture of thanks to her current benefactor. Each of these reasons seems plausible, and a combination of factors may have led to her departure in form and chronology. It is also possible that Macaulay was attracted to the epistolary form for its marketability. The form had proved popular with enthusiastic audiences and profitable to historians and novelists. She returned to epistolary writing in her final conduct book, *Letters on Education* (1790), but she left no documented rationale for undertaking the *History in Letters*, save her opening letter to Wilson.

The first letter (addressed "To the Rev. Dr. W*****," though he had been named in the dedication) is a paean both to Wilson and to republicanism. Macaulay insists that Wilson has not asked for this dedication and that she addressed the *History in Letters* to him of her own accord: "When you indulged me with the happiness of your correspondence, my excellent friend, it never crossed your imagination, that the satisfaction you gave me the opportunity of enjoying, would be mixed with any alloy; yet, my friend, it has subjected me to an anxious desire of rendering my letters worthy your attention, and my correspondence the source of your amusement" (1).[28] For readers, as curious for clues to scandal as for history, this must have seemed an excellent start, with its mention of indulgence, imagination, satisfaction, and anxious desires. The diction soon cools, however, to "filial piety" outlining the "virtues of your character" (*HL* 2). One of Wilson's virtues is his generosity:

Your moderation in every circumstance of indulgence which regards yourself, whilst you are lavishing thousands on the public cause, and to inlarge the happiness of individuals; the example and regularity of your life; your patience and fortitude, and even chearfulness, under the infirmities of a weak and tender constitution; and lastly, the munificent favors you have conferred on me, are subjects of sufficient power to animate the dullest writer. (2)

Along with generosity, Wilson couples modesty, because these compliments "are subjects, my friend, which I am convinced will please every reader better than yourself" (2). After the birthday party debacle and the statue incident, Wilson's reputation for moderation needed propping up.

If Macaulay's opening seems to promise romantic revelations, readers eager for hints of romance between Wilson and Macaulay must find their hopes dashed. Macaulay writes, "As the love of your country, and the welfare of the human race, is the only ruling passion I have ever discerned in your character, I shall . . . fix your attention by the interesting detail of those causes and circumstances, which have insensibly led us . . . to our present state of danger and depravity" (2). From this point forward Wilson as the recipient of Macaulay's letters drops out of the text. The device of addressing the letters to him falls away. Only an occasional "my friend" punctuates the text, forcing us to recall that we are supposedly reading letters. Even in the laudatory first pages of the book, it is easy to forget that Wilson's presence should be animating the text.

Macaulay's letter 1 covers the Glorious Revolution and the reign of King William III, especially his altercations with James II, France, and Ireland. Continuing with King William's dealings with Parliament, including changing the laws of succession to ensure Protestant rule, letter 2 ends with his death. The third letter contains a long section on the national debt, as well as the reigns of Queen Mary and Queen Anne and the union with Scotland. Despite Macaulay's disclaimer that "descriptions of battles are in general the dullest and least interesting part of an historical narrative" and her promise to her "dear friend" to be short on such subjects, the third and fourth letters contain liberal narrations of hostilities between England and France (181). Because Wilson is fond of Macaulay's characters, letter 4 ends with a description of Queen Anne, completed despite the professed danger of injustice and inaccuracy because this monarch lived too near to the present (270). Letter 5 gives the entire reign of George I and the machinations of the South Sea Company, including an uncharacteristic first-person paragraph on Macaulay's grandfather's role, maintaining his innocence of any intent to defraud the public (306–7).

In letter 6 Macaulay writes the history of George II and Parliament, returning to a discussion of the national debt. She again professes that she has "totally rejected the invidious task of giving characters: in the history of these modern times, I cannot submit to the drudgery of culling panegyric from addresses or birth-day odes, and other researches might lead me into dangerous paths" (355). Again, readers mindful of Macaulay's own birthday odes might be troubled by her hypocrisy. She concludes, however, with a character of Mr. Pulteney, whom she tells us her father admired, and ends on a righteous and hopeful note. Macaulay's last letter shows her unwillingness or inability to recall that her text is fashioned as correspondence and not as straightforwardly narrated history. A tacked-on signoff and signature provide the only indication that we have come to the end of the first volume.

Macaulay has seemed "no letter writer in easy gossiping vein" (Donnelly 204), and her surviving private correspondence reinforces that she did not easily take to the form she twice chose for publication. Her private letter writing habits have been difficult for scholars to determine because "only a few letters, most of them with her friends in America" were available in archives before 1992 (Hill, *Republican Virago* 1). Bridget Hill's biographical research on Macaulay found no extant family papers, and Hill suspects that if there were any, they were lost in an early twentieth-century fire. In 1995 new information surfaced, also documented by Hill ("Links" 178). A considerable collection of Catharine Macaulay's papers were sold in 1992 to what Hill writes was an "unknown" United States buyer; two letters (correspondence between Mary Wollstonecraft and Macaulay) were bought by the New York Public Library ("Links" 178). The remaining items are in the Gilder Lehrman Collection, housed in the Pierpont Morgan Library in New York. This collection includes approximately 190 letters relating to Macaulay and her descendants, including correspondence with John Adams, Mercy Otis Warren, and Horace Walpole. Twenty of the letters were written by Macaulay. From them her everyday epistolary habits may be better surmised.

Macaulay's letters to acquaintances are filled with political anecdotes, conjectures, and questions. On occasion her correspondents seem to reveal underlying frustration with her requests for information. William Livingston writes that he will not send her any account of American activities until he receives notice of which particular details she desires (GLC 1793). Correspondent James Bowdoin proposes that she swap anecdotes and papers on the American Revolution with William Gordon, in exchange for material useful to her *History in Letters,* "if God spared your life" (GLC 1791.02). Second only to political details in the letters are concerns for Macaulay's well-being. In letters to her friends, Macaulay begins with updates on her health. Exchanged letters with the eccentric and melancholy Lord Buchan are most explicit about how her health suffers. In 1770 she confirms to Buchan that the account of her health in the newspaper is true but says that she is now somewhat better and is "impatient for a publication which you can call of more consequence" (GLC 1794.08). In 1771 she writes to him of "a very severe fever of four months continuance" that prevented her from writing sooner and tells of her intention to improve her condition through sea bathing (GLC 1794.10). Sometimes she refers to her daughter's education or to her professional plans, but her two pet topics are political events and poor health.

Macaulay was certainly sickly, but evidence also exists that it was not simply her health that prevented her from answering her correspondence. She apparently detested letter writing. The clearest sense we get of Macaulay's private correspondence is from her daughter's letters. Catherine Sophia's notes are regular, chatty, and loving, but in later years daughter also chides mother for her poor letter writing habits. Catherine Sophia is by turns grateful and upset. She regularly compliments her mother for indulging her, but in the next breath she proclaims, "Dear Mama you must allow me to be a little angry with you" for not writing (GLC 1795.20). One letter contains a long narrative describing her painful wait for her mother's overdue letter, the difficulty of life on fruitless post days, and the frustration involved in receiving letters from "indifferent persons." Catherine Sophia concludes, "For God's sake write often" (GLC 1795.15). Five years later she complains, "really you are grown a bad correspondent of late" (GLC 1795.36). In what is perhaps the definitive word on the matter, daughter lectures mother, "You are in general a punctual correspondent tho' not very fond of letter writing" (GLC 1795.34). Although Catherine Sophia claims her mother was "apt to carry a favorite pursuit too far," letter writing—at least of the "easy gossiping" kind that Catherine Sophia herself wrote and appears to desire—was not among Macaulay's favorite pastimes (GLC 1795.16).

In the *History in Letters,* as in many of her private missives, Macaulay's writing is impersonal, terse, emotionally disengaged, and politically impassioned. Informal asides and directly addressed phrases are most prevalent early on in the *History in Letters.* Well into her project, Macaulay's writing becomes much terser, the reflections are fewer, and the language is more directly suited to advancing her political project. The writing is decisive, without footnotes and with few mentions of other historians except for Burnet, whom she credits frequently in the early letters. Macaulay continues her use of rhetorical questions all in a row, especially to drive home points about inappropriate choices or behavior. The descriptions of battles, especially those of the War of Spanish Succession, are colorful and centered on personalities. More than character descriptions (which she claims to avoid), Macaulay reveals a fixation with numbers—numbers of ships, numbers of soldiers, amounts of money, and debts to the Crown. She narrates with vigor the abuses of Whigs and Tories alike. Her transitions, from letter to letter and even within a given letter, are lackluster. Sometimes there is no sense whatever of leaving one topic for another. Unlike the *History of England,* the *History in Letters* does not provide readers with dates or with events glossed in the margins. Following Goldsmith's lead in epistolary historical form, there are few dates within Macaulay's text. Each of her letters is a discrete entity, wherein the narrative is connected by places and personalities, with a series of linked events followed by a summary of issues discussed and concluded. There is frequent restating and reminding, as well as questions for the reader-friend, claiming to leave interpretations up to his own judgment.

Despite her judicious stance, Macaulay is quick to proclaim her opinions. She introduces readers to her thesis that "the Reformation and the Revolution are the two grand aeras in our history" but that both fell far short of their goals and of Macaulay's ideals (*HL* 3–4). Henry VIII was enriching his coffers and revenging himself on the Roman pontiff (3). The Revolution neglected a "fair opportunity to cut off all the prerogatives of the crown" (4). The plan of settlement "was neither properly digested or maturely formed," and as a result, the revolutionary system was "totally void of improvement" (5). It becomes clear that the letter device constitutes Macaulay preaching to the converted when she concludes, "Your extensive reading in history, my friend, will not, I believe, furnish you with one exception to this rule; that when the succession in the government is changed, without a substantial provision for the security of liberty, its total destruction is accomplished, by the measure intended for its preservation" (5).

Macaulay's volume is addressed to someone who presumably knows all the information that follows, though she is not, of course, writing only to Wilson; she has a larger audience in mind at all times. With Wilson, Macaulay writes to someone whose life has almost run its course, who is learned in historical matters. Wilson has "lived too many years in the world . . . to be surprised" (10). Macaulay writes that she does not "pretend to tell you novelties, or to have any other end in this narration, but to revive your memory on the facts necessary to connect that train of events which have compleated the overthrow of the Whig principles" (10). In short, Wilson, as Macaulay's ideal reader, is not representative of her anticipated audience. If his memory needs to be revived, it is not because he has been an indolent student or because his education was inadequate. It is because, as a man in his late seventies, he is becoming forgetful or even senile—something several of his contemporaries intimated (Hill, *Republican Virago* 107). Few of Macaulay's readers would have wanted to imagine themselves as the "friend" in Wilson's shoes.

Oliver Goldsmith's device in his epistolary history was to address every letter to "Dear Charles" or "Dear Child." Macaulay did not follow this pattern of parent writing to offspring and thus is not addressing someone studying history in the formative years in order to become "a proper member of the community, for filling that station, in which you may hereafter be placed, with honour; and for giving, as well as deriving, new lustre from that illustrious assembly, to which, upon my decease, you have a right to be called" (*History* 3). In Goldsmith's version, the correspondence is set up as a fictional one of a teacher-father to a student-son, "Charles," who is at Oxford and who needs to learn history to take his place in the world. Macaulay, because she wanted to dedicate the text to Wilson, ruled out fictional devices that would have provided a pedagogically appropriate address. Had she chosen to address her daughter, Catherine Sophia, her epistolary history would have been more acceptable to readers as a manual of instruction, and its personal undertones would have seemed maternal rather than suspiciously illicit. Macaulay could not rightly use a conduct book frame in her correspondence with Wilson without infantilizing him. Were she herself younger and less established as a historian, she might have legitimately addressed him as a father figure, but that possibility had long passed. Even worse, if he was not infantilized or paternalized, he must be sexualized as an unmarried adult male with whom Macaulay was living. Another shortcoming of Macaulay's work in comparison with Goldsmith's is her lack of any attempt to entertain readers with the pretense of an actual correspondence. In Macaulay's text, neither the letter writer nor the addressee is shaped as a character. As a result, readers had only the assumptions they brought with them about Macaulay and Wilson to read into the correspondence.

Macaulay worried in her *History in Letters* that she had not provided readers with enough entertainment. After a long section narrating the history of Ireland from James I to the Treaty of Limerick, the first letter contains a formulaic and ill-chosen closing device. In need of an excuse to sign off, Macaulay concludes defensively: "I do not know, my friend, whether you are disposed to be entertained with my narration; but, for my part, I am tired with the subject of public abuses, therefore shall lay down my pen, and endeavor to refresh my wearied spirits with some work of imagination, where government answers its just end, where the princes are all wise and good, and the subjects happy and content" (29). Although her apocalyptic tone and utopian longing are in keeping with the rest of the work, nowhere else is her purpose expressed in terms of entertainment. Macaulay implies that readers (and writers) may be entertained for a time by history but that, if accurately told, history is inevitably wearying. Refreshing reading—just, good, and happy reading—can be found most readily in works of the imagination. The Glorious Revolution had been pointed to as one of the happiest of national endings, precisely the opposite of Macaulay's premise. Macaulay's is a story with a singularly unhappy ending—that republicanism has not yet had its day.

The Reception of the *History in Letters*

Macaulay's *History in Letters,* more than any other of her historical works, vaguely resembles a work of fiction, with its "my friend" asides, its epistolary form, and its lack of footnotes and dates. As she writes at the end of the first letter, however, her history cannot compete with a work of the imagination. Readers who long to be "refreshed" and rejuvenated had better look to another kind of book. Macaulay either misunderstood or ignored the expectations of readers looking to published letters. Instead of setting up a first-person connection to the narration, the letters offered only a dedication to Wilson. Macaulay did not have a firm grasp on what made epistolary forms attractive to readers. She undertook a popular historical (and fictional) subgenre without emulating the elements that made it accessible and compelling. At the end of letter 1 she admits that she puts down her own history for a more entertaining book. She suggests that pleasure must be sacrificed for happiness, but she might have taken the example of Richardson's *Clarissa* and retained a tone of warning and impending disaster while writing her history as a tragic lesson that must be communicated on a personal as well as a national level.

In a study on Jane Austen and feminism, Margaret Kirkham finds occasion to briefly discuss Catharine Macaulay. Though Macaulay and Austen seem to have little in common, Kirkham finds a great deal of overlap in the two authors' approaches to gender equality. Kirkham concludes that in this project Macaulay faced one hardship that the younger Austen did not encounter. Macaulay "lacked but one claim to a central position in the development of Enlightenment feminism: she was not a novelist" (12). There is something to Kirkham's suggestion. Macaulay appears to have had no desire to produce a work of the imagination, but the conclusion to letter 1 shows that she was aware of the appeal and the power of fiction. She sought to reach or satisfy new readers with her 1778 history, geared as it is toward an audience with modest historical education or expectations. She wanted to offer historical instruction in a lighter, more narratively intimate mode, but she was apparently not well equipped for the task.

The novel's epistolary inroads in the second half of the eighteenth century are germane to a discussion of Macaulay and to a larger argument about gender and genre in her work. One difficulty with Macaulay's choice of an epistolary form may have been its temporality. An epistolary history, as she designed it, would be expected to narrate past events. Although Goldsmith's narration has similarities to Macaulay's in terms of treatment of the past, he also created a strong device to tie the events to the present moment—relating them to a much-beloved son in need of historical wisdom. Without a necessary and compelling tie to the present, Macaulay's use of the epistolary form loses one of the benefits of that genre—its immediacy. Frank Gees Black has discussed this immediacy as one reason why certain subgenres of the novel were less suited to an epistolary form: "The increasingly popular historical and Gothic fiction made little use of the letter. The effectiveness of the familiar letter depends upon its informality and idiomatic style. These qualities, rather easily obtainable when the letters are supposed to be contemporary, are difficult to secure in representation of a remoter time" (47). Macaulay faced this difficulty but either did not recognize it or did not find a way around it in her *History*. She wanted to reach a popular audience, but she was not well versed in how best to sustain interest in an epistolary structure.

Several months after she published the *History in Letters,* Macaulay considered putting together a collection of imaginative writings and other literature. In August 1778 she wrote to a young Richard Polwhele, telling him of her plan to publish a volume of a *Miscellaneous Works* that demonstrated republican principles and asking him to consider contributing one of his poems (Hill, *Republican Virago* 90). Because this miscellany was never completed, the closest Macaulay came to producing imaginative literature—as it was then defined and developing and as opposed to historical narrative—was in her epistolary writings. Some of her contemporaries quipped that all her history writing qualified as imaginative literature. The painter Allan Ramsay called Macaulay's history a "romance" in his letter to Hume (qtd. in Schnorrenberg, "Brood Hen" 34). His generic confusion was surely meant to be taken as an insult or a joke rather than straightforwardly. But as a series of letters from a woman to a man known to be widowed and living together, the *History in Letters* indeed resembled a romance slightly more than did Macaulay's other writings. The text's epistolary scenario may have left readers wondering why Macaulay would be writing to Wilson in the first place, unless she had something to say that could not be given voice under their shared roof.

In designing her *History in Letters,* Macaulay did not think through many practical questions—nor, it seems, did her supporters. To add to the absurdities of 1777–78, Capel Lofft, one member of Macaulay's "numerous band of Poets, Patriots, Puppies, Pimps," published an almost immediate panegyric on the *History in Letters,* titled *Observations on Mrs. Macaulay's "History of England" (Lately Published) from the Revolution to the Resignation of Sir Robert Walpole in a Letter Addressed to That Lady.* The *DNB* describes Lofft as a "miscellaneous writer," a student of political law, a Cambridge dropout, a member of Lincoln's Inn (later called to the bar), heir to an independent fortune, a strong Whig, a classical scholar, a lover of fine literature and music, and a natural historian fond of botany and astronomy.[29] Macaulay's *History in Letters,* which reached over four hundred pages, elicits sixty-eight pages of Lofft's paraphrase, quotation, and praise. Lofft's *Observations* functioned as an advertisement for Macaulay's book because it was for all practical purposes an abridgment.

Lofft begins with a justification for his undertaking, because "the public will probably think it reasonable to be informed on what motive the writer of this can have assumed those pretensions to notice which your name prefixed will imply" (1). In characteristically rambling prose, Lofft declares that a "worthy patriotic gentleman" (Wilson?) encouraged him to make his remarks public:

A worthy patriotic gentleman, with whom I had very lately the happiness of becoming acquainted, having asked my sentiments of your late *History* . . . then just published, I thought myself under obligations to give those sentiments in a manner the least injurious of which I was capable: it obviously occurred that verbal observations upon such a work would be the easiest and most prudent in regard of myself, but at the same time they appeared to me not sufficiently respectful with relation to the much esteemed proposer of the question, and to the extent and importance of the question itself: in proposing which, though it was very apparent that an honour was intended me, yet as it came from a person whom I believed with reason not to design an honour to any one without thinking they did, or meaning they should observe it, my desire was rather to appear weak or indiscreet, than negligent or ungrateful in the discharge of so high a trust. On reading of it he was pleased to express an opinion, which it would be improper for me to suppose ill-founded, since it was his opinion: and upon the deference due to that, I have been induced to publish those remarks, which had his private approbation. (1–2)

Lofft's praise of Macaulay is everything an admirer like Wilson must have wanted. Lofft writes: "I must not in this letter, nor can perhaps in any, give a proper and adequate title, but to admire the elegant, the amiable, the benevolent, in conversing, esteem was added to veneration" (2). He admits he has ambitions in writing these *Observations* as well, since he is "endeavouring to transmit myself to posterity as one who had attempted to express his ideas of Mrs. Macaulay's historical character" (3). Lofft's ambitions begin to sound like romantic ones, too, as he professes his feelings in the third person:

[The writer is] one who had the honour and happiness of some share in her acquaintance, and who is not without pride enough to hope that he may die possessed of her friendship: the profession of which hope he considers equivalent to a voluntary obligation of himself, to endeavour a constant perseverance in the paths of sincerity and virtue; and as one of the best methods of entitling himself to a double portion of contempt, if ever he shall become a flatterer or a slave. Some effusions of the heart, in which I indulged myself, when writing to the gentleman whom I mentioned, will now be suppressed: since I consider not only of whom, but to whom I am writing. (2–3)

Lofft is conscious of his choice to speak of his correspondent, if not of himself, in the third person: "For the same reason, I shall generally speak of the author in the third person, and on what I have to say upon the subject, shall endeavor from henceforth to speak in a manner as abstracted from any thing but my ideas of the work itself, as if I were commenting on Thucydides, Sallust, or Tacitus" (3). He tries to maintain an even-keeled, distanced, objective pose, though his is a work of fulsome praise from its title forward.

Lofft usually sticks to commentary on the work itself, though he does digress to second Macaulay's views on Wilson's character (5–6). He comments with pleasure on Macaulay's infrequent first-person narration in the *History*. When, at the end of letter 1, Macaulay expresses a wish to read a work of the imagination, Lofft writes, "I do not wonder, that from these scenes, the benevolent Genius should be disposed to remove awhile to the regions of ideal kings, and happy monarchies of imagination. May that Genius live to see more than imaginary happiness of communities" (13). On Macaulay's concern that she might have tired her reader, Lofft writes,

"For the apology made by the historian, . . . I . . . only [observe], that abject indeed is that situation of a people in which such a genius should despair of interesting the reader" (55). At this point it is Lofft who should be despairing of his ability to interest the reader; his references to the "genius" Macaulay and her "excellent work" grow repetitive. The most bizarre digressions from his rosy summary of and quotation from the "rapid and illuminated detail" of the "benevolent Genius" are his twice mentioning the grief he is experiencing owing to the recent death of his mother (16, 67). He concludes with some general remarks on what history writing should be, suggesting that Macaulay has not only met but exceeded these expectations.

The *Observations* received a few short notices in the periodicals. The *Westminster Magazine* commented that Lofft "manifestly betrays rather too much devotion, and Mrs. Macaulay is his idol." The *Monthly Review* was kinder, calling the *Observations* a "panegyrical review of, or commentary on, Mrs. Macaulay's work, written with great zeal for the honour of the Lady and her performance, and with a decent share of judgment; but unequal in style." [30] The least supportive notice is that in the *Critical Review,* which begins, without introduction, with Lofft's commentary on his mother's death. The reviewer writes, "This, we confess, is a mode of reasoning which we do not well understand, even granting that we are disposed to make 'more than rigourously just allowances.' But this is not the most improbable expectation entertained by the author in respect of the present pamphlet, from which he even seems to presage himself immortality." The reviewer comments on the length of Lofft's letter, sarcastically concluding that "Mr. Loft [*sic*] seems to have been impatient to inform the public that he entertains the highest opinion" of Macaulay's work. Lofft might have undertaken the *Observations* as a favor to Wilson or Macaulay, either of whom may have worried about the *History's* reception. The text also leaves readers with more unseemly questions: Was Lofft looking for a mother figure in Macaulay? Did he have romantic feelings for her? He was a young man at the time—single and in his late twenties, though he was to marry his first wife, Ann Emlyn, five months later, in August 1778. He was already a budding author, having published a poem in praise of poetry in 1775 and a work of legal history in 1776, reporting on recent cases of the Courts of King's Bench, Chancery, and Common Pleas. Lofft's *Observations* added to the overdone encomiums expected from Macaulay's birthday-ode circle. His devotion secured the good reputation neither of the *History in Letters* nor of Macaulay herself and seems to have further annoyed a reading public already suspicious of her male admirers.

Critical response to the *History in Letters,* while not as negative as subsequent critics have led us to believe with their accounts of its failure, was certainly mixed. The most nuanced, contextualized study of Macaulay's reception is Susan Staves's. Staves uses Macaulay's reception to make an argument about prevailing cultural attitudes toward women and women's writing in order to illuminate the social construction versus the rhetoric of natural rights:

In this period, three quite different attitudes seem to have coexisted: first, moralistic insistence that ordinary women of the middling and upper classes embody the virtues of chastity and modesty and that they be psychologically dependent on fathers and husbands for approval and admiration; second, nationalistic celebration of the new literary and cultural achievements of the extraordinary English women, the "British Fair," celebrated as emblems of British Enlightenment; third, self-congratulation that polite society now had become more homosocial, that men and women were increasingly improving each other by rational conversation and mutual correction. Misogynistic attacks on women as a gender had, it seems, become impolite. . . . In this cultural context, seriously to attack a woman merely for having written a book on English history risked seeming impolite, ungentlemanly, unpatriotic, and unreasonable. ("Liberty" 172–73)

Staves's argument suggests why the *History in Letters* was treated gently by most reviewers, as well as why many more "risked" impoliteness. Once Macaulay gave the public something to blame her for other than the notoriety of authorship, she no longer had protection from misogynistic attacks.

Throughout Macaulay's career the *Monthly Review* was favorable in its assessments of her writings. With the *History in Letters,* the *Monthly Review* tried to figure out what motives compelled Macaulay to "publish her account of a later period, with some variation of manner, from the continued gravity of historic detail, to the more easy and familiar form of epistolary style" (112). The review reproduced the first-person asides to Wilson, concluding that Macaulay had grander aims than thanking her friend in the *History in Letters,* considering her instead a British Cassandra who attempts to "shew us what treacherous ground we stand on" (114). After generous excerpts, the reviewer returns to comment on the form of "this very singular history," singular in its author's sex and in its "peculiar form, and the striking, summary, and comprehensive manner in which the narration is conducted—scarcely reconcileable, indeed, with the common received notions of historic compositions" (121). Though advising that the title should be "Commentaries, or Reflections, on the History of England," the first installment of the review ends with characteristic commendatory flourishes (121). The reviewer asks for a second volume of the *"Historical Letters,"* and adds material for an errata sheet, with suggestions for a more correct subsequent edition, "should it be called for" (130–31). The review also makes a final plea for the addition of marginal dates (131–32).

The *Critical Review,* like the *Monthly Review,* begins by wondering why Macaulay "changed her narrative from the direct historical to the epistolary form" and offers several less than supportive possibilities. The review proposes that a "familiar style" was chosen because Macaulay thinks more recent political history is less deserving of serious treatment or because she believes it is important to thank the man who erected a statue of her to "animate her researches" of insipid modern politics (130–31). Referring to Macaulay and Wilson as "platonic lovers," the reviewer duly quotes Macaulay's introductory compliments to Wilson. The review ends with lukewarm praise of Macaulay's "judicious and liberal" observations, "excepting a few digressions, with the apostrophes addressed to her *excellent friend"* (134). On the whole, reviewers questioned Macaulay's stylistic shift and her choice of correspondent more than they did her political interpretations.

Nowhere is the lack of support for Macaulay's style clearer than in the *Westminster Magazine's* "Observations . . . on Mrs. Macaulay's *History,"* which begins its commentary on the *History in Letters* by claiming that Macaulay is "too well known" to require "recommendation or encomium." The review continues with precisely such praise of the "sprightly genius" and "unbiassed Writer" (59). The *History* is deemed a "rational, curious, entertaining, and interesting piece of valuable intelligence" before the reviewer makes "candid" criticisms, in agreement with the *Monthly Review,* that Macaulay's *History* does not even deserve the label: "Mrs. Macaulay is too loose, desultory, and incorrect in her arrangement, to be called an Historian. Her Work carries more the appearance of a Commentary, or Notes Historical and Political, than a regular, compleat History of the Times alluded to" (60). The lack of scholarly apparatus and less stringently chronological structure (with her thematic digressions on national debt and philosophical asides on other topics) makes her history appear irregular or incomplete, but the reviewer goes too far. Though Macaulay's *History* involves historical non sequiturs, it is not without order.

The reviewer also faults Macaulay for a lack of attention to female "worthies," assuming that her writings should operate in Staves's second mode of commentary on women: "It is somewhat extraordinary, that these important Females [Queens Mary, Anne, and Caroline] should be treated with such neglect and contempt by a female pen" (60). A close reading of the *History in Letters* shows that this accusation is only partially accurate. Macaulay treats each of these women, though Mary gets short shrift, her death seemingly included as an afterthought (*HL* 83). Queen Anne is given extended treatment, earning occasional compliments, however backhanded (86–87). Queen Anne's weaknesses are discussed in relation to her stronger, influential, and ill-intentioned friends, such as Sarah Churchill, the duchess of Marlborough. Macaulay includes a long narrative about Queen Anne, the duchess, and her cousin Mrs. Masham. Though flattering on no side, it is a colorful story entertainingly told. The reviewer's comments can be considered accurate only if every woman's discussion of a woman must be made in flattering terms—an imperative to which Macaulay, to her credit, would not stoop.

What seems to rattle the *Westminster* reviewer most is that Macaulay, the "Fair Annalist," is "very irregular in the thread of her History, respecting dates" ("Observations" 60). Again, her lack of dates might be an emulation of Goldsmith's *History*. Goldsmith informs his correspondent, Charles, that the rote memorization of dates is not what the study of history should be about:

Yet, still, nothing can be more useless than history, in the manner in which it is generally studied, where the memory is loaded with little more than dates, names, and events. Simply to repeat the transaction is thought sufficient for every purpose, and the youth, who is applauded for his readiness in this way, fancies himself a perfect historian. But the true use of history does not consist in being able to settle a genealogy, in knowing the events of an obscure reign, or the true epoch of a contested birth; this knowledge of facts hardly deserves the name of science: true wisdom consists in tracing the effects from their causes. To understand history is to understand man, who is the subject. To study history is to weigh the motives, the opinions, and the passions of mankind, in order to avoid a similitude of error in ourselves, or profit by the wisdom of their example. (*History* 3)

Despite their shared disregard for dates, Goldsmith would not have approved of Macaulay's history. Macaulay is accused of creating a history in which the reviewer claims that "none but an experienced Reader of History of England can keep pace with her" ("Observations" 60). The reviewer's comment is not completely correct, but as I discussed earlier, her conceit of addressing the letters to a historical "expert" creates an atmosphere of speaking to authorities rather than amateurs. That difference from Goldsmith, more than a lack of dates, was Macaulay's most momentous generic miscalculation.

The *Westminster* reviewer ends with the critical chivalry that Staves prepares us to anticipate, mentioning Macaulay's "peccadillos," "not with a view to depreciate the Authoress, being like spots or patches on a fine Lady's face; but to caution her against these small blemishes in the succeeding volumes." The reviewer believes that "with a few such gentle corrections, her History will be a most valuable acquisition to the Public" (60). Even before Macaulay's marriage to Graham (revealing her carnal "sins"), her supposed historical shortcomings are imagined as gendered, embodied ones—as spots or patches on a fine face. In "focusing on her sex," as Cecile Mazzucco-Than puts it, "much of the praise and calumny alike failed to separate Macaulay's female body from the body of her *History*" (78).

The linkage of Macaulay's body and writings was never more prevalent than after her second marriage. Her life in the year before this event laid the ground for concentration on her body. Macaulay's admirers and Macaulay herself, as we have seen, provided ammunition for this unfortunately standard connection between woman author and female body: the testimonial to Graham, the birthday party and odes, the well-known relationship with Wilson, and the panegyric by Lofft.[31] Before 1777, personal information about Macaulay could be found briefly and primarily in her own works, in modest statements such as the following, appearing in volume 1 of her *History of England* (1763): "If the execution [of my *History*] is deficient, the intention must be allowed to be meritorious; and if the goodness of my head may justly be questioned, my heart will stand the test of the most critical examination" (1: ix). Her apology, expected and acceptable from female authors of the day, may have warmed readers to receive her writings with chivalry. Subsequent episodes flaunting Macaulay's confidence and self-righteousness were not well calculated to draw popular response. At the same time, her politics were becoming even less acceptable to some as the American Revolution began.

Macaulay's politics have been thoroughly discussed by recent scholars, but the political dimension of her choice of the epistolary form in her *History in Letters* has not been fully considered.[32] As Mary Favret and Nicola Watson have illustrated, by the end of the century the letter form, especially epistolary fiction, became "the belle of the ball, her dance card signed by the literary titans of the age." Letters were "imagined as fluid, spontaneous, and unregulated. Letter writing, more than most forms of writing, might encourage the writer to abandon all sense of propriety" (Favret 22, 24). Though Macaulay may have found beneficial the fluidity and spontaneity that epistolary forms offered, there is no evidence that her *History in Letters* abandons propriety or reveals her heart. In addition to its private connotations, the letter took on at this time specifically political meanings: "The genre of the familiar letter . . . had emerged at the end of the century as the medium of collective political activity" (Favret 30).

Macaulay wrote far in advance of the Traitorous Correspondence Bill of 1793, but perhaps she, like Helen Maria Williams after her, sensed the political possibilities of transforming correspondence from the "familiar and sentimental to the public and political" (Favret 52). Unlike Williams, Macaulay misjudged appropriate ways to join these qualities, eschewing familiarity and sentimentality. Helen Maria Williams successfully "transfers the conventions of epistolary fiction into epistolary history" in her eight-volume *Letters from France* (1791–96) (Favret 94).[33] A decade and a half earlier, Macaulay did not find the means to effectively translate the form into a historiographical medium. Her decision to write an epistolary history when her life was under public scrutiny added to her inability to challenge the feminine and political status quo rather than allowing her to attract new readers.

There is an odd coincidence in the timing of Macaulay's unsuccessful attempt to reach a more popular audience with a less scholarly historical form. In 1778, when her professionalism and her sexual propriety were questioned because of her marriage to a young surgeon's mate, Macaulay sought to reach a wider readership ("common" readers). Her detractors did not fail to remark that she herself had selected a "common" husband. Some predicted that her choice to mingle with less distinguished company would end her career as a historian. Although this fate was widely predicted,

Macaulay's tenacity won out in the short term. She continued to publish works regularly until her death in 1791, but her reputation never regained its former stature. Undoubtedly, in addition to the reception her republican principles faced as a result of the American and French revolutions, the events of Macaulay's life in 1777–78 contributed to her critical devaluation and eventual posthumous disappearance.

Could Macaulay's notoriety and her "failure" as a mainstream national historian have dissuaded some English women from following her into the genre or have tempered their historiographical and political expressions?[34] Charlotte Cowley's *Ladies History of England* (1780), with its formal and feminine propriety, would have benefited from some of Macaulay's writerly verve. Twenty years later Hester Lynch Piozzi, Macaulay's political opposite, also attempted to turn popular historian with little success. In Jane Austen's writings, historical discourse took on another guise entirely. As for Catharine Macaulay, "within a generation of her death, she had become little more than a half remembered name" (Stenton 311). The *History in Letters,* itself a half-remembered book in her career, demonstrates that Macaulay, while unquestionably a gifted historian, was unable—for reasons personal and professional—to combine autobiographical and historical forms with the success of a Hutchinson or a Montagu. Readers and reviewers of the eighteenth century and afterward are certainly culpable for treating Macaulay (and many other women writers) in dismissive ways. We must also acknowledge, however, that even before her marriage to Graham, Macaulay's misperceptions of readers' expectations and generic conventions made mainstream praise of the *History in Letters* and continuing sympathy for it (and her subsequent writings) a more difficult proposition.

6

Hester Lynch Piozzi's Infinite and Exact World History, *Retrospection*

■

In late eighteenth-century Great Britain, women's historical and anecdotal travel writings (like Lady Mary Wortley Montagu's) and historical and political accounts in letters (by Helen Maria Williams and others) received notable attention. Catharine Macaulay's mainstream histories of England, for a while, found critical acclaim. The country was ready for a female writer to take on an even more expansive historical project—or so Hester Lynch Piozzi (1741–1821) must have thought. Having published in a number of genres, Piozzi, like many writers before and after her, moved comfortably from letters, biography, poetry, and travel writing to history. Though she produced "the first world history ever written by an English woman," her results brought her no acclaim (McCarthy, *Hester* 211). Her history, *Retrospection* (1801), was a critical failure that effectively ended her publishing career. After 1801, Piozzi's only known publication was an anonymous anti-Napoleonic broadside, "Old England to Her Daughters" (1803).[1] She outlived almost all of her contemporaries, both of her husbands, and most of her offspring, dying at age eighty.

In her later years, *Retrospection* remained Piozzi's pet book, despite its lack of success. Her friends were baffled by her keen interest in revisiting *Retrospection*. A young admirer, Marianne Francis (the granddaughter of Charles Burney and niece of Frances Burney), carried on a fifteen-year correspondence with Piozzi. Francis had nothing but praise for *Retrospection* in her letters, but in her own diary she wrote, "read 'Retrospection.' 2nd. vol.— I think it a strange confused work. I like neither the manner nor the matter" (27 July 1805) (qtd. in Menagh 329). Piozzi valued the work so highly that Francis may have been reluctant to admit her confusion. Whenever Piozzi came across a friend's copy, she offered to annotate and correct it. On her own copy she "corrected throughout, with her pen, the printer's mistakes, of which there were a large number" (Merritt, *Piozzi Marginalia* 141). In addition to corrections, she filled the margins of friends' copies with abundant comments, apparently personalized for each book owner (142).[2] Piozzi, worried about the continuation of her celebrated, misunderstood, and intense friendship with the young actor William Augustus Conway, decided that, so he would "not forget her," she would "annotate copies of her books for him. . . . She began with *Retrospection*" (Tearle 81).[3]

The marginalia in that copy have been printed, and they reveal Piozzi's continuing relationship with *Retrospection* a decade after its publication. Her annotations consist of elaborations of fact, changes in phrasing, or musings on her interpretation of or response to an event, a person, or an author. In her marginal comments, she airs her grievances about the production of the book, extending to the quality of paper, which she found too thin and akin to "Blotting Paper" (Merritt, *Piozzi Marginalia* 149). Piozzi also inserts herself into her narrative. She adds marginal information about her lineage, remarking of the son of the reigning duke of Bavaria that "the Author—or rather Compiler of these Books" is descended from him (151). Her annotations demonstrate the close relationship she maintained with *Retrospection* to the end of her life, rereading it and reviewing it as she made additions and corrections, although modestly reminding herself and her readers of her unassuming role as "compiler" rather than "author." In a sense Piozzi never stopped writing, evaluating, and lobbying on behalf of *Retrospection*. It became her own retrospective task to rewrite it, relive it, and hope for its posthumous reevaluation.

Retrospection was the book in which Piozzi was most interested in the last decades of her life, but it is the only one of her published works that has not been either reprinted or translated since her death. Most nineteenth-century writers, when they discussed Piozzi apart from Samuel Johnson, got bogged down in the hoax of her "love letters" to Conway. Her position as an author has not been secure, in large part because, as William McCarthy argues, her "recognition as a writer is not so certain. . . . Conventionally her writings have been valued as sidelights on Johnson or disesteemed as imitations of him; her very career as a writer has often been thought to be an accident produced by her association with him" ("Writings" 129). Piozzi was not an accidental author. For several decades she wrote and sought publication with an almost single-minded deliberateness. She is best known for her *Anecdotes of the Late Samuel Johnson* (1786) and *Letters to and from the Late Samuel Johnson* (1788), which went through several editions, as did her less successful travel memoir, *Observations and Reflections Made in the Course of a Journey through France, Italy and Germany* (1789).[4]

Piozzi's later publications, *British Synonymy* (1794) and *Retrospection*, have been generally ignored. The following assessment of her late writings is typical: "In the rest of her long life she wrote several more books, of very minor importance, partly for money and partly because authorship had become a habit. . . . In 1794 she wrote 'British Synonyms' [*sic*]. That this is worthless was hardly her fault, for scientific etymology was unborn. 'Retrospection' (1801), an attempt at universal history, has not that excuse" (Esdaile 193). In some accounts of her life, Piozzi's last works were not even mentioned by title. As one writer put it, Piozzi "published a volume of travels and busied herself with several other works, the very names of which are forgotten except by the curious in such matters" (Newton 216). Few remain curious. *Retrospection* "is regarded as dull even by [Piozzi's] fans" (Mandelkern 259). As long as we think of Piozzi as a figure of the "Age of Johnson," we mistakenly diminish the significance of and interest in her last writings.

This chapter discusses a Piozzi less familiar to us—one not centered on Johnson but rather nearing the end of her publishing career at the close of the century. By moving the focus away from her salon days, we avoid the error of concluding, as does *The Macmillan Dictionary of Women's Biography*, that Piozzi's "only writings, apart from travel and personal reminiscences published in 1789 and 1801, were the very popular *Anecdotes of the Late Samuel Johnson*" (Uglow 466). What this dictionary refers to as "personal reminiscences" must be quite differently described. The 1801 text is her disappointing historical magnum opus, the full title of which is *Retrospection, or A Review of the Most Striking and Important Events, Characters, Situations and Their Consequences, Which the Last Eighteen Hundred Years Have Presented to the View of Mankind*. Far from personal reminiscence, Piozzi's work attempts a concerted historical look backward—one that brings together an impressive amount of material in the name of creating "an anecdotal abridgment of history for general readers" (Brownley, "Samuel" 636).

A study of *Retrospection* might begin with a nod to the received wisdom that its critical failure arose from poor writing and insufficient scholarship.

Some suggest that Piozzi's push to have *Retrospection* in print by 1 January 1801 ensured its critical demise. Careering through the composition and proofreading, she missed "hundreds of errors of facts and typography" (Clifford 401). Piozzi maintained that not she but an insurrection of the printers was to blame for the poor typesetting (Merritt, *Piozzi Marginalia* 141). Piozzi's biographer James Clifford calls *Retrospection* "Mrs. Piozzi's most uninteresting book" and says that it cannot be recommended to modern readers (402). Others have faulted not her writing or the errors but the form of the book, concluding that Piozzi was not a self-confident or well-trained scholar and therefore lacked the skills needed to produce a successful world history.[5]

Patriarchal literary practices have also been implicated. McCarthy's discussions of *Retrospection* provide a valuable starting point for readers interested in feminist theoretical questions that range beyond Clifford's sound biographical treatment. McCarthy spends much of his chapter outlining Piozzi's rhetorical honesty and her quasi-feminist leanings (*Hester* 211). According to McCarthy, *Retrospection* "failed not because she was incompetent but because she could not overcome her fear of being incompetent. Its defeat is no disgrace to her and signifies much more than her own failure to surmount the emotional obstacles to success. Its defeat, rather, is a condemnation of the sexual politics of literature" (250). McCarthy ultimately sees Piozzi as a less than able historian but as a modern historiographer, finding humanism in her conservatism and blaming sexism for her lack of acclaim. McCarthy provides an interesting psychological interpretation and a provocative political recuperation of Piozzi, but to fully comprehend the critical demise of her work necessitates considering larger issues of generic context and reception. Although *Retrospection* can hardly be classed a compelling page turner, it is valuable to our histories of history.

I argue that *Retrospection* did not live up to its promise because its reviewers and its readers did not know what to make of it as a kind of writing and because Piozzi did not follow through with the form and content she promised to deliver. McCarthy points the way for such a reading when he asserts: "Considered as a summary for the instruction of unlearned readers, *Retrospection* must be said to defeat its own purpose by being too learned. Considered as an attempt at learned history writing, it proclaims itself, again and again, a failure. . . . *Retrospection* is less a history than a meditation upon history. . . . The effect is not fortuitous" (*Hester* 238–39).

Piozzi's contributions to historiography, in the form of historical anecdotes or "meditations upon history," were not recognized as properly historical by a public that increasingly looked to women writers of national history to address other women or children, to turn history into appropriate moral lessons, and to defer to historical authorities. Additionally, Piozzi's antagonistic stance toward fiction shaped the kind of history writing she produced and the ways her history was received. Piozzi did not perceive or could not meet the conflicting needs of her vast intended audience. A discussion of *Retrospection*'s composition and contents demonstrates Piozzi's inability to construct the history she set out to write.

Piozzi Composes History

Retrospection was not the product of original research. It could not have been. As a history of Western civilization from the birth of Christ to 1800, its contents were culled haphazardly from a host of works, most of them accessible to contemporary readers, though some (apparently unknown to Piozzi) were sadly out of fashion (Bloom and Bloom 3: 13).[6] There is no evidence that Piozzi consulted private collections of primary materials, as Catharine Macaulay did in her history of seventeenth-century England. Piozzi did not have opportunity or occasion to use resources at the British Museum or elsewhere. Her goals for *Retrospection* were far more modest than Macaulay's aims for her histories. Piozzi set out to write a new kind of anecdotal popular history. Like Macaulay, she had a political agenda, but she had also a temporal agenda, hoping to market her book to coincide with the beginning of a new century. *Retrospection,* in its aim to elevate schoolroom history to a higher literary plane, failed to identify and to speak effectively to Piozzi's motley intended audience. Understanding her unfounded expectations of the literary marketplace adds nuance to accounts that see *Retrospection*'s "failure" merely as the result of the responses of sexist reviewers. The book was a victim not only of the demands of the reading public but of its author's own naïveté about the changing milieu for (women's) historical texts—a situation Piozzi shares with Catharine Macaulay.

When Piozzi first conceived of *Retrospection,* sometime in 1795, she noted in a letter to her eldest and often disapproving daughter, Hester Maria Thrale (known as "Queeney"), that the present "Commotions in Civil and political Life" made her contemplate turning to world events for material:

"Tis a wonderful World truly, and displays such Changes of Colour in its last State of Existence, as dazzle and confound an Observer. Yet I could make a pretty Book too to bring out on the last Days of 1799 or the first of 1800 could I get Materials cleverly round me, and Time for Study: as Anecdotes of the late Century—not a History" (*PL* 2: 233). Anecdotes had been Piozzi's forte, and "history" may have seemed too weighty a word for someone who envisioned difficulty in getting materials to consult at Brynbella, her home in Wales. By the time she began the project in February 1796, her conception appears to have become more grand, or as Edward and Lillian Bloom put it, her "intention expanded" (2: 18). By February 1796 Piozzi wrote to Queeney, "My Spirits are not low, for last Monday I begun upon a Literary Work of no inconsiderable Magnitude. Its title would be anticipated if I let any body know it, but when we meet I shall tell it you under the promise of Secrecy, and shew you as far as it will be gone by that Time. But I do not work hard" (2: 317 n. 2). Her claim not to work hard soon fades as well, and two years later she refers to her "heavy Work" that "creeps on" "slowly" (2: 506) and to getting up early "to work at my heavy Book" (2: 510). Because of the effort demanded by *Retrospection,* at the end of 1798 Piozzi sought relief for her impaired health with a trip to Bath (2: 543).

One can follow Piozzi's composition of *Retrospection* through her letters, initially peppered with cryptic references to the project. She was slow to tell her daughter what she was working on, but she hinted, "I am the foolishest among them all: undertaking a Work wch. should be written in All Souls College Oxford, that I might have Books at hand, just where I have *no* Books to consult" (qtd. in Clifford 393). Piozzi worked diligently in spite of these constraints, borrowing sources from neighbors and making do without books when necessary. She tells Queeney that she is forced to use Mrs. Heaton's copy of Gibbon "perpetually as a Consulting Book" and fears getting it dirty (*PL* 2: 319). In March 1796 Piozzi confides to Queeney, "I don't tell him [the Reverend Mr. Chappelow] about my Book, I tell nobody that but You, and I am dying to see whether you will like it" (2: 317). Piozzi then changes the subject to a linen fabric patterned with tiny flowers, a swatch of which she sends to her daughter, asking her to look for others of its sort and to bring the material to her next summer. The end of the letter compares the history to the fabric: "My Book will then be big enough to shew you just such a sample as I enclose of the Linen" (2: 317). Belittling her work by comparing it to a swatch, Piozzi keeps her own and Queeney's expectations low, but she was apparently putting a great deal of effort into *Retrospection*. Alongside mundane requests for fabric, she also asked Queeney to get her copies of histories (2: 320 n. 6, 321 n. 13).

Piozzi's assessment of her project's potential in the literary marketplace seems to have risen by degrees, since she considered that her style would be particularly appropriate for the kind of world history she planned. She wrote confidently to Queeney, "I think that Wit's Work done by a Scholar, never pleases the Public but that Scholar's Work done by a Wit, always pleases" (2: 330) and "Said I well that many Folks gain Title by their Fortune! but I shall make my Fortune by my Title" (2: 342). Penelope Pennington, then a highly regarded friend, exchanged letters with Piozzi as frequently as two or three times a week (Thorpe 106).[7] In April 1798 Piozzi tells Pennington, "I am in the middle of a big book; heaven send it may not for that very Reason be a dull one; but I will be A good Hoper myself" (*PL* 2: 492). Still, the secrecy surrounding the project persisted, as Piozzi tells Pennington, "Of My heavy Work I can give a better account by Word than Letter—You shall see it if we come to the West" (2: 512). She later lets others into her design for *Retrospection*. It will be a popular history, a summary of events of the past 1,800 years, "interspersed with Reflections & c. and a Table of immense Length," as well as mention of ancient and modern names for cities and rivers, projected to fill four quarto volumes (qtd. in Clifford 394). Though the references to *Retrospection* are often tacked onto the end of her letters or mentioned in passing in foreboding discussions of current events or fault-filled fictional works, Piozzi's "pose of insouciant author did not disguise her diligence," according to Edward and Lillian Bloom (*PL* 3: 10).

In January 1799, Piozzi calculated that her work would appear at the beginning of the next century, which she marked as 1 January 1801. She was concerned about events in France and about being able to complete her research and writing: "In two years from this Day the heavy Work of Retrospection will get out of Dock; if things continue in their present State I mean, and no strange Event happens to close my last Volume" (3: 52). Piozzi became more and more anxious about the way her work would be received: "I am working hard; pleasing myself one Day with hopes of Success,—frighting myself another Day with Fears lest it should not succeed" (3: 96). She made plans to be in London to "begin the new century" so that she could watch over the publishing process, "lest I should . . . have to lament those errors of the Press which can be avoided only by close Atten-dance on the Printers" (3: 123). This fear, repeated in another letter, proved well founded (3: 207). A year later Piozzi was negotiating with publishers, trying to secure the best terms possible for *Retrospection,* a work that the periodicals had finally gotten wind of and referred to as "another *tier*" in the "Temple of her *Literary Reputation*" (3: 124).

In the 1790s the number of histories published had doubled compared with the previous decade (Feather, "British Publishing" 43). From the beginning, Piozzi believed that *Retrospection* would bring her financial gain and critical acclaim. In June 1800 she asked publishers for the unbelievably large advance of £1,000. Some publishers thought the book too long, even though she had much reduced her initial design, excluded the table, and squeezed 1,800 years into two quarto volumes.[8] Piozzi assumed that the first edition would be swiftly followed by an octavo edition, sure to be much in demand in schoolhouses. No publisher would agree to her requested advance. In November 1800 Piozzi and John Stockdale came to an agreement whereby she would have a half interest in the profits and he would pay all expenses. Stockdale rushed the manuscript to the printers, and the Piozzis moved into a hotel near the printers' shop (Clifford 400).

Piozzi seemed pleased that the book landed in the "loyal shop" of Stockdale, whom she wrongly referred to as an "aristocrat" and who was the publisher of Johnson's *Works* (*PL* 3: 242). At first orders came in quickly. In December 1800 Piozzi wrote, "We publish on Newyear's Day—and Stockdale seems in high Glee when he looks at his *Order Book*. My own Nerves are not so strong; and I see many a sneering Face, even before anything but the Attempt, can have provoked them to sneer" (3: 249). The book sold well initially, after its publication in January 1801, but negative reviews appear to have brought sales to a virtual standstill by the following summer. The final accounts with the publisher show that 516 of the first 750 quarto sets were purchased; Piozzi's net profit was something less than £100, and to her profound disappointment, *Retrospection* never saw a second edition (Clifford 405). There was no call for an octavo edition to use in schools. There was no applause for her attempt to fill what she perceived as a gap in the market for historical reading.

A Retrospect of *Retrospection*

Retrospection was a departure in genre for Piozzi, but according to Martine Watson Brownley it was also a change in the range of Johnson's continuing influence on her authorship. Brownley argues that she "had always enjoyed history, but her decision to make her fifth book, *Retrospection,* a popularized world history probably derived partly from a desire to escape completely from any possible imputation of Johnsonian influence." Historiography, which Piozzi "could legitimately consider hers alone, would firmly establish her authorial independence" ("Samuel" 636). Critics could not accuse *Retrospection* of being plagiarized from Johnson's unpublished manuscripts, as they had done with Piozzi's *British Synonymy.* The book should not, however, be understood only as a vehicle by which she attempted to separate herself from Johnson's perceived or actual influence. For one thing, Johnson is mentioned appreciatively throughout *Retrospection* and twice in its defensive preface—once in the very first sentence.

Piozzi begins *Retrospection* by warning readers that they will not always be satisfied with her selection of material:

> If the Rambler is right when he says, "That no man ever obtains more from his most zealous endeavours, than a painful conviction of his own defects," how strongly must that conviction press upon her mind, who having collected all these facts together, presents them as an object of *Retrospection* to the Publick. Of those who turn them over, how different, how numerous will be the censures! while each expects his favourite hero, his best-remembered incident to be dilated and brought forward;—instead of which others perhaps appear, and take the lead. (1: n.pag.)[9]

Acknowledging with pro forma modesty the defects of her own authorship, Piozzi anticipates "censures" but characterizes them as a matter of readers' idiosyncratic tastes. As she puts it, "Different observers attach to every object, different degrees of importance" (1: n.pag.). No world history can fulfill multiple wishes of emphasis.

Retrospection contains a constant mix of high and low material, similar to the combinations criticized in Piozzi's previous books, especially her material on Johnson. The book is made up of her favorite historical anecdotes, though she makes no overarching claims as to her authority to select material. She even includes an anecdote to explain her unusual choice of anecdotes:

If however, I should have made improper choice of facts, and if I shall be found at length most to resemble Maister Fabyan of old, who writing the Life of Henry the Fifth, lays heaviest stress on a new weather-cock set up on St. Paul's steeple during that eventful reign; my book must share the fate of his, and be like that forgotten: reminding before its death perhaps, a friend or two, of a poor man living in later times, that Doctor Johnson used to tell us of: who being advised to take subscriptions for a new Geographical Dictionary, hastened to Bolt-court and begged advice. There, having listened carefully for half an hour,—"Ah, but, dear sir!" exclaimed the admiring parasite, "if I am to make all this eloquent ado about Athens and Rome, where shall we find place do you think for Richmond or Aix la Chapelle?" The perplexity was laughable enough—yet such are the perplexities of a compiler; and for a mere compilation stretched to two quarto volumes, the apology must be a serious one. (1: n.pag.)

Piozzi compares herself to Robert Fabyan and to the butt of a Dr. Johnson joke. The comparison to Fabyan is not as humble as it may seem or as it may have been intended. Fabyan, a draper, alderman, sheriff, and historian, wrote *New Chronicles of England and France* in 1504 (published posthumously in 1516). A recent assessment of Fabyan claims his "contribution to historiography was not limited to the transmission of the London chronicles to the modern period." A learned and ambitious historian, he was more than a compiler in that he "attempted to take over and pass on the whole of the English medieval tradition of historical writing," using both modern trends and medieval authorities, beginning at the Creation and attempting to give the work universal scope (Gransden 246). Fabyan, a loyal Lancastrian, wanted, like the "virtuous prince" Henry VII, to promote friendly relations with France (247). Piozzi too had political aims that shaped her historical project, aims that went beyond collection and compilation to sophisticated if idiosyncratic narration. She may have claimed that "*Retrospection* is not history" (*R* 2: 323), but she created a work that even she placed within a historical tradition. Like her sometime friend Frances Burney, who preferred to have her novel *Camilla* called a work, Piozzi might have lobbied for her history to be given another label. Another label did not stick, however, and it is difficult to categorize her historical efforts as something else today.

Piozzi's preface assumes educated readers, but she claims that she wishes to reach young beginners and those who long ago left the formal study of history. This dual audience is possible, she maintains, because of the confusing era in which the British find themselves at the turn of the century. No one has time to study or to recall how history led up to the contemporary conflictual moment:

To an age of profound peace and literary quiet I should have considered such an abridgment as insulting: to our disturbed and busy days abridgments can only be useful. No one has leisure to read better books. Young people are called out to act before they *know,* before they could have *learned* how those have acted who have lived before them. History is voluminous, and fashionable extracts are *so* perpetually separated from each other by verses or by essays, that they leave little trace of information on the mind: a natural consequence, and manifest disadvantage attendant upon all selections, where no one thing having any reference to another thing, each loses much of its effect by standing completely insulated from all the rest. Our Work, though but a frontispiece and ruin, contains between the two some shaded drawings, such as we find in rudiments of painting, and will, like them, be good for young beginners. Perhaps too, those who long ago have read, and long ago desisted from reading histories well-known, may like to please their fancies with the *Retrospect* of what they feel connected in their minds with youthful study, and that sweet remembrance of early-dawning knowledge on the soul. (1: n.pag.)

Piozzi creates *Retrospection* to fill what she sees as an absence in historiography. People had access to histories well known, which were once read by those who enjoyed the "profound peace and literary quiet" in which to study them. Fashionable extracts or miscellanies also circulated, some of them including historical material, but they did not allow readers to retain information or to understand it in a sufficiently broad context.[10] Though previous authors had abridged history, particularly national history (the abridgment of Goldsmith's history remained popular enough that the young Jane Austen found it an appropriate object for burlesque), Piozzi ignores these works. Later she refers offhandedly to "my competitors, the little table books" (*R* 2: 107).[11] Her penchant for conceiving of *Retrospection* as a diminutive visual artifact recurs throughout, as she refers to her work as a painted portrait (2: 15).[12] Piozzi imagines *Retrospection* as a "frontispiece" (as in the preface), hoping that an allusive work will appeal to readers old and young.

It is the seasoned readers whose historical knowledge has lapsed, not the students of history, to whom Piozzi addresses herself and repeatedly apologizes. In selling the concept of *Retrospection* to educated readers, she anticipates their criticism. She hopes to "disarm" their complaints with "a pleasant story" to divert them and "a tender tale" to affect them (1: n.pag.). She downplays her didactic aims:

No insolently obtrusive opinions through these pages, no air of arrogance will offend, or provoke such readers to *say,* however they may *think,* that the necessity of dilating, as it advances, like an inverted cone or sugar-loaf, robs my whole building of that solid basis which many fabricks boast, on which, after all, little sometimes is reared. A moment's thought indeed will shew such criticks, that any other way would have been worse: and half a moment will suffice to prove, that whilst the deep current of grave history rolls her full tide majestick, to that ocean where Time and all its wrecks at length are lost; our flashy *Retrospect,* a mere *jet d'eau,* may serve to soothe the heats of an autumnal day with its light-dripping fall, and form a rainbow round. Did no such book catch the occurrences, and hold them up, however maimed and broken, before the eyes of our contemporaries, we really should very soon forget all that our ancestors had done or suffered. The fever of these last ten or twelve years has formed a heat sufficient to calcine the images upon our minds to dust and ashes, which once seemed strong as if engraved on marble; and if some facts of characters have been called back, 'twas for the use of consultation they were fetched, then thrown again into the general heap, like papers we have done with, doomed to burn. In such a furnace, such an all-devouring crucible, events can scarce retain their proper value, and the mushroom of a night has equal chance to come forth unhurt, as has the oak of a century. (1: n.pag.)

It is difficult to imagine young readers enjoying this often abstruse, flowery prose. Far from being a *jet d'eau,* Piozzi's nightmarish fantasy of grave history's full tides and destruction, of maimed and broken ancestors, and of devouring fires in furnaces intones the rhetoric of gothic novels or of those who saw in the French Revolution (as Piozzi did) an apocalyptic event. Far from avoiding obtrusive opinions to dwell on diverting tales, her history—particularly the second volume—combines them, creating a Royalist narrative that is neither a traditional history nor a tale.

Piozzi incorporated biblical elements in her narrative that also truncated her desired light and airy effect. That she begins with Christ's birth illustrates her religious conception of history, but she establishes herself and her genre as the natural instrument for worshiping God. Her epigraph argues that a biography of a sovereign, as the story of one man, cuts readers off from the national context. One nation's history can provide only a fragmentary account of God's plan. Even the globe itself is but a spot in God's universe, a "short chapter in the grand history, the universal volume of our Creator's works." As Piozzi concludes, the fragmentary nature of history is a fact of human existence and need not prevent us from seeking knowledge: " 'Tis by darkening the glasses that we look at brightest objects; and spots in the sun could never be discerned unless we first abridged him of his splendour" (1: n.pag.). For Piozzi, an author plays god over his or her written creation, making choices that shine light on certain objects or moments. She reminds us that all authors are fallible before the great author. Her project, though not perfect, is a necessary though pale imitation of God's work.

Emphasizing her fallibility, Piozzi fills her preface with apologies. She confesses that she had thought to give the work an authoritative boost with a planned dedication to Thomas Pennant that she ultimately dismissed: "Here then begin we a summary account of what has happened in these eighteen centuries. I thought to have given some importance to the work, by prefixing on its first page the name of one of my earliest and most respected friends—than whom no wit, no scholar, nor no man of general knowledge, ever had more reason to delight in *Retrospection:* but Pennant is gone, and I will search no further for a patron" (1: n.pag.). Possibly Piozzi considers recognizing Pennant, her distant relative, a famed naturalist and traveler who lived near Brynbella, because he and several other scholars provided her with opportunities for intellectual conversation after she moved back to her native country (Clifford 384). She may have chosen to focus on Pennant to emphasize her learned family connections or to reinforce that she had continued to associate with educated company after her unpopular second marriage.[13] Her wish for a patron functions as a plea for literary protection and wider approbation.

Piozzi desperately tries to win readers over to her side. Her final request in the preface flatters her supportive readers, calling them into a comradeship against the reviewers. Resembling a pessimist's version of Austen's famous defense of novels in chapter 5 of *Northanger Abbey,* Piozzi's preface ends with a plaintive request for a gentle reception:

The same kind and encouraging Publick which has ever looked up on my labours with a tenderness, and a good-natured desire of being pleased, more flattering far than hard-earned approbation, shall take as it is; and if they feel themselves pleased with the colours presented in the varying changeful mass, will try to hinder some critic's heavy hand from breaking it; remembering that an opal loses all power of playing before the eye, soon as a crack is made in its thin surface.

But I will not run down my own book no more. The duty of an author is discharged, when what the title promises has been performed. Yet let it not be said of *Retrospection,* as once by a French wit, when Ferrand's Erotica, a dull dissertation upon the passion of love, came out, ". . . The title inspir'd me a strong inclination, But reading the book, I was cur'd of my passion." (1: n.pag.)

Hoping that her readers (even her young readers) would experience a strong inclination verging on "passion" in reading *Retrospection,* Piozzi misjudges the characteristics that had been and would continue to be assigned to history writing. Histories had by the late eighteenth century been touted as an antidote to the kinds of passion one courted by reading novels and romances. Though Charlotte Cowley had also tried to link the arena of the heart to historical composition in her *Ladies History,* passion was a word more easily linked to fiction than to histories, whether the latter were "dull dissertations" or more compelling texts.

Piozzi's historiographical method is more often displayed than described, but we do by degrees get a sense of what she hopes *Retrospection* will accomplish. Her method at the beginning of the work was regular. The first volume consists of twenty-four chapters, each covering between fifty and one hundred years. In these chapters she covers the Romans to the sacking of Constantinople in 1455. All chapters include in their titles periodizing markers and names of Roman rulers or, later, of leaders and events such as "Charlemagne" or "The First Crusade." Piozzi further divided chronological blocks within chapters by region or empire (Europe, Great Britain, Turks, or Italians). She reminded her readers of the title of her work with annoying frequency—approximately once per page—with statements like "Let *Retrospection* too survey" or "Here then may *Retrospection* rest awhile." The repetition of the title throughout the text, in addition to its anthropomorphizing function, frames the narration as though it derives from the historical voice of a deity. Piozzi appears as the scribe behind *Retrospection*'s divine will.

Neither Piozzi nor *Retrospection* claims historical omniscience. Piozzi shares her sources with readers, as when she refers to Gibbon's account in order to disagree with it (1: 26, 400). William McCarthy traces *Retrospection*'s borrowings from Edward Gibbon and Piozzi's countering them with biblical qualities, and he examines her skirmishes with David Hume and her denial of his "history as progress" to argue for apocalypse (*Hester* 211). I will not retrace McCarthy's steps here. It is enough to note that Piozzi read and retooled the work of her country's most respected historians as well as lesser-known writers. Her narrative has overarching political aims—to prove the benefits of monarchical government and to predict the downfall of Western civilization. But her narrative does not have a discernible story line. It includes generous discussions of royal history, church history, and military history. Less frequently Piozzi detours into social history, mentioning the going price of books or wine. She includes information about daily life (e.g., sedan chairs), references to literature, details about commerce, asides on fate, and philosophical discussions of invention and truth. There are very few footnotes, never more than one or two every ten pages. When footnotes are added, they are often used to cite sources such as the *Annual Register*. Piozzi reminds her readers, "There are few notes to this superficial work, which is itself of notes a mere collection" (*R* 2: 371).

Piozzi is unusually clear in volume 2 about her reasons for omitting footnotes, but she hides this explanation in a relatively obscure section of the narrative. She explains why she avoided a scholarly apparatus, using Robertson as her foil:

Robertson says wisely, that if historians are not exact in quoting their authorities, all history is but an amusing tale. He would not, however, have required such care from superficial summaries like mine; epitomized from all, and so confined, that quoting the authorities would make it a long book, and hinder it from being even an amusing tale. This work is just what it professes to be, *Retrospection:* and we need not have quoted [Miguel de Cervantes] Saavedra to prove that Spain is now no longer what she has been; that the bulk of her present subjects are lazy, proud, and poor. (2: 65)

Making an argument about Spain's fall from power is of a different order from "proving" that its citizens are lazy, but this is of no concern to Piozzi. As an amusing tale, as a superficially summarized history, *Retrospection* need not take such care in its assertions. Later she complains about having to emphasize fact at all in her work, preferring to dismiss it because in one case "facts call off attention from conjectures" that she would rather make (2: 153). Piozzi writes what she likes in the name of the *spirit* of the truth. She prefers conjecture to fact (or story to event), eschews authorities (though she draws on them), and finds a new historical path that need not follow Robertson's "wise" rules.

Piozzi writes near the end of volume 1 that her book will focus on developments in the arts and sciences rather than on dates, events, and individual men: "If we would console the *Retrospector's* eye, we must not let it turn to men but things: not to the blood-red page of historic annals, but to the verdant field where springing arts and growing sciences promise, by still fresh improvement, perpetual green. No period of time will shew people much better than those of another period" (1: 359). In preferring verdant green to blood red, Piozzi suggests that she would rather dwell on the manners of an age than on its wars. Because she does not perceive much human or moral progress throughout history, she does not think it necessary to waste time on good and evil "men." Her first volume jumps from story to story, using fabricated dialogue and bombastic prose with copious exclamation points. Her distaste for bloody war narratives continues into the second volume, where she refers to the red-stained glass of *Retrospection* as sickening (2: 17).

Piozzi occasionally gives sustained attention to political if not martial issues. The most overtly political section of *Retrospection* is its two-page digression on three types of government, in which she details a regression of rule from monarchy to aristocracy to democracy. She links monarchy to the quality of love and to one's youth. Aristocracy she connects to ambition and manhood. Democracy is linked to the fall of civilization, avarice, and old age:

Covetousness, to enlarge each his own regal circuit, drives the possessors to unthought on practices; and when even valour's self feels fatigued with encroachment, intrepidity tired of perpetual defence, and honour wearied out by warding off reiterated attackers on each untenable post; money must purchase, and traffic must barter. Commerce points to the safe way of obtaining riches and, as the man yields up his weak remains of life to the guidance of avarice, last passion of human nature, so does the general aggregate of all men, like him breaks down to a general dependance, seek only who shall be wealthier, not who shall be wiser or stronger than his neighbour; for where every thing is to be sold, there, as assuredly, to be bought; and gold buries virtue in the mine he sprang from. (2: 47)

Despite her lack of enthusiasm for democratic rule, Piozzi is not oblivious to the concerns of the masses. She often discusses economic issues, sometimes with interpretations resembling those of modern-day liberals. She dwells on the evils of poverty, which she fears "suspends parental tenderness" because children cannot be expected to live when not properly fed (2: 60). In his assessment of *Retrospection,* McCarthy focuses on details of this kind in order to defend Piozzi's conservative, Royalist politics as more humane than we have previously assumed (*Hester* 211).

Piozzi shows most pleasure when the events she recounts are from the

British tradition: "Our *Retrospection* has however been too long detained from Britain" (*R* 1: 359). Perhaps her preference for British history is one reason she much preferred volume 2 to volume 1. In volume 2, from 1455 to the present, Great Britain plays a prominent role. Recent critics have seconded her preference. Margaret Doody suggests that a Hester Piozzi reader, should one be compiled, ought to contain a chapter from *Retrospection*'s second volume, specifically from its eighteenth-century coverage (Clifford xlv). When Piozzi arrives at the eighteenth century, her material becomes more compelling. The eighteenth-century chapters begin in blocks of twenty-five years, shortened to a decade from 1780 to 1790, then 1790 to 1796, and finally, 1796 to 1800. The last chapters are fascinating ones, with short descriptions of child prodigies, cats, murders, the fashion of suicides, Farinelli, Newgate, music, art, and Montagu's inoculation against smallpox. It is difficult to imagine what kind of historical picture uniformed readers would bring away from her detailed, moralizing anecdotes.

Toward the end of volume 2, quirkiness slides into sloppiness as Piozzi indulges in personal remembrances she enjoyed while creating *Retrospection*. She includes, alongside supposed facts, parenthetical observations such as "(I remember)" or "(I believe)" (*R* 2: 196). Her reliance on memory becomes even more egregious, as she acknowledges: "I first did read this story at a book-stall many years ago; but it recurred to my memory now" (1: 199) or, on the five principal Indian nations, "I forget both the other two" (2: 223). Her haste to finish the project is evident when she mentions "a passage I once copied out but mislaid" (2: 274). Piozzi sounds less and less like an authoritative historian, able either to educate the young or to delight those who need their memory jarred. She herself seems at several points to need a historical refresher course. Piozzi is candid about her scholarly weaknesses when she admits, "Those who read *my* book are in no danger of becoming too *learned*" (2: 275). Such a claim might have worked to her benefit with women readers, since conduct books instilled a fear that women who studied history would become too learned, as we saw in chapter 1. But Piozzi's plea to have written an unlearned book would have been more likely to succeed in a historical subgenre with a reputation for difficulty. Becoming too learned from a work of popular history ostensibly pitched to children was not perceived as a danger.

Retrospection's addresses to "young readers" are uncommon in the second volume (2: 336). Piozzi's diction is sophisticated, and her dour apocalyptic notes, examples of immorality, and stories of lovers, passion, oozing blood, and mistresses would not have been considered suitable for children. As Piozzi nears the end of *Retrospection,* she recalls that she set out to reach young readers, stating, "Even in this shallow book young readers may have learned" (2: 414). The conclusion offers up a final apology and hope for a friendly reception: if *Retrospection* is "found at last too short for use, too long for entertainment, the writer will be sorry" (2: 521). Piozzi conceived of a work of history pitched to many audiences. Her defensive conclusion demonstrates that she fears she has not delivered the book she promised. To be more useful to the educated, *Retrospection* would need expanded treatment of historical events, with greater coverage and cohesion. It would benefit from the apparatus of a mainstream history—an index, a table of contents, marginal dates, and such. To be more appropriate for the young, the book would require greater brevity, simplicity, morality, and entertainment. It could be a collection of historical anecdotes, making no claim to complete coverage. Piozzi's contradictory historiographical goals led to a book that combined traditional historical material, romantic and fantastic stories, everyday habits, economic essays, and outlandish digressions. She created a historical miscellany, with no sense of which classics her beauties originally came from.

Retrospection and the Reviewers

Piozzi must have been gravely disappointed as it became clear that *Retrospection* was almost universally disliked. One critic concluded, "The whole performance was damned by every reviewer who took the trouble to write about it" (Vullaimy 306).[14] Few reviewers accepted Piozzi's terms; most rejected her project by belittling it with feminine comparisons to domestic tasks. They did not couch their disdain in chivalrous language. Reviewers refused to consider that Piozzi was trying to create a new kind of history, ignoring her pleas that *Retrospection* be judged on different grounds from traditional histories. They repeatedly stated their views that she did not have the proper training to complete a work of historical merit. They attributed her lack of historiographical skill to her sex. The reviews were so virulent that Piozzi chose to address them in a published response.

Many reviewers found her choice of historical form hubristic. The *London Review* could not accept Piozzi as a universal historian (rather than a national or a local one): "In a word, female vanity never set itself forth more conspicuously, nor more absurdly, than in the assumption of *universal knowledge* which runs through the whole compilation" (188). The reviewer implies that Piozzi, without a classical education, must be vain to attempt a volume that required not only extensive reading but universal knowledge. The *Critical Review* concurred: "Mrs. Piozzi is already known to the literary world by some publications of merit, which induced us to entertain favourable expectations of the present work, — however unadapted such a labour might appear to a female pen, as requiring at once infinite and exact reading" (28). Piozzi's hallmark style applied to a historical work was deemed affected, obscure, abrupt, and quaint. The *London Review* challenged, "We defy the most learned Critic to decide, to what class of literature this pretty piece of female patch-work belongs" (188). The reviewer could not have known that the damning comparison of *Retrospection* to fabric swatches originated with the author.

Even the conservative *British Critic,* which tried to be more even-handed and sympathetic to its compatriot Piozzi, did *Retrospection* no favors with its lukewarm praise. Its reviewer displayed less surprise, seeing *Retrospection* as a continuation of Piozzi's other writings: "But how shall we characterize a work so perfectly singular? An universal history from the Christian era, translated into chit-chat language; the result of much, very much reading, containing facts and characters put together certainly as they were never put before; a string of reflections chronologically arranged, full of good sentiments, but so expressed — as what, shall we say? — as the Anecdotes, Letters, Travels, and Synonymes of Mrs. Piozzi!" (355). The oddity of *Retrospection* was its universality (and therefore presumed gravity) coupled with its colloquial language. A "string of reflections chronologically arranged" sounds like a history, but the reviewer sees the form as "singular." Instead of imagining *Retrospection* as a new kind of history, the reviewer considers it an amalgam of recycled Piozzi writings. That conclusion is in some respects a strange one, because in *Retrospection* Piozzi employs no epistolary elements, nor does she ruminate on travels. That her history contains anecdotes would not necessarily differentiate it from others currently in vogue. Her interest in "synonymes" (synonymy), which does appear in *Retrospection,* cannot be similarly defended. Some critics accused Piozzi of lacking originality, but from today's vantage point she might be credited with an abundance of it.

Piozzi's originality was considered eccentricity. The *Anti-Jacobin Review* was by far the harshest on *Retrospection*'s form. The reviewer first laments that Johnson is no longer living, because if "this work had been submitted to his perusal in manuscript, we are well convinced that he would have rejected one half of it, and added to the other some reflections and observations to render it worthy of public attention" (241).[15] The reviewer twice describes Piozzi as a cook rather than an author: "This [passage] reminds us of mincing a surloin of beef and reducing it to soup for the purpose of affording nourishment to very weak stomachs, without the labor of digestion" (242). Piozzi's retrospective meal is likened to lighter fictional fare: "Mrs. Piozzi has here attempted to form a new dish for English stomachs. History cooked up in a novel form reduced to light reading for boarding school misses, and loungers at a watering place, during the Dog Days" (241). The *London Review* also employed a culinary analogy: "Like a careful housewife, who keeps by her strings of dried orange and lemon peels, to give a zest to her culinary compositions, so has she hoarded up threads of poetry, to entwine with the annals of the Roman Emperors, and the religious contests of the early Christians" (188). Piozzi's work is conceived of as a historical potluck supper. One reviewer grudgingly saw originality in her ideas. The *Anti-Jacobin Review* insultingly allowed that Piozzi had invented a new kind of work: "We are fully convinced that no general description, no comparison with antient or modern authors, either in poetry or prose, can convey the smallest idea of this lady's style, and the lucidus ordo of her ideas. This is a work *sui generis*" (242).

The reviewers were unable to accept that a world history could be undertaken successfully by a female autodidact. As McCarthy concludes, *Retrospection* "failed in part because it was perceived to have overstepped the generic limits allowed to women writers" (McCarthy, "Hester" 255). I would add that those generic limits did not include all historical discourse. On the contrary, women had been publishing historical fiction and correspondence to some acclaim. To presume to write a world history of the previous 1,800 years, however, was to aspire to an achievement greater in scope than Gibbon's, which covered roughly 1,400 years with one national focus. If Piozzi had written the anecdotal world history for children that she proposed, the reviewers would surely have greeted it more enthusiastically.

She tried to create a history in the tradition of a Christianized Tory Gibbon crossed with Hannah More. What she came up with frustrated readers' expectations.

After troubling over the form of the work, many of the reviews lamented its lack of accuracy. The *Critical Review* homed in almost entirely on the mistakes found in the work, registering that it was "disgusted with its infinitude of puerile errors, of all kinds" (28). Because of *Retrospection*'s alleged mistakes, the reviewer found it "ill adapted to any class of readers. To the learned, it must appear as a series of dreams by an old lady. . . . Far less is it fit for the perusal of youth, of either sex; since the numerous errors, and the air of sufficiency with which they are written, might leave impressions difficult to be eradicated by the genuine page of history" (28–29). The *Critical Review,* in its tirade on Piozzi's supposed errors, also wishes it could be more respectful: "In regard to her sex we are anxious to treat her with all possible lenity; but we should totally fail in our duty if we suffered by the minds of youth, or of female readers, to be contaminated by such a flood of idle tattle and innumerable blunders" (35). Children's minds are more in need of protection than authors' egos.

Piozzi feared sneering reviews, but she must have anticipated greater chivalry. Many of the reviewers mention that they realize they should be more delicate in handling the work of a lady. The *Anti-Jacobin Review,* after offering weak support of Piozzi's aims, claims it cannot rescue her:

It is always more grateful to the critic to praise than to censure. We hope the age of chivalry is not past. We would not try a lady by the severest rules of criticism. We are great admirers of Dr. Johnson, and consider that Mrs. P was once the friend of that good man. She is a firm believer in Revelation, and looks with just abhorrence on the enormities of the French revolution. . . . We cannot flatter her with the hope, that this work will prove any addition to her fame or her fortune. It will not add to the stock of our historical knowledge, and mere novel-readers will start at the sight of two ponderous quartos. At first we were disappointed, that the events and the characters of eighteen centuries, should not have the assistance of an index or a table of contents, but . . . the work is not worth an index. (245–46)

By demonstrating that he knows the critical rules about how to treat a lady author, the reviewer releases himself from them.

Chivalry is a frequent subject even in the sympathetic reviews. The *British Critic* is the only periodical that attempts to restate what Piozzi's form was attempting: "The intention of *Retrospection,* then, is to preserve some traces of general history, at a time when, it seems, nothing else of this instructive kind is likely to be read" (356). Finally, however, the reviewer can praise only by omitting direct criticism:

Thus we have endeavored briefly, to let our readers know what kinds of entertainment is here prepared for them. Much and various amusement there certainly is. The quantity of facts related, or alluded to, is very large; the characters and opinions elucidated, very numerous. The sentiments are benevolent and pious; and if we consider how much time and labor it required to collect and commit the whole to paper, we cannot but wonder at the patience of the author. Her lapses in point of accuracy, or other blemishes, which in a work so extensive might be expected, we shall not endeavor to detect them. It will be a good exercise for those who, for any reason, suspect such failings, to compare our lively lady with more elaborate historians; and instruct themselves, without telling tales of her. (358)

Even among its "friends," *Retrospection* found tepid critical support.

Piozzi's letters document her anxiety about these reviews and her anger at them. In each successive periodical she hoped for, and did not find, a better response. In July 1801 she wrote to the *Gentleman's Magazine* to vindicate herself, after some friends recommended that she publish the letter of complaint she had written. As in *Retrospection* itself, Piozzi was on the defensive. She addressed herself to the "Critical Reviewers"—perhaps because they had been the most vicious. The *Critical Review* referred to the "infinite labour" it would be "to pursue all the mistakes of our authoress" and concluded, "They must be poor scholars, indeed, who informed Mrs. Piozzi" (33). Piozzi, rather than mounting a full-scale defense of her work or commenting on the reviewers' calumny, concentrates on addressing the mistakes the reviewers found. She claims that some of the mistakes (Lusitania for Lithuania and Joseph the Fifteenth for Joseph the First) are compositor's errors ("Mrs. Piozzi's Appeal"). She eagerly points out that the review of *Retrospection* published in the *Critical Review* was itself the victim of "as gross mistakes" by "their own compositor." In her characteristically retributive stance, Piozzi calls the errors in the *Critical Review* "a judgment on the Reviewers" (602). Her rambling defense descends into etymological twists and turns, defending her family's heritage as she defends her book and focusing on irrelevant names. The only thing Piozzi makes clear in the defense of her book is that "it is too hard to be so insulted for *ignorance not one's own*" (603). To be criticized for "*secondhand* learning" seems to her unfair because she had "never boasted any learning at all" (603).[16] Piozzi misses an opportunity to explain to her readers (and to posterity) the value of her work; instead she gets bogged down responding to individual insults.

Retrospection, in a class of its own in 1801, remained so. Rather than spawning additional editions, copycat volumes, or a spate of chronological historical miscellanies, the work languished in a few libraries. More of Piozzi's writings returned to print, but *Retrospection* did not rise in critical estimation. Leonard Benton Seeley's 1891 response was that it was "an enterprise about as hopeful as the 'History of Human Error,' to which Mr. Caxton devoted his life, or the 'Key to All Possible Mythologies,' whereby the Reverend Isaac Casaubon expected to achieve immortality" (309). Although Seeley concedes that "anyone who takes the trouble to turn over a few of those multitudinous leaves will be repaid by lighting on some curious trait of character and manners, some quaint legend, or some interesting piece of unfamiliar history told in a lively and entertaining manner," the damage is more than done with his reference to *Middlemarch*'s Casaubon (309). Piozzi's book is reduced to the fictional unfinished project of a humorless, pedantic drudge.

Likening Piozzi's history to the never-completed work of a character in a novel is a strange proposition. *Retrospection,* however, could not escape from the shadow of novels, whether in its reviews or in its few subsequent notices. The book provides a rich tapestry of European manners and anecdotes, one that would be difficult to find anywhere else but in historical fiction at the moment Piozzi wrote. Conduct books, letters, memoirs, and travel narratives might have provided occasional illustrations of that material, but not of the scope and degree of Piozzi's. Several sections in volume 2 resemble fictional forms, employing conversational, elevated language (e.g., "Silly barons! Short-sighted kings!" [2: 83]). A several-page story of Christopher Columbus in particular is filled with dialogue, anecdote, and romance, typified by the following passage: "Columbus, untired, undismay'd, threw himself once more at Ferdinand's and Isabella's feet; and silently, but with expressive anguish, pointing to his chains, filled them with shame and momentary sorrow; and transferred to his perfidious princes some share of his own ill-deserved mortifications" (2: 49). Despite another Piozzi caveat to avoid focusing a history on the story of one man, Columbus's section is long and told with the flourishes of a gothic romance.

Piozzi, like Johnson, was no supporter of novels. She concurred with the widespread opinion that novels were morally dangerous. As she wrote in a letter to Penelope Pennington, "Our Novel-writers have a right to hate me, who set my face so against fiction, and who have endeavoured (tho' fruitlessly) to make truth palatable" (Knapp 229). Some fictional works rated more highly with her than others. Piozzi singled out the first volume of Sophia Lee's *The Recess* (1783–85) (now categorized by some as the first historical novel), referring to its "peculiar charms" (*British Synonymy* 2: 299). Among the books Piozzi deems novels, she appreciates Charlotte Lennox's "exquisite novel" *The Female Quixote* and the novelists who copy "after manners merely," including Frances Burney, Henry Fielding, and Tobias Smollett. She warns that these authors "must content their love of fame with a limited existence . . . not expecting immortality" (2: 301). The change in customs over time dooms these novels. The novelists who will be remembered are those whose works tear "the human heart," including Samuel Richardson, Jean-Jacques Rousseau, and Laurence Sterne (2: 301–2). The fictional works to which Piozzi accords the highest praise are "moral, or political, or mythological romances" like Johnson's and Fénelon's (2: 302).

Piozzi had clear ideas of what fiction was and should be. *Retrospection,* according to her own definition, falls nowhere in these categories. It does, however, contain elements of good fiction. Piozzi's own statements in her introduction about how to "make truth palatable" argue for textual features that are novelistic. It is no mistake that her reviewers found cause to compare *Retrospection* to novels with such frequency. Piozzi wanted a story that was not filled with freestanding anecdotes, insulated from all the rest. She wanted a narrative in which stories have reference and connection to other stories. She aimed for petty amusement, pleasant narratives, and tender tales. She did not want to distract readers with insolently obtrusive opinions (though of course she frequently did). That she did not produce the text she set out to create was not lost on her reviewers. Piozzi tried to compose a work of historical not-history that would appeal to discriminating readers of popular fictional forms *and* to uninformed youths. *Retrospection* wanted to do for the genre of history what many authors had done for novels—attract and please a diverse group of readers with entertainment and instruction.

In writing a history that drew on what she saw as the successful elements of "moral, or political, or mythological romances," Piozzi tried to meld compiled, "true" history with the attractive qualities of imaginative literature. In the process, she opened herself up to be measured on the qualities most looked for in historians at the turn of the century: accurate and truthful instruction. Had readers been willing to look at *Retrospection* as Piozzi desired, as an entertaining story, they might have been able to accept her collection of tales as worthwhile. To do so necessitated reading *Retrospection* as something other than mainstream history. Because she opted to leave out much of the scholarly apparatus of a history of her time—an index, a table of contents, dates in the margins, and the names of authorities—Piozzi's book did not look enough like history. Its allusive, anecdotal content did not help its case in establishing a resemblance to histories rather than to fiction, letters, or memoir.

Piozzi recognized that not citing authorities would have a cost. It was a choice she made after some thought. In a letter to Pennington she writes, "Those who say my book is merely good for nothing cannot be answer'd. The book says something like that of itself,—but its worthlessness consists in telling people what they knew before, not in telling what is false, for that is the charge that offends me. Much of this obloquy might have been avoided certainly, by quoting authorities, but they would add more to the work's weight than to its value" (*PL* 3: 299). James Clifford, too, notes the omission of citations as one cause of *Retrospection*'s undoing: "Most of the work was based on supposedly standard historical sources, but in many cases the author failed to note her authority. Consequently, errors and false deductions which she had lifted wholesale from out of print volumes were often imputed to her own fertile imagination" (402). In a novel, Piozzi's "fertile imagination" would have been a help. In a history, imagination is used at the writer's peril.

In *Retrospection* Piozzi chose textual features that became associated with novelistic discourse rather than with historical discourse—that is, until we consider it alongside twentieth-century popular histories. *Retrospection* might be seen as a precursor to that genre, as Clifford contends: "The twentieth century is much more adept at popularizing world history, but it must be remembered that Mrs. Piozzi did not have many models to consult" (402). Piozzi lifts her stories of human events from a variety of sources rather than attributing them to authorities. She fundamentally misreads what respectable history is becoming—a genre increasingly antithetical to novels in its form and, to a lesser degree, in its style. History, in its most esteemed branch, would become less a subject for children, requiring a motherly didacticism, and more a subject for professional men (Kent,

"Learning"; P. Levine). History written by women was increasingly history written about women. As Miriam Elizabeth Burstein writes, "Shifting standards in historical evidence meant that women's history and its sentimental peer, the historical novel, were both displaced to the realm of aesthetic pleasure, or, worse, to the realm of pure nonsense" (236). Although, as we have seen, Piozzi's was not a women's history, it did link itself firmly with aesthetic pleasure over solid instruction.

Piozzi "lived to see most of her achievements belittled" (McCarthy, "Hester" 255). Her ambitious choice of world history as her subject was not fortuitous, as women writers continued to gain a more sympathetic readership for their fiction and for their accounts of women worthies. Piozzi's contributions to historiography, in the form of historical anecdotes or "meditations upon history," were not recognized as properly historical by a public that looked to women writers to address other women or children, to turn history into appropriate moral lessons, and to defer to historical authorities. Piozzi's unwillingness to follow these newly forming historiographical dictates for women or to write fiction—and perhaps her lack of opportunity to publish *Retrospection* in an octavo edition, resembling novels in size and affordability—hurt her economically. More lastingly, it damaged her critical legacy. *Retrospection* is a failure on Piozzi's own terms in that she was unable to carry out the project as she designed it. The failure goes beyond her own design and execution, however. Unknown to her, historiography was traveling (and would continue to travel) in a different direction—one that Piozzi, as a result of her education, her commitment to anecdotal forms, and her sex, was not prepared to follow.

7

Reading Jane Austen
and Rewriting "Herstory"

■

Linking Jane Austen (1775–1817) and history was once unthinkable. Critics saw Austen's writing as limited to a "little bit (two Inches wide) of Ivory" and to the milieu of "3 or 4 families in a Country Village" (Austen, *Jane Austen's Letters* 323, 275).[1] The view of her as a novelist of the trivial and local was firmly entrenched and frequently juxtaposed to the "Big Bow-wow strain" of Sir Walter Scott (Southam, *Jane Austen: The Critical Heritage* 106).[2] Scott was believed to cover the weighty worldly matters and Austen the quaint quotidian ones. Biographical details were marshaled to argue that a country spinster could not have had knowledge of—or perhaps even interest in—events beyond her own small sphere. Austen was often denigrated in such accounts, though not purposefully. She and her writings were placed outside history because received wisdom deemed her a genius of the minute human universal, just not the political or the historical realm. "It is a truth universally acknowledged that Jane Austen chose to ignore the decisive historical events of her time," as Raymond Williams facetiously put it (113).[3]

The critical heyday of Austen's ahistoricism is now happily behind us, and myths of her extrahistoricity or subhistoricity appear to have been debunked (Kent, "Learning" 59). The so-called new historicism of the past decades brought attention to a wider range of texts as potential forces of cultural change. Austen and history emerged as a viable area of study.[4] Critics noted historical events and sociohistorical material in her novels: "There are passing allusions to a contemporary history that included the flogging of soldiers, the slave trade, the enclosure of commons, new seed drills, émigrés eking out livings in London, bloody political riots, major and minor battles

on land and sea, including privateering, even the American War of 1812"
(Tave 61). Revived interest in her historical references contributed to "the
more pervasive trend toward historicizing [Austen's] novels" (J. Thompson,
"Jane" 23). Studies appeared on Austen's relation to the French and American revolutions, the industrial revolution, the economics of the marriage
market, and the literary marketplace (Roberts; Butler, *Jane;* R. Williams;
Fergus, *Jane Austen: A Literary Life;* Kroeber).[5] The political implications of
her writings—once seen either as nonexistent or as tacitly Tory, following
her family—provoked new debates.[6] Critics argued about her progressive-
ness or conservatism on such matters as gender, class, race, religion, imperialism, and sexuality.[7] Austen as a writer concerned with history—political
and social—has arrived.

Despite the emergence of scholarship on Austen and history, she remains, in Nancy Armstrong's words, "a particularly hard nut for historical critics to crack" ("Nineteenth-Century Jane Austen" 227).[8] What com-
pounds the problem is that some who have taken a crack at it limit their
commentary to Austen's sparse textual references about "great events." Setting up her use of history as a critical curio, these interpretations of historical minutiae—though not without merit—rarely go far enough, as James
Thompson has contended.[9] What is meant by history or historical context
in Austen studies remains "as vague and various as ever" (24).[10] History has
too often been defined narrowly where Austen is concerned, even among
historically attuned critics. Narrow definitions in Austen studies have been
carried out in the name of critical accuracy: "By placing Jane Austen within
her genre," Marilyn Butler has argued, "we help define her meaning" (4).
One way to see history more accurately in her writings, however, is to consider its meanings beyond her genre of the novel.[11]

In recovering the forces that informed Austen's relationship to fiction and histories, my investigation helps explain why, for nearly 150 years,
claims about her connection to historical matters were viewed as untenable. Her letters and a piece from her juvenilia, the *History of England,* help
show how she positioned her texts in relation to historiographical trends
and to historical novels. *Northanger Abbey,* arguably the most fruitful text
for discovering Austen's philosophy of history, has been perceived by many
critics as a response and a corrective to the sentimental or gothic novels
of the 1790s. Others have viewed it as Austen's plea for the need to add
women to histories. But there is more at stake than either of these accounts

allows. Austen's writings were competing for readers at a time when novels were not yet considered a fully polite form and when histories were experiencing a decade of "revival" (Feather, "British Publishing" 43). She made light of histories and defended novels in *Northanger Abbey,* usurping certain elements from historical discourse while making romance probable. She was defining her text not just against other kinds of novels or novelists but against other kinds of writing, including histories. In effect, Austen combined genres that were said to be masculine or feminine into a new kind of text that retained elements of both. She did not avoid history. On the contrary, she engaged it directly, grappled with it, and refashioned it for her own purposes.

Austen uses the words "history" and "historian" a mere sixty-six times in her published writings (De Rose and McGuire 3: 516). In *Pride and Prejudice* and *Northanger Abbey* we are offered a "history of . . . acquaintance." Catherine Morland gives "her own history" to Eleanor Tilney three times. *Mansfield Park* presents the "history of [Mr. Yates's] disappointment" about not getting to play the character he wanted to in the private theatricals at Ecclesford. In *Lady Susan,* Manwaring tells his wife's history; recent visits are often said to be worthy of "histories," and accounts of "history and character" abound. Modest Fanny Price has a history, as does Jane Fairfax. Mr. Weston gives his audience a "history of engagements" in the neighborhood. In almost all these references, history is not political history (not an account of past events of national import) but something we might call novelized history or history as fiction—that is, history as an account of the local details of a character's life. Even in *Northanger Abbey,* where political history is commented on directly as a genre, there are few explicit references to macrohistorical events.

The meanings of history that Austen employs in her novels have largely dropped out of common usage. "Let me tell you my history" has become in today's parlance a "story." According to the *Oxford English Dictionary,* history once signified "a relation of incidents (in early uses, either true or imaginary; later only those professedly true); a narrative, tale or story." Other definitions of history, most now obsolete, implied "a story represented dramatically" (examples from 1596 to 1877) or "a pictorial representation" in addition to what we now consider history—a branch of knowledge recording past events, often in writing—for which *Northanger Abbey's* "real solemn history" is itself used as an *OED* example. Some scholars have asserted that the novel's eighteenth-century "rise" provided the major textual vehicle for promoting a sense of history as a chronicle of human development and subjectivity. Helpful as these arguments are, they contribute to misleading assumptions about the status of the novel in the eighteenth century in relation to other kinds of writing. To compare Austen's writings with what we might now, following the lead of Christopher Kent, call "schoolroom history," we must ask questions about how she envisioned herself as an author in a broader field of letters ("Learning").

Austen's Letters, Gender, and Genre

Various self-understandings of Austen's authorship appear in her collected *Letters*. She reveals an interest in her own tight-knit community but also demonstrates that she was well aware of the literary marketplace beyond, that she read the writings of her contemporaries, and that she puzzled over the best way to construct her own books so as to appeal to an audience. Her letters on these topics are frequently mentioned in critical studies, but it is useful to reevaluate them in the context of genre. In a famous letter of 1813, Jane Austen wrote to her sister Cassandra that she felt *Pride and Prejudice* was "too light & bright & sparkling;—it wants shade" (*JAL* 203). The way she contemplated achieving this shade illustrates the kinds of writing she believed readers wanted "mixed" with their fiction: "[*Pride and Prejudice*] wants to be stretched out here & there with a long Chapter—of sense if it could be had, if not of solemn specious nonsense—about something unconnected with the story; an Essay on Writing, a critique on Walter Scott, or the history of Buonaparte—anything that would form a contrast & bring the reader with increased delight to the playfulness & Epigrammatism of the general stile.—I doubt your quite agreeing with me here—I know your starched Notions" (203).[12] Austen's account of what her novel should be in order to please her anticipated audience focuses on history and literary criticism, which she implies range in value from "sense" to "solemn specious nonsense." She considers her proposed additions so as to add weight and historical depth to her prose and to highlight the pleasing jocularity and pithy phrases throughout. She may be characteristically ironic when she notes that these historical and critical digressions will, by contrast, remind readers how much amusement is found in other parts of the book. Regardless of her level of sincerity, Austen demonstrates an awareness that she is competing for readers with histories and historical novels, though she appears unwilling to modify her prose to resemble them. Subsequent letters intimate why.

A year later, in 1814, Austen expresses her anxiety that Sir Walter Scott's historical novels will challenge the success of her own. Writing to her niece Anna, she complains: "Walter Scott has no business to write novels, especially good ones.—It is not fair.—He has Fame & Profit enough as a Poet, and should not be taking the bread out of other people's mouths.—I do not like him, & do not mean to like Waverly if I can help it—but fear I must. . . . I have made up my mind to like no Novels, really, but Miss Edgeworth's, Yours [Anna's], & my own" (*JAL* 277–78). Why does Austen worry about Scott's novels but not Edgeworth's? Edgeworth's earnings from one book rivaled the amount that Austen made during her entire lifetime.[13] It cannot be simply a matter of profit. Perhaps what is at issue is her conception of Scott as a threat to the popularity of her fictional product. Scott's *Waverly* differed in kind from Austen's fiction and was therefore viewed as a rival form, whereas Edgeworth's sentimental novels (which Austen may have seen as more like her own) were not.[14] The position that Scott might carve out for himself as a historical novelist could have forced out a comic, domestic novelist like Austen unless she followed his generic lead into a new subgenre of fiction.

The real or perceived battles among fictional genres change their color when the circulation of novels is clarified. In the eighteenth century, novels were primarily borrowed rather than bought. Late in the century the war with France contributed to a jump in the price of new books, and though libraries continued to purchase books, those with smaller collections were at risk (Hodge 75). Circulating libraries (which effectively rented books) helped build the market for novels but did little to establish them as books one would feel compelled to add to one's personal library (Feather, *History* 97, 99). As John Feather concludes, "From the trade's point of view, the significance of the novel lay not in its literary merit but in its essential triviality. It was seen as an ephemeral production to be read once and then forgotten. This meant that, once the demand had been created, a continuous supply of new novels was needed to fill it. Waves of fashion swept over the novel" (*History* 97). Austen's concerns about Scott's success might have arisen from more than a desire for sales or "bread." She may have feared that Scott, as an author who was already established in the more respected genre of poetry, could carry his authorial respectability over to his historical novels rather than to all types of fiction. Historical novels, if they became the ruling fashion, might diminish the demand for novels like Austen's. Riding the coattails of well-regarded and popular histories, historical novels could become a more exalted and acceptable form than domestic novels, long denounced as feminine trash. Austen may have recognized this potential valuation, preferring that her own novels be seen as neither trivial nor ephemeral, though not as historical in either a factual or a romantic strain.

Austen's wariness of history far predates Scott's novel-writing days. How did her skeptical stance toward history arise?[15] Her letters show her contending with historical writing, especially in her often-cited correspondence with James Stanier Clarke, the librarian and chaplain of the prince regent (later George IV). Clarke was subsequently librarian of Prince Leopold of Saxe-Coburg, husband of the prince regent's daughter Charlotte. Clarke and Austen exchanged letters about her willingness to dedicate a novel to the prince regent, which she did with *Emma* in 1816. Along the way, Clarke made free with suggestions for topics he believed she should pursue, insisting that she should write about a clergyman. Clarke went so far as to propose that material from his own life might be used to build a plot. Austen's negative responses to these suggestions, couched as modesty rather than outright defiance, need not be read straightforwardly. She tells Clarke that she cannot write about a clergyman because she is "the most unlearned, & uninformed Female who ever dared to be an Authoress"—probably a polite plea to be released from Clarke's unwelcome ideas (*JAL* 306).

Undaunted, Clarke's advice continued in subsequent letters. He asked Austen to consider dedicating her next work to Prince Leopold and said it might be "any Historical Romance illustrative of the History of the august house of Cobourg," which Clarke claimed would "just now be very interesting" (*JAL* 311). Her response was, again, a pointed refusal:

You are very, very kind in your hints as to the sort of Composition which might recommend me at present, & I am fully sensible that a Historical Romance, founded on the House of Saxe Cobourg might be much more to the purpose of Profit or Popularity, than such pictures of domestic Life in Country Villages as I deal in—but I could no more write a Romance than an Epic Poem.—I could not sit seriously down to write a serious Romance under any other motive than to save my Life, & if it were indispensable for me to keep it up & never relax into laughing at myself or other people, I am sure I should be hung before I had finished the first Chapter.—No—I must keep to my own style & go in my own Way; And though I may never succeed again in that, I am convinced that I should totally fail in any other. (312)

It is difficult to know how much of this letter to Clarke is deliberate posturing and how much true confession. I agree with Donald Greene, who detects "no sense of real limitation in [Austen's] expression of inability" in this letter (152). However, Austen does not explain her distaste for writing historical fiction out of an ignorance of history per se, as she implied before. If this letter is to be believed, her refusal resulted from her wish *not* to be "serious." Clarke's proposal would have involved pleasing royalty with her characterizations—perchance at penalty of her life and livelihood. If she followed his suggestions to compose a historical romance, Austen would have had to paint Saxe-Coburgian characters, despite their shortcomings, in high heroic fashion. She must have believed that in her comic, ironic style she was better able to set down the general moral truths she wanted to tell.

Austen initially pleads her sex as the reason she should not tackle historical fiction, implying that "unlearned" female authors must not dare to attempt such work. She must have known this was fallacious. Austen knew the gothic historical fiction of Charlotte Smith and Harriet Lee. Her mother's cousin, "Aunt Cooke," had published anonymously a historical novel set in the interregnum, *Battleridge, an Historical Tale Founded on Facts,* which the family was "expected to read" (Tomalin 149). Even closer to home, her brother James's periodical the *Loiterer* published an issue on history's virtues.[16] Austen was by no means uninformed when it came to history or historical fiction. We need to turn to her earlier writings to make sense of the ways she opposed her novels to histories, because, as Clifford Siskin has maintained, she "poses not just an individual enigma but a disciplinary one" (52). Austen's relationship to history arose from more than a predilection for comic forms. Though her surviving letters may imply otherwise, she clearly gave a lot of thought to historical discourse.

History and Austen's Juvenilia

More than twenty years before Austen wrote these letters, she confronted history in comic form. Though her engagement with historical material may once have been little known, today's scholars have gone a good distance toward making it well appreciated. Austen's *History of England from the Reign of Henry the Fourth to the Death of Charles the First* (ca. 1790) — a burlesque composed when she was just fifteen years old — has enjoyed three reprintings in the 1990s and was adapted for the stage and performed in Great Britain.[17] This is a significant amount of attention for a slight work of thirty-four manuscript pages that includes illustrations added by her sister Cassandra. Jane and Cassandra Austen's "rowdy mock-history" (Lascelles 9) has long charmed readers with its humorous wit, its wry intelligence, and its incisive characterizations, displaying the younger sister's promise as a writer long before her novels appeared.[18] What the *History of England* has that Austen's novels, for the most part, do not have is a "wild early irony" (*HE* vi) and a "saucy disrespect" (Kent, "Real Solemn History" 93) for English political history. Austen is reverent and irreverent by turns in the *History*. Although she claims at the outset that she is a "partial, prejudiced, & ignorant Historian" and that her text will include "very few Dates," her wide reading in history is implicitly and explicitly on display (1).[19]

Austen's *History of England* begins, "Henry the 4th ascended the throne of England much to his satisfaction in the year 1399, after having prevailed on his cousin & predecessor Richard the 2nd to resign it to him, & to retire for the rest of his Life to Pomfret Castle, where he happened to be murdered" (2). With this opening she sets the tone for the rest of the work — mocking, sardonic, and light, even in the face of far more serious charges and events. Austen moves from monarch to monarch, and Cassandra provides coin-sized pictures of most of the personalities involved. The drawings and the prose expose each subject's humanity and foibles, with little concern for maintaining royal dignity. Henry V "grew reformed and amiable, forsaking all his dissipated Companions" (4). Henry VI's entry gives Austen the opportunity to express her anti-Lancastrian sentiments: "I suppose you know all about the Wars between him & the Duke of York who was of the right side; if you do not, you had better read some other History" (5). Austen makes it clear to her readers that she intends to "vent . . . Spleen," to "shew . . . Hatred," and "not to give information" (5). In describing Edward IV, Austen notes his beauty and courage and concentrates on his romantic entanglements. She writes, "One of Edward's Mistresses was Jane Shore, who has had a play written about her, but it is a tragedy & therefore not worth reading" (7). She concludes by noting ironically that after all these "noble actions" Edward IV died, and his son was crowned. When Austen comes to Henry VIII she again demonstrates that she has placed her readers' needs (though not their expectations) at the forefront: "It would be an affront to my Readers were I to suppose that they were not as well acquainted with the particulars of this King's reign as I am myself" (11). Austen provides four pages on her partialities and prejudices in regard to his case.

Queen Elizabeth I receives the longest account. Her treatment of her cousin Mary Stuart, queen of Scotland, provokes Austen's wrath. Though she is accused of many crimes, including ordering Mary's execution, Elizabeth's first fault is having had "bad Ministers" (20). The reference to "bad ministers" is the first of many descriptions purportedly about Elizabeth that turn out to be focused on others. Much of the Elizabeth section concentrates on redeeming Mary, who was "entirely Innocent" (23). Austen concludes: "Having I trust by this assurance entirely done away every Suspicion & every doubt which might have arisen in the Reader's mind, from what other Historians have written of her, I shall proceed to mention the remaining Events that marked Elizabeth's reign" (24). Her tone is somewhat less flippant in the Elizabethan descriptions than in other sections of the *History,* but her mocking extravagance continues until the conclusion, which notes that because Charles I was a Stuart, he must have been a better ruler than was commonly believed: "The Events of this Monarch's reign are too numerous for my pen, and indeed the recital of any Events (except what I make myself) is uninteresting to me; my principal reason for undertaking the History of England being to prove the innocence of the Queen of Scotland, which I flatter myself with having effectually done, and to abuse Elizabeth, tho' I am rather fearful of having fallen short in the latter part of my Scheme" (33–34). Austen claims in her *History* to invent her own version of events. She keeps to what is interesting and deals exclusively in justifying or damning royal personalities, the most important of whom happen to be women.

As a piece of writing, the *History of England* is engaging, like other Austen texts, but it is by no means an accomplished work. It would be foolish to see this short piece—undertaken to amuse family members—as the foundation for the rest of her fiction. Nevertheless, it deals with issues that reappear in altered form in later writings. Austen defines herself as a "Historian" in this piece, but she produces something that looks like neither standard political history nor domestic fiction. In effect she generates comic history, implicitly disavows schoolroom history, and draws heavily on what we would now call literary sources in constructing an account of England from the reign of Henry IV to the death of Charles I. The last point— Austen's use of fictional historical texts and her commentary on them— deserves further exploration.

Those who have written about Austen's *History of England* examine how it parodies Oliver Goldsmith's *History of England, in a Series of Letters from a Nobleman to His Son* (1764). Austen made comments in the margins of her family's copy of Goldsmith's book, which she read when she was twelve or thirteen years old.[20] Goldsmith's epistolary history, as well as his four-volume *History of England from the Earliest Times to the Death of George III* (1771), and its subsequent abridgments, was often used to educate children. Goldsmith's *History* went through fifty editions in the one hundred years after it was published (Kent, "Learning" 63). Goldsmith was therefore an easy target for Austen's early burlesque. Many critics have focused on the political motivations of Austen's *History*. Her Stuart allegiances have been described as a correction to Goldsmith's anti-Stuart bias.

Understanding Austen's political position as at base familial, Brigid Brophy sees the *History of England* as Austen family history writ large.[21] Tracing her preference for the Stuarts to the Leighs' (Austen's mother's family) assistance to Charles I during the Civil War, Brophy speculates on the ways the Austen family may have considered itself similarly dispossessed a century later. In Brophy's reading the *History of England* is reduced to autobiography, revealing the young author's psychological state: "Jane Austen was simultaneously writing, in metaphor, a history of her family and a history of herself to date" (31). Though her interpretation is thought provoking, it verges on repeating the myth of Austen's ahistoricism. In Brophy's account Austen is again stealthily writing about her own small sphere rather than about the wider world. Her political differences with Goldsmith are understood as personal differences. Considering the *History* in a first-person frame prevents us from asking larger questions about Austen and history.

Psychological readings such as Brophy's have not been dominant in discussions of Austen's juvenilia. Seeing these works as the most feminist and radical of her writings, however, is a newer critical development (Austen, *Catharine* ix–xxxviii). The *History of England* has been part of this trend, used as evidence of her commitment to the stories of real as well as fictional women, particularly Mary, Queen of Scots. Seventeen women are featured in Austen's history, as are twenty-six men—a high proportion of women to men, as Jan Fergus notes (Austen, *History* [1995] iv).[22] Not all of Austen's historical females are queens or wives and daughters of monarchs. Joan of Arc, Jane Shore, and Lady Jane Grey also grace her "parade of female characters." Oliver Goldsmith's history, by contrast, mentions "just four women and twenty men in . . . the reign of Henry VII" (Austen, *History* [1995] iv). Austen's larger percentage of women is notable, but its importance cannot be determined by a contrast to Goldsmith alone. Her choice to ignore many signal events of political and military history may have been unusual for schoolroom histories of the time, but her inclusion of women was not revolutionary. Several histories with precisely this goal had appeared in the decades before Austen wrote.

Some recent critics have shown us how Austen's *History* might be comprehended as an explicitly feminist text, citing its historically revisionist tendencies, for one, as a feminist impulse. It would be easy and even self-evident, as Antoinette Burton notes, "to argue that part of what makes this history 'feminist' is that it insists on placing a wronged woman at its center" in the form of Mary, Queen of Scots (43). Burton shows that Austen's feminism goes beyond sympathy for Mary, especially in the courageous choice to highlight how women too can be implicated in "the operations of patriarchy" rather than opting to present an easy (and disingenuous) historical "sisterhood" (44). Both Burton and Jan Fergus are convincing in their arguments that Jane and Cassandra Austen created a collaborative feminist text in the *History,* one that was involved in "questioning conventional notions of history and revising history itself" (Austen, *History* [1995] i). Austen's *History,* as Burton concludes, "testifies to the power of history to allow women to reinvent the past and so too perhaps to differently imagine their own future" (46). Such arguments have helpfully paved the way for studying related aspects of Austen's *History,* such as gender and genre.

The aim of Austen's juvenilia, Claudia Johnson has claimed, "is demystification: making customary forms subject to doubt by flaunting their conventionality" ("Kingdom" 48).[23] Austen's flaunting has been examined primarily as a send-up of sentimental novels. When conventions are discussed in relation to her *History,* they are frequently historiographical ones.

Christopher Kent identifies her burlesque as "revenge on history—on schoolroom history—a species of history as subject, still very much with us, that was largely a creation of the eighteenth century" ("Learning" 60). Schoolroom history "was reduced for childhood consumption into facts and dates" and was considered especially appropriate for girls (61). Regarded as polite knowledge, histories gave women material for acceptable conversation. We can see evidence of this emphasis on girls' knowing history in *Mansfield Park,* where the more accomplished and thoroughly annoying Bertram sisters gracelessly complain of their cousin Fanny Price's ignorance. Fanny is ridiculed because, though she is ten years old, she does not yet "repeat the chronological order of the kings of England, with the dates of their accession, and most of the principal events of their reigns" (18).

Austen's early burlesque on history is more than a feminist attack on the way the past is textualized, more than a tribute to the Stuarts, and more than a clever pupil's revenge on schoolroom history. The generic significance of her allusions in the *History* ought to be added to previously mentioned understandings. Brigid Brophy's psychological reading of the *History of England* rightly points out that the text models itself heavily on "gothick novelists." By using a vaguely dated costume-drama historical form, Austen shows that she was "thoroughly conversant with the gothick metaphor" (Brophy 31). Her familiarity with the gothic may seem de rigueur. Gothic novels, with their centuries-old foreign settings, labyrinthine castles, supernatural occurrences, villainous men, and innocent heroines (who were often alone or orphaned), were popular reading material and would become even more fashionable as the 1790s progressed. We might ask, however, what part gothic novels could play in a burlesque of history.

Studying Austen's literary manuscripts, B. C. Southam speculates that her treatment of the duke of Norfolk in the *History* is indebted to *The Recess* and that Delamere's appearance there is drawn from Charlotte Smith's novel *Emmeline* (1788) (Austen, *Volume* 215).[24] Both Lee's and Smith's texts have been referred to in the notes accompanying Austen's *History* by A. S. Byatt, Jan Fergus, and Margaret Doody and Douglas Murray, all of whom find the connections meaningful but do not elaborate on them.[25] Though the allusions to Smith and Lee are only implied, there are direct references to other fictional texts in Austen's *History.* Richard Sheridan's play *The Critic* (1781) and Nicholas Rowe's *The Tragedy of Jane Shore* (1714) secure a mention, as do several of Shakespeare's plays, including *Henry IV, Part 2,* and

Henry V. Austen's allusions are to imaginative literary sources rather than factual historical ones.

From Austen's use of allusions I conclude that she believed history owed its color and life to fictional, imaginative texts, not to supposedly objective, impartial reconstructions of the past. The *History's* pronouncement that it will have "very few dates" is not just Austen's joke (*HE* 1). It is a textual cue taken from Goldsmith, whose history eschewed dates. Austen may use her lack of dates for more than parody. Goldsmith claims in his *History* that filling minds "with little more than dates, names, and events" constitutes "uselessness" (3). He otherwise assumes that his readers must start with the basics. Austen, on the other hand, points out that it would be foolish for her to repeat in her *History* those details that her readers must already know, whether dates, names, events, or anecdotes (*HE* 11–12). Goldsmith assumes he must present certain kinds of historical information to his novice readers, who will not know it. He envisions them as a historical tabula rasa, needing to be filled with historically significant information. Austen's imagined audience (again, likely a family one) is educated, and so her *History,* like her novels, begins in medias res rather than at some imagined origin. Her texts are not aimed at the historically uninformed; she does not instruct beginners. Her *History* deconstructs historical material and then reconstructs it in a fictional mold, claiming with tongue in cheek that truth is "very excusable in an Historian" (27). For Austen, truthfulness ("telling it like it is") requires a skilled author of instructive fiction.

Austen's truths are of a distinctive type. They are present-day truths, as we will also see in *Northanger Abbey.* In his reading of Austen's juvenilia, Marvin Mudrick maintains that "History, for Jane Austen as for most people, is a world not here and now" (25). I am arguing precisely the opposite. In her *History* Austen ties anecdotes to the present, mentioning herself, her neighbors, and other living people (22). The portraits Cassandra provided to accompany the text also depict historical figures in present-day dress and manner.[26] Austen treats historical events as "the occurrences of everyday life" and historical personalities "as if their characters and feelings were fully known" (Southam, *Jane Austen's Literary Manuscripts* 28).[27] She makes the history of England not only a present-day concern but a reflection of the current moment's manners, fashions, and interpretations. Her history is self-conscious about contemporary uses and apprehensions of the past.

Austen's concentration throughout the *History* is on romantic affairs of state rather than the "prominent features of war and turbulence" that Goldsmith sees as constituting history (*History* 403). Austen's choices may be viewed as evidence of a feminist or feminine concern, but we should also entertain the possibility that hers are generic concerns. Kent believes she does not present herself as a rival to historians in the *History* ("Real Solemn History" 94, 102). I believe she was implicitly doing so, not as a historian herself per se but as a substitute historian—a writer of worthy fiction. Novels about war and political turbulence became part of nineteenth-century literary history to an extent undreamed of in the late eighteenth century.[28] Austen, who could not foresee this shift in the content of esteemed novels, may have written her *History* as an indirect plea for the historical value of fiction. Beyond being interested in the relative merits of reading and writing history as a student and reader, she was self-interested as a budding novelist.

Northanger Abbey: Novel Approaches to History

Because her name has long been synonymous with restraint, Austen is rarely thought of as combative; but in *Northanger Abbey,* even more than in the *History of England,* we glimpse her as she engages in written warfare. The stakes were high—success or failure as a writer. Her place in the literary market, and ultimately in the history of letters, was being determined. We can read back from the outcome as she could not.[29] *Northanger Abbey* has gained a reputation as the definitive commentary on the history of late eighteenth-century fiction, as A. Walton Litz maintains (19). Austen's comments go beyond the realm of fiction writing, however. Her first completed novel (and her last published) shows most directly how she understood her fiction's relation to history writing and how she differentiated her work from historical texts.[30] Viewing Austen's struggle in the context of late eighteenth-century genres other than fiction allows us to speculate about why she may have sought distance from them.[31]

The question whether schoolroom history helped to mold sensible and qualified females—implicit in the *History of England*—is taken up directly in *Northanger Abbey.* Though the novel has received more attention as a result of renewed critical interest in gothic and sentimental novels, its place in Austen's oeuvre remains somewhat unstable.[32] In relation to the gothic tradition, *Northanger Abbey* has been extricated from it as parody (M. Williams) and implicated in it as imitator (Wilt).[33] It has been called the "most political of Jane Austen's novels" (Hopkins) as well as the "shortest and lightest" (Anderson) and the "most trivially entertaining" (G. Levine). On the level of character, Catherine Morland has been defined as a self-actualized heroine (Reddy; Morgan) and as a colonized protagonist (Cottom 21), and Henry in turn has been considered a benevolent mentor and a bully. Though these critical debates may tell us more about today's literary criticism than about Austen, there are parallels to be noted between her day and our own. Austen too was involved in labeling and classifying her work as a particular kind of writing—a task that involved differentiating novels like hers from other genres, notably history.

Although *Northanger Abbey* is "structured like a Chinese box of fiction within fictions within fictions," as Laura Mooneyham has described it, the plot is relatively uncomplicated (1). An unremarkable young woman (Catherine Morland) is taken by her chaperones to Bath, where—unknown to her and to the reader—she is mistakenly thought to be an heiress. Her initial circle of acquaintance forms a crucial subplot. The sycophantic Thorpes hinder rather than advance the novel's most significant romance. Catherine meets a rich and eligible man (Henry Tilney) whose father (General Tilney) promotes the match and invites her to stay at their home, Northanger Abbey. When the general finds out that Catherine is of much more modest means than he was led to believe, he rudely sends her away, much to the horror of his son and his amiable daughter (Eleanor Tilney). Eventually all is forgiven, Catherine is deemed morally exemplary, and she and Henry are wed, having secured the blessings of both families. What makes this novel far more entertaining than this sketch might suggest is Catherine's unworthiness as a heroine and her misguided penchant for seeing the world as a gothic novel. As a quixotic woman, Catherine is quaintly lovable like Arabella in Charlotte Lennox's *The Female Quixote* (1752), though she has neither Arabella's panache nor her fortune.[34] The eerie gothic novel that Austen uses as Catherine's false reality is in some ways a more vivid foil than Arabella's chivalric French romances. At issue in both books is what constitutes dangerous reading for young women—and what does not—though Lennox and Austen encountered different contexts for the reception of their fiction.

By the late eighteenth century, the caveat against women's reading fiction—prevalent in earlier decades—had softened. In 1798 Austen did not face the same struggle for legitimacy as did the previous generation of fiction writers, but novels like hers did not yet benefit from high status or stable ground. What a novel should include, how it was to be defined, and how it should be weighed against other kinds of writing were still being negotiated. Austen attempted to convince readers that fiction could be authoritative and educational rather than just trivial, entertaining, or morally dangerous. In *Northanger Abbey* the narrator several times justifies her undertaking— defining the elements of good and bad reading and writing. Austen reveals through this defense that novels were not established to the degree she would have liked. In the end her novels helped change the definition of valuable and educational, as well as "literary" and "historical," writing.

The famous justification of the novel in *Northanger Abbey*'s chapter 5 has been a favorite with critics, and most recognize that "in writing her first novel, Jane Austen was . . . concerned to stake out her literary territory" (Monaghan, *Jane Austen: Structure* 16). Austen's narrator maintains that when any narrator or heroine disparages novels, the authors who express these opinions (and the readers who embrace them) necessarily become ludicrous:

Yes, novels;—for I will not adopt that ungenerous and impolitic custom so common with novel writers, of degrading by their contemptuous censure the very performances, to the number of which they are themselves adding—joining with their greatest enemies in bestowing the harshest epithets on such works, and scarcely ever permitting them to be read by their own heroine, who, if she accidentally take up a novel, is sure to turn over its insipid pages with disgust. Alas, if the heroine of one novel be not patronized by the heroine of another, from whom can she expect protection and regard? I cannot approve of it. Let us leave it to the Reviewers to abuse such effusions of fancy at their leisure, and over every new novel to talk in threadbare strains of the trash with which the press now groans. Let us not desert one another; we are an injured body. Although our productions have afforded more . . . pleasure than those of any other literary corporation in the world, no species of composition has been so much decried. From pride, ignorance, or fashion, our foes are almost as many as our readers. (*Northanger Abbey* [1966] 37) [35]

The amusing passage defending novels also alludes to serious matters, as most readers agree.[36] By calling on her audience to join her in healing the injured and unfashionable body of her text—to take pride in the purveyed intelligence and pleasing form she implies that her novel offers—Austen argues that her book offers readers the same benefits formerly believed to be the provenance of other genres.

When interpreting this passage, some critics have been quick to see the injured body she invokes as an injured female body. They point to a subsequent statement—" 'Oh! it is only a novel!' "—after which the narrator proclaims: " 'It is only Cecilia, or Camilla, or Belinda'; or, in short, only some work in which the greatest powers of the mind are displayed, in which the most thorough knowledge of human nature, the happiest delineation of its varieties, the liveliest effusions of wit and humour are conveyed to the world in the best chosen language" (*NA* 38). With its references to the writings of Frances Burney and Maria Edgeworth, this statement has been used by some to argue that Austen invokes a women's literary tradition, creating a bond with her sister authors. As I have proposed elsewhere, it is also possible that she is using Burney and Edgeworth for her own purposes.[37] Austen's literary "sisters" did not label their productions novels. Edgeworth called *Belinda* (1801) "a moral tale" because she considered novels immoral.[38] Burney insisted that *Camilla* (1796) was a "work" and not a novel. Rather than embracing these female authors as comrades, Austen co-opted them to advance her own classificatory cause. She may not have meant Edgeworth or Burney any harm, but she preferred to forge a literary relation to these authors on her own terms rather than on theirs.

In delineating what reviewers should applaud in novels, Austen's narrator mocks the "abilities of the nine-hundredth abridger of the *History of England*" and "the man who collects and publishes in a volume some dozen lines of Milton, Pope, and Prior with a paper from the Spectator and a chapter from Sterne" (*NA* 37). She sees these miscellanies and abridgments as garnering too much praise and attention. But is this a feminist critique? Margaret Kirkham answers yes, claiming that each of the authors chastised is sexist: "Jane Austen's skepticism about 'History' is a feminist skepticism in which she anticipates a later age. . . . The 'man' of whom she speaks contemptuously is a miscellanist and incurs scorn because he lacks the original creative gifts of the novelist, but his choice of authors also has a feminist point. Milton, Prior, and Pope had all written works to which a feminist might take exception" (69). Kirkham's is a possible reading. Equally convincing to me is the idea that Austen views putting together "elegant extracts" as a worthless, unoriginal act that does not deserve commendation.

After holding the novel above history and poetry (and above collections of excerpts of "great works"), the narrator describes a mock female reader who would not be afraid to show people that she was reading something like the *Spectator*. The narrator concludes that this reader is foolish because the *Spectator* does not show good taste. If we take the narrator's word, the "greatest powers of the mind" and "thorough knowledge of human nature" are no longer to be found in past accounts, like the abridger's or the *Spectator*'s: "the substance of [the *Spectator*'s] papers so often consisting in the statement of improbable circumstances, unnatural characters, and topics of conversation, which no longer concern any one living; and their language, too, frequently so coarse as to give no very favorable idea of the age that could endure it" (*NA* 38). By devaluing the writings and opinions of the past, Austen's narrator claims for the emerging novel the primary connection to current events and opinions—things that concern those "now living." The *Spectator* is faulted because its subject and its diction, its old-fashioned qualities and improprieties, will reflect poorly on the current age. Instead of concentrating on past history, or even on Whig histories illustrating how the present is shaped by lessons learned from the past, *Northanger Abbey* implies that reading present-tense "histories" (in the form of the novel of manners) offers readers the best option.

Northanger Abbey must be viewed within the generic context in which it was written, a task that has proved difficult for critics when dealing with Catherine Morland and her comments on history.[39] The well-meaning Catherine devalues history, but she is shown to be a naive reader. She thinks the world operates in the same manner as her favorite gothic novels, rife with haunted abbeys, suspected murderers, kidnappings and other dark deeds. In addition to being a devotee of gothic novels, Catherine says she hates reading history. She disparages historical writings for their lack of entertainment value, not primarily for their lack of probability or contemporary relevance, though these issues too arise. In chapter 14, when Catherine is on a walk at Beechen Cliff with her soon-to-be-hero Henry Tilney and his sister Eleanor, the conversation turns to the premier gothic novelist, Ann Radcliffe, and her *Mysteries of Udolpho* (1794), which each of them has read and enjoyed. Catherine tells Eleanor that she does "not much like any other" reading than novels, except perhaps poetry, plays, and travels. "History," she says, "real solemn history, I cannot be interested in" (108). "Real solemn history" signifies schoolroom history for Catherine Morland, but Eleanor counters that she enjoys reading history. Catherine launches into an often-quoted critique of that genre: "I read it a little as a duty, but it tells me nothing that does not either vex or weary me. The quarrels of popes and kings, with wars or pestilences, in every page; the men all so good for nothing, and hardly any women at all—it is very tiresome; and yet I think it very odd that it should be so dull, for a great deal of it must be invention . . . [which] is what delights me in other books" (108).

Eleanor responds that she finds history to be good reading and that she believes it is as true or as false as anything that one does not observe oneself. Eleanor likes in history what Catherine does not find there: imaginative speeches, whether they are produced by Hume and Robertson or by Caractacus, Agricola, or Alfred the Great (109). In effect, Eleanor (who has been characterized as better educated and wiser than Catherine) reads history to be entertained by human nature—the things for which novels, and specifically Austen's, would become valued. Even while perusing schoolroom history, Eleanor envisions herself as a reader of what we might call history as fiction, whereas Catherine understands schoolroom history to be the furthest thing from the gothic novels she enjoys reading. I agree with Christopher Kent that Eleanor, rather than Catherine, is the character whose views the novel endorses.[40] Eleanor does not criticize histories or historians. Instead she uses their words on her own terms. She seeks neither dates nor events but insights into the history and character of important personalities. Eleanor reads histories as if they were novels.

The conversation of Catherine, Eleanor, and Henry turns to the role history has traditionally played in educating young people. Catherine responds that she knows only men who read history by choice. She says that she will take Eleanor's example of enjoying history and no longer feel sorry for the writers of it: "If people like to read [histories], it is all very well, but to be at so much trouble in filling great volumes, which, as I used to think, nobody would ever willingly look into . . . always struck me as a hard fate, and though I know it is all very right and necessary, I have often wondered at the person's courage that could sit down on purpose to do it" (109). Catherine does not merely question the historian's "courage," she criticizes the messenger and the message. History is a necessary cultural evil, she implies, but it is so boring that its practitioners deserve pity as much as praise. Henry believes the historian has a higher aim than Catherine assigns him—to instruct and not to torment himself or his readers. At issue is what kind of reading is frivolous and what edifying, as well as what kind is best used to educate the young. Catherine's point is not fully articulated, how-ever, and the conversation moves to matters of taste about which Catherine "had nothing to say" (110). Henry has the upper hand and persuades both women to come around to his point of view (110–11).

After this discussion and another on the picturesque, the conversation devolves once again from a comment that Catherine makes. Catherine has heard that "something very shocking indeed, will soon come out in Lon-don" (112), referring to a gothic novel. Eleanor mistakes her meaning, be-lieving that she describes a "dreadful riot" in the making (112). Henry serves as the all-knowing buffer, clearing up the misunderstanding between the two with his characteristically pompous explanation:

My dear Eleanor, the riot is only in your own brain. . . . Miss Morland has been talking of nothing more dreadful than a new publication which is shortly to come out, in three duodecimo volumes. . . . And you, Miss Morland, my stupid sister has mistaken all your clearest expressions. You talked of expected horrors in London— and instead of instantly conceiving, as any rational creature would have done, that such words could relate only to a circulating library, she immediately pictured to herself a mob of three thousand men assembling in St. George's Fields; the Bank attacked, the Tower threatened, the streets of London flowing with blood. . . . Forgive her stupidity. (113)

This passage has become a favorite with critics of *Northanger Abbey* and history, who have tried to determine which riot Austen alluded to. The anti-Catholic Gordon Riots of 1780, in which there was widespread destruction and three hundred people were killed, have been raised as a possibility, as have subsequent riots in the 1790s in which St. George's Fields was a cen-tral location.[41] The conclusion I draw from this section resembles Nancy Armstrong's: this conversation among Catherine and the Tilneys "takes place against a landscape where fiction displaces history" ("Nineteenth-Century Jane Austen" 235). Armstrong sees *Northanger Abbey*'s displace-ment as a "narrowing down" of history in Austen's writings as a whole, allowing for the achievement of particular political effects (236–37). Her displacement of history also allows for novelistic effects. Beginning with a discussion of novels and moving on to history and the picturesque (land-scape), *Northanger Abbey*'s chapter 14 displaces history twice—once in the form of "real solemn history" and once in the form of "riots"—only to re-turn us on each occasion to the topic of fiction, as well as to the fiction we continue to read, the second half of *Northanger Abbey*.[42]

Austen and "Herstory"

Northanger Abbey makes light of more than gothic conventions. At the least, it makes light of histories too, perhaps going so far as to oppose itself to them.[43] Many have viewed the "novel as opposed to history" maneuver as Austen's attempt to change the status of women in standard historical accounts. Some have cited Catherine's words as meaning that Austen was making a prescient call for "herstory," for historical accounts that—as a corrective—centered on women rather than on men. In such arguments Catherine's pronouncements are taken to be Austen's own. Austen is then congratulated for realizing before her time that women were excluded from histories. To accept such a formulation is to miss a more complex relationship between women and history at work in this novel. Histories by, about, and for women were not unheard of in the decades before Austen wrote these lines, though they by no means dominated the field. Histories of women's history have been neglected, in part as a result of the power of writers like Austen. By the late twentieth century, women's relationship to history in the early modern era was believed to resemble Catherine Morland's picture of it, however ironically Austen may have meant to render it when she wrote *Northanger Abbey*.

Contemporary feminist critics have used Catherine's conclusions about history, fiction, and women toward a variety of ends. Cataloging the uses of Catherine's pronouncements provides a glimpse into how critics in recent decades have appropriated Austen on the subject of history and gender. Educator Lyn Reese begins her Women in the World Curriculum Resources workshops for teachers by citing Catherine as an authority on both history and women. In *The Women's History of the World*, Rosalind Miles uses Austen as an authority to ground her own authorial undertaking, putting Catherine Morland's words directly into Austen's mouth. Miles writes, "As Jane Austen demurely remarked, 'I often think it odd that history should be so dull, for a great deal of it must be invention'" (xii). In a chapter titled "Woman's Work," Miles takes Catherine's "real solemn history" speech as its epigraph (117). David Nokes, in his recent biography of Austen, writes of Catherine Morland's comments on history, "These were Jane's thoughts, too" (124).

Even writers who address a scholarly audience have similarly mischaracterized *Northanger Abbey*. In their far-ranging and useful multivolume study

A History of Women in the West, Georges Duby and Michelle Perrot sum up their introduction with Catherine Morland's words, professing a hope that Jane Austen would find their own efforts less tiresome (ix–xxiii). Duby and Perrot introduce their study with assumptions similar to Catherine's: that history and women were, and had long been, categories that did not overlap. Susan Groag Bell and Karen Offen's collection of eighteenth- and nineteenth-century historical writings, *Women, the Family and Freedom: The Debate in Documents,* on the other hand, takes this section of *Northanger Abbey* for its epigraph, partially to argue against it:

The omission of women from the histories discussed by Jane Austen's characters is misleading. The debate about women was unmistakably present in the dialogues of popes and kings, and in the consideration of wars and natural disasters, even though the chroniclers did not refer to it. Indeed, the "woman's question" may be the most central, yet overlooked, "quarrel" in the political and intellectual history of Western nations. It became an issue precisely because it challenged long-standing ideas of male dominance, which had remained implicit in Western political and social thought—published by men—until the seventeenth century. (1)

Bell and Offen rightly conclude that Catherine's claims about the omission of women from history are misleading because the woman question has received a good deal of unacknowledged historical attention. At the end of this section, however, they claim of their own anthology, "Here, in contrast to the books read by Jane Austen and her contemporaries, women are on every page" (1).[44] Bell and Offen present a contradictory tension: Austen misleads us by suggesting that the woman question was not present in the chronicles of history, but in the case of "the books read by Austen and her contemporaries," women were indeed often absent. This statement takes Catherine Morland at her word once again, mistaking her for an authority on books.

The most extreme—and certainly the most influential—example of Austen as a proponent of "herstory" can be found in Sandra Gilbert and Susan Gubar's *The Madwoman in the Attic* (1979), a one-time Goliath in feminist literary criticism that has been both appreciatively cited and widely criticized in the two decades since its publication. Though Gilbert and Gubar rightly conclude that "Austen attempted through self-imposed novelistic limitations to define a secure place," they make the suspect claim that her writings "imply a criticism, even a rejection, of the world at large" (108). Gilbert and Gubar equate Austen with Catherine, asserting that "both Catherine and Austen realize that history and politics . . . have been completely beyond the reach of women's experience" (134). They believe that Austen shows "sympathy and identification with Catherine Morland's ignorance" (133). Although they recognize that Catherine's views are raised only to be criticized within the novel, Gilbert and Gubar determine that Catherine "is, after all, correct, for the knowledge conferred by historians does seem irrelevant to the private lives of most women" (32). I might add, using this standard, that history is irrelevant to the lives of most men as well.

Gilbert and Gubar make a final, incredible argument about Austen and history that sums up their views: "Ignoring the political and economic activity of men throughout history, Austen implies that history may very well be a uniform drama of masculine posturing that is no less a fiction (and a potentially pernicious one) than gothic romance. She suggests, too, that this fiction of history is finally a matter of indifference to women, who never participate in it and are almost completely absent from its pages" (134). They attribute Austen's supposed motives to feminist anger, commenting that her novel is "not unfittingly pronounced North/Anger" (135). Austen's anger (if it can be so described) may well have been an authorial anger, a generic anger—the anger of a writer who was competing for readers with historical texts—both "real solemn" histories and historical gothic novels. To say that in Austen history is a "matter of indifference to women" is patently untrue.[45] History was of paramount importance to Austen.

Recent feminist scholarship has theorized British women's writings to better effect for at least two reasons. First, an abundance of previously little known and unknown texts have now come to light, and second, theories of women's writing have begun to address historical and cultural differences. In a discussion of women's historical writings, for example, Isobel Grundy alludes to Catherine Morland's characterization of history. Grundy recognizes that Austen's Catherine is not a precocious expert on women and history:

Women's history before the nineteenth century—history written about, or by, or for women—is generally assumed to be non-existent, a classic absence or silence. Examination, however, shows that the presumed absence is merely an absence of what we have mistakenly expected to find. Fully-fledged female writers of mainstream, national political history emerged late: Catherine Macaulay in Britain, 1763, and Mercy Otis Warren in the USA, 1805. The differences of these women from their male peers (though they exist and merit attention) are less immediately striking than their likenesses. Their great works fall under the stricture of Jane Austen's Catherine Morland about history writing. ("Women's History?" 126)

Grundy's reading shows that Catherine is correct in her assumptions not only about histories written by men but about those written by women as well. That Macaulay and Warren produced histories similar to those of their male contemporaries is an accurate but, in some circles, potentially unpopular feminist critical claim. If we agree with Grundy, Catherine not only is disparaging male writers of history, she must necessarily be seen as criticizing women writers too. The fact of women's sometime adherence to the mainstream of historical discourse should give pause to those who posit Austen the herstorian. Perhaps the point is not that Austen's *Northanger Abbey* presents us with a male versus female issue in its comments on history but that it is a matter of stereotypically masculine versus feminine discourses in Austen's time. History was never completely identified as "male" in its production or content, just as novels were not wholly "female." Each, however, had aspects of conventionally perceived femininity and masculinity grafted on to it. In her writing, Austen did not replicate these assumed gender divisions, nor did she seek to overturn them. Instead she attempted to integrate them. She took the "masculine" benefits that were said to accrue to female readers of experiential, true genres (like history) and joined them to the "feminine" novel to create something that was, at least at the moment of its combination, not easily classified in terms of gender.[46]

The strongest argument against viewing *Northanger Abbey* as a call for "herstory" involves a return to the novel's plot. Until the end of the book, when she is lectured by Henry and cured of her gothic predilections, Catherine cannot be mistaken for a trustworthy authority on anything. Chapter 14 also shows that *Northanger Abbey* is not a text that empowers women to make their voices heard. At the end of her critique of history, Catherine is silenced by Henry, and the narrator ironically suggests that the woman unfortunate enough to know anything should "conceal it as well as she can" (111). This sentence puzzles critics, who either take the sentiment at face value and see Austen's conservatism or believe her statement is sarcastic evidence of feminist anger. Whether the narrator's aside is meant to instruct the naive Catherine, the more accomplished Eleanor, or Austen's readers remains unclear. Whether it is meant as a critique of society, of Henry, or of assertive, intelligent women or as another of Austen's trademark ironic asides cannot easily be determined. The novel encourages us to laugh at the characters, at society, and at ourselves. In Austen's fictional world, novels (as opposed to "shaded," dry histories) make us laugh. In addition, novels teach what history cannot—how to function in the present. For Austen, novels offer edifying pleasure without haughty, didactic pain.

Walter Anderson is surely right when he opines that in *Northanger Abbey* "Austen intends her work, through its superiority in reality and substance, to compete with and ultimately to outstrip Gothic Romances," but there were additional competitors to face (495).[47] Austen matched her novel to history as well, when the boundaries of what both genres might be (or become) were shifting. *Northanger Abbey* proposes leaving behind the pedantry of schoolroom history while keeping its supposedly good qualities of probable events and natural behavior. Probability and naturalness were factors considered missing from history as fiction (especially gothic historical fiction), which was put down for its fancifulness. Austen gives her history as fiction a more substantive turn. In taking certain elements from schoolroom history and historical fiction and in making romance probable, she offers a reconciliation in her own writings. *Northanger Abbey* is hardly the only vehicle through which history exits and literature enters as more edifying reading material. Enlisting history as its "secret partner" and thereby "enacting a sophisticated reclassification of itself," as Joseph Litvak puts it, *Northanger Abbey* improves its status ("Charming Men" 255).[48] Austen's novel is an important artifact in valuing novels over histories, complicitous in change that we might now be tempted to see as inevitable.

Austen lived and wrote on the threshold of a new era of and for history. For her, novels and histories were presented as competitors more often than as coconspirators. If we attempt to move beyond Catherine Morland's easy distinction of "male equals history, female equals fancy (or fiction)," we find ourselves in less charted waters. The name "Morland" has offered critics material for interpreting *Northanger Abbey*'s economic meanings, and it offers similar possibilities for understanding generic implications. Morland as a proper noun might signify Catherine as a site through which "more land" will be accrued in the joining of property through marriage, as Maaja Stewart has suggested (16).[49] We might also imagine Austen's era as interested in the lay of the land of newly forming written genres. Austen's building up of novels at the expense of history may be an attempt to acquire "more land" for the burgeoning field of literature.

Austen has a legitimate place in the pantheon of British feminist writers, but she should no longer simplistically prop up arguments about the absence of women in mainstream national histories during the eighteenth and early nineteenth centuries. Catherine's views of history must not be assigned to Austen, and Austen's views of history (as illustrated in *Northanger Abbey*'s chapter 5, in the *History of England,* and in her *Letters*) must continue to be examined in broader generic contexts. Unlike many of her predecessors and contemporaries, male and female, Austen positioned her writings in a way that gave them extraordinary posthumous staying power in literary history. To attribute this fact to the universality of her subject matter or to her literary genius is to ignore her professional savvy and ultimate generic good fortune, as well as to imply that other forgotten writers have deserved the attention they did not (or do not) receive. It is even possible that, rather than standing before us as a founder of herstory, Austen and her writings worked against the larger cultural recognition of the contributions of women to historiography. Austen's nineteenth-century literary success and twentieth-century lionization may have inadvertently propelled forces that prevented women's history and history by women from emerging as a widespread scholarly concern for more than a century and a half after her death. More to her credit, Austen is responsible for attracting many of us to a life of historically focused feminist literary study.

Notes

■

One: Introduction

1. Not all second-wave accounts made such assumptions, though as Mary O'Dowd and Sabine Wichert recently noted, "Some of the published work on women's history which dates from [the 1970s] was imbued with political rhetoric and lacked scholarly detachment and objectivity" (x).

2. In the *Dictionary of Feminist Theory,* "herstory" is defined as "women's history. The theory of, and documentation about, past and contemporary lives, groups, language and experience of women" (Humm 94). Most practitioners now would not equate "herstory" with "women's history," the latter category being more all-encompassing. "Herstory" frequently sought collective female experience that was ignored, suppressed, or downplayed.

3. Gerda Lerner stresses that "women have been left out of history not because of the evil intent of male historians, but because we have considered history only in male-centered terms" (109). I argue that women as a subject (an object?) have not been entirely left out of history and that women historians themselves sometimes wrote history in "male-centered terms," if that means mainstream historiographical forms.

4. On Astell, see Perry, *Celebrated Mary Astell.*

5. In his useful article on women and history writing, D. R. Woolf mentions Cowley but provides no reading of her text beyond noting that "it was intended specifically for women rather than for the reading public at large" (645). Cowley is not included in any of the recent dictionaries of women's writing.

6. Crosby focuses on texts by George Eliot, William Thackeray, Charles Dickens, Wilkie Collins, and Charlotte Brontë, among others.

7. See Todd, *Dictionary;* Schleuter and Schleuter; Blain, Clements, and Grundy; Buck; Shattock; and Horwitz. Anthologies are too numerous to mention, though the best known is Gilbert and Gubar, *Norton Anthology.*

8. Important early studies include Spencer, *Rise;* Spender, *Mothers;* and Todd, *Sign.*

9. For instance, Bridget Hill's important biography of Catharine Macaulay, *The Republican Virago,* the first book-length treatment Macaulay has ever received, did not examine her in the context of other eighteenth-century women contributors to historical discourse. The only other woman historian who is discussed is Macaulay's American correspondent and friend Mercy Otis Warren. See Hill, esp. 125–29.

10. Essays on early American women historians have also appeared. See Messer, Scott, and Sklar.

11. Scholars who have asked about history's gender include Davis, "History's Two Bodies," and Pocock, *Virtue,* esp. 98–100.

12. In the category of what we would now call literature, poetry was by far the most popular genre, accounting for almost half of the publications (Feather, "British Publishing" 42). For an excellent discussion of conditions of authorship for women and of the cultural position of novels, see Fergus, *Jane Austen: A Literary Life* 1–27.

13. Kenyon notes that the first active professor of modern history at Cambridge was William Smyth (1807–49), who lectured almost exclusively from Hume (56). See also Sharpe.

14. Ancient history apparently fared little better at Oxford and Cambridge, where, according to Joseph Levine, the ancient history chairs went "swiftly into a decline that lasted until the nineteenth century" (279) and "neither the ancients nor the moderns won any advantage in the university" (279).

15. On Elstob, see also M. Green; Hughes; and Wallas.

16. Fitzsimons (141) contends that Burnet modeled his history on that of Jacques-Auguste de Thou (1553–1617).

17. Additional writers included in Janet Todd's *A Dictionary of British and American Women Writers, 1660–1800* who deserve consideration for their historical contributions include Jane Barker, Elizabeth Ogilvy Benger, Elizabeth Bentley, Matilda Betham, Margaret Coghlan, Mary Deverell, Susannah Dobson, Anne Dutton, E. M. Foster, Anne Fuller, Mary Ann Hanway, Elizabeth Helme, Anna Maria McKenzie, Anna Riggs Miller, Mary O'Brien, Lucy Peacock, M. Peddle, Mary Pix, R. Roberts, Mary Scott, Marianna Stark, Elizabeth Thomas, Elizabeth Tollett, Elizabeth Sophia Tomlins, and Maria Julia Young.

18. John Essex's 1722 abridgment of Fénelon also quotes this line. Nancy Armstrong brought Fénelon's quotation on history to my attention (*Desire* 104).

19. More than fifty years later, this format remained appealing, though assembled with more sophistication. See W. Butler.

20. Gearhart suggests that history is not a genre but several genres, especially during the Enlightenment (58). Although I agree with the spirit of her remarks, I refer to history as a genre throughout this book.

21. Braudy keeps history and novel in place as discrete eighteenth-century categories, thus separating his work from subsequent studies that acknowledge jockeying and mixing. For Braudy history and literature have individual natures,

and texts have artistic unity that merely reflects an emerging unity of structure (3, 7, 6). It is in this respect that Braudy might be said to illustrate what Lee Patterson calls the remnants of "extrinsic literary historicism" or "old historicism" (258).

22. McKeon's version of generic mixing is worth noting: "Typologies of fiction, romance, history, and novel are posited, take root, sprout subcategories, and quickly send out feelers that intersect with one another whose very existence finally must vitiate the discriminatory function of the original taxonomy. It is easy enough to see why this happens. The common understanding that the novel 'rose' around 1740 provides a terminus ad quem which appears to organize all that follows within the ample boundaries of the great modern form, but which also requires that what precedes this founding act will resemble chaos" (25).

23. Haywood examines the status of what was variously deemed "history" in "fiction"—and vice versa. He focuses on the status of ancient poetry as historical knowledge in order to contextualize the forgeries of Macpherson and Chatterton. In the process, the contingency of history and literature—specifically of fact and fiction—is revealed.

24. I have found Hunter's study very useful, especially his notion that fiction took advantage of "border disputes" of genres in the eighteenth century (343).

25. To give one brief and often-cited example, Clara Reeve's *The Progress of Romance* (1785) connects romance with history and brackets off the novel, concluding that "the effects of Romance, and true History are not very different" (102).

Two: The True and Romantic History of Lucy Hutchinson's *Memoirs of the Life of Colonel Hutchinson*

1. The *Memoirs* was published in an abridged version in Edinburgh in 1825. It was reedited and published in Bohn's Standard Library in 1846. An edition by C. H. Firth was published with modern spellings in 1885. Harold Child's 1904 edition returned to the original spelling, and in 1906 Firth's revised volume published documents relating to the Hutchinsons. Helen Kendrick Hayes edited *Colonel Hutchinson: Roundhead,* yet another edition of the *Memoirs,* in 1909.

2. Green explains that because they lived during revolutions (the English Civil War and the French Revolution, respectively), Hutchinson and Macaulay experienced fertile growing conditions for their historiography. Women write historical texts only when "history" itself (here limited to war) encroaches on their lives, Green maintains. She ignores the fact that Macaulay published historical work long before the French Revolution or the American War of Independence and that Hutchinson too engaged in writing and translating before the Civil War began. On Green, see McDowell.

3. Subsequent references to Hutchinson's *Memoirs* are cited from the 1995 edition, using the abbreviation *MJH*. Other editions are cited as *Memoirs* with the date. For the 1995 edition, N. H. Keeble edited the *Memoirs* from the manuscript, held in the Brewhouse Yard Museum in Nottingham. When the *Memoirs* manu-

script resurfaced in 1922, the manuscript of the autobiographical fragment did not. See Race, "Notes." Although most twentieth-century critics have seen the comparison to Cavendish as detrimental to Hutchinson, Anna Battigelli argues that it "never benefited Cavendish," who is seen as lacking "poise and restraint" (4).

4. Norbrook tentatively attributes a 1679 poem versification of Genesis, *Order and Disorder,* to Hutchinson ("Devine Originall").

5. Robert Mayer's argument that Hutchinson was ignored because of "a difference in early modern and twentieth-century views of the relationship between life writing and history-writing" (76) overlaps with my own, although Mayer does not give particular attention to the gendered aspects of this difference.

6. "Note Book," British Library (hereafter BL), Add. MSS 25,901. This is the text from which *The Norton Anthology of English Literature* draws its excerpt and the text the *Memoirs* appears to be based on. Julius Hutchinson called it a "diary," but as Margaret Bottrall notes, "it was not a record kept while the story was unfolding itself; rather, it was a notebook, fuller in some respects and more particularized, which Mrs. Hutchinson used as a basis for the *Memoirs*" (Hutchinson, *Memoirs* [1968] x). Bottrall writes that no edition has yet appeared that systematically traces the relation between the *Memoirs* in its final form and the draft that preceded it, but it is clear that Hutchinson suppressed several details from the notebook in her *Memoirs,* particularly those that "reflected adversely on her husband" (xii). See also Race, "Colonel Hutchinson: Manuscript."

7. Lucretius, *De rerum natura,* BL, Add. MSS 19,333. For an excellent discussion of this translation, see Barbour. Hugh de Quehen has edited this translation (1996).

8. This translation was viewed by Sydney Race in 1923 when it was in the possession of the Reverend C. A. Hutchinson (Julius Hutchinson's great-grandson). Race describes three volumes of writings by Lucy Hutchinson that he examined:

1. A volume described on the first leaf as "The writings of Lucy Hutchinson," and partly in her own handwriting. It contains some unpublished writings by her on religious subjects, a translation of part of the "Aeneid," and transcriptions of some contemporary poems and ballads.

2. A volume, wholly in Mrs. Hutchinson's handwriting, of theological writings. Some large parts of these are nearly identical with parts of the printed volume, "On the Principles of Christian Religion."

3. A small unbound volume, in the hand of an amanuensis, containing transcriptions of poems by Mrs. Hutchinson, probably made under her supervision. ("Notes" 165)

David Norbrook notes that Hutchinson did not translate Virgil; she merely recopied Denham's and Godolphin's versions. Norbrook worked with these manuscripts, located at the Nottinghamshire Archives since 1953 ("Lucy Hutchinson's 'Elegies' "). As Norbrook reports, Christopher Hill seems to be the only scholar who has quoted from the manuscripts, in his "Colonel John Hutchinson." Hugh De Quehen has discussed Hutchinson's supposed translation of the *Aeneid.* He suggests that "the belief spread by (1891) that Hutchinson herself translated part of the *Aeneid* may well have originated with [the transcripts now at Nottinghamshire], if the attributions at the end were overlooked" (Lucretius 5).

9. Norbrook has edited a manuscript of twenty-four of Lucy Hutchinson's poems, published along with an article ("Lucy"). Before this, only a few of Hutchinson's poems were available in print. See Hutchinson, *Memoirs* (1906) 383–85 and Greer et al. 220–23.

10. If Norbrook is correct that Hutchinson published a poem anonymously in 1679, versions of her as a private author will be easily overturned. See Norbrook, "Devine."

11. Women's writings on the Civil War often found publication years after their authors' deaths: for example, Ann, Lady Fanshawe (published 1829); Anne, Lady Halkett (published 1875); Brilliana, Lady Harley (published 1854); and Alice Thornton (published 1874).

12. Though she cannot be accused of intending to belittle Hutchinson, Joan Thirsk uses Hutchinson as her first example of a female family historian. Thirsk contends that "Hutchinson's contribution [was] to *family* history, even though its main concern was her husband's career during the Civil War" ("Women Local and Family Historians" 498). I do not view Hutchinson's book as merely family history, nor do I think its actual (rather than ostensible) "main concern" can be said to be her husband's career.

13. Norbrook points out, "We do not know nearly enough about Hutchinson's later life to generalize securely about the circulation of her writings, but there is no reason to believe that she saw herself as falling completely silent" ("Lucy" 484). Susan Cook argues that "there was no hope that a Cavalier government would allow the wife of a regicide to print a memoir that might vindicate Colonel John's motives and beliefs" (272).

14. On providence, see K. Thomas 104–12 and Donagan. Donagan states, "Although the belief that God's providential hand guiding the nation did not die at the Restoration, and although trust in providence remained a source of consolation and reassurance, the part allotted to human action was greatly diminished" (443).

15. In her preface to the translation of Lucretius's *De rerum natura,* Hutchinson apologizes both for her choice of subject and for her method. She labels Lucretius "vain philosophy, (which even at the first I did not employ any serious study in for I turned it into English into a room where my children practised the several qualities they were taught with their tutors, and I numbered the syllable of my translation by the threads of the canvase I wrought in, and set them down with a pen and ink that stood by me: how superficially it must needs be done in this matter, the thing itself will show)." BL, Add. MSS 19,333. Her apologies here sound similar to those she makes in the autobiographical fragment about her ability to recite amorous sonnets—a mixture of shame and pride.

16. BL, Add. MSS 19,333.

17. A possible exception to this is Lucy Hutchinson's use in the *Memoirs* of sections of her husband's account of his imprisonment, written while he was in the Tower of London. John Hutchinson published *A Narrative of the Imprisonment and Usage of Col. John Hutchinson of Owthorpe . . . Now Close Prisoner in the Tower. Written by Himself on the 6th of April 1664 . . . for the Satisfying His Relations and Friends of His Innocence* (1664). It is interesting that, among all the speculation that John Hutchinson wrote some or all of the *Memoirs,* there has been no speculation that Lucy Hutchinson had a direct or indirect hand in the composition of this *Narrative.*

18. On May's friendship with Clarendon, see Trevor-Roper 39.

19. Hutchinson's comments on Elizabeth I are reprinted as the sole excerpt from the *Memoirs* in Taylor.

20. Sandra Findley and Elaine Hobby interpret this technique as one that allows Hutchinson to dissociate herself from the proscribed obedient woman by allowing the "I" of the text to stand outside marriage—thus giving us a stance of writerly authority (26). Note, however, that other possibilities may be entertained. The use of "she" is also a way for Hutchinson to attempt to *reinscribe* female (and paradoxically, authorial) silence. Hobby goes some distance toward avoiding this stumbling block. In *Virtue of Necessity,* Hobby labels Hutchinson's two "selves" a dutiful wife who is pleased to be so and an "I" who is the author and creating artist outside the relationship (79). Hobby's thesis of the split self (one who creates a self-fashioned "virtue" from a socially given "necessity") is valuable, but Hutchinson's text seems to present something more than merely a double—more than an I/she split of a guilt-ridden or subversive author.

21. Not all critics have agreed. For example, Dale Spender discusses the "distance" of Hutchinson's "third-person narration" as strategy: "Lucy Hutchinson . . . wrote in the third person. Whether this was because she believed then, as so many academics do now, that the use of the third person automatically makes an account more truthful and magically removes the 'personal' and subjective, or whether she wanted to conceal her identity, one can only guess. But she certainly made use of the convention of removing her 'self' from the record and this practice persists in many forms to the present day, justified on the very spurious grounds that it permits disinterest and promotes authenticity" (*Mothers* 32). Spender's reading fails to take into account that Hutchinson's writings are not entirely in the "academic" third person as well as discounting the fact that the regular use of "I" and "we" must complicate the possibility of concealing her identity.

22. For a savvy account of Lucy Hutchinson's authorial contradictions, see N. H. Keeble, "Colonel's Shadow."

23. About this section of the *Memoirs* Antonia Fraser concludes, "It was a romance stirred not by a pair of gloves, a favour or a fan, but by a shelf of books in the Latin language" (*Weaker Vessel* 136). Again, this points up the ways Hutchinson has indeed written something akin to "romance" (at least for contemporary readers) despite her protestations to the contrary.

24. Other editions have rendered "honour" as "humor." See Hutchinson, *Memoirs* (1973) 239–40.

25. This letter (dated 5 June 1660) is in the Public Record Office, cataloged as an example of Lucy Hutchinson's handwriting. In the letter, "John" Hutchinson petitions: "I cannot but beg the honorable House would not exclude me from the refuge of the Kings most gratious pardon, and pluck me from the horns of that sacred altar, to become his sacrifice who if thus escape being made a burnt offering, I shall make all my life, all my children, & all my enjoyments, a perpetuall dedication to his M^ties service, bewailing much more my incapacitie of rendring it, so as I might else have done, then any other wretched selfe my most deplorable crime hath brought upon me in whom life will but lengthen an insupportable afliction, that to the grave will accompany, Your most obidient and most humble servant" (PRO/SP 29 3).

26. According to Margaret Bottrall, John Hutchinson's involvement in his wife's "forgery" was more complicated: "He may indeed have regretted his wife's intervention, but he did not repudiate the letter. . . . Far from disowning this appeal, Colonel Hutchinson followed it up with a petition to the House of Lords, dated some six weeks after the Commons had acceded to his request for liberty" (Hutchinson, *Memoirs* [1968] xi). Bottrall notes that both letters are reprinted in Firth's 1906 edition of the *Memoirs*.

27. Cook notes that the *Memoirs* has "no single characteristic style. It is at the same time a virtual hagiography, military and political history, and theological comment" (272) as well as a romance. Cook argues that Hutchinson had to "create a style peculiar to the situation, which allows her to repaint the ideals of heroism in terms of republican and Puritan values" (274).

28. On women of the Civil War, see also Plowden.

29. Hobman concludes, "The political sections of the book are occasionally involved and long drawn out, but there are times when Lucy Hutchinson can rise to the heights of literary style. . . . The Memoirs of Colonel Hutchinson should not be allowed to fall into neglect, for the sake of the book's literary and historical value, but above all because of the living portrait which, perhaps unconsciously, it has preserved of the best type of humane, cultivated and Liberal-minded English gentlewoman" (118).

30. Compare this with Myra Reynolds, who writes that Lucy Hutchinson "wields a pen vigorous, racy, and unafraid. She had a genius for picturesque characterization, and her scornful descriptions of cowards and traitors are veiled by no feminine softness of phrase" (73).

31. BL, Ashley 4780, 155. On visual imagery in Hutchinson's writings, see Norbrook, "Lucy."

32. This section is in keeping with Nancy Armstrong's often-cited argument about how the formation of modern subjectivity first found expression in discourses about women in conduct books and novels (*Desire;* "Gender Bind").

33. Lest we think such rhetoric has left the critical scene, a look at Mar-

garet George's chapter "Lucy Hutchinson, Keynote Speaker" proves otherwise. Hutchinson is held up as authorial paradigm and womanly paragon: "Mrs. Hutchinson had no way of knowing how many other women sat in their closets writing secret memoirs and diaries. Nor do we. How many in this England of four or five million souls? One thousand? One hundred? Twenty? But it is safe to say that Lucy Hutchinson was very special, and that she knew she was special and took pride in it" (16). Despite the pervasiveness of notions such as George's, recent research debunks these authorial myths. Patricia Crawford's study of known seventeenth-century women writers names 300 women writers and over 800 first editions. Hilda Smith and Susan Cardinale's bibliography of seventeenth-century women's writings counts 637 texts by women. It is not difficult to imagine how speculations such as George's have taken hold as "fact" when, as Margaret Ezell shows, the prevailing idea of second-wave feminist literary critics and historians has been that women authors before 1800 were rare and eccentric (*Writing* 39–65).

34. The entry on Hutchinson is adapted from Sarah Hale's longer work *Woman's Record* (1853).

35. References to these works can be found in Race, "Notes" 166. Making a literary figure out of Hutchinson's character continues today, though on a smaller scale. For instance, Antonia Fraser dubs Lucy Hutchinson "one of the most attractive of the gallery of seventeenth-century women," concluding, "Although she sprang into print in order to write a justificatory memoir of the husband she adored, . . . it is the witty independent, ever courageous character of Lucy which animates the text, rather than that of the Puritan John Hutchinson" (135). Compare this with Keeble, who maintains, "Colonel Hutchinson is, then, the unchallenged protagonist of the *Memoirs*" ("Colonel's Shadow" 231). See also George, who concludes: "But once more, or finally, it is *Mrs.* Hutchinson, the matchless model of the married lady, who should be kept in mind. So above the pitch of ordinary women she is no 'typical' reference point of the bourgeois wife. Rather, she was the *best*" (*Women* 32).

36. After the Restoration, Zillah gives up her Puritan doctrine and returns to England as Hastings's wife.

37. This connection has its basis in the *Memoirs,* where Lucy Hutchinson acts as a surgeon and physician to the wounded soldiers of both sides. The governor's wife "dressed all their wounds (whereof some were dangerous, being all shots) with such good success that they were all well cured in convenient time" (*MJH* 129). After their own men's wounds were dressed, Lucy Hutchinson bound up and dressed the wounds of the prisoners and replied that "she had done nothing but what she thought was her duty in humanity to them, as fellow-creatures, not as enemies" (129). Many have speculated that she learned these skills from her mother, Lucy St. John Apsley, who cared for sick prisoners (13). Apsley is also said to have assisted Sir Walter Raleigh with his experiments while he was a prisoner in the Tower, where he also wrote his *History of the World.* Raleigh and Hutchinson

share the philosophy that history should teach by example and exhibit the divine plan of providence.

38. Bromley purchased the Hutchinsons' estate at Owthorpe in the nineteenth century. According to Lina Chaworth Musters, the Bromleys removed the picture of Mrs. Hutchinson to Stoke, where they also kept the relics of Prince Rupert, one of their distant ancestors (383). On the authenticity of these images, see Race, "Notes," and Race, "Colonel Hutchinson, the Regicide."

39. According to Keeble, this is akin to what Hutchinson herself does in the *Memoirs:* "Lucy Hutchinson has stolen the Royalists' clothes: John Hutchinson excels in precisely those accomplishments upon which Royalists prided themselves, which, indeed, they supposed distinguished their Cavalier culture from the vulgarity of all rebels and fanatics" (*MJH* xxii).

40. Anecdotes about Hutchinson's children are not central features of her own writings or of the fictional representations of her. She had eight children: Thomas, Edward, Lucius, John, Barbara, Lucy, Margaret, and Adeliza. See Race, "Colonel Hutchinson, Governor" 39.

41. Another connection the Hutchinsons had was to the earl of Rochester's family. Anne Wilmot (second wife of the first earl and mother of the poet, John) was a cousin of Lucy Hutchinson (*MJH* 372 n. 317). On Hutchinson and Rochester, see Norbrook, "Lucy" 484–85. See also De Quehen's translation of Lucretius. De Quehen notes that Lucy Hutchinson and John Wilmot dined with Anglesey on 2 September 1676 (Lucretius 12).

42. Hutchinson's writings cannot easily be called "herstorical" or feminist. Royce MacGillivray states that Hutchinson was "very far from being a feminist and expresses her views very strongly on the due subordination and the inferiority of women to the stronger sex" (*Restoration* 174). On ambiguous understandings of female subordination in Puritan circles, see M. Todd 96–117.

43. After a fine discussion of the ambiguities of genre in Hutchinson's work, Susan Cook makes the case for the *Memoirs* as a protonovel: "Her very subjectivity, while perhaps detracting from the value of the *Memoirs* as a factual document (though on the whole its history is accurate) looks towards the development of the novel, which demands a presentation of a story to an audience, and the communication of one continuum to another" (276). For a more traditional account of the role of Puritan literature in the development of the novel, see Kettle.

Three: Lady Mary Wortley Montagu

1. Though Srinivas Aravamudan makes a compelling case for retitling this work *Letters from the Levant during the Embassy to Constantinople, 1716–18,* following the lead of an 1838 editor, I retain the more widely recognized title "Turkish Embassy Letters." See Aravamudan, "Lady Mary" 69 and Montagu, *Letters* (1838). See also Aravamudan's 1999 book *Tropicopolitans.*

2. I agree with Isobel Grundy in referring to Lady Mary Wortley Montagu

by name. As Grundy notes, "The socially correct 'Lady Mary' sounds right to eighteenth-century scholars, but to others it may sound either over-familiar or obsequious" (Montagu, *Essays and Poems* vi; subsequent references are cited parenthetically in the text as *EP&S*). Grundy addresses this problem by "according to context, using generally 'Lady Mary' for the woman and 'Montagu' for the author" (*EP&S* vi). I have followed the same principle in referring to Lady Louisa Stuart as either Lady Louisa or Stuart, depending on the context.

3. For a history and interpretation of Stuart's anecdotes and the supplement, see Rubenstein, "Women's Biography." For Lady Louisa's stance on women authors and publication, see Rubenstein, "Familiar Letter." See also Stuart, *Letters*. Lady Mary, according to Isobel Grundy, "pitied her cousin Sarah Fielding for the financial need which drove her to publish." As Grundy concludes, however, "modern readers may be inclined to regret the material comfort which preserved Montagu from any such need." The same may be said for Lady Louisa. See Montagu, *Romance Writings*. Subsequent references are cited parenthetically in the text as *RW*.

4. Halsband and Grundy published an edited version of the "Biographical Anecdotes." For the complete text, see "Biographical Anecdotes of Lady M. W. Montagu" (Montagu, *Letters and Works* [1837]).

5. Montagu, *Complete Letters of Lady Mary Wortley Montagu* 3: 18. Subsequent references are cited parenthetically in the text as *CL*.

6. Note that though she did not write anything that survives on Augustus Caesar, Lady Mary did compose "Caesar," a dramatic monologue in which Brutus justifies his conspiring against Julius Caesar (*EP&S* 150–53).

7. In his study of Lady Mary, Walter Bagehot mentions her and Lucy Hutchinson together, though more for their historical connections than for their historiographical ones. As Bagehot notes, Hutchinson's *Memoirs* "contains a curious panegyric on *wise William* Pierrepont," who was Lady Mary's great-grandfather (2: 222). Bagehot's essay was first published in 1862. In *MJH*, many other members of the Pierrepont family are mentioned.

8. On *The Nonsense of Common-Sense*, see *EP&S* 105–49. The periodical was also reprinted by AMS Press in 1970. This edition was originally published in 1947 by Northwestern University Press and includes an introduction by Halsband. For criticism of Montagu's periodical, see Sherman and Campbell. On Lady Mary's response to works published under her name, see Grundy, "Politics."

9. On Lady Mary's relationship with Pope, see Halsband, *Life* 113–14, 131–32, 135–37; Spacks, "Imaginations"; Rumbold 131–50; Wall; and Lowenthal, *Lady Mary* 52–79. For an earlier essay on Lady Mary and Pope, see Tillotson. As Dervla Murphy has put it, "Pope's enraged sneering stained Lady Mary's reputation during her lifetime and has proved an indelible dye" (Montagu, *Embassy* 22).

10. Montagu's penchant for masquerade has been more frequently seen as involving gender. As Isobel Grundy writes, Montagu "is fond of masquerading as her Other. . . . She crosses and re-crosses gender barriers at a bound" (*EP&S* xiv).

11. The circumstances of the publication of the 1803 edition may have in-

cluded something akin to blackmail by the publisher Richard Phillips, who returned to Lady Bute's eldest son some of Lady Mary's letters that had come into his hands in return for permission to publish an edition of other (more decorous) letters. See Halsband, *Life* 289–90. According to Halsband, the "Account of the Court of George I" was first printed in 1837 and first edited in his own edition. See *EP&S* 4.

12. Croker's review puts it even more baldly. He writes, "The lady deals in personal, the gentleman in political, scandal" (174). He concludes that "Lady Mary's sketches are more general and more satirical. Her *Account* is really a curious piece of court gossip, worthy to stand by the side of Horace Walpole's sprightly, but very inaccurate, *Reminiscences*" (175–76).

13. Jill Rubenstein calls Lady Louisa "Tory to the bone, never having forgiven the pain inflicted on her father by the scurrilous personal attacks of Wilkes and others." Rubenstein likens Lady Louisa's Tory politics to those of her friend Sir Walter Scott, "a principled and consistent conservatism" ("Giving" 232).

14. Halsband cites Eduard Vehse in *Geschichte der deutschen Höfe seit der Reformation* (vol. 18, 1853) and Wolfgang Michael in the first volume of *Englische Geschichte im achzehnten Jahrhundert* (1837) (*EP&S* 82). Grundy, in her recent biography of Montagu, opines that "historians are becoming less sure" of Montagu's interpretations of George I (*Lady Mary Wortley Montagu* 83), though the "Account" "sparkles with cynical wit and trenchant analysis of personal power-relations" (529). Grundy also discusses Edward Wortley Montagu's account (112–13).

15. Some scholars of the "Account" confirm Hatton's fears. Dervla Murphy writes that Montagu's "long, lovely and perceptive essay on George I's court is now regarded as a valuable historical document" and was part of the "idiosyncratic history of her own time" (Montagu, *Embassy* 37). In her biography of George I, Joyce Marlow quotes amply from Montagu's "Account," noting that Montagu's "thumbnail sketches of many of her contemporaries . . . make witty reading even today." John M. Beattie draws on Montagu's "Account" for information while simultaneously labeling her malicious and ill informed.

16. There is no consensus today on when the "Account" was written or whether it may have been a part of Montagu's "History." In 1960 Robert Halsband echoed Stuart, arguing that the "Account" was a fragment of the "History" that "escaped the flames" (*Life* 272). By 1977 Halsband has qualified his earlier surmise, stating that "it is tempting to see [the 'Account'] as a fragment of what she called 'the History of my own time,' " but he agrees more with Croker, who believed Montagu's "Account" was probably written early in the reign of George I (*EP&S* 82; Croker 181). Halsband, following Croker, thinks that internal evidence points to a composition date of 1715. Halsband concludes, "Lady Mary would have been a remarkably disciplined artist to have written in 1752 a memoir which so rigorously excludes anything that happened after 1715," though "if true that she wrote the Account in 1715 it is also remarkable that in the brief span of a few months she should have been able to compose a memoir so brilliant and incisive" (*EP&S* 82). Lady

Mary may have written this piece in much the same way the "Turkish Embassy Letters" appear to have been composed and revised—using material drawn from her "voluminous" journal.

17. On Montagu and fiction, see also Grundy "Trash."

18. The memoir describes Lady Mary's being swindled by Count Palazzi. Montagu, according to Grundy, is "regularly made the scapegoat for her own plight" in "circumstances worthy of a Gothic novel" (335). Furthermore, "Lady Mary wrote the Italian Memoir in a dearth of generic models. . . . It is remarkable, however, how many parallels exist between the Memoir and works of fiction, mostly by women, mostly as yet unwritten" (343). Grundy compares Montagu's efforts to those of Burney and Radcliffe. Elsewhere she notes that Montagu's memoir is "curiously drained of affect" (*RW* xix).

19. Rumors circulated in 1755 that called Princess Augusta's virtue into question; the man named as her lover was Lady Bute's husband, as Grundy notes (*RW* xv–xvi).

20. Soon after Montagu wrote Louisa's tale, Charlotte Lennox translated into English La Beaumelle's *Memoirs for the History of Madame de Maintenon and of the Last Age,* although Madame de Maintenon was a notorious and well-known historical figure in Great Britain long before. Isobel Grundy speculates that "Louisa" was written either between 1742 and 1746 or, more likely, from 1746 to 1756 (*RW* xix).

21. On Montagu's feminism, see also Halsband, "Condemned," and Benkovitz.

22. In a chapter titled "The Rebel," Alice Hufstader claims that Montagu "had far more in common with the feminists of today and yesterday than had her gentler successors. It was to remain her cast-iron conviction that life is a bad bargain, and that women have the worst of it" (7). About Montagu's trip to Turkey, Hufstader writes, "Here, as in her campaign for women's intellectual integrity, Lady Mary was in advance of her time. . . . In her letters from the East, Lady Mary suspended the sarcasm with which she so expertly satirized Western society. As she approached the Ottoman frontier, she addressed herself without mockery to an unknown culture. . . . It is this tone of sincere inquiry that sets apart her Embassy Letters from her familiarity-breeds-contempt vignettes of London, and makes them more, or less, favored depending upon their readers' tastes" (33, 40).

23. Elsewhere Rogers asserts that Montagu's "insistence on the happy liberty of Mohammedan Turkish women functions as a wicked comment on the Englishman's complacent assumption that England was 'the paradise of wives'; but it is upsetting to note that she defined woman's liberty in terms of spending money and carrying on adulterous affairs with impunity. She had radical ideas about women, but evidently felt the need to camouflage them" (*Before Their Time* x). For Rogers, Montagu's "feminism is typically veiled in apology or flippancy," and "Montagu prided herself on being a properly conducted aristocrat and a tough-minded ratio-

nalist, and she ruthlessly suppressed feminist feelings that seemed to conflict with these ideals" (*Feminism* 93).

24. On Astell and Montagu, see Perry, "Two." On Astell, see Perry, *Celebrated Mary Astell.*

25. Some see the issue as competing discourses *within* Montagu's own work and social milieu, rather than as Montagu's misplaced application of the European romantic model onto her Turkish situation. Lisa Lowe, for instance, finds dual tendencies in Montagu's work, which she calls a rhetoric of identification and a rhetoric of differentiation with Turkish women. The rhetoric of identification is "an emergent feminist discourse" that speaks of common experiences among women of different societies; the rhetoric of differentiation follows in the tradition of Orientalism that Said has outlined—one of "othering" (32). Lowe's remarks provide a corrective to those who would simplistically hold up Montagu as a feminist heroine: "Montagu's idealization of the liberty of Turkish women, however, which targets and challenges the male orientalist attack on European women, must also be scrutinized for its bias; her claim that Turkish women are 'the only free people in the Empire' misrepresents and appropriates Turkish female experience for the purpose of defending English feminism" (44).

26. See Said, *Orientalism,* and Said, "Orientalism." Said does not mention Montagu. Joseph Lew's article on Montagu and Orientalism "examine[s] how, in the Letters Written during Mr. Wortley's Embassy, Lady Mary drew upon, yet characteristically and self-consciously distanced herself from, an already flourishing Orientalist discourse" (432). Lew's project is like Lowe's in that both want to show that Orientalisms do not hold as the monoliths Said makes them out to be. Lew reinstitutes another kind of monolith: women's discourse. Lew discusses Western perceptions of Muslim veiling practices. He points to the work of Abu-Lughod and Mernissi, to which also might be added that of Ahmed; F. Davis; Keddie and Baron; Mabro; Melman, *Women's Orients;* and Yegenoglu, among others.

27. On Montagu's (and Augustan) attitudes toward issues of race, see MacKinnon.

28. Montagu's "going native" and dressing according to Turkish fashion is well documented. Halsband reports that she kept her Turkish costumes and that Alexander Pope commissioned Godfrey Kneller to paint her in Turkish dress in 1720 (*Life* 88, 98–99). While in Turkey, Montagu went out veiled, and she delivered her daughter in accordance with Turkish childbearing practices.

29. It is interesting to juxtapose Montagu's utopian commentary on Turkish women's freedom with that of a contemporary Turkish man visiting Europe for the first time. Mehmed Efendi, the first Ottoman ambassador to Paris, had this to say about French women in 1719: "In France, esteem for women prevails among men. The women can do what they want and go where they desire. To the lowest, the best gentleman would show more regard and respect than necessary. In these lands, women's commands are enforced. So much so that France is the paradise of

women. They have no hardships or troubles at all—it is said that they obtain their wishes and desires without any resistance whatsoever" (qtd. in Gocek 45).

30. See Hamalian, where this is the lead-off letter in a selection of six from Montagu.

31. On the difference in connotation of the Italianate *bagnio* and its synonymous *hammam* (or public bath), see Melman, *Women's Orients* 88–90. Melman notes that the word *bagnio* was also used to designate a brothel and that "the women's public-baths were identified as the loci sensuales in the erotically charged landscape of the Orient" (89).

32. On Oriental painting, aestheticism, and Montagu, see Bohls, Pointon, and Yeazell. On female homoeroticism in Montagu's "Turkish Embassy Letters," see Nussbaum, *Torrid Zones*. On cultural relativism or hybridity, see Aravamudan.

33. Nochlin focuses on several painters to make her argument, finding that Jean-Léon Gérôme's 1860 works (for instance, *Snake Charmer*) illustrate "that this Oriental world is a world without change, a world of timeless atemporal customs and rituals, untouched by the historical processes that were . . . drastically altering Western society at the time" (35–36).

34. It must further be remarked that the date on this particular letter, 1 April, seems as mysterious as its unnamed addressee, Lady ——. There are nine "Turkish Embassy Letters" dated 1 April 1717. In a surviving "Heads of Letters" briefly describing contents of her missives, dated 1 April 1717 (*CL* 344–45), Montagu lists seventeen letters to various correspondents.

35. Mary Jo Kietzman maintains that "Turkey, as a space 'beyond' Montagu's culture of origin, is not a static concept for her" (549). I argue the opposite, at least as far as Montagu's depictions of Turkish women are concerned.

36. Even Lady Mary's status as a maker of history in introducing smallpox inoculation to England has been called into question. Genevieve Miller contends that accepting Lady Mary as the introducer of smallpox inoculation "is analogous to believing literally that George Washington was the father of our country. In fact Washington probably played more of an important role in founding the United States than Lady Mary did in bringing inoculation 'into fashion' in England, as she expressed it" (3). Lady Mary's place in scientific history is also discussed in Alic 88–92.

Four: Charlotte Lennox and the Study and Use of History

1. In her poem "To Delia," included in the text of her first novel, Lennox writes: "Beneath a cypress' spreading shade / . . . / Repeating Pope's harmonious lays: / Now Homer's awful leaves turn o'er, / Or graver history explore; / Or study Plato's sacred page, / Uncommon to our sex and age." See Lennox, *Life* 266.

2. Critical work on Lennox took on new life in the 1960s with the important discovery of fifty letters to and from Lennox (painstakingly annotated by Duncan Isles). See Isles, "Lennox Collection." The letters were first summarized and

discussed in Isles, "Unpublished Johnson Letters." After Isles's work came the detailed study of Lennox's American connections by Philippe Séjourné. His study, originally a Sorbonne dissertation, remains the most reliable source of information about Lennox in America.

3. The genre of history in Lennox's *Female Quixote* is given some treatment in essays by Dorn; Gallagher; Motooka, "Coming"; and Spencer, "Not Being."

4. See also Gustavus Maynadier's earlier and more speculative study of Lennox's American connections. For recent work on Lennox's transatlantic fiction, see Ellison and Berg.

5. For a review more skeptical of Séjourné's arguments, see Cowie.

6. As Goldgar illustrates, the relative value placed on different kinds of history (e.g., Whig versus Tory, distanced versus eyewitness) may have played a part in the creation and classification of fiction by Fielding and others. On the subject of Fielding and history, see also Braudy and Burke.

7. Spencer's discussion, an important starting point on Lennox and history, does not aim to be exhaustive on the subject; *The Female Quixote* is one of three texts Spencer touches on in her essay "Not Being a Historian." See also Catherine Gallagher's more detailed discussion of fiction, romance, and history in *The Female Quixote.*

8. Judith Dorn has made a similar point, that "in exalting women's positions as readers of events, however, Lennox replicated the contemporary use of women as perceivers rather than as subjects of history" (8). Ultimately, Dorn has more faith than I do in a feminist Lennox.

9. For Elizabeth Bergen Brophy, Lennox typifies conservatism, "advocating quiet diffidence"; Lennox "does not radically challenge the standards of her age, but she does realistically show the strains this model could produce" (250–51). The tendency to find conservatism or realism in Lennox's work has been countered by attempts to locate subversive potential. Margaret Doody sees Lennox as a "solitary dissenter" whose *Female Quixote* is "covertly polemical beneath its facade of compliance and conformity" (307). Katherine Sobba Green believes that within *The Female Quixote,* though we cannot say that "feminism successfully routs patriarchy," Lennox "seeks rather to demystify marriage" (50–51). Regina Barreca claims that Lennox saw Arabella's "cure" as a demise and reads the climax as Arabella's ironic dwindling into a wife, a "double-voiced" subversive ending (47, 60). Kate Levin gives a more convincing combinatory view, proposing that Lennox "suffered from flouting the social consensus" and that she "became a 'woman writer' according to her society's specifications" in order to achieve professional success (278). Joseph Bartolomeo more accurately, to my mind, sees Arabella as an "icon of both morality and feminism" (171). Thus he views Lennox as neither "progressive" nor "conservative" in terms of her gender politics throughout her life but as negotiating the pulls and consequences of competing ideologies.

10. On Lennox's plays, see Small 164–83 and Cave. Lennox's dramatic works deserve more sophisticated critical treatment.

11. On the speculation that Lennox was not liked by women, though a favorite with men, I agree with Dale Spender: "There is constant intimation that Charlotte Lennox was disliked by her own sex. I do not know if this is true. I do wonder if it is relevant" (*Mothers* 198).

12. *The History of Eliza* (1766) has been tentatively attributed to Lennox by Isles, "Lennox Collection" (1970–71), based on the proposals for publishing her *Works,* never printed.

13. On Lennox's eleven numbers of the periodical the *Lady's Museum* in 1760–61, see Dorn. Lennox's short-lived periodical was the "last magazine for women conducted by an author of talent or reputation until the nineteenth century" (Mayo 292).

14. On Lennox and Johnson's collaboration on translation, see Gray.

15. On Johnson and history, see Vance; Brownley, "Samuel Johnson and the Writing"; and Davies. Johnson and Lennox appear to share some beliefs on history, just as they shared some beliefs about fiction.

16. William Strahan printed *The Age of Lewis XIV* for Robert Dodsley in July 1752. *The Female Quixote* was published by Andrew Millar (printed by Richardson) in March 1752. A second edition was published in July 1752 (Richardson and Strahan each printed one volume) (Isles, "Lennox Collection" [1970] 342–43).

17. Several essays have appeared on Lennox's translations. Vogler discusses the multiple sources she drew on and their literary historical reception in her translation of the *Memoirs of the Countess of Berci* (1756). Lennox's *Memoirs of the Duke of Sully* (1751), which went through more than a dozen editions, has been discussed most often in the context of copyright law (Gallagher, *Nobody's Story* 199; Isles, "Lennox Collection" [1971] 178). Lennox also translated the aforementioned *Age of Lewis XIV* (1752) and the *Memoirs for the History of Madame de Maintenon and of the Last Age* (1757). The latter was reviewed by Oliver Goldsmith as an "amphibious production" of history and romance (*Miscellaneous Works* 3: 466). Goldsmith's review was originally published in the *Monthly Review* 17 (1757): 80–81. With the help of Johnson, the earl of Orrery, and acknowledged others, Lennox translated *The Greek Theatre of Father Brumoy* (1759).

18. That work, begun just after *The Female Quixote,* was made possible by the lessons in Italian she received from Giuseppe Barretti in return for tutoring him (apparently with little skill) in English (Small 16).

19. For a sketchy and not entirely reliable summary of *Shakespear Illustrated,* see Ralli 26–32. Lennox's position on Shakespeare might have been positively received earlier in the eighteenth century, but it was not a study that would be popular by the nineteenth, as many have remarked. On *Shakespear Illustrated* and gender, see Doody and S. Green.

20. Critics have not reached consensus on *The Female Quixote*'s quality. As early as 1810, Anna Laetitia Barbauld found the plot "spun out too much." Some contemporary critics have agreed, finding "certain defects in the writing" and believing, as Sandra Shulman does, that Lennox could have learned from contempo-

rary romance novelists "their economy of style and the tight plotting that necessitates" (Lennox, *Female Quixote* [1986] xiii). Others have considered the novel well crafted and thought Lennox's style "satirically comical and her structure distinctly clever" (Spender, *Mothers* 201). Critics have long agreed that *The Female Quixote* is Lennox's best work (MacCarthy, *Female Pen* 293–304).

21. On the "mysteries" of Lennox's life (many of them seemingly self-created), see Isles, "Lennox Collection" (1970–71); Séjourné; Small; and Beasley.

22. For information on Don Quixote–inspired and female quixote–inspired novels, see Small 64–117. See also Staves, "Don Quixote"; Hoople; and Sloman. On *Don Quixote* and history, see Wardropper. Bruce Wardropper claims that Cervantes' "chief butt was man's gullibility . . . about alleged historical facts. But . . . he chose to satirize human credulity in a dangerous way: by encouraging, by seeking to some extent to cultivate, in his reader the very defect he was ridiculing" (10). On Don Quixote and quixotism in the British tradition see Motooka; Reed; and Paulson, *Don Quixote.*

23. Katherine Sobba Green adds the following novels to the list of Lennox-inspired productions: Frances Burney's *Camilla,* Mary Wollstonecraft's *Mary,* Maria Edgeworth's *Belinda,* and Eaton Stannard Barnett's *The Heroine* (47).

24. For Lennox's surviving correspondence with Johnson and Richardson on the subject of her novel, see Isles, "Lennox Collection" (1970). See also Walker. On the influence of Johnson and Richardson on *The Female Quixote,* see Spacks, *Desire and Truth;* Isles, "Johnson, Richardson"; and Marshall.

25. Subsequent references are cited parenthetically in the text as *FQ* and refer to the 1989 Oxford University Press edition edited by Margaret Dalziel.

26. In addition to aforementioned work, see Gardiner; Gordon; Langbauer; Lynch; Malina; Ross; Rothstein, "Woman"; Roulston; H. Thomson; and Warren.

27. If the amount of literary criticism produced is any indication, contemporary readers suffer from the same reluctance. There is a dearth of criticism in English on French romances and their relation to British literature. See Haviland and H. Hill. On Scudéry, see Donawerth and McDougall.

28. On Bellmour's use of romance and its lack of integrity, see Gardiner.

29. Ronald Paulson notes that *Don Quixote* "served as a vehicle for both sides in the epistemological controversy known as the Battle of the Ancients and the Moderns" (*Don Quixote* xii).

30. Subsequent references are cited parenthetically in the text as *MC.* David Marshall has also discussed the influence of *Mock-Clelia* on *The Female Quixote* (122–27).

31. On probability, see Patey.

32. Kate Levin concludes: "Lennox thus created the perfect marketing strategy. She made reading, and reading her, not only permissible but necessary to female readers. Only her novels could teach them to 'regulate' rather than 'suppress,' 'restrain' rather than 'subdue.' . . . she constructed herself as the indispensable cure for what ailed her female readers" (285). Susan Auty believes that in *The*

Female Quixote the novel is raised above the "historically interesting" to show the complexity of human nature (78). Relatedly, Catherine Gallagher writes that *The Female Quixote* "pretends to explore the history of fiction, thereby implying that fiction had been around for centuries, just waiting to be recognized" (179–80). What I add to these accounts is the way history was used within *The Female Quixote* to play a role in this "marketing strategy," as a partner to novels rather than just a foil or a competitor.

33. Joseph Bartolomeo has also connected this passage to Lennox's novel (170).

34. On this passage, see Christine Roulston, who concludes that "the question of genre, in this sense, is marked by the question of gender, in terms of who has the authority to legitimise particular modes of representation" (28). Her argument resembles Helen Thomson's in its assignment of masculine and feminine to particular genres, though mine overlaps with Roulston's in the conclusion that there is an "uneasy relation between romance and history" in the novel (39).

35. Isles also holds Samuel Richardson at least in part responsible for the flaws of Lennox's novel, because of his "misguided" if "well-intentioned" advice for revising the plot (Isles, "Lennox Collection" [1970] 341).

36. Joel Weinsheimer too discusses Bolingbroke's *Letters* in relation to the quixote tradition and Lennox. See Weinsheimer 88–89. On Weinsheimer, Bolingbroke, and Lennox, see Rothstein, "Woman" 274 n. 28.

37. As Nadel notes, Voltaire's *Défense de Milord Bolingbroke* (1752) reads "as if he had not properly read the *Letters* he was defending in that pamphlet" and "may suggest that, having read them long ago, he saw no reason to study them again in 1752" (556). In another interesting though unrelated similarity between Lennox and Bolingbroke, one apologist for Bolingbroke made him out to be quixotic, claiming that "prejudices had disorder'd his mind" (Fleming 11–12). On Voltaire and Bolingbroke, see Kramnick's introduction to Bolingbroke's *Historical Writings,* esp. xxxiv–xxxv.

Five: "Deep Immers'd in the Historic Mine"

1. Bridget Hill compares Macaulay's and Piozzi's marriages (*Republican Virago* 113). See also Myers 256–57. Sylvia Myers discusses Elizabeth Montagu's reactions to Macaulay's marriage in letters to Piozzi. Montagu thought Macaulay's marriage came about "from . . . adopting Masculine opinions & masculine manners" (qtd. in Myers 256). Montagu and the Bluestockings were later no happier with Piozzi's May-December marriage.

2. Gilbert Burnet's marriages to one much older woman and one much younger one (both wealthy) were also the subject of satire earlier in the century. Satire about age- and class-appropriate spouses was not reserved for women writers, though it often was more brutal in their cases. On Burnet, see Kenyon 35.

3. On Macaulay's readership in the past two centuries, see Hill, *Republican*

Virago 233–51. Some modern editions of Macaulay's writings have begun to appear. Her *Letters on Education* has been reprinted most frequently. See Macaulay, *Letters* (1974, 1994, and 1996). Macaulay's "An Address to the People of England, Ireland, and Scotland on the Present Important Crisis of Affairs" was reprinted in 1972. Most recently, her pamphlet in response to Burke was reissued (*Observations*). That Macaulay's *History* is difficult to find has recently been documented by Mary Ellen Waite. In her entry on Macaulay, Waite writes, "I have not been able to obtain the *History*. . . . I therefore rely on the survey article by Boos and Boos for an assessment of the *History*" (3: 218).

4. On Macaulay's self-identification with Clio, see Mazzucco-Than. On images that circulated of Macaulay as the muse of history, see Fox.

5. "The Histories of the Tête-à-Tête" in the *Town and Country Magazine* was a regular scandal sheet feature offering its readers stories of couples whose identities were thinly veiled. At the end of 1776, Wilson and Macaulay were featured, called "the POLITICAL and PLATONIC LOVERS." A 1771 "History of the Tête-à-Tête" may also have been about Wilson and Macaulay. See Hill, *Republican Virago* 81–82.

6. On the *History in Letters* as a "ninth volume," see Staves, "Liberty" 163. On the *History in Letters* as a "new history," see Schnorrenberg, "Catherine Macaulay" 229.

7. On Wollstonecraft and Macaulay, see Hill, "Links." See also J. Wordsworth's introductions to Macaulay, *Letters* (1994) and *Observations,* and Gardner.

8. Despite his exclusionary title, Kenyon deals with Macaulay's writings for several pages, calling her Hume's "one serious rival" (54). He concludes, "She was not Hume's equal as a prose stylist, but she was far from being a dull writer" (55).

9. Linda Kerber, while labeling Macaulay a feminist, does not find that her historiography displays feminist qualities: "Not even so articulate a feminist as Catharine Macaulay felt the need to discuss women in her histories and essays, though she did discuss women's education elsewhere. . . . Macaulay, who was confident enough to plunge directly into public political debate and to criticize . . . without even a passing apology for the frailties of her sex, apparently felt no need to address the responsibilities of women to political society. Perhaps she believed she had made her position clear by implication and practice. But her direct comments speak of the private responsibilities of women—even reformed, chaste, nonfrivolous women—to individual men" (53).

10. Florence and William Boos echo Mary Hays's assessment of 1807. Hays argues that Macaulay's "talents and powers could not be denied; her beauty was therefore called in question, as if it was at all concerned with the subject; or that, to instruct our understandings, it was necessary at the same time to charm our senses" (2: 292). Evidence that Macaulay was thought a good mother may now be established by letters from her daughter Catherine Sophia Macaulay, later Gregorie. Catherine Sophia's thirty-eight letters to "My Dear Mama" refer frequently to maternal tenderness, concern, and generosity. These letters are from the Catharine Macaulay Papers, housed in the Gilder Lehrman Collection on deposit at the Pier-

pont Morgan Library, New York. Subsequent references are cited parenthetically in the text by accession number as GLC. Macaulay's side of the correspondence with her daughter apparently does not survive.

11. On the influence of Hollis, see Hill, *Republican Virago* 164–72. On John Sawbridge, see Hay, "John."

12. Bridget and Christopher Hill refer to Graham's "successful electrical treatment" ("Catharine Macaulay and the Seventeenth Century" 383). See also Hill, *Republican Virago* 90–96. Marianne Geiger sees the treatments as less beneficial: "When seeking to explain Macaulay's bizarre behavior, one must consider the real possibility of her psychological balance being impaired by a bad reaction to Graham's ether treatments" (286). The *Dictionary of National Biography* writes that Graham though "a quack, and possibly a madman, was not without some knowledge." He was against eating flesh, drinking too much alcohol, and wearing too much clothing and believed in the benefits of cold bathing, open windows, sleeping on mattresses, and mud baths up to the neck. Graham's property was seized for debt in 1782; in later years he became a religious man. Before his death in 1794, he was for some time confined in his own house, as the *DNB* writes, "as a lunatic."

13. In 1767, according to a friend, Macaulay had "adopted a diet of milk and vegetables in the hope of curing a chronic 'bilious complaint'" (Beckwith, "Catharine" [1953] 30). Beckwith notes that Macaulay's ailment "must have been more chronic than critical at the time that she went to Bath to reside, for it did not prevent her from enjoying a liberal portion of the city's social life" (30).

14. On Georgiana, duchess of Devonshire, see Colley 242–50. There are many interesting overlaps in the ways Macaulay and Georgiana were treated by an unsympathetic press. On James Graham's life and career, see Schnorrenberg, "A True Relation," and Schnorrenberg, "Medical Men."

15. See Hill, *Republican Virago* 94–98, and Donnelly 185–86 for very different treatments of this event. Hill, who describes the party as "out of character" for Macaulay, attributes her behavior to the "depressing time" many English radicals were experiencing and her possible "dejection" to a realization that her "fame was coming to an end" (98). Donnelly less sympathetically characterizes her as "ill and restless" (186). The most extensive treatment of the party is in Beckwith, "Catharine" (1953) 33–36. This dissertation is especially helpful on Macaulay's reception. Beckwith published a small portion of the dissertation as "Catharine Macaulay: Eighteenth-Century Rebel" (1958). Doris Mary Stenton also includes a colorful one-page description of the party (309).

16. Macaulay's history writing shares with Hutchinson's the appellation "nervous." In eighteenth-century parlance, nervous signified muscular or strong.

17. For Hill's discussion of *The Female Patriot,* see *Republican Virago* 115–17. See also Staves, "Liberty" 176 and 183 n. 35. Staves's reading of the poem is excellent, if brief. She concludes that "Joddrell cannot reconcile his idea of natural womanhood with his idea of ambitious historical writing" (176).

18. Wilson apparently "left legacies many thousands more than he was worth"

(Hill, *Republican Virago* 120). Catherine Sophia's letters indicate that she felt she was being treated fairly by Wilson's executors. In a 1786 letter she writes to her mother, "I know you will be glad to hear that my legacy is perfectly safe tho' it may be some time before it is paid, as the Executors have put the management of the late Doctor's affairs into the care of Chancery" (GLC 1795.24).

19. Although in her future writings Macaulay signed herself "Macaulay Graham," she was often referred to in the press as "Macaulay" until her death.

20. Macaulay also wrote *Loose Remarks on Certain Positions to Be Found in Mr. Hobbes's "Philosophical Rudiments of Government and Society"* (1767). Marianne Geiger notes, "In view of her unique position as a female writing for the political world, Macaulay ought to have been exceedingly careful about the titles of her works, yet she betrayed a great naivete," using "loose" and "modest" in the titles, opening the way for double entendres (268). *A Remarkable Moving Letter!* makes much of Macaulay's "loose thoughts" (7).

21. For a caricature of William Graham as a boy "not yet of age," see "Auspicious Marriage." The account features a Hamlet-inspired soliloquy in which the fictionalized Macaulay muses, "To marry, or not to marry, that is the question— Whether is it nobler in the mind to pass my days with an old dotard, who can afford me no joys but what arise from political animadversion, sarcastic observation, and ministerial invective—or fly to the arms of the dear beloved youth, who burns with rapture to embrace me. . . . Shall I not be lampooned in the rooms, burlesqued in the papers, satyrized, perhaps wooden blocked in the Magazines!—ay there's the rub" (624). The account, signed "An Admirer of Consistency," ends with Macaulay reportedly "casting from her the implements of writing, and devoting herself entirely to the impulse of her amorous passion" (624).

22. J. G. A. Pocock's essay is useful in its careful explication of Macaulay's political and historiographical commitments, as well as in its recognition of the limits of her feminism ("Catharine").

23. This letter calls those making "defamatory aspersions" "illiberal or unthinking" and charges, "Never before, in any Instance or private concern, was a slight imprudence so stigmatized as a crime, and a venial error so ridiculed as a folly, or satirized as a vice" (52). The letter writer holds Wilson, and the "ludicrous medley" surrounding him, partly responsible for Macaulay's weaknesses. Both her "thirst after literary fame" and her "ignorance of the world, and strong natural desires" led to her "late extraordinary step" ("Vindication" 52).

24. On Macaulay's pamphlets or political tracts, see Schnorrenberg, "Brood Hen."

25. On Macaulay and the seventeenth century, see Bridget and Christopher Hill, "Catharine Macaulay and the Seventeenth Century."

26. Elsewhere Schnorrenberg also concludes that the *History in Letters* "showed none of the careful research and conclusions of the *History.* . . . Horace Walpole, who strenuously objected to the new work's unflattering picture of his father, was not alone in his condemnation of it. This poor reception, coupled with

Macaulay's break with Wilson in late 1778, resulted in there being no further volumes of this work. Although weak as history, the *History . . . from the Revolution* provides a summary of Macaulay's views on the immediate consequences of 1688" ("Opportunity" 233).

27. The review Macaulay apparently took too hard was published in the *Monthly Review* 36 (1767): 300. According to Bridget and Christopher Hill, "All the first five volumes of her *History* have extensive footnotes. She must have noted, however, a criticism made of her third volume by the *Monthly Review*. It 'will not be thought altogether so interesting as those which preceded it. The notes are very numerous, and chiefly consist of tedious and dry extracts from Rushworth and the parliamentary history, the substance of which had better been comprised in the context, with such observations as the several subjects suggested.' With volume IV, Macaulay began to weave formerly footnoted material into the text itself and included a note explaining her choice to readers" ("Catharine Macaulay's *History*" 271).

28. Subsequent references to Macaulay's *History of England from the Revolution to the Present Time: In a Series of Letters to a Friend* are cited parenthetically as *HL*.

29. The *DNB* does not mention Macaulay in its entry on Lofft, nor does it include his *Observations* in its list of his publications.

30. The review concludes, "Mr. Lofft has been happy in pointing out many excellencies in Mrs. M's history, which might escape the observation of ordinary readers" (234).

31. That Macaulay's relationship with Wilson is still exaggerated and misunderstood can be seen in one of the reviews of Bridget Hill's biography. L. G. Mitchell seems to invoke Wilson when he writes, "The success of the work certainly brought its author intense public scrutiny, the pressures of which would have taxed the most level-headed. Its effect on a woman who created a scandal by marrying a man much older than herself and then compounded the felony by marrying a man much younger, is not hard to imagine" (762). Though George Macaulay was indeed older than Catharine, that marriage was never a scandal. The reviewer must be mistakenly assuming that Wilson and Macaulay's scandalous relationship was a marital one.

32. For commentary (not already mentioned) on Macaulay's political views, see Ditchfield; Hay, "Catharine Macaulay"; Letzring; and Withey.

33. On Williams, fiction, history, and gender, see Jones and Fruchtman.

34. Macaulay directly influenced French and American women who undertook the writing of history. Mercy Otis Warren and Madame Roland both expressed a desire to follow in Macaulay's footsteps. On Roland, see Hill, *Republican Virago* 40. On Warren and Macaulay, see Geiger. See also Baym, who does not discuss Macaulay.

Six: Hester Lynch Piozzi's Infinite and Exact World History, *Retrospection*

1. Piozzi's broadside was reprinted (without attribution) in Klingberg and Hustvedt 76–79. The manuscript is held at the John Rylands Library in Manchester.

2. According to Morris Brownell, "Perhaps only Horace Walpole can rival Mrs. Piozzi as an annotator of books" (99). Brownell writes, "This passion for book annotation reflects the 'perennial urge to authorship' in a literary career which encountered many frustrations common to the eighteenth-century woman writer. Just as she wrote her own diary with the thought of its eventual publication, she may have considered her annotated books as a kind of publication in limited editions of a single copy" (99).

3. On the strange critical history of Piozzi and Conway's friendship, see Merritt, *True Story.*

4. For information on the editions printed of each of these works, see Clifford, *Hester* 462–63. Though *Observations and Reflections* has found fewer readers over the years, John Dussinger has recently called it "probably her best published work" with "firmer narrative control" ("Hester" 46). The reviewer for the *European Magazine* was not so generous, claiming that "beauties and defects are so closely intermingled in almost every page of this desultory and heterogeneous performance, that the acutest powers of criticism might find it an arduous, and perhaps impracticable task entirely to decompose them" (332). On Piozzi's travel writings, see also Hamalian.

5. On Piozzi's lack of scholarly self-confidence, see Spacks, *Female Imagination* 264. On literary skill, see Spacks, "Scrapbook."

6. Subsequent references are cited parenthetically in the text as *PL.*

7. James Thorpe also notes that Pennington visited Piozzi occasionally, for as long as four months at a time (106). See also Knapp.

8. A draft and the final manuscript of *Retrospection* are at the John Rylands Library. There are four folio notebooks containing rough drafts of the preface and of several long sections, a manuscript of 504 pages—the final draft—from which part of the short preface and four leaves of text are missing, and several miscellaneous notebooks with historical summaries. See Tyson, "Unpublished Manuscripts" 477–78.

9. Subsequent references are cited parenthetically in the text as *R.*

10. The *London Review*'s reviewer saw Piozzi's work as guilty of the things it pretends to despise: "The work itself is subject to the same animadversion—facts half related, and in many instances left so unfinished, that they cannot possibly afford either information or instruction to young readers—anecdotes breaking off the thread of history, intruded without order or connexion; interlarded with scraps of poetry, the very accusation she brings against the compilers" (188).

11. Far from dismissing "little table books," however, Piozzi rates them highly, expressing the belief that such books "commonly" give "the truest account of such

matters" such as who was "the first female who ever used pins in England." The answer, according to Piozzi and her table books, is Catherine Howard (*R* 2: 107).

12. On the visual nature of *Retrospection,* see McCarthy, *Hester* 239.

13. On responses to Piozzi's second marriage to the Italian music master, see Myers 256–57.

14. C. E. Vullaimy refers to *Retrospection* as a "ponderous farrago" and calls Piozzi's mention of the printers' insurrection "wholly inexplicable" (306).

15. The *Critical Review* thought no one would have been able to rescue the book: "Upon the whole we wish, for the sake of Mrs. Piozzi's reputation, she had never committed these volumes to the press; nor could her most learned friend have remedied the mischief, as the errors exceed every power of correction" (35).

16. The entirety of this section of Piozzi's argument reads: "What makes our Critical Reviewers so outrageous? I expected more candour from *these* enemies, and censure better founded. They *know* the word *Lusitania* for *Lithuania* is, and *must* be, an error of the Press. I have called Poland by the name of *Lithuania* not once, but *many* times, in the course of the work. . . . As a judgment on the Reviewers, however, their own compositor makes as gross mistakes" ("Mrs. Piozzi's Appeal" 602).

Seven: Reading Jane Austen and Rewriting "Herstory"

1. Subsequent references to Le Faye's edition of Austen's letters are cited parenthetically in the text as *JAL.*

2. Christopher Kent demonstrates that the comparisons to Scott in Austen studies "opened in the mid-Victorian period" when Richard Simpson "cast doubt upon the historicity of [Austen's] novels" in 1870. See Kent, "Real Solemn History" 87.

3. Williams describes the ways Austen's writings are implicated in history. For a study of Austen's writings in relation to Regency England that goes much further, see Sales.

4. For other early studies on Austen's relation to history, debunking her supposed "limitations," see Greene; Wiesenfarth, "Austen" 46–47, 59–63; Wiesenfarth, "History"; Southam, "Regulated Hatred"; and Hopkins.

5. For an account of Austen by a historian who argues that she presents "access to the felt reality" of her times and is the first and finest "historian's novelist," see MacDonagh ix.

6. For an engaging article that labels Austen a Tory but takes issue with the ways "Tory" has been defined by today's critics, see Neill. Edward Neill refers to Austen as having been "Bastilled for life" by critics who view her as ahistorical or anti-Jacobin (207). He contends that Austen's novels are politically "contradictory amalgams" (211). For an account of the history of Austen's reputation as "political," see Kelly 155–56. Unlike James Thompson, who locates a more recent critical change, Kelly believes that the turn in the tide toward seeing a political Austen began in the 1950s with the commentary of Rebecca West.

7. For a summary of this criticism, see Monaghan, *Jane Austen in a Social Context* 1–8, and Johnson, *Jane* xxiv–xxv, 48. For arguments claiming a feminist Austen, see Kirkham; Sulloway; and L. Smith. For an account that distances Austen from feminism, see Butler, *Jane.* Marilyn Butler asserts that "Jane Austen's novels belong decisively to one class of partisan novels, the conservative" (*Jane* 3). On Austen and imperialism/slavery, see Said, *Culture,* and Fraiman. Duckworth's *Improvement of the Estate* (1994 [1971]) is often credited with transforming Austen studies through its infusion of careful historicizing.

8. Armstrong persuasively argues, "That we tend to see the Austen text as a limited one ultimately says more about the limits of our notion of history, then, than about the limits of her world" ("Nineteenth-Century Jane Austen" 237).

9. For an insightful account of criticism on historical and ahistorical Austens, see Kent, "Real Solemn History" 86–93.

10. Thompson concludes, "Despite its mass Austen studies still have a long way to go before we can begin to restore and uncover the repressed history embodied in the novels," noting that what passes for history in Austen studies is often conventional background or annotation (30).

11. Tara Ghoshal Wallace's article on *Northanger Abbey*'s "collision of genres" focuses on fictional genres (parody, romance, and the realistic novel). Frank Kearful similarly states that "Austen is writing what is not simply a novel of satire, a burlesque or a parody, a comedy or a tragedy, a romance or an anti-romance. She is, rather, combining elements of all of these" (527). Even Edward Neill, in his correct claim that the label "novelist" has limited our range of comparisons for Austen's work, restricts his call for further comparison to "radical male poets" (212). Most critics see *Northanger Abbey* and the juvenilia as combining literary subgenres, but few look to histories and other nonliterary genres as points of comparison.

12. On Scott's career as it compares with Austen's, see Millgate.

13. Jane Austen, during her lifetime, made £685 from her writing. On Austen and Edgeworth, see Hodge 84.

14. On Edgeworth and Austen, see M. Butler, esp. chap. 5. Edgeworth also wrote historical novels, "broad and much more masculine sketches of national life," some of which were said to have influenced Scott, including *Ennui, The Absentee,* and *Ormond* (M. Butler 132). The Edgeworth novels that Austen values most appear, from other references, to have been her "philosophical novels," including *Belinda* and *Tales from a Fashionable Life.*

15. John Dussinger has suggested three possible answers: "Austen's silence about such momentous historical happenings may be attributed to one or more of the following causes: 1) a provincial's indifference toward the public world in general; 2) a comic novelist's aesthetic distancing of her story from local history; and 3) a late eighteenth-century woman writer's reluctance, or inability, to enter into the discourse of patriarchal politics" ("Jane" 33). This chapter and future work on Austen should add more possibilities to Dussinger's list.

16. David Nokes discusses history and the *Loiterer* in relation to Austen's writings, finding hers a feminist answer to her brother's positions (123–24).

17. See Austen, *History of England* (1993 and 1995), and Austen, *"Catharine"* *and Other Writings.* In an edition of Austen's early writings published before these, the *History of England* was not even included (Austen and Brontë). A fifty-minute play based on Austen's *History of England* was adapted and directed by Tim Heath and performed by Rebecca Blech in the summer of 1996 at the Theatre Royal, Bath, at the Cannizaro House, Wimbledon, and at Chawton. Subsequent references to Austen's *History of England* are cited parenthetically from Byatt and Le Faye's 1993 edition as *HE.* Though most critics comfortably label her piece a burlesque, Marilyn Butler disagrees (168). Few see Oliver Goldsmith's *History* as anything other than "real solemn" historiography. Marvin Mudrick departs from this view, distancing Goldsmith's text from history, calling it a "potboiler" and "gossip masquerading as history" (23).

18. Admirers of Austen's juvenilia in general and the *History* in particular go back as far as the text was known. See Austen, *"Love and Friendship,"* and Southam, *Jane Austen's Literary Manuscripts.*

19. As Mary Lascelles notes, Austen's *Volume the Second* (of juvenilia) is "evidently allusive, sprinkled with references to which a list of the books that were then in the Steventon rectory would be a key" (9–10).

20. On these marginal comments, see Austen-Leigh 26–28, 33. They include material on Cromwell and his men: "Oh! Oh! The Wretches!" (26); on the verdict against the Stuart family, "A family who were always ill-used, BETRAYED OR NEGLECTED, whose virtues are seldom allowed, while their errors are never forgotten" (27); on Charles I's being called unworthy, "Unworthy, because he was a Stuart, I suppose—unhappy family!" (27); and on Anne's forsaking her father's cause for her brother-in-law: "Anne should not have done so, indeed I do not believe she did" (28). Austen did not always disagree with Goldsmith; she agrees with him on the destitution of the poor after the Revolution: "How much are the poor to be pitied, and the Rich to be Blamed!" (33). Park Honan reprints some of these marginalia (74–75).

21. Valerie Grosvenor Myer shares Brophy's view of *History of England* as a demonstration of family political sympathies (125). B. C. Southam proposes alternatively that the *History of England* is "not a sufficient vehicle for [Austen's] view of life" (*Jane Austen's Literary Manuscripts* 3).

22. Christopher Kent sees the proportions as closer to half and half: "Nearly half its characters are women, and half its space is devoted to their exploits" ("Learning" 67). Kent also notes that "a third of the people Austen chose to mention in her history met violent deaths—mostly beheadings" ("Learning" 66).

23. As Julia Epstein points out, Jane Austen's juvenilia reveal "her comprehensive knowledge of eighteenth-century prose traditions, her interest in the nature of women's voices in eighteenth-century narrative, and her sense of how those traditions and voices might be recast" (401).

24. Southam points out that "Charlotte Smith is the only contemporary novelist whose works are referred to in the juvenilia" (in *Catharine*) though he is count-

ing only direct references (*Jane Austen's Literary Manuscripts* 10). Indirect references would expand this number. On Austen and Smith, see Ehrenpreis.

25. Doody notes that "Jane Austen sustains the use of dramas as sources for history" and that "once again, Jane Austen cites drama rather than history" (Austen, *"Catharine"* 329, 332).

26. Though this feature of the *History*'s illustrations has been noticed by many critics, Jan Fergus et al. were the first to identify the source of two of the portraits. A 1780 engraving by W. H. Bunbury provided the model for Cassandra's illustrations of Henry V and Edward IV (Austen, *History* [1995] ii–iii).

27. As Ellen Martin puts it, "The whole notion of a great narrative of causation linking events is regarded as inadequate by an artist devoted to sapping what passes for consequence and celebrating the connections made by the private, eclectic fancy" (93).

28. Of course, Jacobin and anti-Jacobin novels dealt with militaristic materials in their accounts of the French Revolution. See M. Butler. Eighteenth-century novels such as *Tom Jones* and *Tristram Shandy* also used war as a narrative feature or backdrop.

29. Language as melodramatic as my own is used by Katrin Burlin: "Jane Austen's motive is to fight for her craft, to prove that it is the responsible novelist who protects us by teaching us through his art to recognize and discriminate among the fictions of life and art alike" (89–90).

30. On the dates of composition of *Northanger Abbey* (which are not easy to fix), see Chard 133–36; Emden; Mansell 40–41; and Southam, *"Sanditon"* 4. On the questionable claim that the Bath section and the Abbey section were written at different times, see Moler 31. Cassandra Austen, who was responsible for naming the novel *Northanger Abbey,* dates it from 1798. Austen had titled the novel *Susan* when she sold it to Crosby in 1803. Crosby did not publish it, and Austen eventually bought it back from him in 1816 for the price he had paid: £10. Austen referred to it at this time as *Miss Catherine.* Internal evidence proves revisions must have been made after 1798, though how much the novel was revised is subject to debate. The work was published posthumously, with *Persuasion,* in 1818. Meenakshi Mukherjee speculates that Austen's "playful subversion of some of the conventions of the popular novel in *Northanger Abbey* resulted in the non-publication of the manuscript in her lifetime, even though a publisher had paid for it," but the reasons it was not published have not been substantiated (31). B. C. Southam suggests that Crosby may have "thought that the Gothic market was over-crowded" (Southam, *"Sanditon"* 4).

31. In my article "(Re)Making Fiction and Philosophy: Austen's *Northanger Abbey*" I consider *Northanger Abbey* in comparison with philosophical as well as historical discourse.

32. In 1976 B. C. Southam wrote, "While each of the other novels has attracted a substantial body of critical writing and possesses its own individual critical tradition, *Northanger Abbey* has inspired rather little, the unstated implication

being that [it is] . . . the least in need of commentary" (*Jane Austen: "Northanger"* 20). This can no longer be argued, though *Northanger Abbey* has never received the unequivocal critical praise given the other novels. Typical is Joan Aiken's assessment that the novel is an "exuberant, faulty masterpiece" (54).

33. Amy Elizabeth Smith maintains that readings of *Northanger Abbey* to date have been "somewhat lopsided" in their consideration of gothic novels and lack of focus on the reverberations with the sentimental genre (40).

34. George Whalley believes that "At best *Northanger Abbey* is a sort of *Donna Quixote*" (127). See also Kauvar. Rachel Brownstein notes that Catherine cannot truly be a Quixote figure because she is "too modest to presume herself a heroine of romance" and because "it would be hard for any girl to do so in a world like hers, where people read novels and discuss them together" (40).

35. Subsequent references are to this edition and are cited parenthetically in the text as *NA*.

36. Everett Zimmerman writes, "In her juvenilia Jane Austen burlesqued these failings of popular fiction; in *Northanger Abbey* she attempts to resuscitate the fiction and certain values on which it is based" ("Function" 62).

37. See my introduction to *Jane Austen and Discourses of Feminism,* esp. 8–9. Without engaging issues of feminist criticism, Frank Bradbrook remarks on this reference to Edgeworth as a possible reproach (113), and he points to an even earlier source for this reading: C. Thomson (45–46).

38. Edgeworth too wanted to change the way novels were labeled, wishing that a name could be devised to distinguish "philosophical novels" from "trifling, silly productions" (M. Butler 131).

39. "In *Northanger Abbey,*" Jocelyn Harris has convincingly declared, "Jane Austen transforms philosophy into fiction, but what she attacks in that fiction is history. Her defence of the novel, like other famous defences of the imagination, claims superiority to them both" (26). Harris makes the provocative case that in chapter 5 Austen implies that "historical writing soon looks out-of-date" (27) and that it is "in effect the essay that she said she omitted from *Pride and Prejudice*" (30). Harris further argues, "The upstart novelist challenges the philosopher and the historian, standing (as Sidney said of the poet) between the precepts of one and the examples of the other. . . . she stakes the bold claim that fiction usurps poetry as well" (32–33). Harris's argument has been important in formulating my own. It opens up questions similar to those I have been discussing by comparing and contrasting *Northanger Abbey,* John Locke's *Essay concerning Human Understanding,* and Sir Philip Sidney's *Apology for Poetry.* In making these important comparisons, Harris necessarily brackets off the question of how Austen's novel might be gauged in a larger field of writings.

40. As Kent writes, "There is every reason to believe that Eleanor Tilney, who was 'fond of history,' better represented Jane Austen's own mature views than did Catherine Morland" ("Learning" 68). On Eleanor, Catherine, and imagination in the Beechen Cliff episode, see Morgan, "Guessing" 117–18. In Frans De Bruyn's

interesting article "Edmund Burke's Gothic Romance" these insights are given to Catherine. De Bruyn claims that Catherine Morland "acknowledges a close generic kinship between histories and novels and pertinently questions the consistency of her own taste, given her avowed love of fiction" (415). Some of De Bruyn's arguments, including that "the stated aims of historians and novelists often converged remarkably in the period" and that Austen belongs to a tradition of " 'historical' novel-writing," overlap with my own (415).

41. On the "something shocking" passage as a historical reference, see Litz 64; Southam, "Regulated Hatred" 124–26; Hopkins 216–17; Rothstein, "Lessons" 29; Paulson, *Representations* 216; and Loveridge 4. Rothstein notes that "St. George's Fields were the common gathering ground of any riotous mob from the early seventeenth century on" (29).

42. In Eric Rothstein's view, the Beechen Cliff conversation is not about the triumph of fiction over history but about the components of gothic fiction: "One can see that the subjects discussed are really an analysis of the Gothic novel into components: words, pleasure for readers, history, didacticism, picturesque scenery, and the violence of life which it professes to imitate" ("Lessons" 18–19).

43. As Ronald Paulson has maintained, however, the gothic and history should not be strictly opposed: "We notice the difference between gothic fiction and history, but also the similarity. . . . The gothic did in fact serve as a metaphor with which some contemporaries in England tried to understand what was happening across the channel in the 1790s" (*Representations* 217).

44. For another account that understands Catherine's complaint as anticipating today's feminist criticism, see Tanner 44.

45. Christopher Kent has asserted that "Sandra Gilbert and Susan Gubar have recently attempted to 'dehistoricize' Austen in the name of feminist literary criticism. They choose to identify her with Catherine Morland and maintain that she 'refused to take historical "reality" seriously.' . . . This feminist version of history is the mirror image of the conventional chauvinistic view of history as a men's club. Happily, this gender stereotyping of history as a subject (one which, if it existed in Austen's time, was if anything reversed) is currently dissolving" ("Learning" 69).

46. Ina Ferris has made a similar but opposite claim—that Sir Walter Scott incorporated the masculine world of political or public history into the form of the novel, a largely female domain, thus changing the ground on which the novel was classified. That Scott's novels have been subsumed by Austen's in the canon tells us more about the twentieth century than about previous judgments.

47. As Mark Loveridge has noted, *Northanger Abbey* "has recently come to be recognized as a transitional work in a much wider sense: as a work highly suggestive of changes in novelistic technique that were taking place between the eighteenth and nineteenth centuries" (2). I think, however, that Loveridge's "wider sense" could be wider still.

48. Litvak and I agree on the role that historical discourse plays in *Northanger Abbey,* but he finds Catherine Morland's thoughts on "real, solemn history" to be

Austen's "rather sophisticated feminist critique"—a conclusion I disagree with. Litvak's essay goes on to argue for *Northanger Abbey* as a preparation for the "homophobic aversion therapy" found in the nineteenth-century novel ("Charming Men"). Litvak's work on *Northanger Abbey* also appears in his *Strange Gourmets*.

49. Stewart writes, "Catherine Morland's name reflects her fate: she gains more land through marriage" (16).

Works Cited

■

Abrams, M. H., et al., eds. *The Norton Anthology of English Literature.* New York: W. W. Norton, 1993. 2 vols.

Abu-Lughod, Lila. "The Romance of Resistance: Tracing Transformation of Power through Bedoin Women." *American Ethnologist* 17 (1990): 41–55.

Adams, H. G. *A Cyclopedia of Female Biography; Consisting of Sketches of All Women Who Have Been Distinguished by Great Talents, Strength of Character, Piety, Benevolence, or Moral Virtue of Any Kind: Forming a Complete Record of Womanly Existence or Ability.* London: Groombridge, 1857.

Ahmed, Leila. *Women and Gender in Islam: Historical Roots of a Modern Debate.* New Haven: Yale UP, 1992.

Aiken, Joan. "How Might Jane Austen Have Revised *Northanger Abbey?*" *Persuasions* 7 (1985): 42–54.

Aikin, Lucy. *Epistles on Women, Exemplifying Their Character and Condition in Various Ages and Nations: With Miscellaneous Poems.* London: J. Johnson, 1810.

Alexander, William. *The History of Women, from the Earliest Antiquity, to the Present Time, Giving Some Account of Almost Every Interesting Particular concerning That Sex among All Nations, Ancient and Modern.* Dublin: J. A. Husband, 1779.

Alfred. "Letter to the Editor." *Westminster Magazine* 6 (1778): 681–82.

Alic, Margaret. *Hypatia's Heritage: A History of Women in Science from Antiquity through the Nineteenth Century.* Boston: Beacon, 1986.

Allen, J. Antisell. *The True and Romantic Love Story of Colonel and Mrs. Hutchinson: A Drama in Verse.* London: Elliot Stock, 1885.

Allen, M. D. "The New Path: English Women Travelers in the Middle East." *West Virginia University Philological Papers* 40 (1994): 1–5.

Alliston, April. *Virtue's Faults: Correspondences in Eighteenth-Century British and French Women's Fiction.* Stanford: Stanford UP, 1996.

Anderson, Walter E. "From Northanger to Woodston: Catherine's Education to Common Life." *Philological Quarterly* 63 (1984): 493–509.

Aravamudan, Srinivas. "Lady Mary Wortley Montagu in the *Hammam:* Masquerade, Womanliness, and Levantinization." *ELH* 62 (1995): 69–104.

———. *Tropicopolitans: Colonialism and Agency, 1688–1804.* Durham: Duke UP, 1999.

Armstrong, Nancy. *Desire and Domestic Fiction: A Political History of the Novel.* New York: Oxford UP, 1987.

———. "The Gender Bind: Women and the Disciplines." *Genders* 3 (1988): 1–23.

———. "The Nineteenth-Century Jane Austen: A Turning Point in the History of Fear." *Genre* 23 (1990): 227–46.

Astell, Mary. *The Christian Religion, as Profes'd by a Daughter of the Church of England.* London: W. B. for R. Wilkin, 1717 [1705].

"The Auspicious Marriage." *Town and Country Magazine* 10 (1778): 623–24.

Austen, Jane. *"Catharine" and Other Writings.* Ed. Margaret Doody and Douglas Murray. Oxford: Oxford UP, 1993.

———. *The History of England.* Ed. A. S. Byatt and Deirdre Le Faye. Chapel Hill, NC: Algonquin, 1993.

———. *The History of England.* Ed. Jan Fergus et al. Edmonton: U of Alberta, 1995.

———. *Jane Austen's Letters.* Ed. Deirdre Le Faye. New ed. Oxford: Oxford UP, 1995.

———. *"Love and Friendship" and Other Early Works.* Ed. G. K. Chesterton. London: Chatto and Windus, 1922.

———. *Mansfield Park.* Ed. R. W. Chapman. 3rd ed. Vol. 3. Oxford: Oxford UP, 1966.

———. *"Northanger Abbey" and "Persuasion."* Ed. R. W. Chapman. 3rd ed. Vol. 5. Oxford: Oxford UP, 1966.

———. *Volume the Second.* Ed. B. C. Southam. Oxford: Clarendon, 1963.

Austen, Jane, and Charlotte Brontë. *The Juvenilia of Jane Austen and Charlotte Brontë.* Ed. Frances Beer. Harmondsworth, Eng.: Penguin, 1986.

Austen-Leigh, Mary Augusta. *Personal Aspects of Jane Austen.* New York: E. P. Dutton, 1920.

Auty, Susan G. *The Comic Spirit of Eighteenth-Century Novels.* Port Washington, NY: Kennikat, 1975.

Bagehot, Walter. *Literary Studies.* Ed. Richard Holt Hutton. Vol. 2. London: Longmans, Green, 1910. 3 vols.

Barbour, Reid. "Between Atoms and the Spirit: Lucy Hutchinson's Translation of Lucretius." *Renaissance Papers,* 1994, 1–16.

Barnett, George L., ed. *Eighteenth-Century British Novelists on the Novel.* New York: Meredith, 1968.

Barreca, Regina. *Untamed and Unabashed: Essays on Women and Humor in British Literature.* Detroit: Wayne State UP, 1994.

Bartolomeo, Joseph F. "Female Quixotism v. 'Feminine' Tragedy: Lennox's Comic

Revision of *Clarissa.*" *New Essays on Samuel Richardson.* Ed. Albert J. Rivero. New York: St. Martin's, 1996. 163–75.

Battigelli, Anna. *Margaret Cavendish and Exiles of the Mind.* Lexington: UP of Kentucky, 1998.

Baym, Nina. *American Women Writers and the Work of History, 1790–1860.* New Brunswick: Rutgers UP, 1995.

Beasley, Jerry C. "Charlotte Lennox." *Dictionary of Literary Biography.* Vol. 39. Detroit: Gale Research, 1981–. 306–12.

Beattie, John M. *The English Court in the Reign of George I.* Cambridge: Cambridge UP, 1967.

Beckwith, Mildred Chaffee. "Catharine Macaulay, Eighteenth-Century English Rebel: A Sketch of Her Life and Some Reflections on Her Place among the Historians and Political Reformers of Her Time." Diss. Ohio State U, 1953.

———. "Catharine Macaulay: Eighteenth-Century Rebel." *Proceedings of the South Carolina Historical Society,* 1958, 12–29.

Bell, Susan Groag, and Karen M. Offen, eds. *Women, the Family and Freedom: The Debate in Documents.* Palo Alto, CA: Stanford UP, 1983.

Benkovitz, Miriam J. "Some Observations on Woman's Concept of Self in the Eighteenth Century." *Women in the Eighteenth Century and Other Essays.* Ed. Paul Fritz and Richard Morton. Toronto: Hakkert, 1976. 37–54.

Berg, Temma F. "Getting the Mother's Story Right: Charlotte Lennox and the New World." *Papers on Language and Literature* 32.4 (1996): 369–98.

Biographia Gallica, or The Lives of the Most Eminent French Writers of Both Sexes in Divinity, Philosophy, Mathematics, History, Poetry &C. From the Restoration of Learning under Francis I to the Present Time. London: R. Griffiths, 1752.

Black, Frank Gees. *The Epistolary Novel in the Late Eighteenth Century: A Descriptive and Bibliographical Study.* Vol. 2. Eugene: U of Oregon, 1940.

Black, J. B. *The Art of History: A Study of Four Great Historians of the Eighteenth Century.* New York: Russell and Russell, 1965.

Blain, Virginia, Patricia Clements, and Isobel Grundy. *The Feminist Companion to Literature in English: Women Writers from the Middle Ages to the Present.* New Haven: Yale UP, 1990.

Bloom, Edward, and Lillian Bloom, eds. *The Piozzi Letters.* Newark: U of Delaware P, 1989. 6 vols.

Bohls, Elizabeth. *Women Travel Writers and the Language of Aesthetics, 1716–1818.* Cambridge: Cambridge UP, 1994.

Bolingbroke, Henry St. John, Lord Viscount. *Letters on the Study and Use of History.* London: A. Millar, 1752.

Boos, Florence, and William Boos. "Catharine Macaulay: Historian and Political Reformer." *International Journal of Women's Studies* 3.1 (1980): 49–65.

Boswell, James. *Life of Johnson.* Ed. R. W. Chapman. Oxford: Oxford UP, 1980.

Bradbrook, Frank W. *Jane Austen and Her Predecessors.* Cambridge: Cambridge UP, 1966.

Braudy, Leo. *Narrative Form in History and Fiction.* Princeton: Princeton UP, 1970.

A Bridal Ode: On The Marriage of Catherine and Petruchio. London: J. Bew, 1779.

Brophy, Brigid. "Jane Austen and the Stuarts." *Critical Essays on Jane Austen.* Ed. B. C. Southam. London: Routledge, 1968. 21–38.

Brophy, Elizabeth Bergen. *Women's Lives and the Eighteenth-Century English Novel.* Tampa: U of South Florida P, 1991.

Brown, John Henry. *Love's Labyrinth: A Play.* London: Catty and Dobson, 1876.

Brownell, Morris R. "Hester Lynch Piozzi's Marginalia." *Eighteenth-Century Life* 3 (1977): 97–100.

Brownley, Martine Watson. *Clarendon and the Rhetoric of Historical Form.* Philadelphia: U of Pennsylvania P, 1986.

———. "Samuel Johnson and the Printing Career of Hester Lynch Piozzi." *Bulletin of the John Rylands University Library* 67.2 (1985): 627–40.

———. "Samuel Johnson and the Writing of History." *Johnson after Two Hundred Years.* Ed. Paul J. Korshin. Philadelphia: U of Pennsylvania P, 1986. 97–110.

Brownstein, Rachel. "*Northanger Abbey, Sense and Sensibility,* and *Pride and Prejudice.*" *Cambridge Companion to Jane Austen.* Ed. Edward Copeland and Juliet McMaster. Cambridge: Cambridge UP, 1997. 32–57.

Buck, Claire, ed. *The Bloomsbury Guide to Women's Literature.* New York: Prentice Hall, 1992.

Buds of Genius, or Some Account of the Early Lives of Celebrated Characters: Who Were Remarkable in Their Childhood. 2nd ed. London: Darton, Harvey, and Darton, 1818.

Burke, John J., Jr. "History without History: Fielding's Theory of Fiction." *A Provision of Human Nature: Essays on Fielding and Others in Honor of Miriam Austen Locke.* Ed. Donald Kay. University: U of Alabama P, 1977. 45–63.

Burlin, Katrin Ristkok. "'The Pen of the Contriver': The Four Fictions of *Northanger Abbey.*" *Jane Austen: Bicentenary Essays.* Ed. John Halperin. Cambridge: Cambridge UP, 1975. 89–111.

Burnet, Gilbert. *History of His Own Times.* London: J. M. Dent, 1906.

Burstein, Miriam Elizabeth. "From Good Looks to Good Thoughts: Popular Women's History and the Invention of Modernity, ca. 1830–1870." *Modern Philology* 97.1 (1999): 46–75.

———. "'The Reduced Pretensions of the Historic Muse': Agnes Strickland and the Commerce of Women's History." *Journal of Narrative Technique* 28.3 (1998): 219–42.

Burton, Antoinette. "'Invention Is What Delights Me': Jane Austen's Remaking of 'English' History." *Jane Austen and Discourses of Feminism.* Ed. Devoney Looser. New York: St. Martin's, 1995. 35–50.

Butler, Marilyn. *Jane Austen and the War of Ideas.* Oxford: Clarendon, 1975.

Butler, William. *Miscellaneous Questions relating Principally to English History and Biography: Designed for the Use of Young Ladies.* London: S. Crouchman, 1818.

Campbell, Jill. "Lady Mary Wortley Montagu and the Machinery of Female Identity." *History, Gender and Eighteenth-Century Literature.* Ed. Beth Fowkes Tobin. Athens: U of Georgia P, 1994. 64–85.

Cave, Wendy Nelson. "Charlotte Lennox, First American Woman Playwright." *New Rambler* 29 (1978): 3–20.

Cavendish, Margaret, Duchess of Newcastle. *"The Life of William Cavendish Duke of Newcastle": To Which Is Added "The True Relation of My Birth, Breeding, and Life."* Ed. C. H. Firth. 2nd rev. ed. London: George Routledge, 1914.

Certeau, Michel de. *The Writing of History.* Trans. Tom Conley. New York: Columbia UP, 1988.

Chard, Leslie F., II. "Jane Austen and the Obituaries: The Names of *Northanger Abbey.*" *Studies in the Novel* 7 (1975): 133–36.

Chudleigh, Lady Mary. *The Poems and Prose of Mary, Lady Chudleigh.* Ed. Margaret J. M. Ezell. Oxford: Oxford UP, 1993.

Clifford, James. *Hester Lynch Piozzi (Mrs. Thrale).* 2nd ed. New York: Columbia UP, 1987.

Clingham, Greg, ed. *Making History: Textuality and the Forms of Eighteenth-Century Culture.* Bucknell UP, 1999.

Coleman, Linda S. "Public Self, Private Self: Women's Life-Writing in England, 1520–1720." Diss. U of Wisconsin–Milwaukee, 1986.

Colley, Linda. *Britons: Forging the Nation, 1707–1837.* New Haven: Yale UP, 1992.

Collins, Irene. *Jane Austen and the Clergy.* Rio Grande, OH: Hambledon, 1993.

Cook, Susan. " 'The Story I Most Particularly Intend': The Narrative Style of Lucy Hutchinson." *Critical Survey* 5.2 (1993): 271–77.

Cottom, Daniel. *The Civilized Imagination: A Study of Ann Radcliffe, Jane Austen, and Sir Walter Scott.* Cambridge: Cambridge UP, 1985.

Cowie, Alexander. Rev. of *Mystery of Charlotte Lennox,* by Philippe Séjourné. *American Literature* 40 (1969): 553–54.

Cowley, Charlotte. *The Ladies History of England; from the Descent of Julius Caesar, to the Summer of 1780. Calculated for the Use of the Ladies of Great-Britain and Ireland; and Likewise Adapted to General Use, Entertainment, and Instruction.* London, 1780.

Craft, Catherine A. "Reworking Male Models: Aphra Behn's *Fair Vow-Breaker,* Eliza Haywood's *Fantomina,* and Charlotte Lennox's *Female Quixote.*" *Modern Language Review* 86.4 (1991): 821–38.

Craig, W. H. *Dr. Johnson and the Fair Sex: A Study of Contrasts.* London: Sampson Low, Marston, 1895.

Crawford, Patricia. "Women's Published Writings: 1600–1700." *Women in English Society, 1500–1800.* Ed. Mary Prior. London: Methuen, 1985. 211–82.

Croker, John Wilson. Rev. of *Letters and Works of Lady Mary Wortley Montagu,* ed. Lord Wharncliffe. *Quarterly Review* 58 (1837): 147–96.

Crosby, Christina. *The Ends of History: Victorians and "the Woman Question."* New York: Routledge, 1991.

Davies, Godfrey. "Dr. Johnson on History." *Huntington Library Quarterly* 12 (1948): 1–21.

Davis, Fanny. *The Ottoman Lady: A Social History from 1718 to 1918.* Westport, CT: Greenwood, 1986.

Davis, Lennard J. *Factual Fictions: The Origins of the English Novel.* New York: Columbia UP, 1983.

Davis, Natalie Zemon. "Gender and Genre: Women as Historical Writers, 1400–1820." *Beyond Their Sex: Learned Women of the European Past.* Ed. Patricia H. Labalme. New York: New York UP, 1980. 153–82.

———. "History's Two Bodies." *American History Review* 93 (1988): 1–30.

De Bruyn, Frans. "Edmund Burke's Gothic Romance: The Portrayal of Warren Hastings in Burke's Writings and Speeches on India." *Criticism* 29.4 (1987): 415–38.

De Rose, Peter L., and S. W. McGuire. *A Concordance to the Works of Jane Austen.* New York: Garland, 1982.

Directions for a Proper Choice of Authors to Form a Library. [Signed N. N.] London: John Whiston, 1766.

Ditchfield, G. M. "Some Literary and Political Views of Catharine Macaulay." *American Notes and Queries* 12 (1974): 70–76.

Donagan, Barbara. "Understanding Providence: The Difficulties of Sir William and Lady Waller." *Journal of Ecclesiastical History* 39.3 (1988): 433–44.

Donawerth, Jane. "'As Becomes a Rational Woman to Speak': Madeleine de Scudéry's Rhetoric of Conversation." *Listening to Their Voices: The Rhetorical Activities of Historical Women.* Ed. Molly Meijer Werthheimer. Columbia: U of South Carolina P, 1997. 305–19.

Donnelly, Lucy. "The Celebrated Mrs. Macaulay." *William and Mary Quarterly* 6 (1949): 173–207.

Doody, Margaret. "Shakespeare's Novels: Charlotte Lennox Illustrated." *Studies in the Novel* 19 (1987): 296–310.

Dorn, Judith. "Reading Women Reading History: Form in Charlotte Lennox's 'The Lady's Museum.'" *Historical Reflections/Réflexions Historiques* 18.3 (1992): 7–27.

Douglas, David C. *English Scholars.* London: Jonathan Cape, 1939.

Duby, Georges, and Michelle Perrot. "Writing the History of Women." *A History of Women in the West.* Vol. 1. Ed. Georges Duby and Michelle Perrot. Cambridge: Harvard UP, 1992. 3 vols. ix–xxiii.

Duckworth, Alistair. *The Improvement of the Estate: A Study of Jane Austen's Novels.* 1971. Baltimore: Johns Hopkins UP, 1994.

Dussinger, John. "Hester Piozzi, Italy, and the Johnsonian Aether." *South Central Review* 9.4 (1992): 46–58.

———. "Jane Austen's Political Silence." *Dolphin* 19 (1990): 33–42.

Edgeworth, Maria, and Richard Lovell Edgeworth. *Practical Education.* Ed. Gina Luria. New York: Garland, 1974. 2 vols.

Ehrenpreis, Anne. "*Northanger Abbey:* Jane Austen and Charlotte Smith." *Nine-teeth-Century Fiction* 25 (1970): 343–48.

Ellison, Julie. "There and Back: Transatlantic Novels and Anglo-American Careers." *The Past as Prologue: Essays to Celebrate the Twenty-fifth Anniversary of ASECS.* Ed. Carla H. Hay and Syndy M. Conger. New York: AMS, 1995. 303–23.

Elstob, Elizabeth. *The Rudiments of Grammar for the English-Saxon Tongue, First Given in English: With an Apology for the Study of Northern Antiquities. Being Very Useful towards the Understanding Our Ancient English Poets, and Other Writers.* London: W. Bowyer, 1715.

Emden, Cecil S. "The Composition of *Northanger Abbey*." *Review of English Studies* 19.75 (1968): 279–87.

Epstein, Joseph. "Wise, Foolish, Enchanting Lady Mary." *New Criterion* 13.5 (1995): 8–17.

Epstein, Julia. "Jane Austen's Juvenilia and the Female Epistolary Tradition." *Papers on Language and Literature* 21 (1985): 399–416.

Esdaile, Arundell. "Hester Thrale." *Quarterly Review* 284 (1946): 179–94.

Essex, John. *The Young Ladies Conduct, or Rules for Education, under Several Heads; with Instructions upon Dress, both before and after Marriage. And Advice to Young Wives.* London: John Brotherton, 1722.

Ezell, Margaret J. M. *The Patriarch's Wife.* Chapel Hill: U of North Carolina P, 1987.

———. *Writing Women's Literary History.* Baltimore: Johns Hopkins UP, 1992.

Favret, Mary A. *Romantic Correspondence: Women, Politics, and the Fiction of Letters.* Cambridge: Cambridge UP, 1993.

Feather, John. "British Publishing in the Eighteenth Century: A Preliminary Subject Analysis." *Library* 8 (1986): 32–46.

———. *A History of British Publishing.* London: Routledge, 1988.

Fénelon, François de Salignac de La Mothe-. *The Accomplish'd Governess, or Short Instructions for the Education of the Fair Sex. Abridg'd from a Long and Curious Dissertation on That Interesting Subject, Composed Originally in the French Tongue.* London, 1752.

———. *Instructions for the Education of Daughters.* Trans. George Hickes. Glasgow: R. and A. Foulis, 1750.

Fergus, Jan. *Jane Austen: A Literary Life.* New York: St. Martin's, 1991.

———. *Jane Austen and the Didactic Novel: "Northanger Abbey," "Sense and Sensibility," and "Pride and Prejudice."* Totowa, NJ: Barnes and Noble, 1983.

Ferris, Ina. *The Achievement of Literary Authority: Gender, History, and the Waverley Novels.* Ithaca: Cornell UP, 1991.

Fielding, Henry. *Tom Jones.* Ed. Sheridan Baker. 2nd ed. New York: W. W. Norton, 1995.

Findley, Sandra, and Elaine Hobby. "Seventeenth-Century Women's Autobiography." *1642: Literature and Power in Seventeenth-Century England*. Ed. Francis Barker et al. Essex: U of Essex P, 1981. 11–36.

Firth, C. H. "The Development of the Study of Seventeenth-Century History." *Transactions of the Royal Historical Society* 7 (1913): 25–48.

Fitzsimons, M. A. "Political Histories and Memoirs in the Seventeenth Century." *The Development of Historiography*. Ed. M. A. Fitzsimons et al. Harrisburg, PA: Stackpole, 1954. 133–45.

Fleming, Caleb. *An Apologetical View of the Moral and Religious Sentiments of the Late Right Honourable Lord Viscount Bolingbroke. Taken from His Letters on the Study and Use of History*. London: J. Noon and R. Baldwin, 1754.

Forfreedom, Ann. *Women out of History: A Herstory Anthology*. Los Angeles: Everywoman, 1972.

Foucault, Michel. *The Order of Things: An Archaeology of the Human Sciences*. New York: Random House, 1970.

Fox, Claire Gilbride. "Catharine Macaulay, an Eighteenth-Century Clio." *Winterthur Portfolio* 4 (1968): 129–42.

Fraiman, Susan. "Jane Austen and Edward Said: Gender, Culture, and Imperialism." *Critical Inquiry* 21 (1995): 805–21.

Fraser, Antonia. *The Weaker Vessel*. New York: Vintage, 1984.

Fruchtman, Jack, Jr. "Public Loathing, Private Thoughts: Historical Representation in Helen Maria Williams' *Letters from France*." *Prose Studies* 18.3 (1995): 223–43.

Fussner, F. Smith. *The Historical Revolution: English Historical Writing and Thought, 1580–1640*. New York: Columbia UP, 1962.

Gallagher, Catherine. *Nobody's Story: The Vanishing Acts of Women Writers in the Marketplace, 1670–1820*. Berkeley: U of California P, 1994.

Gardiner, Ellen. "Writing Men Reading in Charlotte Lennox's *The Female Quixote*." *Studies in the Novel* 28.1 (1996): 1–11.

Gardner, Catherine. "Catharine Macaulay's Letters on Education: Odd but Equal." *Hypatia* 13.1 (1998): 118–37.

Gearhart, Suzanne. *The Open Boundary of History and Fiction: A Critical Approach to the French Enlightenment*. Princeton: Princeton UP, 1984.

Geiger, Marianne B. "Mercy Otis Warren and Catharine Sawbridge Macaulay: Historians in the Transatlantic Republican Tradition." Diss. New York U, 1986.

George, Margaret. *Women in the First Capitalist Society: Experiences in Seventeenth Century England*. Urbana: U of Illinois P, 1988.

Gilbert, Sandra M., and Susan Gubar. *The Madwoman in the Attic: The Woman Writer and the Nineteenth-Century Literary Imagination*. New Haven: Yale UP, 1979.

———. *The Norton Anthology of Literature by Women: The Tradition in English*. 2nd ed. New York: Norton, 1996.

Gocek, Fatma Muge. *East Encounters West: France and the Ottoman Empire in the Eighteenth Century*. New York: Oxford UP, 1987.

Goldgar, Bertrand. "Fielding on Fiction and History." *Eighteenth-Century Fiction* 7.3 (1995): 279–92.

Goldsmith, Oliver. *An History of England, in a Series of Letters from a Nobleman to His Son*. London: J. Newberry, 1764. 2 vols.

———. *Miscellaneous Works of Oliver Goldsmith*. Ed. James Prior. Vol. 3. London: John Murray, 1837. 4 vols.

Gooch, G. P. *History and Historians in the Nineteenth Century*. Boston: Beacon, 1959.

Goodwill, Jasper. "The History of England by Question and Answer." *Ladies' Magazine* 1.1 (1749): 1–2+.

Gordon, Scott Paul. "The Space of Romance in Lennox's *Female Quixote*." *Studies in English Literature* 38 (1998): 499–516.

Gossman, Lionel. *Between History and Literature*. Cambridge: Harvard UP, 1990.

Graham, James. *A Short Inquiry into the Present State of Medical Practice, in Consumptions, Asthmas, Nervous Disorders, & c. and a More Elegant, Speedy, and Certain Method of Cure, by Means of Certain Chemical Essences, and Aërial, Aetherial, Magnetic, and Electrical Vapours, Medicines, and Applications—Recommended*. 2nd ed. London: F. Newbery, 1777.

Gransden, Antonia. *Historical Writing in England II: c. 1307 to the Early Sixteenth Century*. London: Routledge and Kegan Paul, 1982.

Gray, James. "Dr. Johnson, Charlotte Lennox, and the Englishing of Father Brumoy." *Modern Philology* 83 (1985): 142–50.

Green, A. S. *Woman's Place in the World of Letters*. London: Macmillan, 1913.

Green, Katherine Sobba. *The Courtship Novel, 1740–1820: A Feminized Genre*. Lexington: UP of Kentucky, 1991.

Green, Mary Elizabeth. "Elizabeth Elstob: The Saxon Nymph." *Female Scholars: A Tradition of Learned Women before 1800*. Ed. J. R. Brink. Montreal: Eden, 1980. 137–60.

Green, Susan. "A Cultural Reading of Charlotte Lennox's *Shakespear Illustrated*." *Cultural Readings of Restoration and Eighteenth-Century Theater*. Ed. J. Douglas Canfield and Deborah C. Payne. Athens: U of Georgia P, 1995. 228–57.

Greene, Donald. "The Myth of Limitation." *Jane Austen Today*. Ed. Joel Weinsheimer. Athens: U of Georgia P, 1975. 142–75.

Greer, Germaine et al., ed. *Kissing the Rod: An Anthology of Seventeenth-Century Women's Verse*. New York: Farrar, Straus and Giroux, 1988.

Grundy, Isobel. *Lady Mary Wortley Montagu*. Oxford: Oxford UP, 1999.

———. "Lady Mary Wortley Montagu's 'Italian Memoir.'" *Age of Johnson* 6 (1994): 321–46.

———. "The Politics of Female Authorship: Lady Mary Wortley Montagu's Reaction to the Printing of Her Poems." *Book Collector* 31.1 (1982): 19–37.

———. "'Trash, Trumpery, and Idle Time': Lady Mary Wortley Montagu and Fiction." *Eighteenth-Century Fiction* 5.4 (1993): 293–310.

———. "Women's History? Writing by English Nuns." *Women, Writing, History:*

1640–1740. Ed. Isobel Grundy and Susan Wiseman. Athens: U of Georgia P, 1992. 126–38.

Hale, Sarah Josepha Buell. *Woman's Record, or Sketches of All Distinguished Women, from "the Beginning" till A.D. 1850: Arranged in Four Eras. With Selections from Female Writers of Every Age.* London: S. Low, 1853.

Halsband, Robert. "'Condemned to Petticoats': Lady Mary Wortley Montagu as Feminist and Writer." *The Dress of Words: Essays on Restoration and Eighteenth Century Literature in Honor of Richmond P. Bond.* Ed. Robert B. White Jr. Lawrence: U of Kansas P, 1978. 35–52.

———. "Lady Mary Wortley Montagu and Eighteenth-Century Fiction." *Philological Quarterly* 45 (1966): 145–56.

———. *The Life of Lady Mary Wortley Montagu.* New York: Oxford UP, 1960.

Hamalian, Leo, ed. *Ladies on the Loose: Women Travellers of the Eighteenth and Nineteenth Centuries.* New York: Dodd, Mead, 1981.

Handley, George M. *Notes on the Memoirs of Colonel Hutchinson.* London: Normal, 1905.

Harris, Jocelyn. *Jane Austen's Art of Memory.* Cambridge: Cambridge UP, 1989.

Hatton, Ragnhild. *George I: Elector and King.* Cambridge: Harvard UP, 1978.

Haviland, Thomas Phillip. "The Roman de Longue Haleine on English Soil." Diss. U of Pennsylvania, 1931.

Hay, Carla H. "Catharine Macaulay and the American Revolution." *Historian* 56.2 (1994): 301–16.

———. "John Sawbridge and 'Popular Politics' in Eigtheenth-Century Britain." *Historian* 52.4 (1990): 551–65.

Hays, Mary. *Female Biography.* Philadelphia: Birch and Small, 1807. 3 vols.

Haywood, Ian. *The Making of History: A Study of the Literary Forgeries of James MacPherson and Thomas Chatterton in relation to Eighteenth-Century Ideas of History and Fiction.* Rutherford, NJ: Fairleigh Dickinson UP, 1986.

Heath, Tim, adapt. and dir. "The History of England." By Jane Austen. Perf. Rebecca Blech. Unpublished manuscript, 1996.

Hicks, Philip S. *Neo-classical History and English Culture: From Clarendon to Hume.* New York: St. Martin's, 1996.

Hill, Bridget. "The Links between Mary Wollstonecraft and Catharine Macaulay: New Evidence." *Women's History Review* 4.2 (1995): 177–92.

———. *The Republican Virago: The Life and Times of Catharine Macaulay, Historian.* Oxford: Clarendon, 1992.

Hill, Bridget, and Christopher Hill. "Catharine Macaulay and the Seventeenth Century." *Welsh History Review* 3 (1967): 381–402.

———. "Catharine Macaulay's *History* and Her Catalogue of Tracts." *Seventeenth Century* 8.2 (1993): 269–85.

Hill, Christopher. "Colonel John Hutchinson, 1615–1664: A Tercenary Tribute." *Transactions of the Thoroton Society of Nottinghamshire* 69 (1965): 85–86.

Hill, Herbert Wynford. *La Calprenède's Romances and the Restoration Drama.* Ed. Committee on Publications. Vols. 2.3 and 3.2. Chicago: U of Nevada [U of Chicago P], 1910–11.

"Histories of the Tête-à-Tête Annexed, or Memoirs of the POLITICAL and PLATONIC LOVERS." *Town and Country Magazine* 8 (1776): 674–78.

Rev. of *History of England from the Revolution to the Present Time* by Catharine Macaulay. *Critical Review* 45 (1778): 130–34.

Rev. of *History of England from the Revolution to the Present Time,* by Catharine Macaulay. *Monthly Review* 58–59 (1778): 111–21; 289–95; 124–32.

Hobby, Elaine, and Elspeth Graham et al., eds. *Virtue of Necessity: English Women's Writing, 1649–88.* London: Routledge, 1990.

Hobman, D. A. "A Puritan Lady." *Contemporary Review* 176 (1949): 115–18.

Hodge, Jane Aiken. "Jane Austen and Her Publishers." *Jane Austen: Bicentenary Essays.* Ed. John Halperin. Cambridge: Cambridge UP, 1975. 75–88.

Honan, Park. *Jane Austen: Her Life.* London: Weidenfeld and Nicholson, 1987.

Hoople, Sally C. "The Spanish, English, and American Quixotes." *Annales Cervantinos* 22 (1984): 119–42.

Hopkins, Robert. "General Tilney and Affairs of State: The Political Gothic of *Northanger Abbey.*" *Philological Quarterly* 57 (1978): 213–24.

Horwitz, Barbara. *British Women Writers, 1700–1850: An Annotated Bibliography of Their Works and Works about Them.* Lanham, MD: Scarecrow, 1997.

Hudson, Roger. *The Grand Quarrel: From the Civil War Memoirs of Mrs. Lucy Hutchinson; Mrs. Alice Thornton; Ann, Lady Fanshawe; Margaret, Duchess of Newcastle; Anne, Lady Halkett, and the Letters of Brilliana, Lady Harley.* London: Folio Society, 1993.

Hufstader, Alice Anderson. *Sisters of the Quill.* New York: Dodd, Mead, 1978.

Hughes, S. F. D. "Mrs. Elstob's Defense of Antiquarian Learning in Her *Rudiments of Grammar for the English-Saxon Tongue* (1715)." *Harvard Library Bulletin* 27 (1979): 172–91.

Hull, Suzanne. *Chaste, Silent and Obedient: English Books for Women, 1475–1640.* San Marino, CA: Huntington, 1982.

Humm, Maggie. *The Dictionary of Feminist Theory.* Columbus: Ohio UP, 1990.

Hunter, J. Paul. *Before Novels: The Cultural Contexts of Eighteenth Century English Fiction.* New York: W. W. Norton, 1990.

Hutchinson, John. *A Narrative of the Imprisonment and Usage of Col. John Hutchinson of Owthorpe . . . Now Close Prisoner in the Tower. Written by Himself on the 6th of April 1664 . . . for the Satisfying His Relations and Friends of His Innocence.* London, 1664.

Hutchinson, Lucy. *Colonel Hutchinson: Roundhead.* Ed. Helen Kendrick Hayes. London: Sisley's, 1909.

———. *Memoirs of the Life of Colonel Hutchinson.* Ed. Julius Hutchinson. 4th ed. London: Longman, Hurst, Rees, Orme, and Brown, 1822.

——. *Memoirs of the Life of Colonel Hutchinson.* London: George Bell, 1863.

——. *Memoirs of the Life of Colonel Hutchinson.* Ed. C. H. Firth. London: George Routledge, 1906.

——. *Memoirs of the Life of Colonel Hutchinson.* Ed. Julius Hutchinson. Intro. Margaret Bottrall. London: J. M. Dent, 1968.

——. *Memoirs of the Life of Colonel Hutchinson.* Ed. James Sutherland. London: Oxford UP, 1973.

——. *Memoirs of the Life of Colonel Hutchinson.* Ed. N. H. Keeble. London: Everyman, 1995.

——. *"On the Principles of Christian Religion," Addressed to Her Daughter; and "On Theology."* London: Longman, Hurst, Rees, Orme, and Brown, 1817.

Isles, Duncan. "Johnson and Charlotte Lennox." *New Rambler* 3 (June 1967): 34–48.

——. "Johnson, Richardson, and *The Female Quixote*." *The Female Quixote.* Ed. Margaret Dalziel. Oxford: Oxford UP, 1970. 419–28.

——. "The Lennox Collection." *Harvard Library Bulletin* 18 (1970): 317–44.

——. "The Lennox Collection." *Harvard Library Bulletin* 19 (1971): 36–60, 165–86, 416–35.

——. "Unpublished Johnson Letters." *Times Literary Supplement* 29 (July 1965): 666.

Italiano, Gloria. "Two Parallel Biographers of the Seventeenth Century: Margaret Newcastle and Lucy Hutchinson." *Critical Dimensions: English, German, and Comparative Literature Essays in Honour of Aurelio Zanco.* Ed. Mario Curreli and Alberto Martino. Cuneo, Italy: SASTE, 1978. 241–51.

Jeffrey, Francis. Rev. of *Memoirs of the Life of Colonel Hutchinson,* by Lucy Hutchinson. *Edinburgh Review* 13.25 (1808): 1–25.

Joddrell, Richard Paul. *The Female Patriot: An Epistle from C-t-e M-c-y to the Rev. Dr. W-l-n on Her Late Marriage.* London: J. Bew, 1779.

Johnson, Claudia L. *Jane Austen: Women, Politics, and the Novel.* Chicago: U of Chicago P, 1988.

——. " 'The Kingdom at Sixes and Sevens': Politics and the Juvenilia." *Jane Austen's Beginnings: The Juvenilia and "Lady Susan."* Ed. J. David Grey. Ann Arbor: UMI, 1989. 45–58.

Johnson, Samuel. *Selected Essays from the "Rambler," "Adventurer," and "Idler."* Ed. W. J. Bate. New Haven: Yale UP, 1968.

Jones, Vivien, ed. *Women in the Eighteenth Century: Constructions of Femininity.* New York: Routledge, 1990.

——. "Women Writing Revolution: Narratives of History and Sexuality in Wollstonecraft and Williams." *Beyond Romanticism: New Approaches to Texts and Contexts, 1780–1832.* Ed. Stephen Copley and John Whale. New York: Routledge, 1992. 178–99.

Kauvar, Elaine M. "Jane Austen and *The Female Quixote*." *Studies in the Novel* 2 (1970): 211–21.

Kearful, Frank J. "Satire and the Form of the Novel: The Problem of Aesthetic Unity in *Northanger Abbey*." *ELH* 32 (1965): 511–27.

Keddie, Nikki R., and Beth Baron, eds. *Women in Middle Eastern History*. New Haven: Yale UP, 1991.

Keeble, N. H. " 'The Colonel's Shadow': Lucy Hutchinson, Women's Writing and the Civil War." *Literature and the English Civil War*. Ed. Thomas and Jonathan Sawday Healy. Cambridge: Cambridge UP, 1990. 227–47.

Kelley, Donald R., ed. *Versions of History from Antiquity to the Enlightenment*. New Haven: Yale UP, 1991.

Kelley, Donald R., and David Harris Sacks, eds. *The Historical Imagination in Early Modern Britain: History, Rhetoric, and Fiction, 1500–1800*. New York: Cambridge UP, 1991.

Kelly, Gary. "Religion and Politics." *Cambridge Companion to Jane Austen*. Ed. Edward Copeland and Juliet McMaster. Cambridge: Cambridge UP, 1997. 149–69.

Kent, Christopher. "Learning History with, and from, Jane Austen." *Jane Austen's Beginnings: The Juvenilia and "Lady Susan."* Ed. J. David Grey. Ann Arbor: UMI, 1989. 59–72.

———. " 'Real Solemn History' and Social History." *Jane Austen in a Social Context*. Ed. David Monaghan. London: Macmillan, 1981. 86–104.

Kenyon, John. *The History Men: The Historical Profession in England since the Renaissance*. Pittsburgh: U of Pittsburgh P, 1984.

Kerber, Linda. *Toward an Intellectual History of Women*. Chapel Hill: U of North Carolina P, 1997.

Kettle, Arnold. "The Precursors of Defoe: Puritanism and the Rise of the Novel." *On the Novel: A Birthday Present for Walter Allen on His Sixtieth Birthday*. Ed. B. S. Benedikz. London: J. M. Dent, 1971. 201–16.

Kietzman, Mary Jo. "Montagu's *Turkish Embassy Letters* and Cultural Dislocation." *Studies in English Literature* 38 (1998): 537–51.

Kirkham, Margaret. *Jane Austen, Feminism, and Fiction*. Sussex: Harvester, 1983.

Klingberg, F. J., and S. B. Hustvedt, eds. *The Warning Drum: The British Home Front Faces Napoleon: Broadsides of 1803*. Berkeley: U of California P, 1944.

Knapp, Oswald G., ed. *The Intimate Letters of Hester Piozzi and Penelope Pennington, 1788–1821*. London: John Lane, 1914.

Knipp, Christopher. "Types of Orientalism in Eighteenth-Century England." Diss. U of California–Berkeley, 1974.

Kramnick, Isaac. *Bolingbroke and His Circle: The Politics of Nostalgia in the Age of Walpole*. Cambridge: Harvard UP, 1968.

Kramnick, Jonathan Brody. "Reading Shakespeare's Novels: Literary History and Cultural Politics in the Lennox-Johnson Debate." *Modern Language Quarterly* 55.4 (1994): 429–53.

Kroeber, Karl. "Jane Austen as an Historical Novelist: Sense and Sensibility." *Persuasions* 12 (1990): 10–18.

Kucich, Greg. "Romanticism and Feminist Historiography." *Wordsworth Circle* 24.3 (1993): 133–40.

———. "Staging History: Teaching Romantic Intersections of Drama, History, and Gender." *Approaches to Teaching British Women Poets of the Romantic Period.* Ed. Stephen C. Behrendt and Harriet Kramer Linkin. New York: MLA, 1997. 88–96.

———. "'This Horrid Theatre of Human Sufferings': Gendering the Stages of History in Catharine Macaulay and Percy Bysshe Shelley." *Lessons of Romanticism: A Critical Companion.* Ed. Thomas Pfau and Robert Gleckner. Durham: Duke UP, 1998. 448–65.

La Beaumelle, Laurent. *Memoirs for the History of Madame de Maintenon and of the Last Age.* Trans. Charlotte Lennox. London: A. Millar and J. Nourse, 1757. 5 vols.

Langbauer, Laurie. *Women and Romance: Consolations of Gender in the English Novel.* Ithaca: Cornell UP, 1990.

Lascelles, Mary. *Jane Austen and Her Art.* Oxford: Oxford UP, 1939.

Lee, Sophia. *The Recess, or A Tale of Other Times.* New York: Arno, 1972. 3 vols.

Lennox, Charlotte. "The Art of Coquetry." *Gentleman's Magazine* 20 (November 1750): 518–19.

———. *The Female Quixote.* Ed. Sandra Shulman. New York: Pandora, 1986.

———. *The Female Quixote.* Ed. Margaret Dalziel. Oxford: Oxford UP, 1989.

———, ed. *The Lady's Museum.* 2 vols. London: J. Newbery, 1760–61.

———. Letter to Unknown Addressee ("Sir"). 3 February 1952. Gunther Collection, Chicago Historical Society, Chicago.

———. *The Life of Harriot Stuart, Written by Herself.* Ed. Susan Kubica Howard. Teaneck, NJ: Fairleigh Dickinson UP, 1995.

———. *Poems on Several Occasions. Written by a Young Lady.* London: S. Paterson, 1747.

———. *Shakespear Illustrated, or The Novels and Histories, on Which the Plays of Shakespear Are Founded, Collected and Translated from the Original Authors with Critical Remarks.* London: A. Millar, 1753–54. 3 vols.

———. *The Sister: A Comedy.* 2nd ed. London: J. Dodsley, 1769.

Lerner, Gerda. *The Creation of Feminist Consciousness: From the Middle Ages to Eighteen-Seventy.* New York: Oxford UP, 1993.

———. "The Necessity of History and the Professional Historian." *The Vital Past.* Ed. Stephen Vaughan. Athens: U of Georgia P, 1985. 104–15.

Leslie, Doris. *A Toast to Lady Mary.* London: Hutchinson, 1954.

"Letter from a Gentleman in Town to His Friend in the Country, concerning Celebrated Fair Historians." [Signed P. N.] *Town and Country Magazine* 1 (1796): 91–92.

Letzring, Monica. "Sarah Prince Gill and the John Adams–Catharine Macaulay Correspondence." *Proceedings of the Massachusetts Historical Society* 88 (1976): 107–11.

Levin, Kate. " 'The Cure of Arabella's Mind: Charlotte Lennox and the Disciplining of the Female Reader." *Women's Writing* 2.3 (1995): 271–90.

Levine, George. "Translating the Monstrous: *Northanger Abbey.*" *Nineteenth-Century Fiction* 30 (1975): 335–50.

Levine, Joseph M. *The Battle of the Books: History and Literature in the Augustan Age.* Ithaca: Cornell UP, 1991.

Levine, Philippa. *The Amateur and the Professional: Antiquarians, Historians and Archaeologists in Victorian England, 1838–1886.* Cambridge: Cambridge UP, 1986.

Lew, Joseph W. "Lady Mary's Portable Seraglio." *Eighteenth-Century Studies* 24.4 (1991): 432–50.

Lewis, Jayne Elizabeth. " 'Ev'ry Lost Relation': Historical Fictions and Sentimental Incidents in Sophia Lee's *The Recess.*" *Eighteenth-Century Fiction* 7.2 (1995): 165–84.

Litvak, Joseph. "Charming Men, Charming History." *On Your Left: Historical Materialism in the 1990s.* Ed. Ann Kibbey et al. New York: New York UP, 1996. 248–74.

———. *Strange Gourmets: Sophistication, Theory, and the Novel.* Durham: Duke UP, 1997.

Litz, A. Walton. *Jane Austen: A Study of Her Artistic Development.* New York: Oxford UP, 1965.

Lofft, Capel. *Observations on Mrs. Macaulay's "History of England" (Lately Published) from the Revolution to the Resignation of Sir Robert Walpole in a Letter Addressed to That Lady.* London: Edward and Charles Dilly, 1778.

Looser, Devoney, ed. *Jane Austen and Discourses of Feminism.* New York: St. Martin's, 1995.

———. "(Re)Making History and Philosophy: Austen's *Northanger Abbey.*" *European Romantic Review* 4.1 (1993): 34–56.

Love, Harold. *Scribal Publication in Seventeenth-Century England.* Oxford: Clarendon, 1993.

Loveridge, Mark. "*Northanger Abbey,* or Nature and Probability." *Nineteenth-Century Literature* 56.1 (1991): 1–29.

Lowe, Lisa. *Critical Terrains: French and British Orientalisms.* Ithaca: Cornell UP, 1991.

Lowenthal, Cynthia. *Lady Mary Wortley Montagu and the Eighteenth-Century Familiar Letter.* Athens: U of Georgia P, 1994.

Lucretius Carus, Titus. *Lucy Hutchinson's Translation of Lucretius, "De Rerum Natura."* Ed. Hugh de Quehen. Ann Arbor: U of Michigan P, 1996.

Lynch, James J. "Romance and Realism in Charlotte Lennox's *The Female Quixote.*" *Essays in Literature* 14.1 (1987): 51–63.

Mabro, Judy, ed. *Veiled Half-Truths: Western Travellers' Perceptions of Middle Eastern Women.* London: I. B. Tauris, 1991.

Macaulay, Catharine. "An Address to the People of England, Ireland, and Scotland on the Present Important Crisis of Affairs." *English Defenders of American Freedoms, 1774–8.* Ed. Paul H. Smith. Washington, DC: Library of Congress, 1972. 113–22.

———. *The History of England from the Accession of James I, to That of the Brunswick Line.* Vol. 1. London: J. Nourse, 1763. 8 vols.

———. *The History of England from the Accession of James I, to the Elevation of the House of Hanover.* Vol. 1. London: Edward and Charles Dilly, 1769. 5 vols.

———. *The History of England from the Revolution to the Present Time: In a Series of Letters to a Friend.* Vol. 1. Bath: R. Crutwell, 1778.

———. *Letters on Education.* New York: Woodstock, 1994.

———. *Letters on Education.* Brookfield, VT: Pickering and Chatto, 1996.

———. *Letters on Education: With Observations on Religious and Metaphysical Subjects.* Ed. Gina Luria. New York: Garland, 1974.

———. *Loose Remarks on Certain Positions to Be Found in Mr. Hobbes's "Philosophical Rudiments of Government and Society." With "A Short Sketch of a Democratical Form of Government," in a Letter to Signor Paoli.* London: T. Davies, 1767.

———. *A Modest Plea for the Property of Copy Right.* London: E. and C. Dilly, 1774.

———. *Observations on the Reflections of the Right Hon. Edmund Burke, on the Revolution in France, in a Letter to the Right Hon. the Earl of Stanhope on Burke's Reflections on the French Revolution.* New York: Woodstock Books, 1997.

MacCarthy, B. G. *The Female Pen: Women Writers and Novelists, 1621–1818.* Cork: Cork UP, 1994.

———. *Women Writers: Their Contribution to the English Novel, 1621–1744.* Oxford: Cork UP, 1946.

MacDonagh, Oliver. *Jane Austen: Real and Imagined Worlds.* New Haven: Yale UP, 1991.

MacGillivray, Royce. *Restoration Historians and the English Civil War.* The Hague: Martinus Nijhoff, 1974.

———. "The Upham Thesis and the Literary Debts of Mrs. Lucy Hutchinson." *Revue de l'Université d'Ottawa* 40 (1970): 618–30.

MacKinnon, A. H. "The Augustan Intellectual and the Ignoble Savage: Houyhnhnm versus Hottentot." *Essays on English and American Literature and a Sheaf of Poems.* Ed. J. A. Verleun J. Bakker and J. V. D. Vriesenaerde. Vol. 63. Amsterdam: Rodopi, 1987. 56–63.

Maitzen, Rohan Amanda. *Gender, Genre, and Victorian Historical Writing.* New York: Garland, 1998.

———. " 'This Feminine Preserve': Historical Biographies by Victorian Women." *Victorian Studies* 38.3 (1995): 371–93.

Malina, Debra. "Rereading the Patriarchal Text: *The Female Quixote, Northanger Abbey,* and the Trace of the Absent Mother." *Eighteenth-Century Fiction* 8.2 (1996): 271–92.

Mandelkern, Michael. "Hester Lynch [Thrale] Piozzi." *Dictionary of Literary Biography.* Vol. 142. Detroit: Gale Research, 1981–. 251–60.

Mansell, Darrel. "The Date of Jane Austen's Revision of *Northanger Abbey.*" *English Language Notes* 7 (1969): 40–41.

Marlow, Joyce. *The Life and Times of George I.* London: Weidenfeld and Nicolson, 1973.

Marshall, David. "Writings Masters and 'Masculine Exercises' in *The Female Quixote.*" *Eighteenth-Century Fiction* 5.2 (1993): 105–35.

Martin, Ellen E. "The Madness of Jane Austen: Metonymic Style and Literature's Resistance to Interpretation." *Jane Austen's Beginnings: The Juvenilia and "Lady Susan."* Ed. J. David Grey. Ann Arbor: UMI, 1989. 83–94.

May, Thomas. *The History of the Parliament of England: Which Began November the Third, M.DC.XL. With a Short and Necessary View of Some Precedent Yeares.* London: Moses Bell, for George Thomason, 1647.

Mayer, Robert. *History and the Early English Novel: Matters of Fact from Bacon to Defoe.* Cambridge: Cambridge UP, 1997.

Maynadier, Gustavus. *The First American Novelist?* Cambridge: Harvard UP, 1940.

Mayo, Robert D. *The English Novel in the Magazines, 1740–1815.* Evanston, IL: Northwestern UP, 1962.

Mazzucco-Than, Cecile. " 'As Easy as a Chimney Pot to Blacken': Catharine Macaulay 'the Celebrated Female Historian.' " *Prose Studies: History, Theory and Criticism* 18.3 (1995): 78–104.

McCarthy, William. "Hester [Lynch Thrale] Piozzi." *Dictionary of British and American Women Writers, 1660–1800.* Ed. Janet Todd. Totowa, NJ: Rowman and Littlefield, 1987. 253–56.

———. *Hester Thrale Piozzi: Portrait of a Literary Woman.* Chapel Hill: U of North Carolina P, 1985.

———. "The Writings of Hester Lynch Piozzi: A Bibliography." *Bulletin of Bibliography* 45.2 (1988): 129–41.

McDougall, Dorothy. *Madeleine de Scudéry: Her Romantic Life and Death.* London: Methuen, 1938.

McDowell, R. B. *Alice Stopford Green: A Passionate Historian.* Dublin: A. Figgis, 1967.

McKeon, Michael. *The Origins of the English Novel: 1600–1740.* Baltimore: Johns Hopkins UP, 1987.

McVeagh, John, ed. *All Before Them: 1660–1780.* Vol. 1 of *English Literature and the Wider World.* London: Ashfield, 1990.

Melman, Billie. "Gender, History, and Memory: The Invention of Women's Past in the Nineteenth and Early Twentieth Centuries." *History and Memory* 5.1 (1993): 5–41.

———. *Women's Orients: English Women and the Middle East, 1718–1918.* 2nd ed. London: Macmillan, 1995.

Rev. of *Memoirs of the Life of Colonel Hutchinson,* by Lucy Hutchinson. *Censura Literaria* 4 (1807): 49–69, 181–93.

Rev. of *Memoirs of the Life of Colonel Hutchinson,* by Lucy Hutchinson. *Critical Review* 10 (1807): 66–89.

Rev. of *Memoirs of the Life of Colonel Hutchinson,* by Lucy Hutchinson. *Eclectic Review* 3 (1807): 16–25.

Rev. of *Memoirs of the Life of Colonel Hutchinson,* by Lucy Hutchinson. *Flower's Political Review and Monthly Register* 3 (January–June 1808): 241–43, 363–64, 102–5.

Menagh, Diane. "The Life of Marianne Francis; With an Account of Her Letters to Mrs. Piozzi, an Old Friend of the Family." *Bulletin of the New York Public Library* 80.3 (1977): 318–44.

Mendelson, Sara Heller. *Mental World of Stuart Women.* Brighton, Eng.: Sussex, 1987.

Mernissi, Fatima. *Beyond the Veil: Male-Female Dynamics in a Modern Muslim Society.* New York: Schenkman, 1975.

———. *Women and Islam: An Historical and Theological Enquiry.* Oxford: Basil Blackwell, 1991.

Merritt, Percival, ed. *Piozzi Marginalia, Comprising Some Extracts from the Manuscripts of Hester Lynch Piozzi and Annotations from Her Books.* Cambridge: Harvard UP, 1925.

———, ed. *The True Story of the So-Called Love Letters of Mrs. Piozzi: "In Defense of an Elderly Lady."* Cambridge: Harvard UP, 1927.

Messer, Peter C. "Writing Women into History: Defining Gender and Citizenship in Post-Revolutionary America." *Studies in Eighteenth-Century Culture* 28 (1999): 341–60.

Meynell, Alice. *Essays.* London: Burns and Oates, 1914.

Miles, Rosalind. *The Women's History of the World.* New York: Harper and Row, 1990.

Miller, Genevieve. "Putting Lady Mary in Her Place: A Discussion of Historical Causation." *Bulletin of the History of Medicine* 55.1 (1981): 2–16.

Millgate, Jane. "Prudential Lovers and Lost Heirs: *Persuasion* and the Presence of Scott." *Jane Austen's Business: Her World and Her Profession.* Ed. Juliet McMaster and Bruce Stovel. New York: St. Martin's, 1996. 109–23.

Mitchell, L. G. Rev. of *Republican Virago,* by Bridget Hill. *English Historical Review* 110 (1995): 761–62.

Mitchell, Rosemary Ann. "'The Busy Daughters of Clio': Women Writers of History from 1820 to 1880." *Women's History Review* 7.1 (1998): 107–34.

Moler, Kenneth L. *Jane Austen's Art of Allusion.* Lincoln: U of Nebraska P, 1968.

Momigliano, Arnaldo. "The Introduction of History as an Academic Subject and Its Implications." *The Golden and the Brazen World: Papers in Literature and History, 1650–1800.* Ed. John Wallace. Berkeley: U of California P, 1985. 187–204.

Monaghan, David. *Jane Austen in a Social Context*. London: Macmillan, 1981.

———. *Jane Austen: Structure and Social Vision*. London: Macmillan, 1980.

Montagu, Mary Wortley, Lady. *The Complete Letters of Lady Mary Wortley Montagu*. Ed. Robert Halsband. Oxford: Clarendon, 1965. 3 vols.

———. *Embassy to Constantinople: The Travels of Lady Mary Wortley Montagu*. Ed. Christopher Pick. Intro. Dervla Murphy. New York: New Amsterdam, 1988.

———. *Essays and Poems and "Simplicity, a Comedy."* Ed. Robert Halsband and Isobel Grundy. Oxford: Clarendon, 1977.

———. *Indamora to Lindamira*. Ed. Isobel Grundy. Edmonton: Department of English, U of Alberta [Juvenilia Press], 1994.

———. *Lady Mary Wortley Montagu: Select Passages from Her Letters*. Ed. Arthur R. Ropes. London: Grolier Society. 190?

———. *The Letters and Works of Lady Mary Wortley Montagu*. Ed. Lord Wharncliffe. Philadelphia: Carey, Lea and Blanchard, 1837. 2 vols.

———. *Letters from the Levant during the Embassy to Constantinople, 1716–18*. Ed. J. A. St. John. London: Joseph Rickerby, 1838.

———. *The Nonsense of Common-Sense*. Ed. Robert Halsband. New York: AMS, 1970.

———. *Romance Writings*. Ed. Isobel Grundy. Oxford: Clarendon, 1996.

Mooneyham, Laura J. *Romance, Language, and Education in Jane Austen's Novels*. New York: St. Martin's, 1988.

Morgan, Susan. "Guessing for Ourselves in *Northanger Abbey*." *Jane Austen: Modern Critical Views*. Ed. Harold Bloom. New York: Chelsea, 1986. 109–28.

Motooka, Wendy. *The Age of Reasons: Quixotism, Sentimentalism, and Political Economy in Eighteenth-Century Britain*. New York: Routledge, 1998.

———. "Coming to a Bad End: Sentimentalism, Hermeneutics, and *The Female Quixote*." *Eighteenth-Century Fiction* 8.2 (1996): 251–70.

Mudrick, Marvin. *Jane Austen: Irony as Defense and Discovery*. Princeton: Princeton UP, 1952.

Mukherjee, Meenakshi. *Jane Austen*. New York: Macmillan, 1991.

Murry, Ann. *Mentoria, or The Young Ladies Instructor, in Familiar Conversations on Moral and Entertaining Subjects: Calculated to Improve Young Minds in the Essential, as Well as Ornamental Parts of Female Education*. 6th ed. London: Charles Dilly, 1791.

Musters, Lina Chaworth. *A Cavalier Stronghold: A Romance of the Vale of Belvoir*. London: Simpkin, Marshall, Hamilton, Kent, 1890.

Myer, Valerie Grosvenor. *Jane Austen, Obstinate Heart: A Biography*. New York: Arcade, 1997.

Myers, Sylvia. *The Bluestocking Circle: Women, Friendship, and the Life of the Mind in Eighteenth-Century England*. Oxford: Clarendon, 1990.

Nadel, G. H. "New Light on Bolingbroke's Letters on History." *Journal of the History of Ideas* 23 (1962): 550–57.

Narveson, Katherine. "The Source for Lucy Hutchinson's *On Theology.*" *Notes and Queries* 36 (1989): 40–41.

Neill, Edward. "The Politics of 'Jane Austen.'" *English: The Journal of the English Association* 40.168 (1991): 205–13.

Newman, Barbara. "On the Ethics of Female Historiography." *Exemplaria* 2.2 (1990): 702–6.

Newton, A. Edward. *The Amenities of Book-Collecting and Kindred Affections.* Boston: Atlantic Monthly Press, 1918.

Nicolson, Harold. *Development of English Biography.* New York: Harcourt, Brace, 1928.

Nochlin, Linda. *Politics of Vision: Essays on Nineteenth-Century Art and Society.* New York: Harper and Row, 1989.

Nokes, David. *Jane Austen: A Life.* New York: Farrar, Straus and Giroux, 1997.

Norbrook, David. "A Devine Originall: Lucy Hutchinson and the 'Woman's Version.'" *Times Literary Supplement* 19 March 1999: 13–15.

———. "Lucy Hutchinson's 'Elegies' and the Situation of the Republican Woman Writer." *English Literary Renaissance* 27.3 (1997): 468–521.

Nussbaum, Felicity. *Torrid Zones: Maternity, Sexuality, and Empire in Eighteenth-Century English Narratives.* Baltimore: Johns Hopkins UP, 1995.

O'Brien, Karen. *Narratives of Enlightenment: Cosmopolitan History from Voltaire to Gibbon.* Cambridge: Cambridge UP, 1997.

Rev. of *Observations and Reflections Made in the Course of a Journey of France, Italy, and Germany,* by Hester Piozzi. *European Magazine* 16 (1789): 332–34, 403–4.

"Observations on, and Extracts from, Mrs. Macaulay's *History of England from the Revolution to the Present Time.*" *Westminster Magazine* 6 (1778): 59–63.

Rev. of *Observations on Mrs. Macaulay's History,* by Capel Lofft. *Critical Review* 45 (1778): 320.

Rev. of *Observations on Mrs. Macaulay's History,* by Capel Lofft. *Monthly Review* 59 (1778): 234.

Rev. of *Observations on Mrs. Macaulay's History,* by Capel Lofft. *Westminster Magazine* 6 (1778): 230.

O'Dowd, Mary, and Sabine Wichert, eds. *Chattel, Servant or Citizen: Women's Status in Church, State and Society.* Belfast: Institute of Irish Studies, 1995.

Okie, Laird. *Augustan Historical Writing: Histories of England in the English Enlightenment.* Langham, MD: UP of America, 1991.

Orr, Bridget. "'The Only Free People in the Empire': Gender Difference in Colonial Discourse." *De-scribing Empire.* Ed. E. Tiffin and A. Lawson. London: Routledge, 1994. 152–68.

Orr, Linda. "The Revenge of Literature: A History of History." *New Literary History* 18 (1986–87): 1–22.

Patey, Douglas Lane. *Probability and Literary Form: Philosophic Theory and Literary Practice in the Augustan Age.* Cambridge: Cambridge UP, 1984.

Patterson, Lee. "Literary History." *Critical Terms for Literary Study*. Ed. Frank Lentricchia and Thomas McLaughlin. Chicago: U of Chicago P, 1990. 250–62.

Paulson, Ronald. *Don Quixote in England: The Aesthetics of Laughter*. Baltimore: Johns Hopkins UP, 1997.

———. *Representations of Revolution (1790–1820)*. New Haven: Yale UP, 1983.

———. *Satire and the Novel in Eighteenth-Century England*. New Haven: Yale UP, 1967.

Pennington, Lady Sarah. *An Unfortunate Mother's Advice to Her Absent Daughters*. New York: Garland, 1986.

Perry, Ruth. *The Celebrated Mary Astell: An Early English Feminist*. Chicago: U of Chicago P, 1986.

———. "Two Forgotten Wits." *Antioch Review* 39.4 (1981): 431–38.

———. *Women, Letters and the Novel*. New York: AMS, 1980.

Pierpoint, Robert. " 'History': The Marble Statue in the Entrance Hall of Warrington Town Hall." For private circulation, 1908. Rpt. from the *Warrington Guardian,* December 1908.

Pilkington, Mary. *A Mirror for the Female Sex: Historical Beauties for Young Ladies. Intended to Lead the Female Mind to the Love and Practice of Moral Goodness. Designed Principally for the Use of Ladies' Schools*. London: Vernor and Hood, 1798.

Piozzi, Hester. *British Synonymy*. Ed. R. C. Alston. Menston, Eng.: Scolar, 1968. 2 vols.

———. "Mrs. Piozzi's Appeal against the Critical Reviewers." *Gentleman's Magazine* 71 (1801): 602–3.

———. *Retrospection, or A Review of the Most Striking and Important Events, Characters, Situations and Their Consequences, Which the Last Eighteen Hundred Years Have Presented to the View of Mankind*. London: Stockdale, 1801. 2 vols.

Plaisant, Michele. "Les lettres turques de Lady Mary Wortley Montagu." *Bulletin de la Sociétés d'Études Anglo-Américaines des XVII et XVIII Siècles* 16 (1983): 53–75.

Plowden, Alison. *Women All on Fire: The Women of the English Civil War*. Thrupp, Eng.: Sutton, 1998.

Pocock, J. G. A. *The Ancient Constitution and the Feudal Law*. New York: W. W. Norton, 1967.

———. "Catharine Macaulay: Patriot Historian." *Women Writers and the Early Modern British Political Tradition*. Ed. Hilda L. Smith. Cambridge: Cambridge UP, 1998. 243–58.

———. *Virtue, Commerce, and History*. Cambridge: Cambridge UP, 1985.

Pointon, Marcia. *Hanging the Head: Portraiture and Social Formation in Eighteenth-Century England*. New Haven: Yale UP, 1993.

Preston, Thomas R. "Historiography as Art in Eighteenth-Century England." *Texas Studies in Literature and Language* 11 (1969–70): 1209–21.

Race, Sydney. "Colonel Hutchinson, Governor of Nottingham Castle, and Regicide." *Notes and Queries* 174 (1938): 39.

———. "Colonel Hutchinson: Manuscript and Printed Memoirs." *Notes and Queries* 199 (1954): 160–63, 202–4.

———. "Colonel Hutchinson, the Regicide." *Notes and Queries* 197 (1952): 32–33.

———. "Notes on Mrs. Hutchinson's Manuscripts." *Notes and Queries* 145 (1923): 3–4, 26–28, 165–66.

Rafferty, Deirdre. *Women and Learning in English Writing, 1600–1900.* Dublin: Four Courts, 1997.

Ralli, Augustus. *A History of Shakespearian Criticism.* London: Oxford UP, 1932. 2 vols.

Reddy, T. Vasudeva. *Jane Austen: The Dialectics of Self-Actualization in Her Novels.* London: Oriental UP, 1987.

Reed, Walter L. *An Exemplary History of the Novel: The Quixotic versus the Picaresque.* Chicago: U of Chicago P, 1981.

Reese, Lyn, and Jean Wilkinson, eds. *Women in the World: Annotated History Resources for the Secondary Student.* Metuchen, NJ: Scarecrow, 1987.

Reeve, Clara. *The Progress of Romance.* New York: Facsimile Text Society, 1930.

A Remarkable Moving Letter! Which Was Suggested by an Extraordinary Epistle Sent by Her on Her Second Marriage to Her Clerical Admirer. London: R. Faulder, 1779.

Rendall, Jane. "Writing History for British Women: Elizabeth Hamilton and the *Memoirs of Agrippina.*" *Wollstonecraft's Daughters: Womanhood in England and France, 1780–1920.* Ed. Clarissa Campbell Orr. Manchester: Manchester UP, 1996. 79–93.

Rev. of *Retrospection,* by Hester Lynch Piozzi. *Anti-Jacobin Review* 8 (1801): 241–46.

Rev. of *Retrospection,* by Hester Lynch Piozzi. *British Critic* 19 (1802): 355–58.

Rev. of *Retrospection,* by Hester Lynch Piozzi. *Critical Review* 32 (1801): 28–35.

Rev. of *Retrospection,* by Hester Lynch Piozzi. *London Review and Literary Journal* 39 (1801): 188–93+.

Reynolds, Myra. *The Learned Lady in England: 1650–1760.* Boston: Houghton Mifflin, 1920.

Roberts, Warren. *Jane Austen and the French Revolution.* New York: St. Martin's, 1979.

Rogers, Katharine M. *Before Their Time.* New York: Frederick Ungar, 1979.

———. *Feminism in Eighteenth-Century England.* Urbana: U of Illinois P, 1982.

Rogers, Pat, ed. *The Eighteenth Century: The Context of English Literature.* New York: Holmes and Meier, 1978.

Rose, Mary Beth. "Gender, Genre and History: Seventeenth-Century English Women and the Art of Autobiography." *Women in the Middle Ages and the Renaissance.* Ed. Mary Beth Rose. Syracuse: Syracuse UP, 1986. 245–78.

Ross, Deborah. "Mirror, Mirror: The Didactic Dilemma of *The Female Quixote.*" *SEL* 27.3 (1987): 455–73.

Rothstein, Eric. "The Lessons of *Northanger Abbey.*" *University of Toronto Quarterly* 44.1 (1974): 14–30.

———. "Woman, Women, and *The Female Quixote.*" *Augustan Subjects: Essays in Honor of Martin C. Battestin.* Ed. Albert J. Rivero. Newark: U of Delaware P, 1997. 249–75.

Roulston, Christine. "Histories of Nothing: Romance and Femininity in Charlotte Lennox's *The Female Quixote.*" *Women's Writing* 2.1 (1995): 25–42.

Rousseau, G. S., and Roy Porter, eds. *Exoticism in the Enlightenment.* Manchester: Manchester UP, 1990.

Rubenstein, Jill. "The Familiar Letter between Women: The Letters of Lady Louisa Stuart to Miss Louisa Clinton." *Wordsworth Circle* 19.3 (1988): 122–29.

———. "Giving the Devil His Due: Lady Louisa Stuart and Henry Lord Brougham." *Wordsworth Circle* 12.4 (1981): 232–42.

———. "Women's Biography as a Family Affair: Lady Louisa Stuart's 'Biographical Anecdotes' of Lady Mary Wortley Montagu." *Prose Studies* 9.1 (1986): 3–21.

Rumbold, Valerie. *Women's Place in Pope's World.* Cambridge: Cambridge UP, 1989.

Said, Edward. *Culture and Imperialism.* New York: Vintage, 1993.

———. *Orientalism.* New York: Random House, 1978.

———. "Orientalism Reconsidered." *Literature, Politics and Theory: Papers from the Essex Conference, 1976–84.* Ed. Francis Barker et al. London: Methuen, 1986. 210–29.

Sales, Roger. *Jane Austen and Representations of Regency England.* London: Routledge, 1994.

Salzman, Paul. *English Prose Fiction, 1558–1700.* Oxford: Oxford UP, 1985.

Sandford, Mrs. John [Elizabeth]. *Lives of English Female Worthies.* Vol. 1. London: Longman, Rees, Orme, Brown, Green, and Longman, 1833.

Scanlon, Jennifer, and Sharon Cosner. *American Women Historians, 1700s–1990s: A Biographical Dictionary.* Westport, CT: Greenwood, 1996.

Schleuter, Paul, and June Schleuter. *An Encyclopedia of British Women Writers.* New York: Garland, 1988.

Schnorrenberg, Barbara Brandon. "The Brood Hen of Faction." *Albion* 2.1 (1979): 33–43.

———. "Catharine Macaulay." *Dictionary of Literary Biography.* Vol. 104. Detroit: Gale Research, 1981–. 226–32.

———. "Medical Men of Bath." *Studies in Eighteenth-Century Culture* 13 (1984): 189–203.

———. "An Opportunity Missed: Catherine Macaulay on the Revolution of 1688." *Studies in Eighteenth-Century Culture* 20 (1990): 231–40.

———. "A True Relation of the Life and Career of James Graham, 1745–1794." *Eighteenth-Century Life* 15 (1991): 58–75.

Schofield, Mary Anne. *Masking and Unmasking the Female Mind: Disguising Romances in Feminine Fiction, 1713–1799.* Newark: U of Delaware P, 1990.

Schwartz, Kathryn Carlisle. "The Rhetorical Resources of Lady Mary Wortley Montagu." Diss. Ohio State U, 1976.

Scott, Joan Wallach. *Gender and the Politics of History.* New York: Columbia UP, 1988.

Seeley, Leonard Benton. *Mrs. Thrale, Afterwards Mrs. Piozzi: A Sketch of Her Life and Passages from Her Diaries, Letters, and Other Writings . . . with Nine Illustrations after Hogarth, Reynolds, Zoffany, and Others.* London: Seeley, 1891.

Séjourné, Philippe. *The Mystery of Charlotte Lennox: First Novelist of Colonial America (1727?-1804).* Vol. 62. Aix-en-Provence: Publications des Annales de la Faculté des Lettres, 1967.

Sharpe, K. "The Foundation of the Chairs of History at Oxford and Cambridge." *History of Universities* 2 (1982): 127–52.

Shattock, Joanne. *The Oxford Guide to British Women Writers: Over Four Hundred Writers from Aphra Behn to Jeanette Winterson.* Oxford: Oxford UP, 1994.

Sherman, Sandra. "Instructing the 'Empire of Beauty': Lady Mary Wortley Montagu and the Politics of Female Rationality." *South Atlantic Review* 60.4 (1995): 1–26.

Siskin, Clifford. "Jane Austen and the Engendering of Disciplinarity." *Jane Austen and Discourses of Feminism.* Ed. Devoney Looser. New York: St. Martin's, 1995. 51–70.

Six Odes, Presented to That Justly-Celebrated Historian, Mrs. Catharine Macaulay, on Her Birth-Day, and Publicly Read to a Polite and Brilliant Audience, Assembled April the Second, at Alfred-House, Bath, to Congratulate That Lady of the Happy Occasion. Bath: R. Cruttwell, 1777.

Rev. of *Six Odes Presented to . . . Mrs. Catharine Macaulay. Monthly Review* 57 (1777): 145–49.

Sklar, Katherine Kish. "American Female Historians in Context, 1770–1930." *Feminist Studies* 3.1–2 (1975): 171–84.

Sloman, Judith. "The Female Quixote as an Eighteenth-Century Character Type." *Transactions of the Samuel Johnson Society of the Northwest.* Ed. Robert H. Carnie. Vol. 4. Calgary: Samuel Johnson Society of the Northwest, 1972. 86–101.

Small, Ian. *Conditions for Criticism: Authority, Knowledge, and Literature in the Late Nineteenth Century.* Oxford: Clarendon, 1991.

Smith, Amy Elizabeth. " 'Julias and Louisas': Austen's *Northanger Abbey* and the Sentimental Novel." *English Language Notes* 30 (1992): 33–42.

Smith, Bonnie G. "The Contribution of Women to Modern Historiography in Great Britain, France, and the United States, 1750–1940." *American Historical Review* 89.3 (1984): 709–32.

———. *The Gender of History: Men, Women, and Historical Practice.* Cambridge: Harvard UP, 1998.

Smith, Hilda L., and Susan Cardinale, eds. *Women and the Literature of the Seven-*

teenth Century: An Annotated Bibliography Based on Wing's Short Title Catalogue. Westport, CT: Greenwood, 1990.

Smith, Leroy W. *Jane Austen and the Drama of Womanhood.* New York: St. Martin's, 1983.

Southam, B. C., ed. *Jane Austen: "Northanger Abbey" and "Persuasion." A Casebook.* London: Macmillan, 1976.

———. *Jane Austen's Literary Manuscripts.* Oxford: Oxford UP, 1964.

———, ed. *Jane Austen: The Critical Heritage.* London: Routledge and Kegan Paul, 1968.

———. " 'Regulated Hatred' Revisited." *Jane Austen: "Northanger Abbey" and "Persuasion": A Casebook.* Ed. B. C. Southam. London: Macmillan, 1976. 122–27.

———. "*Sanditon:* The Seventh Novel." *Jane Austen's Achievement.* Ed. Juliet McMaster. New York: Barnes and Noble, 1975. 1–26.

Spacks, Patricia Meyer. *Desire and Truth: Functions of Plot in Eighteenth-Century English Novels.* Chicago: U of Chicago P, 1990.

———. *The Female Imagination.* New York: Avon, 1972.

———. "Imaginations Warm and Tender: Pope and Lady Mary." *South Atlantic Quarterly* 83.2 (1984): 207–15.

———. "Scrapbook of a Self: Mrs. Piozzi's Late Journals." *Harvard Library Bulletin* 18 (1970): 221–47.

Speck, W. A. *Society and Literature in England, 1700–1760.* Dublin: Gill and Macmillan, 1983.

Spencer, Jane. "Not Being a Historian: Women Telling Tales in Restoration and Eighteenth-Century England." *Contexts of Pre-novel Narrative: The European Tradition.* Ed. Roy Eriksen. Berlin: Mouton de Gruyter, 1994. 319–40.

———. *The Rise of the Woman Novelist: From Aphra Behn to Jane Austen.* Oxford: Basil Blackwell, 1986.

Spender, Dale. *Mothers of the Novel: One Hundred Good Women Writers before Jane Austen.* London: Pandora, 1986.

———, ed. *Women of Ideas: And What Men Have Done to Them.* London: Pandora, 1982.

Staves, Susan. "Don Quixote in Eighteenth-Century England." *Comparative Literature* 24 (1972): 193–215.

———. " 'The Liberty of a She-Subject of England': Rights Rhetoric and the Female Thucydides." *Cardozo Studies in Law and Literature* 1.2 (1989): 161–83.

Stenton, Doris Mary. *The English Woman in History.* London: George Allen and Unwin, 1957.

Stewart, Maaja A. *Domestic Realities and Imperial Fictions: Jane Austen's Novels in Eighteenth-Century Contexts.* Athens: U of Georgia P, 1993.

Stuart, Lady Louisa. *Gleanings from an Old Portfolio: Containing Some Correspondence between Lady Louisa Stuart and Her Sister Caroline, Countess of Portarlington and Other Friends and Relatives.* Ed. Mrs. Godfrey Clark. Edinburgh: David Douglas, 1895. 3 vols.

———. *Letters of Lady Louisa Stuart to Miss Louisa Clinton.* Ed. James A. Home. Edinburgh: David Douglas, 1901–3. 2 vols.

Subligny, Perdou de. *The Mock-Clelia: Being a Comical History of French Gallantries, and Novels, in Imitation of Dom Quixote.* London: L. C., 1678.

Sulloway, Alison. *Jane Austen and the Province of Womanhood.* Philadelphia: U of Pennsylvania P, 1989.

Sutherland, James. *English Literature of the Late Seventeenth Century.* Oxford: Clarendon, 1969.

Swift, Jonathan. *Prose Works of Jonathan Swift.* Ed. Herbert Davis. Oxford: Basil Blackwell, 1962. 14 vols.

Tanner, Tony. *Jane Austen.* Cambridge: Harvard UP, 1986.

Tave, Stuart M. "Jane Austen and One of Her Contemporaries." *Jane Austen: Bicentenary Essays.* Ed. John Halperin. Cambridge: Cambridge UP, 1975. 61–74.

Taylor, Philip A. M., ed. *The Origins of the English Civil War: Conspiracy, Crusade, or Class Conflict?* Lexington, MA: D. C. Heath, 1960.

Tearle, John. *Mrs. Piozzi's Tall Young Beau: William Augustus Conway.* Rutherford, NJ: Associated UP, 1991.

Tenney, Tabitha Gilman. *Female Quixotism.* Ed. Cathy N. Davidson. New York: Oxford UP, 1992.

Thirsk, Joan. "The History Women." *Chattel, Servant or Citizen: Women's Status in Church, State and Society.* Ed. Mary O'Dowd and Sabine Wichert. Belfast: Institute of Irish Studies, 1995. 1–11.

———. "Women Local and Family Historians." *Oxford Companion to Local and Family Historians.* Ed. David Hey. Oxford: Oxford UP, 1996. 498–504.

Thomas, Keith. *Religion and the Decline of Magic.* London: Weidenfeld and Nicolson, 1971.

Thomas, Peter. "Mrs. Macaulay, the Contrary Historian." *Times Literary Supplement* 19 June 1992: 11.

Thompson, James. "Jane Austen and History." *Review* 8 (1986): 21–32.

Thompson, James Westfall. *A History of Historical Writing.* New York: Macmillan, 1942. 2 vols.

Thomson, Clara Linklater. *Jane Austen: A Survey.* London: H. Marshall, 1929.

Thomson, Helen. "Charlotte Lennox's *The Female Quixote:* A Novel Interrogation." *Living by the Pen: Early British Women Writers.* Ed. Dale Spender. New York: Teacher's College, 1992. 113–25.

Thomson, Mark A. *Some Developments in English Historiography during the Eighteenth Century.* London: H. K. Lewis, 1957.

Thorpe, James. "Friend to Mrs. Piozzi: Penelope Pennington in Miniature." *Princeton University Library Chronicle* 21 (1960): 105–10.

Tillotson, Geoffrey. "Lady Mary Wortley Montague and Pope's *Elegy to the Memory of an Unfortunate Lady.*" *Review of English Studies* 12 (1936): 401–12.

Todd, Janet, ed. *A Dictionary of British and American Women Writers, 1660–1800.* Totowa, NJ: Rowman and Allanheld, 1985.

————. *The Sign of Angellica: Women, Writing and Fiction, 1660–1800*. New York: Columbia UP, 1989.

Todd, Margo. *Christian Humanism and the Puritan Social Order*. Cambridge: Cambridge UP, 1987.

Tomalin, Claire. *Jane Austen: A Life*. London: Viking, 1997.

Trevor-Roper, H. R. "Clarendon and the Practice of History." *Milton and Clarendon*, 21–50. Los Angeles: William Andrews Clark Memorial Library, University of California, 1965.

Turner, Cheryl. *Living by the Pen: Women Writers in the Eighteenth Century*. London: Routledge, 1992.

Tyson, Moses. "Unpublished Manuscripts, Papers, and Letters of Dr. Johnson, Mrs. Thrale, and the Frinds, in the John Rylands Library." *Bulletin of the John Rylands Library* 15 (1931): 467–88.

Uglow, Jennifer S., ed. *The Macmillan Dictionary of Women's Biography*. London: Macmillan, 1984.

Upham, A. H. "Lucy Hutchinson and the Duchess of Newcastle." *Anglia* 36 (1912): 200–220.

Vance, John A. *Samuel Johnson and the Sense of History*. Athens: U of Georgia P, 1984.

"Vindication of Mrs. Macaulay's Late Marriage." *Westminster Magazine* 7 (1779): 51–52.

Vogler, Frederick W. "Vital d'Audiguier and Charlotte Lennox: Baroque Studies, Women's Studies, and Literary Resurrection." *Romance Notes* 36.3 (1996): 293–99.

Voltaire, M. de. *The Age of Lewis XIV*. Trans. Charlotte Lennox. 1752. 2 vols.

Vullaimy, C. E. *Mrs. Thrale of Streatham*. London: J. Cape, 1936.

Waite, Mary Ellen, ed. *A History of Women Philosophers: Modern Women Philosophers, 1600–1900*. Boston: Kluwer Academic Publishers, 1991. 4 vols.

Walker, Eric C. "Charlotte Lennox and the Collier Sisters: Two New Johnson Letters." *Studies in Philology* 95.3 (1998): 320–32.

Wall, Cynthia. "Editing Desire: Pope's Correspondence with (and without) Lady Mary." *Philological Quarterly* 71.2 (1992): 221–37.

Wallace, Tara Ghoshal. "*Northanger Abbey* and the Limits of Parody." *Studies in the Novel* 20.3 (1988): 262–73.

Wallas, Ada. *Before the Bluestockings*. New York: Macmillan, 1930.

Walpole, Horace. *Horace Walpole's Correspondence*. Ed. W. S. Lewis et al. Vol. 9. New Haven: Yale UP, 1937–83.

————. *Memoirs of King George II*. Ed. John Brooke. New Haven: Yale UP, 1985. 3 vols.

Warburton, Eliot. *Reginald Hastings: Or, A Tale of the Troubles in 164–*. New York: Harper, 1850.

Wardropper, Bruce W. "Don Quixote: Story or History?" *Modern Philology* 63.1 (1965): 1–11.

Warfel, Harry R. Rev. of *Mystery of Charlotte Lennox,* by Philippe Séjourné. *Early American Literature* 3 (1968): 216.

Warren, Leland E. "Of the Conversation of Women: *The Female Quixote* and the Dream of Perfection." *Studies in Eighteenth Century Culture* 11 (1982): 367–80.

Watson, Nicola J. *Revolution and the Form of the British Novel 1790–1825: Intercepted Letters, Interrupted Seductions.* Oxford: Clarendon, 1994.

Weinsheimer, Joel C. *Eighteenth-Century Hermeneutics: Philosophy of Interpretation in England from Locke to Burke.* New Haven: Yale UP, 1993.

Whalley, George. "Jane Austen: Poet." *Jane Austen's Achievement.* Ed. Juliet McMaster. New York: Barnes and Noble, 1975. 106–34.

Whalley, Peter. *An Essay on the Manner of Writing History.* Ed. Keith Stewart. Vol. 80. Los Angeles: William Andrews Clark Memorial Library, University of California, 1960.

Wharton, Grace, and Philip Wharton. *The Queens of Society.* New York: Harper, 1861.

Wheare, Degoraeus. *The Method and Order of Reading Both Civil and Ecclesiastical Histories: In Which the Most Excellent Historians Are Reduced into the Order in Which They Are Successively to Be Read; and the Judgements of Learned Men, concerning Each of Them, Subjoin'd.* Trans. Edmund Bohun. London: Charles Brome, 1685.

Wiesenfarth, Joseph. "Austen and Apollo." *Jane Austen Today.* Ed. Joel Weinsheimer. Athens: U of Georgia P, 1975. 46–63.

———. "History and Myth in Jane Austen's *Persuasion.*" *Literary Criterion* 11 (1974): 76–85.

Williams, Michael. *Jane Austen: Six Novels and Their Methods.* New York: St. Martin's, 1985.

Williams, Raymond. *The Country and the City.* New York: Oxford UP, 1973.

Wilt, Judith. *Ghosts of the Gothic.* Princeton: Princeton UP, 1980.

Withey, Lynne E. "Catharine Macaulay and the Uses of History: Ancient Rights, Perfectionism, and Propaganda." *Journal of British Studies* 16.1 (1976): 59–83.

Wollstonecraft, Mary. *A Vindication of the Rights of Woman.* Ed. Carol Poston. 2nd ed. New York: W. W. Norton, 1988.

Women of Worth: A Book for Girls. New York: W. A. Townsend, 1861.

Womersley, D. J. "Lord Bolingbroke and Eighteenth-Century Historiography." *Eighteenth Century* 28.3 (1987): 217–34.

Woodward, Carolyn. " 'My Heart So Wrapt': Lesbian Disruptions in Eighteenth-Century British Fiction." *Signs* 18.4 (1993): 838–65.

Woolf, D. R. "A Feminine Past? Gender, Genre, and Historical Knowledge in England, 1500–1800." *American Historical Review* 102.3 (1997): 645–79.

Wordsworth, Christopher. *Scholae Academicae: Some Account of the Studies at the English Universities in the Eighteenth Century.* Cambridge: Cambridge UP, 1877.

Yeazell, Ruth. "Public Baths and Private Harems: Lady Mary Wortley Montagu and the Origins of Ingre's *Bain Turc.*" *Yale Journal of Criticism* 7.1 (1994): 111–38.

Yegenoglu, Meyda. *Colonial Fantasies: Towards a Feminist Reading of Orientalism.* New York: Cambridge UP, 1998.

Zimmerman, Everett. *Boundaries of Fiction: History and the Eighteenth-Century Novel.* Ithaca: Cornell UP, 1996.

———. "The Function of Parody in *Northanger Abbey.*" *Modern Language Quarterly* 30 (1969): 53–63.

Index

■